SOCIOLOGY
Alive!

Third Edition

Stephen Moore

First published in 1987 by:
Stanley Thornes (Publishers) Ltd
Second edition 1996

Third edition published in 2001 by:
Nelson Thornes Ltd
Delta Place
27 Bath Road
CHELTENHAM
GL53 7TH
United Kingdom

01 02 03 04 05 / 10 9 8 7 6 5 4 3 2 1

A catalogue record for this book is available from the British Library.

ISBN 0 7487 5464 4

Illustrations by Steve Ballinger and Shaun Williams
Typeset by Northern Phototypesetting Co. Ltd, Bolton

Printed and bound in Italy by STIGE

CONTENTS

PREFACE

Welcome to the third edition of *Sociology Alive!* It reflects many of the changes in sociology and society since the last edition was published.

Although the contents and the look may have changed, the aim is just the same as in the two previous editions – to excite and challenge you with the world of sociology. Sociology, in my opinion, is more than just another exam to be passed – it ought to shock and enlighten you, making you examine your preconceived ideas. Nothing is more fun to me than a lively group of students genuinely outraged by ideas which they have just encountered, and desperate to get the class to listen to their views on the subject under discussion. This challenge to received wisdom shouldn't be the preserve of university students – but at every level of the education system.

No apologies too if some parts use difficult words or make you struggle a bit. How else are you going to learn? Why else is there a teacher in the classroom?

When I teach, I rarely allow the students the comfort of working together as a whole class. Instead, I divide the class into groups and get them to do different exercises – when they have finished, it is their job to 'teach' the others. The main text carries all the sociological information you require, and you can just pick and choose the exercises you want to illustrate the main points. Whatever way you choose to teach and study, there is a huge amount of information available to you – drawn from a very wide range of sources and as up-to-date as any book published at any level.

I really do hope that the book makes studying and teaching sociology an exciting and exhilarating experience.

Stephen Moore
January 2001

ACKNOWLEDGEMENTS

Thanks to all those who have bought and used previous editions of the book, I do appreciate the positive comments made – and the fact that you keep buying it!

Thanks also to my 'children' – Sarah, Claudia and Michael for driving me on (mainly by requesting large sums of money to maintain their lifestyle). For those of you who have read the previous editions and followed the biographies of my family, here is the update. Remember those little kids who used to pester me? Well, Sarah who once 'did a wee' over the original typescript is now at university. Claudia who ate a page of *Social Trends* is now studying A-level Sociology. Michael, who used to adore me, has now (perfectly reasonably) shifted his attentions to adoring a succession of young girls.

My special thanks to my wife Paola, who despite writing her own books (and being much more organised about it than me), has found time to support and encourage me (and I have to confess, at times, threaten me).

I remain at Anglia Polytechnic University (APU) in Cambridge, where I have been 'elevated' to the grand position of Reader in Social Policy. In case, you don't know, this is a position reserved for those who are generally considered to be a little too dim ever to be a professor.

Stephen Moore

The author and publishers are grateful to the following for permission to reproduce previously published material:

Addison Wesley Longman for extract from *The New British Politics* by I. Budge, I. Crewe, D. McKay and K. Newton (p 367) ● Associated Book Publishers Ltd for extracts from *Coal is our Life* by N. Dennis, F. Henriques and C. Slaughter (p 186) and *The Family* by A. Wilson (p 158) ● Barnardo's for advertisement (p 131) ● British Journal of Sociology for extract from *Mealtime rituals: power and resistance in the construction of mealtime rules* by S. Grieshaber (p 30) ● The British Psychological Society for adapted material from 'Self-reported delinquency among schoolboys and their attitudes to the police' by H. B. Gibson, *British Journal of Social and Clinical Psychology*, 6 (p 345) ● John Calder Ltd for adapted material from *The Assembly Line* by R. Linhart, translated by M. Crossland, 1981, originally published by Editions de Minuit, Paris (p 288) ● Commission for Racial Equality for information (pp 102, 108, 109, 110, 122,) ● Child Poverty Action Group for extracts from *Putting the Treasury First – The truth about child support* by A. Garnham and E. Knights (p 181); *Poverty: Journal of the Child Poverty Action Group* (pp 386-7, 390) and *Poverty: The facts* by C. Oppenheim (pp 388-9, 391) ● Comedia Publishing Company Ltd for an extract from *The British Media* by M. Grant (p 207) ● Daily Express for extracts (pp 127, 174, 421) ● Daily Mail for extracts from *The Daily Mail*, © *Daily Mail* (pp 88, 95, 126, 209, 269) ● Faber and Faber Ltd, for adapted material from *Married Life in an African Tribe* by I. Shapera (p 163) ● Gower Publishing Company Ltd for extracts from *Police and People in London* by D. Smith and J. Gray (p 112); and *Sex, Gender and Society* by A. Oakley (p 79) ● The Guardian for extracts from various issues, © *The Guardian* (pp 2, 4, 25, 66, 73, 80, 85, 105, 109, 116, 133, 167, 173, 187, 197, 204, 205, 206, 209, 234, 264, 266, 267, 284, 296, 336-7, 414) and Ian Jackson's *Where you rate in the new social order* (p 55) ● Help the Aged for an extract from *People not Pensioners* (p 150) ● Her Majesty's Stationery Office for statistical information (pp 56, 147, 169, 175, 177, 176, 178, 179, 180, 190, 210, 227, 230, 234, 237,259, 260, 261, 279, 303, 306, 309, 333, 335, 337, 415, 417) and tables from DfEE website (p 252) ● The Home Office for material by C. Mirrlees-Black, T. Budd, S. Partridge, and P. Mayhew, (1998) *The British Crime Survey*. Home Office Statistical Bulletin 21/98. (pp 332, 342, 346) ● Eileen Krige for an extract from *The Realm of a Rain Queen* by J. and J. D. Drige, Juta & Co. Ltd, South Africa (p 253) ● Macmillan Publishers Ltd for an extract from *Sociology in Context* by J. Nobbs (p 48) ● Mail on Sunday for material (p 20) ● William Morrow & Co. Inc. for an extract from *Male and Female* by Margaret Mead, Greenwood Press, 1977 (p 9) ● National Children's Bureau for extract from *Understanding Families: Children's Perspectives*, by V. Morrow (p 154) ● New Internationalist Publications Ltd for adapted material from *The New Internationalist* (pp 129, 354, 374) ● *New Society* for material from various editions (pp 172, 217, 300, 351, 361) ● Newspaper Publishing plc for extracts from *The Independent*, © *The Independent* (pp 49, 80-81, 111, 114, 150, 424) ● NI Syndication for material from The Sun (p 201) ● The Observer for cartoon by Ian Jackson (p 50) ● Office of National Statistics for extracts from *Social Trends 30*, National Statistics © Crown Copyright 2000 (pp 28, 87, 196, 286, 301) ● OfSTED for extract from *Raising the Attainment of Minority Ethnic Pupils* (p 271) ● Penguin Books Ltd for extracts from *Just Like a Girl: How Girls Learn to be Women* by S. Sharpe © 1976 S. Sharpe (p 273); and *Working for Ford* by H. Beynon, first published as Penguin Education 1973, © 1973, 1984 H. Beynon (p 243) ● Philip Allan Publishers Ltd for extracts from *Sociology Review (formerly Social Studies Review)* (pp 35, 62, 104, 142, 161, 202, 307, 313, 316, 360, 385, 396) ● Laurence Pollinger Ltd on behalf of Colin Turnbull for extracts from *The Mountain People* (pp 4-5, 134) and *The Forest People* (pp 10, 188), Jonathan Cape Ltd ● Price Waterhouse Coopers for advertisement (p 86) ● Routledge and Kegan Paul for extracts from *Family and Class in a London Suburb* by P. Willmott and M. Young (p 186); *World Revolution and Family Patterns* by W. J. Goode (p 182); *Social Class and the Comprehensive School* by J. Ford (p 251); *Human Societies* by G. Hurd *et al.* (p 173) and from issue of 20.6.69 of *The British Journal of Sociology* (p 424) ● Sylvia Secker for an extract from *The Ragged Trousered Philanthropists* by R. Tressell, Panther, 1965 (p 410) ● Times Newspapers Limited for extracts © *The Times* (pp 64, 209, 302, 342); © Haldane/Times Newspapers Limited 1999 (p 302); © Cole/Times Newspapers Limited 1993, for cartoon (p 168) ● The Telegraph for various extracts (pp 112, 113, 118, 265) ● Times Supplements Limited for extracts from *The Times Educational Supplement* (pp 264, 269) ● Unwin Hyman Ltd for extracts from *Poor Britain* by J. Mack and S. Lansley (pp 381, 384, 405)

We are grateful to the following for permission to reproduce illustrations and for providing prints:

Associated Press, photo (p 330), photo (p 420), photo left (p 352), photo right (p 352) ● John Birdsall Photography, photo (p 274), photo left (p 3) ● Adam Butler/Associated Press, photo (p 130) ● Camera Press/Newsmakers, photo (p 78) ● Christian Charisius/Reuters, photo (p 374) ● Commission for Racial Equality, advertisement top (p 116) ● Valdir Cruz, photo (p 2) ● Chris Davies/Network, photo (p 231) ● Mary Evans Picture Library, photo (p 133) ● Kieran Doherty/Reuters, photo (p 148) ● Ronald Grant Archive, photo (p 199) ● Judy Harrison/Format Photographers, photo (p 51) ● Yves Herman/Reuters, photo (p 254) ● INS, photo (p 416) ● Don McPhee/The Guardian, photo (p 195) ● Modus Publicity, image bottom (p 116) ● Sam Morris/Associated Press, photo (p 154) ● Egberto Nagueira/Reuters, photo (p 174) ● Newsteam International, photo (p 50) ● North News & Pictures, photo (p 295) ● David Perrett & Duncan Rowland/University of St Andrews/Science Photo Library, image (p 94) ● Brenda Prince/Format Photographers, photo left (p 383) ● Diary of an Amateur Photographer/Graham Rawle/Picador, photo (p vi) ● Sean Smith/Camera Press, photo right (p 45) ● Paula Solloway/Format Photographers, photo centre (p 3) ● Graham Turner/The Guardian, photo left (p 45) ● Penny Tweedie/Network Photographers, photo (p 12) ● Ulrike Press/Format Photographers, photo (p 298) ● Garry Weaser/The Guardian, photo centre (p 45)

Every attempt has been made to contact copyright holders, and we apologise if any have been overlooked.

INTRODUCTION

Michael is attending an evening course in photography. Here is an extract from his diary about the first time he shows a photograph to the teacher and the class:

Nature's eiderdown

Same day. 9.55 p.m.

Very good meeting, though rather poor turnout. Only eight in attendance this week.
   Alistair chose my picture (among others) to pin on the wall for discussion. Unfortunately he hung it upside-down like this, thinking it was a bird instead of Mrs. Eckersby's cat. He congratulated me on handling potentially tricky lighting conditions so I didn't say anything.

Source: G. Rawle, *Diary of an Amateur Photographer: A Mystery* (Picador, 1998)

Well, as you can see, not everything is as it appears! There is usually another way of looking at things – and that is the task of sociology. We take normal, everyday, taken-for-granted life and turn it upside down, looking for other meanings. Very often we end up seeing things very differently from most people.

UNDERSTANDING SOCIOLOGY

Chapter contents

What is sociology?

Sociology is the subject which studies the social world around us, how this social world operates and how it influences our daily lives.

We all tend to accept the 'social arrangements' which we grow up with as being somehow natural or, at most, too complicated to understand. So, the family is the *natural* way to bring up children and schools are the *obvious* place for young people to learn.

For most people then, the social world is 'just there', channelling our lives. We cannot change it and it is not really worthwhile trying to understand it.

There is a consequence of this argument – that the social world is fixed and natural – which is very important. That is when people try to understand their own position in society, rich or poor, isolated or popular, they usually do so by saying that it is their own personal abilities and weaknesses which cause them to be as they are.

Well, sociologists do not agree with most of this! We regard it as our job to understand society and the way it influences us. We tackle this task by using:

- certain 'building block' concepts such as values, beliefs, norms and identity
- theories – that is explanations which link a number of different social events together and which show how these social events affect each other
- special, tried and tested methods to study social life.

Finally, we try to avoid putting forward our own personal ideas as if they were 'facts'.

In this chapter we will concentrate on the 'building blocks' mentioned above. In Chapter 2 we will look at methods and theories.

Stone Age tribe

In 1996, a researcher finally encountered a tribe that had been isolated from the rest of the world since the dawn of history. Even today, there are societies which remain isolated and which have totally different cultures and ways of life. This is how the researcher finally encountered the 'lost' tribe.

Since records began in 1928, at least 50 people have met their deaths – some by arrows, some clubbed, many with the flesh ripped from their bones – at the hands of the 'undiscovered' Stone Age tribe … The Korubo owe their survival to their awe-inspiring violence and their inaccessible home in the thick rainforest frontier between Brazil and Peru. …

In 1996, Possuelo decided to try to contact the Korubo. With a team that included Indians from nearby tribes, he made several expeditions through the virgin rainforest, looking for the footprints and broken branches which would indicate the presence of human life. On the third trip he found a clearing and a hut of sticks and leaves. "The tension was enormous. No one knew what was going to happen. All previous attempts at getting close had always resulted in death," says Possuelo. "The big problem was that we didn't know how many of them there

The last surviving members of a Stone Age tribe in the Amazon

were. They could have circled us and killed us all."

The Indians didn't appear. Possuelo left presents – knives, pans, an axe – and then left. First contact was only made on a following sortie, after his team had been camped by the Indians'

clearing for a week.

The Indians gradually appeared from behind the trees. First came a man, later identified as Shamabo, naked but for a piece of string tied around his waist to hold up his penis, covered in red paint derived from urucu fruit,

and holding a club. A second man arrived, then a woman. One Korubo took someone's hat and put it on. Another tugged at someone's necklace. Then they moved to the base camp, rifled through the food and took a packet of cheese crackers …

Source: Adapted from *The Guardian*, 7 January 2000

The contact was successfully made and no violence took place.

Technology: mobile phones – an example of social change

Society is dynamic – that is, it is always changing. Sociologists have suggested many complex explanations for social change, but a simple explanation is that changing technology has inevitable social consequences.

Today almost 45 per cent of the British population own mobile phones. Fifteen years ago, the number of mobile phone users was tiny. Be a sociologist – make a list of what social changes are happening and may happen in the future (good and bad) as a result of modern forms of personal communication, such as the mobile phone.

Incidentally, if you want to be a really good sociologist, you might care to suggest some reasons why mobile phones were invented in the first place and why people nowadays want to use them, when perhaps 30 years ago they might not have wanted them.

Culture

A **culture** is the whole set of beliefs and guidelines as to how people *ought* to behave in any society. The overwhelming majority of people in any society regard the culture as natural and normal. It provides all of us with the ability to understand and participate in society.

> **Definition**
>
> **Culture** – a whole way of life that guides our way of thinking and acting. People within a culture regard it as somehow natural; for example, the difference between British values and Italian values

Cultures vary across societies

Every society has a different culture, so that expectations of behaviour are very different in China than in France, for example.

Cultures vary over time

The culture of society changes over time. For example, British culture today is very different from British culture in the 1950s. It is likely to be very different in 2050 too.

Divisions within cultures

> **Definition**
>
> **Subculture** – exists within a culture and is a distinctive set of values that marks off the members of the subculture from the rest of society; for example, youth (sub)culture

Within any culture there may be differences. The larger and more socially complex the society, the greater the likelihood is that there will be a range of different values which coexist within the mainstream culture. These variations in culture are known as **subcultures**. So, young people will share some beliefs and values with older people and may have some distinctive ones of their own.

Cultures: a framework to provide meaning

Cultures vary so much because they are created by people to help them make sense of the world in which they live. Different societies exist in very different circumstances and so cultures will reflect these differences in circumstances.

One planet, different world

There is no such thing as 'normal' behaviour or 'abnormal' behaviour for human beings. Whenever you study another society, rather than thinking how weird/silly/strange their behaviour is, remember that to the members of that society, it is as sensible and normal as our own seems to us.

This is what happened, according to a journalist, when a group of anthropologists (people who study tribal societies) visited a remote Indian tribe in Brazil.

> The Indians sit next to him [the leader of the anthropologists], laughing with him. The chief, Shishu, puts his arm around him for half an hour. Shishu makes us tea by grating a vine over a club encrusted with monkey-teeth, and then wetting and squeezing the result.
>
> One man pulls up my shirt to see if I have breasts and looks down the trousers of Possuelo's long-haired teenage son.

Source: Adapted from *The Guardian*, 7 January 2000

1 What do you think is the significance of making tea? How are you able to understand the significance? How does this help us to understand that humans often wish to express similar emotions or needs, but choose to do so in culturally different ways?

2 The members of the tribe go about naked. How does this help explain their behaviour?

Cultures provide a framework for people to cope with the world around them

John Turnbull studied a tribe in the north of Uganda in the 1950s. The Ik tribe had traditionally been hunters, but the Ugandan government decided that their hunting lands should become a game reserve and resettled them in a mountainous region, with too few animals to hunt and inadequate rainfall to grow crops. In effect, they had been sentenced to death. The Ik responded by developing a new form of culture which allowed them to cope with their desperate circumstances.

The quality of life that we hold as necessary for survival, love, the Ik also dismiss as idiotic and highly dangerous.

So we should not be surprised when the mother throws out her child at three years old. She has breast-fed it, with some ill humor, and cared for it in some manner for three whole years, and now it is ready to make its own way. I imagine the child must be rather relieved to be thrown out, for in the process of being cared for he or she is carried about in a hide sling wherever the mother goes, and since the mother is not strong herself this is done grudgingly. Whenever the mother finds a spot in which to gather, or if she is at a water hole or in the fields, she loosens the sling and lets the baby to the ground none too slowly, and of course laughs if it is hurt. ... Then she goes about her business, leaving the child there, almost hoping that some predator will come along and carry it off. This happened once while I was there – once that I know of, anyway – and the mother was delighted. She was rid of the child and no longer had to carry it about and feed it, and still further this meant that a leopard was in the vicinity and would be sleeping the child off and thus be an easy kill. The men set off and found the leopard, which had consumed all of the child except part of the skull; they killed the leopard and cooked it and ate it, child and all.

Hunger was indeed more severe than I knew, and the children were the next to go. It was all quite impersonal – even to me, in most cases, since I had been immunized by the Ik themselves against sorrow on their behalf. But Adupa was an exception. Her stomach grew more and more distended, and

her legs and arms more spindly. Her madness was such that she did not know just how vicious humans could be, particularly her playmates. She was older than they, and more tolerant. That too was a madness in an Icien world. Even worse, she thought that parents were for loving, for giving as well as receiving. Her parents were not given to fantasies, and they had two other children, a boy and a girl who were perfectly normal, so they ignored Adupa, except when she brought them food

that she had scrounged from somewhere. They snatched that quickly enough. But when she came for shelter they drove her out, and when she came because she was hungry they laughed that Icien laugh, as if she had made them happy. ...

Finally they took her in, and Adupa was happy and stopped crying. She stopped crying forever, because her parents went away and closed the asak [compound] tight behind them, so tight that weak little Adupa could never have moved it if

she had tried. But I doubt that she even thought of trying. She waited for them to come back with the food they promised her. When they came back she was still waiting for them. It was a week or ten days later, and her body was already almost too far gone to bury. In an Ik village who would notice the smell? And if she had cried, who would have noticed that? Her parents took what was left of her and threw it out, as one does the riper garbage, a good distance away.

Source: Adapted from C. Turnbull, *The Mountain People* (Picador, 1974)

1 What are the main values of the Ik, do you think?

2 Why did these values develop, in your opinion?

3 Why was Adupa different?

4 People often claim that most normal parents 'naturally' love and care for their children. Does the extract challenge this in any way?

5 Sociologists argue that no behaviour is 'natural' to mankind; goodness, evil, love, are all products of society. Having read the extract, what is your opinion? Discuss in small groups, then appoint one person to report back to the class.

Beliefs, values and norms

Cultures are composed of three main elements:

- beliefs
- values
- norms.

Beliefs

Definition

Beliefs – very general views on the nature of the world

Beliefs are general feelings or opinions about the nature of the world around us. They provide us with the general framework of our understanding about the world. One general belief, for example, is that human life is sacred.

Values

Definition

Values – ideas about the correct form of behaviour

Values are ideas about correct forms of behaviour, which stress how we ought to behave in general terms. For example, one shared value is that it is wrong to hurt other people.

Norms

Norms are the normal, expected patterns of behaviour which we ought to follow in everyday life if we are to be considered 'normal'. Norms provide us with very clear guidance on how to behave in everyday situations. So people generally join the ends of queues and those who push to the front are criticised by others as behaving improperly (see the poem below).

Norms are crucial to a culture, as they provide clear guidance on how to act and, in doing so, create an orderly and predictable society.

Q.

I join the queue
We move up nicely

I ask the lady in front
What are we queuing for.
'To join another queue,'
She explains.

'How pointless,' I say,
'I'm leaving'. She points
To another long queue.
'Then you must get in line.'

I join the queue.
We move up nicely.
Roger McGough

Source: R. McGough, *Blazing Fruit Selected Poems 1967–87* (Penguin, 1990)

Social roles

Definitions

Social role – a way of acting which is expected of a person in a particular position in society

Society – people acting in a particular set of predictable patterns (known as social roles) and who share a set of common ideas about the world (a culture)

Can you imagine a world where other people are totally unpredictable? You simply do not know what people are going to do next. Clearly, chaos would follow, as you would be unable to plan anything or rely on anyone. So, in order to avoid this, we have developed **social roles**. A social role is a predictable 'bundle' of actions, linked with particular positions in **society** such as a mother or a teacher. This sounds complicated – and it is! But a couple of examples should make it clear. If a woman has the social role of 'mother', then we expect her to love and care for her children. If a man has the role of 'teacher', we expect him to maintain order in the classroom and to pass relevant knowledge and ideas to the students. We also expect him to dress moderately well (though not too well!), to be educated and generally to live a fairly conventional life.

If the mother preferred to go out each night and ignored her children, we would be shocked; just as we would if the teacher spent his classroom time playing on a computer game.

If you can imagine society as a complicated form of model kit, like Lego, then roles are the parts of the kit you fit together. If a part is missing or faulty, the model cannot be made. So, without the millions of social roles, society could not exist as we know it today.

To simplify this incredibly difficult task of having to live in everyone else's mind as well as our own, the number of social roles are restricted. People do not behave just as they wish, they conform to what is generally considered to be the correct behaviour for a particular role. By and large, the behaviour of students is predictable, so is that of teachers, of shop assistants and policemen. We all know what these people ought to do, and it does not matter too much which individual fits into the role – he or she will behave roughly the same. So, I fit my role (for example, at the moment as writer and teacher) to your role (as reader and student).

Multiple roles

Nobody plays one role in life – all of us play a number of different roles. The person reading this might be a student, a mother, a sister, a carer and a friend. Each role requires different behaviour and carries different responsibilities.

Activities

1   Play the game where a person has to guess what his or her role is. The tutor shows one group of students a particular social role (for example, teacher). One person is not allowed to see what the tutor has written. The group has to give one-word clues until the person guesses what the role is. The words you use will make clear what expectations you all have of a particular role.

2   To illustrate the strength of social roles, a famous sociologist, Gafinkel, once got his students to play 'wrong' roles in particular situations. In one experiment, students went home and pretended that they were staying in a hotel, to the puzzlement of their parents.

Why not try a similar experiment? At lunchtime for five minutes, talk and act towards your friends (who are not in this class) as if they were distant acquaintances whom you had met just once before. What are their reactions? How do they try to get you back into your role?

Role conflict

Most of the time, we juggle these multiple roles about quite successfully, but there is often a conflict between the different roles in terms of what they demand from us. For example, a woman may be a student, but is also caring for her disabled mother. There may well be a conflict between the amount of time she needs for studying and for looking after her mother.

So, roles provide us with clear-cut guidance, or scripts, on how to behave. Unfortunately, they may at times clash. Generally, the society will give us a 'nudge' to suggest which of the roles is more important – though this is not always the case. Which do you think is the more important role for the woman above, looking after her mother or studying for an exam?

Question

You are a doctor in a hospital and you hear there has been an accident with the local school bus. Your daughter is seriously injured and, along with five others, might possibly die. However, your daughter is not in the very worst state; there are two other children in a worse state. Who do you operate on first? Explain your answer.

What does this tell us about values and norms?

Main points ▶ Sociology studies the social world around us, how it operates and how it influences our lives.

▶ In order to do so, there are certain building blocks, which provide the framework for us to understand society.

▶ The building blocks include values, norms, beliefs and identity; the use of theory and correct research methods.

▶ Cultures provide meaning, and they vary across society and time. There are even divisions within cultures.

▶ Beliefs are general opinions about the world.

▶ Values are general ideas about how we ought to behave.

▶ Norms are much more specific guidelines on how to behave.

▶ Social roles provide the predictability which makes society possible.

▶ Everyone must perform a number of roles – sometimes they conflict.

Socialisation and social control

Definitions

Socialisation – the process of learning how to behave 'correctly' in a society

Social control – people learn the expectations and values of society (culture) through socialisation and if they do not follow the guidelines of society, then they are punished in some way (social control)

Well, now we have the basic building blocks to understand society. People share a common culture which is based upon a set of beliefs and values. These provide us with clear guidelines about how we should act in most situations – norms. A society actually functions by people taking on a wide range of social roles which structure and predict actions.

Now this is truly a miracle of complex interaction – but it does not happen naturally – it must be learned and, once learned, people must be persuaded to continue to play their roles. This is the where we need to explore the concepts of **socialisation** and **social control**.

Socialisation

The new-born baby lying in the cot is the centre of attention of her parents and family. They play with her, they smile at her, and eventually she learns to smile back. Months later she learns from tones of voice which actions are not to be done and which actions please her parents. After her parents have constantly repeated words like 'mummy' and 'daddy' to her, she learns that by saying these 'magic' words, she gets a kiss or a drink, or some reward. As time progresses, the child learns more words, and more rules of behaviour. Eventually, the little girl will have learned all the behaviour expected of her in most situations, and of course she will regard this behaviour as perfectly natural. As she grows up, through playing games with her friends, through the example of her parents and later through her studies at school, the girl will come to learn all the appropriate behaviour expected of girls and women in our society.

Socialisation and personality

This extract describes child-rearing in two societies.

The Arapesh treat a baby as a soft vulnerable precious little object, to be protected, fed and cherished. ... When the mother walks about, she carries the child slung beneath her breast ... whenever it is willing to eat even if it does not show hunger, it is fed gently and with attention. Through the long protected infancy, the child is never asked to perform tasks that are difficult or exacting.

The Mundugumor women actively dislike child-bearing and they dislike children. Children are carried in harsh baskets that scratch their skin, high up on their mother's shoulders, well away from the breast. Mothers nurse their children standing up, pushing them away as soon as they are the least bit satisfied. Here we find a character developing that stresses angry, eager greed.

Source: Adapted from M. Mead, *Male and Female* (Penguin, 1962)

1 Suggest two words to describe the Arapesh view of children, and two to summarise the Mundugumor attitude.

2 What sort of personalities do you think that:

a) Arapesh children will have when they grow up?

b) the Mundugumor children will have?

3 What does the extract suggest about the relationship between child-bearing and adult personalities?

Everyone passes through this socialisation process and emerges with similar expectations of behaviour. It is only as a result of this that society is possible, otherwise there would be chaos with people doing exactly what they wanted.

In modern societies, sociologists distinguish between primary and secondary socialisation:

- Primary socialisation is the learning of social behaviour from those closest to you, such as family and friends.
- Secondary socialisation is the learning of social rules that takes place in school and at work, and very importantly, in the mass media (television, radio, newspapers).

Socialisation: learning the skills

The pygmies were mainly hunters who travelled through the forest, only staying in one place for a short time (this is called a nomadic tribe). The extract shows how the children learn the skills necessary to survive as adults in the forest.

Like children everywhere, pygmy children love to imitate their adult idols, and this is the beginning of their schooling, for the adults will always encourage and help them. What else do they have to be taught, except to grow into good adults? So a fond father will make a tiny bow for his son, and arrows of soft wood and with blunt points. He may also give him a strip of a hunting net. The mother will delight herself and her daughter by weaving a miniature carrying basket, and soon boys and girls are 'playing house'. They solemnly collect the sticks and leaves, and while the girl is building a miniature house the boy prowls around with his bow and arrow. He will eventually find a stray plantain or an ear of corn which he will shoot at and proudly carry back. With equal solemnity it is cooked and eaten, and the two may even sleep the sleep of innocence in the hut they have made.

They will also play at hunting, the boys stretching out their little bits of net while the girls beat the ground with bunches of leaves and drive some poor, tired, old frog in towards the boys. If they can't find a frog they go and awaken one of their grandparents and ask him to play at being an antelope. He is then pursued all over the camp, twisting and dodging amongst the huts and the trees. …

And one day they find that the games they have been playing are not games any longer, but the real thing, for they have become adults. Their hunting is now real hunting, their tree climbing is in earnest search of inaccessible honey, their acrobatics on the swings are repeated almost daily, in other forms, in the pursuit of elusive game, or in avoiding the malicious forest buffalo. It happens so gradually that they hardly notice the change at first, for even when they are proud and famous hunters their life is still full of fun and laughter.

Source: Adapted from C. Turnbull, *The Forest People* (Picador, 1976)

1 How do the games the children play relate to their adult lives?

2 Is there any difference between the roles of the girls and boys in their games? What does this suggest?

3 Is there any relationship in our society between the games children play and their adult lives? Provide some examples.

Social control

If people act in a way which does not conform to the expectations of society, then they are punished in some way, either by being regarded as odd and perhaps having no friends or, in extreme cases, by being branded as criminals. These forms of pressure to ensure conformity are known as social control.

There are two types of social control:
- formal
- informal.

Formal social control

Formal social control is when the rules of society are expressed in law or rules within an organisation and they are backed up by official agencies, such as the police and the courts. These rules are almost always written down.

Informal social control

Informal social control is where there are certain expectations of behaviour which are not formally written down, but most people take for granted. When people break these 'rules', then others show their disapproval in a variety of ways, short of involving the law.

Instinct versus learning

Many people reading this for the first time might well argue that sociology ignores our natural **instincts**. They would claim that when women cuddle babies, it is the response to their 'natural' maternal instinct. When wars are fought, it is the result of man's 'natural' aggressiveness and theft is the result of our instinct to possess.

Sociologists are very doubtful about these explanations and the book will rarely mention them.

Are people 'naturally' human beings?

Human beings act in the way they do through copying those around them. If they are isolated from human contact they will adopt other forms of behaviour. The following extract is about a boy who had been brought up by wolves in an isolated area of India.

He heard some squealing, crept up, and saw the boy playing with four or five wolf cubs. He was most emphatic they were wolves.

The boy had very dark skin, finger-nails grown into claws, a tangle of matted hair and callouses on his palms, elbows and knees. [When disturbed] He ran rapidly on all fours, yet couldn't keep up with the cubs as they made for cover. The mother wolf was not in sight. The [man] caught the boy and was bitten. But he did manage to truss him up in his towel, lash him to the bicycle and ride home.

At first Shamdev [as they called him] cowered from people and would only play with dogs. He hated the sun and used to curl up in shadowy places. After dark he grew restless and they had to tie him up to stop him following the jackals which howled round the village at night. If anyone cut themselves, he could smell the scent of blood and would scamper towards it. He caught chickens and ate them alive, including the entrails. Later, when he had evolved a sign language of his own, he would cross his thumbs and flap his hands; this meant 'chicken' or 'food'.

Eventually, [he was] weaned off red meat. He forced rice, dal and chappatis down his throat, but these made him sick. He took to eating earth, his chest swelled up and they began to fear for his life. Only gradually did he get used to the new diet. After five months he began to stand: two years later he was doing useful jobs like taking straw to the cows.

Source: Adapted from *The Sunday Times Magazine*, 30 July 1978

1   What behaviour did the boy display?

2   Can you suggest any reason for this?

3   What does this suggest about the way that we behave?

4   In your opinion, what would happen if a person was left completely alone from birth except to be given food and shelter?

The first, and major, objection to the explanations given above is that if people's behaviour is natural, then it ought to be, by and large, the same all over the world, in the same way that our physical attributes are. Most human beings all over the world have the same *physical needs*, such as eating and sleeping, and the same *physical abilities*, such as walking, running and lifting. But *desires*, *attitudes* and *patterns of behaviour* vary tremendously from one society to another. This simply could not be the case if our behaviour was natural – we would all behave the same way, and so we amend, adapt and invent behaviour according to our cultures, norms and beliefs.

Definition

Learning – behaviour acquired through socialisation and reinforced by social control

The simplest way to prove the importance of **learning** as opposed to instinct is to look at examples of people who have lived their first few years without other human company. The results have always been the same; the person does not have the abilities which we recognise as normal amongst humans. There have been a number of cases where a child was abandoned by parents and have survived by living with animals. These children have adopted the behaviour of the animals with whom they lived – running on all fours, eating raw meat and growling rather than talking in one particular case.

Identity

Definition

Identity – a person's identity is composed of a mixture of personal experiences and wider images of the world and their place in it, provided by schools, the media and people who are important to the individual. It is usually linked to awareness of gender, race and social status, as well as an image of one's own body

The final piece of equipment in our sociological toolbox is the concept of **identity**.

How we act and respond to others is closely related to our sense of who we are. But this belief of what and who we are in the scheme of things is the result of a long and complex learning process which is closely related to socialisation.

For the socialisation process not only teaches us how to behave, but also *who we are* within the many millions of possible identities 'on offer'. Usually identities are 'located' within certain clear boundaries. In Europe for example, we are aware of such things as our gender, our sexual orientation, our skin colour, our nationality (and maybe also a sense of the region from where we come) and our social status. Beyond this, the construction of our identities may become more fragmented and individual, depending upon personal experiences, educational success, friendships, interests and family ideas.

The result of this incredible web of experiences is an individual identity. Look at the photo below. The aboriginal men have retained their 'identity' and their culture despite the introduction of modern technology.

Two aboriginal men telephone relatives to invite them to an initiation ceremony.

Main points ▶ Socialisation is the process by which we learn how to behave 'correctly' in society.
▶ The way people are socialised strongly influences their personalities and how they act.
▶ Different societies socialise their children into different values, beliefs, norms and roles.
▶ Social control is the process whereby people are made to conform to the norms of society.
▶ There are two types of social control: formal and informal.
▶ This shows that people do not act instinctively, but learn their behaviour.
▶ People's identities, that is how they see themselves, are formed through socialisation.

---

1 CHAPTER SUMMARY

1   Sociology explores the social world around us which we take for granted.

2   In order to do so, sociologists use a series of concepts, or 'building blocks', which include culture, beliefs, values, norms, roles, identity, socialisation and social control.

3   A culture is the whole set of beliefs and guidelines as to how people *ought* to behave in any society.

4   Cultures vary over time and across societies. Within cultures there are sometimes variations and these are known as subcultures.

5   Beliefs are very general feelings or opinions about the nature of the world around us.

6   Values are ideas about correct forms of behaviour, which stress how we ought to behave in general terms, but they do not provide a guide to behaviour in specific situations.

7   Norms provide us with very clear guidance on how to behave in everyday situations

8   A social role is a *predictable* 'bundle' of actions, linked with particular positions in society. Everybody plays more than one role and sometimes this can lead to a conflict in the expectations associated with each role.

9   In order to learn how to behave, people are socialised. Socialisation is simply the process of being taught, usually in informal situations, how to survive, both physically and socially, in a society.

10   However, at points in their lives, people may behave in ways which threaten to disrupt the smooth pattern of society – and so they need to be brought back into conformity. This is known as the process of social control. Social control can be either formal or informal.

11   Sociologists believe that all of these building blocks prove that people act in certain ways, not from instinct (like animals), but through learning.

12   The sense of who we are is known as identity and this is learned throughout our lives through socialisation.

Test Your Knowledge

1 Name any three building blocks of sociology.

2 Do cultures remain the same over time and across societies? Explain your answer.

3 What is a norm? Give one example.

4 Give an example of role conflict.

5 What is the difference between socialisation and social control?

6 Why do sociologists reject the idea of instinct as the main explanation for human behaviour?

RESEARCHING SOCIETY

Chapter contents

Common sense and research 'sense'

When people discuss social issues with friends or family, they usually support their argument on the basis of their common sense and experience. Yet these two methods of making sense of the world are of limited use if we really want to tackle problems in a fresh, accurate and unbiased way.

What's wrong with common sense?

An alternative, and rather cynical, view of common sense is that it is just *applying our prejudices* – and, after all, your common sense may not be the same as mine, and who is to say that one is more accurate than the other?

What's wrong with experience?

The other way of approaching problems, through our own experience, is equally dubious, for everyone's experience is limited and memories or perceptions are distorted. Also my experiences may, like my common sense, be very different from yours.

Knowledge through research

Research is another way of trying to arrive at the truth. When a person engages in research, she or he will try to find out as many relevant facts and pieces of information about the area under investigation, without letting personal bias or values influence this process. The researcher will use a range of tools and methods which have been developed by social scientists for over a century.

Properly conducted research can unearth accurate, useful information which provides the basis for well-informed debate. Rather than two people swapping prejudices, we can exchange different pieces of information and try to put them together to help us understand society better.

Social science research is widely used by the British government, for example, to allow it to decide how best to provide educational, health and social services, as well as to plan housing and road-building programmes.

Sociology, fiction and journalism

The aim of sociology is to uncover the rules of society that govern our everyday lives, which we take for granted. This involves exploring people's experiences, describing their lifestyles and understanding their feelings. But sociologists are not alone in this work: novelists and journalists, along with a host of other people, do a very similar thing. But there is a difference. Whereas journalists may embroider their stories, or make their accounts of what happens more exciting in order to sell a few more copies, and novelists may simply use their insights to make up stories, sociologists must describe and explain the social world simply, clearly and accurately for the sole purpose of advancing our knowledge.

Approaches to research

Definition

Positivism – positivists believe that sociology should try to be a science and to use as many of the methods which the physical sciences use as is possible. They conduct surveys and gather statistics and, when possible, use experiments

If you watch an expert craftsperson at work, you will notice that he or she uses the very best tools and follows methods which have developed over years of training and experience. If sociologists want to perform their work accurately, they too must have excellent tools and methods. This chapter is devoted to studying these.

But, as with most subjects, there are very different ways of approaching the study of society. A division exists between **positivists** and **subjective sociologists**. Almost all research falls into one or other of these categories.

Positivists

Positivists follow, very broadly, the same sorts of research methods as natural scientists (physicists, biologists, etc.) and believe this is the very best way to understand society. The methods used include:

- surveys
- official published statistics (such as the crime rates which are published every year)
- historical sources (such as diaries and war records)
- experiments.

Their belief is that as the natural sciences have been so successful in understanding the physical world around us, we should adopt their tried and proven methods to understand the social world.

Subjective sociologists

These sociologists are not convinced that borrowing the methods of the natural sciences is the best way to understand social life. They prefer to try to put themselves in the minds of people whose behaviour they are trying to understand. Only by looking at people's actions from their point of view can we actually understand why they behave the way they do.

This sort of approach is very often used when studying something most of us may find unusual or criminal. The most commonly used methods are:

- observational study
- participant observation.

The difference between observation and participant observation

We will return to this division later and explore how they are both used and how they are both extremely good was of providing different insights.

Main points

▶ Sociology attempts to uncover the reality of the social world by using a series of specific research methods, rather than relying upon common sense or experience.

▶ These methods distinguish the sociologist from journalists and other commentators.

▶ Sociologists all agree on the need to have rigorous research methods, but they disagree about which methods are best.

▶ There are two general approaches sociologists use:
- positivist, which stresses the use of surveys
- subjectivist, which prefers to observe people in their daily lives.

Surveys

The most commonly used research method in sociology is the survey. A survey is simply a series of questions which are given to a cross-section of the group of people you wish to study (known as a *population* in sociology). Perhaps the best known form of survey is the **opinion poll** – the results of which you can read in a newspaper virtually everyday.

For example, when opinion poll companies want to predict the outcome of a general election, they ask a cross-section of British voters which party they intend to vote for. They add the results together and make predictions as to which political party is going to win. Opinion polls are also used to find out our views on a very wide range of other issues from racial prejudice to convenience foods.

Bloodsports, Royalsports, Spoilsports

The passionate debate over whether to ban fox-hunting and other traditional country pastimes is dividing Britain as never before, an exclusive survey reveals.

And, increasingly, it is dragging the Queen and the Royal children into the bitter argument over the Prime Minister's plans to outlaw hunting before the next election.

The Mail on Sunday/MORI poll reveals the growing public belief that the Queen herself should take the lead by discouraging Prince Charles and other members of the Royal Family from taking prt in hunting with hounds. The majority clearly believe that, in supporting bloodsports, the Royals set a bad example. And, while passions continue to run high over fox-hunting, the poll reveals a huge increase in opposition to the shooting of grouse and pheasant, another rural pastime enjoyed by Princes William and Harry.

MORI interviewed 801 adults aged 18 and over across Britain. Interviews were conducted by telephone on July 14 and 15, 1999. Data weighted to match national population profile.

HUNTING WITH DOGS

Where do you live most of the time?	%
In the middle of a city or town	31
In a suburb	38
On the edge of the countryside	23
In the middle of the countryside	9

To what extent do you support or oppose a ban on hunting with dogs in Britain?	%
Strongly support a ban	52
Tend to support a ban	11
Neither support nor oppose a ban	11
Tend to oppose a ban	10
Strongly oppose a ban	14
Don't know/No opinion	2

Fox-hunting is necessary to preserve the balance of country wildlife.

	Feb 95 %	Jul 99 %	Change 95–99 ±%
Strongly agree	4	10	+6
Tend to agree	16	13	−3
Neither agree/disagree	12	5	−7
Tend to disagree	30	22	−8
Strongly disagree	36	47	+11
Don't know/No opinion	2	3	+1

SHOOTING BIRDS

Shooting live game birds such as pheasants and grouse should be banned.

	Feb 95 %	Jul 99 %	Change 95–99 ±%
Strongly agree	27	40	+13
Tend to agree	26	13	−13
Neither agree/disagree	15	10	−5
Tend to disagree	21	21	0
Strongly disagree	10	13	+3
Don't know/No opinion	1	3	+2

FISHING

Fishing with rod and line should be banned.

	Feb 95 %	Jul 99 %	Change 95–99 ±%
Strongly agree	5	10	+5
Tend to agree	7	8	+1
Neither agree/disagree	18	10	−8
Tend to disagree	36	33	−3
Strongly disagree	32	35	+3
Don't know/No opinion	2	4	+2

ROYAL FAMILY AND BLOODSPORTS

The Royal Family set a bad example by taking part in bloodsports.

	Feb 95 %	Jul 99 %	Change 95–99 ±%
Strongly agree	31	47	+16
Tend to agree	33	17	−16
Neither agree/disagree	12	7	−5
Tend to disagree	16	16	0
Strongly disagree	5	12	+7
Don't know/No opinion	3	1	−2

The Queen should take the lead and actively discourage her family from taking part in bloodsports.

	Feb 95 %	Jul 99 %	Change 95–99 ±%
Strongly agree	39	47	+8
Tend to agree	26	17	−9
Neither agree/disagree	12	7	−5
Tend to disagree	15	14	−1
Strongly disagree	6	14	+8
Don't know/No opinion	2	1	−1

Source: Adapted from *The Mail on Sunday*, 25 July 1999

1 How many people were interviewed?

2 How was this done?

3 Are the majority of people in favour of hunting?

4 Why did they ask the question about where people lived?

5 What is the majority view on fishing?

6 Have attitudes towards the Royal Family and hunting changed between 1995 and 1999? In what way?

7 After you have read the full section on surveys, undertake a similar one on attitudes to hunting.

Activity

Collect the newspapers for the past week. Are any survey findings reported? What are they? How many people were asked for their opinions?

For lots of interesting surveys look up the MORI opinion poll company website: http://www.mori.com

Types of survey

There are three different types of survey:

- the **cross-sectional survey**
- the **longitudinal survey**
- the **panel survey**.

Cross-sectional surveys

These surveys, which we have just described above, aim to find out the opinions of a wide range of people. But they have one drawback – everyone is asked their opinion at one time, that is, of course, when the survey takes place. The problem is that people change their minds and so what they think today, they may possibly not think tomorrow. So such surveys are a fixed reflection of one moment in time.

Longitudinal surveys

These are surveys conducted on the same people over quite a long period of time, sometimes over as long as 20 years. They provide us with a clear, moving image of the changes in attitudes over time.

Unfortunately longitudinal surveys are difficult to do, mainly because people drop out of the survey as they get bored answering the questions, or they might move and the researchers lose track of them. If too many people 'drop out', this may make the survey unreliable.

Panel surveys

An alternative version of the longitudinal survey is the panel survey. A panel survey usually lasts for a shorter time than a longitudinal survey and asks questions of panel members on a more frequent basis. Typically, a person may be a member of a panel for a couple of years and be asked questions every month. In a longitudinal survey, they will probably be asked questions only once a year.

A pilot survey for a pilot survey?

Pilot surveys

Before any survey is actually conducted, the researchers will want to conduct a 'dry-run' just to make sure they have got everything right. This dry-run is known as a **pilot survey**. There may be problems with the way the questions have been written so that people cannot understand them, or perhaps there are too many questions so that people get bored. They may also discover that the people they have chosen for the survey may not be appropriate for their purpose.

Main points

▶ Surveys aim to get the views of a cross-section of the population.

▶ There are a number of different types of survey which provide different ways of getting information. These include:
   - cross-sectional surveys – giving a snapshot view of society at any one time
   - longitudinal surveys – giving views of a wide range of people over a long period of time
   - panel surveys – giving highly detailed views over a period of time.

Sampling

Definition

Sampling – a way of finding a small number of people who form a representative cross-section of the population in general

There are about 64 million people in Britain. Finding out *everybody's* views would be terribly expensive and complicated to do. Only the government has the resources to carry out a survey of every household in Britain (known as the Census), and even this is so difficult and expensive that the government only does it once even ten years.

So, in order to find opinions and get information, sociologists have to study a smaller number of people. This is not necessarily a bad thing, as long as the small group chosen (the **sample**) is a true cross-section of people, so that the opinions of this sample represent the opinions of everyone in the population under study. Clearly, if the sample is not a true cross-section, the whole study will be inaccurate.

Definition

Sampling frame – the place, list or resource from which the sample is drawn

Getting an accurate sample of the population you wish to study is therefore one of the most important things that a researcher must do. This is what we need to discuss next. But before we do so, there is one problem we have to mention, that is the **sampling frame**.

The sampling frame

The sample which we want to make must be taken from some source; it could be, for example, every third person walking down the street, it could be a random selection of names from the electoral roll in a town (this is a list of local voters and can be found in the main library of any town), or a selection from the names of people enrolled in an evening class. Each of these is an example of a sampling frame, which can be defined as *the source from which a sample can be drawn.*

If the sampling frame is poor, the sample, and the survey, will be of little use. For instance, it is no use taking names at random from a list of 12-year-olds if the purpose of the survey is to find how people intend to vote in the next election, as you have to be 18 to vote.

Surveys, samples and sampling frames

The following extract is from a leaflet produced by a government research department, the Office for National Statistics. The research was intended to give a clear picture of the eating habits of children under five and to relate this to their health.

2. Why have we come to your household?
To visit every household in the country would take too long and cost far too much money.

Therefore we selected a sample of addresses from the Postcode Address File. The Postcode Address File is compiled by the Post Office and lists all the addresses to which mail is sent. We sent a letter to each selected address asking for details of the age and sex of everybody living there. We chose those addresses in a way that gave everyone the same chance of being selected. From the replies we were able to tell which households contained a child under 5, and from those we selected a sample to be interviewed. Your household is one of those chosen to be interviewed.

Some people think either that they and their family are not typical enough to be of any help in the survey or that they are very different from other people and they would distort the findings. The important thing to remember is that the community consists of a great many different types of people and families and we need to represent them all in our sample survey. It will therefore be appreciated if everyone we approach agrees to take part.

Source: OPCS, 'The Young Children's Dietary Survey', 1992

1 In your own words, explain what a sampling frame is?

2 Which sampling frame was used in this survey?

3 Why did they ask questions about the age and sex of the people living at each address?

4 Why is it important to get a cross-section of the community when conducting a survey?

Question

Say what is wrong with the sampling frame suggested in each case below and suggest a more appropriate one.

Group	**Suggested sampling frame**
a) people over 18 years of age	people who look over 18 in the street
b) students in a college	everyone in your class
c) 'clubbers'	cool-looking people at college
d) Labour Party members	anyone who votes Labour

Methods of sampling

Definition

Random sampling – the cross-section is found by randomly selecting people

There are basically two ways in which sociologists ensure that their sample of the population is accurate:

- random sampling
- quota sampling.

Random sampling

This is based on the idea that if you select people in the population entirely randomly, then you are likely to end up with a sample which is an exact mirror of the population, as each person has an equal chance of being picked.

Activity

If you are studying in a group of 20 or more, try seeing if random sampling works. For every female in the class mark a slip of paper with the letter F, for every male put in a blank slip. If you are in a same-sex class, you might want to make some sort of simple division by age, ethnic group, height, hair colour or anything else you can think of.

Put the slips of paper in a box and then pull eight or ten out at random. You should find that the proportion of males/females (or whatever you chose) reflects the composition of the group.

Quota sampling

Definition

Quota sampling – the cross-section is based on a statistical breakdown of the population, so that researchers are told to get a 'quota' of specific people to fill each statistical category

This form of sampling is used by most commercial market research companies, as it is accurate and very cheap. It is basically the same as *strata sampling* – each interviewer is told to go out and interview an exact number of specifically identified groups of people in direct proportion to their existence in the population as a whole.

For instance, we know that about half the population is female, so half the sample must be female. We also know the proportion of women in each age group, so the interviewers are told to find women in the correct proportion of ages to mirror the population, and so on.

The main problems with this sort of sampling are that it:

- only works when you know a lot about the population you wish to study
- relies upon interviewers correctly spotting the 'right' type of person to fit their quota.

However, so much information has been gathered about the British population that it is rare the commercial market research companies get it wrong. Indeed, it is so accurate that opinion polls based on as few as 1,500 people can usually predict the views of the entire British population.

Quota sampling: The population characteristics required are told to the interviewers.

The interviewers find appropriate people.

Sampling in action

There is overwhelming public backing for the idea that teachers should promote marriage as part of sex education classes in schools. ...
  ICM [a research company]

interviewed a random, countrywide sample of 1205 adults aged 18 and over by phone [over a two-day period], with the results weighted to the profile of all adults.

Source: *The Guardian*, 15 February 2000

1 Which type of sampling method was used?

2 What sampling frame was used?

3 Was an interview or questionnaire used?

4 What problems do you think there might be when using the telephone for conducting research?

5 How large was the sample? Do you think that this is a large enough sample to make the claim that 'there is overwhelming public support'. When you read headlines in the papers which make such claims in the future, what sorts of question should you ask?

Sampling and survey accuracy

This technical note comes from a national survey of attitudes of British people.

Technical Note

[The research company] ... interviewed a representative quota sample of 1,230 people aged 15+ throughout Great Britain.

This size and design of sample [was such that] ... we would expect in 95% of cases to be accurate to plus or minus 3%. ... For example, if we found, as we did, that 57% of our sample said they were married, there would be a 95% probability that the true percentage of married people aged 15 and over would be between 54% and 60% with the greatest probability that the true figure was indeed 57%.

Source: Adapted from E. Jacobs and R. Worcester, *Typically British?* (Bloomsbury, 1991)

1 Explain in your own words what the following sentence means:

'This size and design of sample [was such that] ... we would expect in 95% of cases to be accurate to plus or minus 3%.'

2 What does this tell us about the accuracy of surveys today?

3 If an opinion poll at a general election stated that one political party was going to get 2 per cent more of the votes than its nearest rival, would you believe it?

Main points

▶ Sampling involves choosing a small number of people who are a typical cross-section of society.

▶ A sample is usually taken from a sampling frame – which is the source from which the cross-section are chosen. If this is no good, it will ruin the research.

▶ There are two main types of sampling:

– random sampling, based on the view that random selection will lead to a representative cross-section being chosen. There are a number of types of random sample which ensure greater accuracy or provide greater depth

– quota sampling, where a lot of information is already known about a society or group of people, then one can select a cross-section on the basis of this knowledge. There is only one form of quota sampling.

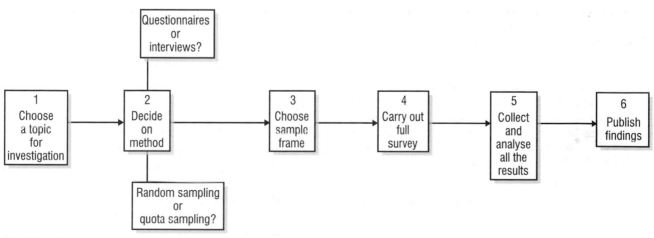

The stages of a survey

Asking questions: questionnaires and interviews

To find out what people actually think, sociologists have to ask them questions. There are two ways of doing this, by using:

- a **questionnaire** – the researcher writes down the questions and leaves people to answer them by themselves.
- an **interview** – the research asks people questions face-to-face.

Activity

Asking questions: accuracy and clarity

When sociologists undertake their research they make sure that their questions:

- are phrased *very carefully* – they must be simply expressed in good English and have only one possible meaning to the respondent (the person being asked)
- guide the *respondent* to give a clear answer, which makes it possible for the researcher to put all of the information together fairly easily.

Below are some questions which you are considering using for your survey. Indicate which questions are:

- helpful in sociological research
- not helpful
- would be better used in interviews than questionnaires.

Remember the distinction between open and closed questions and the different usefulness in interviews and questionnaires. Give reasons for your answers.

Try asking a small sample of people these questions and see how the responses vary in their usefulness to you.

1 What do you think about racism?
2 How many hours' homework do you do each night?
   a) None
   b) less than 1 hour
   c) 1–2 hours
   d) more than 2 hours
3 Why do you think people commit crime?
4 Do you agree or disagree with the following statement: 'Religion is in decline in the UK today.'?
5 Current debates over the nature of financial support to the agro-chemical industries misses the key point, that GM crops will eventually revolutionise the entire agricultural enterprise – especially in the poorer nations. True or false?
6 a) Which political party do you support?
   b) Could you give me any reasons why you support it?
7 Which party did you vote for at the last general election?
8 Wouldn't you agree that private health care is a bad thing?

Questionnaires

Definitions

Questionnaire – a series of written questions which people complete by themselves

Interview – a series of questions or topics asked by a researcher directly to a person and the answers are recorded by the researcher

Questionnaires consist of a series of written questions which are usually posted or handed out to people, although sometimes they are read out to respondents.

The essence of a good questionnaire is that it asks exactly the *right questions* to uncover the information you want to find, in as *clear and simple* a manner as possible and that it is *as short as possible*.

The advantages of questionnaires

Questionnaires are very useful for reaching a large number of people as they can just be handed out or posted to a widely spread group of people, living in different towns in Britain, for example. You can simply put them in the post and they only need the cost of an envelope and postage stamp (plus a stamped, addressed return envelope, of course!).

Often people will reply to rather embarrassing questions about such things as sexual activities or illegal acts if they are contained in a questionnaire, but they would not answer (truthfully) if faced by an interviewer.

The disadvantages of questionnaires

The disadvantages are that very often people cannot be bothered to send a questionnaire back, so the *response rate* (the number of people who reply) is very low. This can make a survey useless, as you do not know if the few who reply are typical in their views of all those who did not reply. So, if the researcher posts 200 questionnaires and gets 20 back, even if they all agree on the answer, the researcher has still received too few to know what the other 180 people think and it is wrong to assume that they all think the same way as the people who replied.

A second problem is it is difficult to go *into depth* in a questionnaire, because the questions need to be clear and simple. So, questionnaires are best used when the answer can be expressed in very clear terms such as numbers (How many hours? How much money? etc.) or in terms of 'Yes' or 'No'.

Finally, you can never be sure that the *correct person answers*. If you want the questions answered by a female in a household, but they cannot be bothered or are to busy, it could be answered, in an idle ten minutes, by a son or husband. The answers would therefore reflect the male as opposed to the female point of view.

Advantages of questionnaires		Disadvantages of questionnaires	
Reach a large number of people	✔	Low response rate	✔
A widely dispersed population	✔	Difficult to go into depth	✔
Good for embarrassing subjects	✔	Never know if correct person answers	✔

Interviews

An interview is a series of questions, or a discussion on a selected topic, asked face-to-face between two people, the researcher and the respondent.

Interviewing skills

SOCIAL SURVEY INTERVIEWERS

The Social Survey Division of ONS have vacancies for permanent interviewers **living in** the following Postcode areas only:

SO BH TA TN DY WV SW SE

GU RG OX G EH DD PE LN NE

NG LE SR DL M WA WN CB

RM W TN CH SA DH CM N WD

The work involves calling on people in their homes and collecting information on a variety of social issues on behalf of the Government by carrying out structured interviews.

Candidates should have a pleasant manner, smart appearance and good communication skills. Own car and telephone are essential. The work is hourly paid at attractive rates plus expenses. Interviewers are required to be available for at least three days and three evenings per week. The Retirement age is 65.

For an application form pleased write to: Central Support Unit, Room 426, Office for National Statistics, St Catherines House, 10 Kingsway, London WC2B 6JP. Postcards only. Or alternatively ring 01329 813002 (lines will be open from 29th May to 5th June 1996. 10a.m.–4p.m. weekdays only).

Closing date for applications: 14th June 1996.

1   What work does a social survey interviewer do?

2   What skills are required? Why?

Structured and unstructured interviews

Interviews can be very tightly organised, with the interviewer simply reading out questions from a prepared questionnaire, or they can be very open and flexible with the interviewer being given scope to ask extra questions or rephrase difficult ones.

The tightly organised interview is known as a *structured interview* and the flexible one is called an *unstructured* or an *in-depth interview*.

The advantages of interviews

If the subject of enquiry is *complex*, or a small survey needs to be done *immediately*, or the sociologists knows that a questionnaire would never be answered, for whatever reason (for example, young children who cannot read properly), sociologists generally use interviews.

Apart from being useful for examining complex issues, the interviewer can also compare his or her own observations with the answers of the respondent, to check if they are telling the truth. So, a person who describes himself as a fitness fanatic who regularly stops the interview for a long cough, a drag on his cigarette and a calming swig of whisky may not be telling the truth.

Finally, there is a much higher response rate with interviews than with questionnaires as the process is so much more personal and it is difficult to refuse a researcher when approached politely.

The disadvantages of interviews

The disadvantages are that the interviewer may influence the replies of the respondent in some way. For instance, a black interviewer asking a white respondent about racial prejudice has been found to receive very different replies from a white interviewer. And, of course, hiring trained interviewers is expensive.

Oh yes, definitely — a fitness fanatic.

Advantages of interviews		Disadvantages of interviews	
Can go into depth	✔	Takes a lot of time	✔
Usually get a higher response rate	✔	Not much use for a large number of people	✔
Good for untangling complex issues	✔	Difficult to discuss embarrassing subjects	✔
		Interviewer bias a possible problem	✔

Interviewing

The researcher in the extract below wanted to examine the views of 'feminist mothers' – those mothers of young children who held strong views about the roles of men and women and wished to gain more power for women.

Fifty-two women were interviewed for this research, twenty in London, sixteen in Leicester and sixteen in Helsinki, … The women were found through friends and acquaintances and through various organisations, and a few I knew from previous research contacts.

The interviews lasted up to two hours. The purpose of the interviews was explained to the women as they were contacted. Some information was obtained in writing, and the rest of the interview was recorded. All the interviews were transcribed [the words on the recording written down] and the transcripts were returned to the interviewees. The interviews were semi-structured, with particular themes I wanted cover. However, if something particular was of interest to the interviewee, this was explained at length, and consequently other areas received less coverage.

Source: T. Gordon, *Feminist Mothers* (Macmillan Education, 1990)

1 How did the researcher obtain her sample? (This method, incidentally is known as snowball sampling.)

2 Do you think that this sample was representative of all women? Did she want it to be representative?

3 Suggest any strength and weakness of snowball sampling.

4 What is meant, do you think, by 'semi-structured interviews'? Why, in your opinion, would she use this rather than a 'highly structured interview'?

5 How did she remember what they said?

6 Why did she return the 'transcripts', do you think?

Case studies

A **case study** is a piece of research where the sociologist chooses one specific group or situation and carries out an intensive study to find out as much information and detail as possible.

A case study of family mealtimes

This study by Susan Grieshaber was about the dynamics of family life. But, unusually, she wanted to explore the ways that young children 'resist' and bargain with their parents and, secondly the differences in the ways that boys and girls are expected to behave. The research focused on mealtimes, which she felt were a particularly important family occasion. Grieshaber actually conducted four case studies so that she would be able to reject the criticism that her work was not typical of most families.

> [The] family was visited a minimum of ten times for at least three hours … Along with other aspects of daily domesticity, mealtime preparation, consumption and cleaning rituals were recorded using a video camera.

Grieshaber found that there were rules concerning appropriate behaviour at the table and that the children tried to 'subvert' these on many occasions. Here are the 'rules' in two of the households:

Adult rules about table manners

Family	Rules
The Haineses	need to ask to use fingers to eat; if child chooses not to eat, still required to sit at the table; what is not eaten that night is eaten the next day; if child is not eating the meal, no chips, milk or soft drink allowed; no talking with mouth full; what is requested must be eaten; what is on the plate must be eaten; knives stay out of mouths; teatime is the only time the family sits down together; child's food preferences have some influence over what is eaten; mother feeds child if necessary; not too much food in the mouth at one time; speak nicely at the table; mouth is to be closed when chewing; sit appropriately at the table, with feet on the floor.
The Andersons	sit at the table to eat; keep hands off food not about to be consumed; once the meal is finished there is nothing else to eat; some fruit is to be consumed each day; some vegetables are to be eaten for the evening meal; utensils to be used to serve food; eat nicely, no playing with food; elbows off the table; children can get own drinks; parents put salt on food; no toys at the table; food dropped on the floor is to be picked up; parents decide how much chocolate, ice cream etc., children can have.

Source: Adapted from S. Grieshaber, 'Mealtime rituals: power and resistance in the construction of mealtime rules', *British Journal of Sociology*, Vol. 48, No. 4, December 1997

Conduct your own case study. What are the rules in your household?

The advantages of case studies

Generally, a case study is expected to provide extremely detailed information which can be applied to other, similar situations and groups of people. This may be useful just to help us understand that situation (for example, bullying in a particular school or place of work). A second use of a case study is as a type of pilot study, to see what problems or main issues need to be looked at in a larger survey or study later (for example, if we want to study children's eating habits to see the effect on health, we study one family first). A third use is to provide evidence to support or to reject a theory .

The disadvantage of case studies

However, the problem is that unlike the survey, it is never certain that group or situation chosen for the case study really is typical and, as a consequence, the results cannot necessarily be used to produce general explanations.

Comparative studies

Experiments are not commonly used in sociology because society is so complex that we just cannot recreate the conditions of a science laboratory. But there have been a few famous experiments. In the late 1960s in the USA, Rosenthal and Jacobson (*Pygmalion in the Classroom*), tricked school teachers in one school into believing that, by using a very new intelligence test they could uncover children with extra potential. They then told the teachers who these children were. Sure enough, after 18 months these children had improved much more than the other children in the classes. In fact, the children had been selected entirely at random. They were no different from the other children at the beginning of the 18 months. The improvement was due to the teachers believing they were clever!

Comparative studies are often claimed to be the sociologist's alternative to experiments. Sociologist often compare the behaviour of similar groups in different situations (or quite different groups in similar situations!) to uncover the key factors which make them behave differently.

Comparisons are made across a range of different social factors, including age groups, ethnicity, gender, geographical position, social class, and an enormous range of other variables.

For example, we know that people who smoke cigarettes have a higher chance of dying from heart disease and lung cancer than those who do not smoke, but otherwise live exactly the same sort of lives as smokers. The following information was obtained from comparative studies:
- The avoidance of smoking would eliminate one third of the cancer deaths in Britain.
- A person who smokes regularly more than doubles his or her risk of dying before the age of 65.

> **Definition**
>
> **Comparative study** – comparing two societies or groups of people to find out in what key ways they differ

Main points ▶ There are two main ways of asking people questions: questionnaires and interviews.

▶ Questionnaires are written questions which people complete and return to the researcher.

▶ Interviews are where people are asked questions face-to-face.

▶ Each method has advantages and disadvantages – so sociologists tend to use them in different situations.

▶ In general, interviews allow greater depth of analysis, whilst questionnaires can be given to a much larger and widely dispersed number of people.

▶ Case studies are when a particular group is studied in very great depth. It is a fairly unusual method in sociology, but is extremely useful for detailed information.

▶ The comparative method is where two societies are compared in order to see what key differences there are between them and what may cause these differences.

▶ Both the comparative method and case studies tend to be used in sociology instead of experiments which are more common in psychology.

Primary and secondary sources

Sociologists must use whatever methods are most appropriate for the situation and group of people they are studying. As a result, they employ a great variety of methods which reflect influences such as how easy it is to obtain access to information, or how up-to-date the information is. The answers to these questions usually determine whether a researcher is going to use **primary** or **secondary sources** of information.

Primary sources

> **Definition**
>
> **Primary sources** – all information that the sociologist has gathered him or herself

Primary sources include all information that the sociologist has gathered him or herself, irrespective of the method used – from questionnaires, interviews, experiments and observational studies, for example.

Problems with primary sources

The strength of primary research – that the researcher has done the work her or himself – is also its greatest weakness Any factual error in the statistics, poorly phrased questions, or even subconscious bias will affect the outcome and usefulness of the research.

Secondary sources

> **Definition**
>
> **Secondary sources** – information initially researched by someone else and which the researcher uses

Secondary sources include all statistics and information not collected directly by a sociologist engaged in research, but which have been collected by other people. For example:
- government statistics on crime, births, deaths, marriages, etc.
- historical documents such as diaries, church records, descriptions of important events and court documents

- media sources, such as newspaper and television stories
- the Internet
- non-fiction publications, such as factually-based novels and autobiographies.

Sometimes, research is based entirely on these sources, particularly if the people being studied are dead, acting illegally or are difficult to trace, but generally sociologists are very wary about using secondary sources. More often, sociologists use these secondary sources as background information to help them understand their primary research better.

Problems with secondary sources

The problems with secondary sources are that they have generally been collected for specific reasons, by people who have varying motives. A diary, autobiography or novel may reflect the values and prejudices of the writer. How much, therefore, can be believed? Statistics on crime are less a reflection on how many crimes are committed a year, and more a reflection of how many of the crimes are actually reported to the police (and we know the majority are not) and how many of these the police take seriously.

Content analysis

Definition

Content analysis – the detailed analysis of one or more of the media (such as newspapers, Internet sites or advertisements) in order to find how a particular group or event is being portrayed

Content analysis is a very common method of research used by sociologists and consists of searching through newspapers and other forms of media to find information on a particular topic. This information is then analysed. Today, most researchers use the Internet to access back copies of newspapers and other forms of media information.

Content analysis has been used to research such things as the portrayal of women, racial stereotyping, images of violence and the reporting of war in the media.

Content analysis In 1992, David Morrisson conducted research which:

set out to explore what the viewer considered the role of television ought to be in covering war and to provide an account of how viewers responded to the images they	did see and the information they received. ... [As part of his research, he] conducted a massive content analysis of the main evening news and current affairs programmes broadcast	during the [Gulf] war on BBC1, BBC2, ITV, Channel 4, CNN and BSkyB. In addition, the news on the following foreign channels was also recorded for the purpose of comparative content	analysis – Germany (BR2), France (TF1), Italy (RAI1) and Russia (the main service carried on the Gorizont satellite).

Source: D.E. Morrisson, *Television and the Gulf War* (John Libbey & Co., 1992)

Various groups of adults and children were then shown all or part of this material and asked for their views.

1 What does the extract mean when it refers to a 'massive content analysis of the main evening news and current affairs programmes broadcast during the [Gulf] war'?

2 What advantages to the research can be gained by using comparative material?

Observational studies

The methods we have examined so far are generally associated with sociologists who believe that sociology ought, as far as possible, to follow the methods of the natural sciences, such as chemistry or physics (positivists). The survey is seen as the substitute for the experiment. However, other sociologists (subjective sociologists) argue that the best way to understand people is to try to get as close to them in their daily lives as possible. These sociologists stress the usefulness of observational methods.

Observational techniques are particularly useful for studying people in circumstances where they would not normally reply to a questionnaire or interview. For example, in a study of youth crime, it would hardly be possible to ask the youths to stop in the middle of committing a burglary so they could complete a questionnaire.

The sociologist should not get too get too close to the group he or she is studying.

The sociologist should always try to retain a neutral attitude.

What normally happens in observational studies is that the sociologist joins a group which he or she wishes to study in depth. The sociologist then has a number of decisions to make.

Participant versus non-participant observation?

Does the sociologist become a full member of the group (perhaps the group is engaged in criminal activities)? This is known as **participant observation**. Or does the sociologist follow them around, simply observing, rather like a 'fly on the wall'? This is known as **non-participation observation**.

If the sociologist becomes a full member of the group, the advantage is that he or she will readily get to see things the way the group does, *but* may be influenced so much by this that the research becomes too biased in favour of the group or prejudiced against them.

If the sociologist acts as a 'fly on the wall', the advantage is that there is far less risk of getting too drawn into the group, so that greater objectivity (seeing things as they really are) results. *But* there is less chance of fully understanding things as the group under study do because the researcher is not really one of them.

Covert versus overt observation?

Whether the researcher engages in participant or non-participant observation, a crucial problem which he or she must solve is the extent to which the presence of an observer influences the group's actions. People just do not act naturally if they know they are being observed.

In certain circumstances, sociologists may prefer to pretend to be a member of the group. Philip Bourgois lived undercover, using **covert observation** whilst studying the lives of those who sold and used crack cocaine in an inner city area of a US city. Had he been discovered, then he faced violence and possible death as a police undercover agent. But Bourgois knew this was the only way to study crack cocaine dealers.

On the other hand, Howard Parker told the gang of petty criminals in his study, *View from the Boys*, exactly what he was doing. This is known as **overt observation**. Firstly, this was morally better as he was not deceiving anyone and, secondly, he found that gang members would confide things in him that they would be embarrassed to tell other gang members, just because he was a trusted outsider.

In actual research, however, a variety of techniques may well be thrown together to ensure that a full picture is drawn of the subject under study.

Real research: observational research and other techniques

Andrew Parker studied what it was like to be a trainee footballer in a professional football club. Parker used the overt participant observer method, joining in training sessions and allowing himself to be treated as a young footballer.

However, when he did the research, he also included a variety of other methods to get at the truth of the situation.

Gaining entry: Parker found it extremely difficult to be allowed to join a club. It took one year to be allowed to attend the club. As he puts it,

'Eventually ... I managed to convince staff at "Colby Town" that I was a relatively harmless "college student" eager to find out what it was like to be a football youth trainee.'

The research technique: This changed over time, as Parker's enquiries progressed:

'I interviewed trainees at least twice over the course of the research period. For the most part I attended the club for three days each week as a participant observer, spending two days training, working and socialising

with trainees and one day at a local college of further education as a fellow student. After the initial three months of participant observation, I began to conduct interviews with trainees ... [and] with various members of club staff and the college tutors directly involved with Colby trainees. ... All the interviews were tape-recorded. To supplement this data, a detailed fieldwork diary was kept throughout the research period.'

[In the article from which I took this information, Parker also gives a list of references which tells us that he also used secondary sources to understand the situation he was researching.]

Problems: The youth team coach

took a dislike to Parker and attempted to turn the trainees against him:

'He regularly made comments, gestures and inferences to trainees indicating his discomfort with my presence. ... He frequently addressed me in a demeaning fashion in front of the youth team players, discouraged them from talking to or about me and at times, completely ignored my existence.'

The positive side of the research: Parker got on well with the trainees and was accepted by them:

'Trainees regularly encouraged and supported my efforts. ... In addition they accepted me as one of their number outside

work and during general leisure time.'

Writing-up: Not as easy as it seemed. First there was the complexity of the task, second the sense of isolation at staying at home writing up the research:

'When the time came to synthesise theory, observations, fieldnotes and seven hundred sides of tape-recorded conversation, the task appeared decidedly unmanageable. ... Feelings of isolation were frequent during the initial months of writing-up, particularly because my days were now devoid of the excitement and activity of "doing" research, and the camaraderie of club solidarity.'

Source: Adapted from A. Parker, 'Staying on-side on the inside', *Sociology Review*, February 1998

1 What research techniques did Parker use?

2 Did this include non-participant or participant observation?

3 What problems did Parker face?

4 Why do you think Parker did not use covert observation?

5 What is 'writing-up'? Why was it so difficult?

Activity

Undertake a piece of observational research yourself. Have you got a part-time job? If so, spend one day as an 'outsider' looking at the what happens in your workplace. You should think about:

- the relationships between the workers and what you think makes them like/dislike each other
- the differences between the males and females
- the different attitudes of workers to their employment
- the way the person in charge treats people differently.

In groups, make a list of other possible points to explore.

Accuracy in research

The problems of reliability, validity and bias

Definitions

Reliable – each interview and questionnaire in a survey is carried out to a standard format, so that the researcher is sure that they are all the same

Valid – the research measures what it is supposed to measure

Unbiased – the personal views and biases of the researcher are kept out of the research

No matter how a piece of research is carried out, there are three important requirements. The piece of research must be:

- **reliable** – each interview and questionnaire in a survey is carried out to a standard format, so that the researcher is sure that they are all the same
- **valid** – the questionnaire or interview actually and accurately measures what it is supposed to measure
- **unbiased** – the personal views and biases of the researcher do not get tangled up with the research.

Reliability

A survey is composed of a number of different interviews or questionnaires which are carried out by one or more interviewers with many different people. The results are added up and at the end of our calculations we can say, for example, that when 100 people were asked about their views on racism and promotion at work:

- 50 people believed there was racial prejudice when it came to promotion
- 30 people said there was not
- 12 people felt that those from ethnic minority backgrounds actually got preference
- 8 people expressed no opinion.

But how do we know that this represents the truth, and that each interview is directly comparable with the others? For example, I am an African-Caribbean researcher asking the questions about racism in employment – will I receive the same answers as my white colleague? Well, we can make a reasonable assumption that some people will adjust their views depending upon the perceived ethnic origin of the interviewer.

The point about this example is that we cannot always assume each interview is exactly the same – things may happen to make one interview different from another. This problem is known as the problem of reliability.

Validity

Validity is the word used by researchers to describe the problem of making sure that the interview or questionnaire actually gets the information that you want it to. For example, if you wish to find out about violence on television and in the cinema, you might ask the question, 'Do you think the media have any effect on people's behaviour?' The respondent may not understand the meaning of the word 'media', but rather than admit this, he or she will reply 'Yes' or 'No' in order to say something.

In this case, the question and answer do not provide us with any idea of the 'truth' – the question is not valid.

Bias and values

Everyone has their own views on the world and their own pet theories, but in doing research, they need to put those views to one side and be as objective, or value-free, as possible. In interviews or questionnaires, it is very easy to influence the respondent by putting one's own views into questions, such as 'Wouldn't you agree that gay men should be allowed to marry?'

In observational studies, the researcher may interpret the behaviour of people through his or her own values, perhaps by being too sympathetic or even intensely disliking the group under study.

Research and opinion

Here is a letter sent to **The Sunday Times** regarding a debate on women's role in society. Read the letter carefully.

Domineering middle-class "feminists" have always been detrimental to ordinary people (*Comment*, last week). A notorious early example was their hijacking of the suffrage movement, turning it into a violent organisation which lost sympathy for the cause. The current contrary motion of the sexes, women going into the workforce while men go into dole queues, merely reflects their respective starting points. Men have left secure skilled work, women have left the home, but both have left secure positions to move down-hill to the labour pool.

Survey after survey of young women (18–24) reports most of them saying their favoured life-style when they reach 30 would be looking after their children full-time , supported by a husband with a secure, reasonably paid job. This after 30 years of feminist propaganda.

Along with their colleagues producing fiscal policies which penalise proper parenthood, the gender warriors are promoting greater exploitation dressed up as "choice" and "liberation".

Source: *The Sunday Times*, 17 October 1999

1 Is this letter based on fact or opinion?

2 How does the writer use the 'research' he cites?

3 Can you see any problem in the way he uses the research to support his argument?

4 Do the writer's values come through very clearly? Give examples of his choice of words.

Main points ▶ Primary sources are the information which sociologists find from their own direct research with people. Most of the methods in this chapter (surveys, case studies, observational studies, etc.) are examples of primary research.

▶ Secondary sources are the research and writings of others which sociologists use in their research. These include official statistics or published research, even diaries and novels.

▶ Content analysis is where sociologists examine published sources, such as newspapers or the Internet, in order to find out how a particular group is portrayed.

▶ Observational research is the method most used by subjectivist sociologists who believe that by watching and even joining in group activities they can understand more than by asking questions.

▶ Observational research has a number of variations. These are participant or non-participant, and covert or overt.

▶ Whatever form of research is undertaken, three issues must always be resolved: reliability, validity and bias.

Which method of research is best?

None of them! A sociologist will have to choose the method which seems most appropriate to the circumstances and aims of the research.

- Usually surveys are preferred if the aim is to find out the opinions of large numbers of people.
- Secondary sources are used to provide background information or to uncover information when there is no one able or willing to answer questions.
- Observational studies are used to help understand the activities of deviant or secretive groups, who when asked questions would not provide a reliable explanation for their behaviour.
- Comparative methods are used where clearly defined groups of people (such as nations or regions) are the focus of the research.

Doing a research project

Many courses in sociology require students to undertake a piece of research, and in this section we will look at the actual process of doing the research.

Choosing the topic

Choose a topic which is relevant to sociology, which is interesting to you, and which you believe you will actually be able to do some research on. Favourite topics followed by students I have taught are related to areas of gender and race, and, less often, social class, religion, crime and deviance (usually attitudes to drugs or the behaviour of [male] football supporters). However, I have read excellent pieces of research on nursing, stress, health and illness, older people, disability, and part-time employment in a fast-food chain. Each of these research projects had two common characteristics: the students were interested in the issues, and they had some knowledge of them before they started.

Always check with your tutor that your topic is relevant to sociology and that it is feasible, before you begin.

Background reading and Internet use

Once you have an idea of what you wish to research, ask your tutor for suggestions for background reading, go to your local library (or better still the town's central library) and ask for help.

Don't forget the Internet, which has a wide range of information, and any relevant CD-ROMs.

Deciding on the most appropriate method

This chapter has explained the different methods of research and the circumstances in which they are normally used, so you should now think carefully about which method would be most useful.

- Questionnaires (which are handed out) can provide a lot of information from a range of different people. The major problem will be getting them returned to you.
- Interviews will provide more detailed information, but they tend to take a lot of time and so you can only interview a small number of people.
- Observation is extremely useful if you wish to look at a group of people that you would normally be a member of, for example your friends' behaviour on your weekly Friday night out. Observation rarely yields much statistical information, although you could follow up observation with questionnaires or interviews.
- Comparative studies are very difficult to do, unless you rely upon secondary data for some, if not all, of your information.
- Experiments are possible, in a narrow range of situations where you might want to compare how people acted differently in different situations and where you are able to alter and control those situations. An example would be if you wanted to study differences in people's behaviour towards people with disabilities and people without disabilities. You could re-enact the same situation (person unable to open a door), but sometimes you would have a person with a disability (or appearing to have a disability) unable to open the door and sometimes a person without a disability.

Definition

Triangulation – using a number of methods to carry out a research project

Remember, you do not have to use just one method. Indeed, it is quite normal in contemporary social science research to use a number of different methods together. This is called **triangulation**.

The sample

Having selected your method, you must think about your sample. In some cases, the sample selects itself, such as your place of (part-time) employment – although you would need to decide whether this case study is typical of other organisations, or not. However, if you are doing a questionnaire or a series of interviews, you need to think carefully about the effect the sample you have chosen may have on the outcome of your research. Most people use friends, colleagues or family for their interviews, but there are obvious problems with doing this if you are seeking a cross-section of opinion.

Analysing data

Observational studies

You should have already isolated some themes by now that seem particularly interesting or important. You could group your information under these headings.

Questionnaires and interviews

If your school or college has IT facilities, you can use a spreadsheet. This has particular advantages when it comes to writing up your research project. If you cannot use a computer, or do not have access to one, then a simple way to analyse data is to make a grid like the one below.

	Response code			
Question no.	1	2	3	4
1	1111	1111 1111	11	111
2				
3				

By coding the answers to the questions, the grid allows you to easily 'read' the types of replies across a large number of questionnaires. In the above example, there are six questions and four possible replies to each one. The first question was:

1 In your opinion, which of the four things mentioned below is the single most important cause of crime today:

    1 unemployment?
    2 breakdown of family life?
    3 drug use?
    4 lack of discipline at school?

Five more questions followed. Twenty people answered in total, and their replies were as follows:

- five people chose 'breakdown of family life'
- ten people chose 'unemployment'
- two people chose 'drug addiction'
- three people chose 'lack of discipline at school'.

Presenting data

Numerical data can be presented in many ways, but the most common are:

- tables
- line graphs
- bar charts (another form of graph really)
- pie charts (another form of graph).

Remember to explain clearly the meaning of the data in your main text.

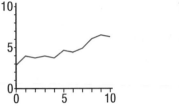

A line graph

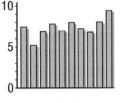

A bar chart

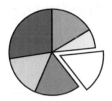

A pie chart

Writing the assignment

Introduction

Start with the background to your study, explaining why you are doing it and what you intend to prove, or what issue you are going to explore. You should include any evidence of background reading or examples of studies which interested you and seem relevant.

The methodology

Explain the methodology you have used, in particular discussing why you used your chosen method(s) rather than any other method. You should always point out the weaknesses of your methodology.

The results

Work through the study and describe what information you have obtained, and how it relates to other published studies.

The discussion

Discuss your study and draw conclusions from it, saying how they do, or do not relate to your original idea.

Conclusion

Go back over the assignment summarising and clarifying the main points as you see them. Criticise yourself and your methods if you genuinely feel there are weaknesses. Say how you would improve the study if you had to repeat it.

Assignment and essay writing hints

- *Short paragraphs* Always write in short, clear paragraphs. A paragraph of, say, four to eight lines should consist of one point that you are trying to explore.
- *Linked paragraphs* Each paragraph should be linked to the previous one in some way. Don't leave paragraphs floating by themselves and expect your tutor or the examiner to make sense of the links. Use simple link words or phrases to start a paragraph, for example, 'As a result of this', 'Another example of this', 'However', 'So', 'In contrast to', 'Furthermore', 'Also', etc.
- *Signposts* You should insert a paragraph after every page and a half which acts as a signpost to the reader: 'So far we have … and now we will look at …' This allows the reader to see clearly the argument you have presented and understand what the various relationships are.
- *Appendices* Graphs and tables can either go in the main text in the appropriate place or they can be placed in an appendix (plural = appendices) which is a number of pages inserted at the end of your assignment. If you use the appendix, it usually does not form part of the word count of the assignment.
- *Bringing essays and assignments to life* You can add other things in the appendix, such as transcriptions of interviews, copies of the questionnaire, examples of the replies, photographs, tape recordings and even videos.

---

2 CHAPTER SUMMARY

1   Sociology attempts to uncover the reality of the social world by using a series of specific research methods, rather than relying upon common sense or experience.

2   These methods distinguish the sociologist from journalists and other commentators.

3   Sociologists all agree on the need to have rigorous research methods, but they disagree on which methods are best.

4   There are two general approaches sociologists use – positivist, which stresses the use of surveys, and subjectivist, which prefers to observe people in their daily lives.

5   There are a number of different types of surveys which provide different ways of getting information. These include cross-sectional surveys, longitudinal surveys, panel surveys.

6   Sampling involves choosing a small number of people from a sampling frame

7   There are two main types of sampling – random sampling and quota sampling.

8   There are two main ways of asking people questions – questionnaires and interviews

9   Questionnaires are written questions which people complete and return to the researcher.

10   Interviews are where people are asked questions face-to-face.

11 In general, interviews allow greater depth of analysis, whilst question-naires can be given to a much larger and widely dispersed number of people.

12 Case studies are when a particular group is studied in very great depth.

13 The comparative method is where two societies are compared in order to see what key differences there are between them and what may cause these differences.

14 Primary sources are the information which sociologists find from their own direct research with people.

15 Secondary sources are the research and writings of others which sociologists use in their research.

16 Observational research is the method most used by subjectivist sociologists who watch and even join in group activities.

17 There are two types of observational research – participant and non-participant.

18 Whatever form of research is undertaken, three issues must always be resolved: reliability, validity and bias.

Test Your Knowledge

1 Identify the differences between sociology and journalism.

2 Explain the difference between a positivist sociologist and a subjective sociologist.

3 Name and describe any two types of survey.

4 Why do sociologists 'sample'?

5 Explain the difference between a questionnaire and an interview.

6 What are primary sources? Give two examples.

7 When would a sociologist use participant observation?

Chapter 3

SOCIAL DIVISIONS AND SOCIAL CLASS

Chapter contents

- **Differentiation, stratification and life chances**

  We examine the meanings of these terms, how they link to each other and just how important they are for understanding society. What we find is that people live very different lives depending upon what financial and social resources they have. These resources are not randomly scattered throughout the population, but are clearly linked to social class, gender and race.

- **Social stratification over time and place**

  We explore a few examples of how other societies in history have 'stratified' people, and what the consequences are.

- **The importance of social class**

  As, arguably, the main form of stratification in society, we start the rest of the chapter by looking at how important class is in affecting people's lives today. You may be surprised just how significant it is.

- **Explaining social class**

  Why societies should separate people into classes and not just accept them as individuals has been one of the enduring debates in sociology. Here we introduce three of the most famous explanations for the existence of social class.

- **Measuring social class**

  In research, what sociologists need to do is construct very clear definitions of what class is and which people belong to each social class. Sociologists have found the most accurate way of dividing people into social classes is to use their occupations.

- **The changing social classes**

  Society is dynamic, that is, it is always changing. This dynamism applies just as much to social class as to any other element of society. Here we look at the three most important elements of change in the social classes.

- **The working class**

  A detailed exploration of the changes which have happened to this class in the last 30 years. In particular we look at the way that it has split between the more affluent and successful and those who have been left behind.

- **The middle class**

  This is a class which has grown greatly over the last 30 years, reflecting the changes in British society and in particular the types of occupations which dominate Britain today.

- **The upper class**

  This is a small group of the population which has largely retained its wealth and income, and which has succeeded in 'incorporating', that is accepting, new 'rich' people, so that it remains powerful.

- **Social class: an outdated idea?**

  The entire chapter has been based on the belief that social class is very important. But many sociologists today are raising doubts about this and arguing that it is an old-fashioned idea. This section explores the debate and suggests new ways of looking at social divisions.

- **Social mobility**

  A large proportion of people move social classes in their lifetimes and, over the last 40 years, even more have changed their class from that of their parents. We examine what social mobility is, how we can measure it and why it happens.

- **Wealth and income**

  The last part of the chapter explores the inequalities of wealth and income which exist in society. The figures show that only a very few people hold an extremely large proportion of the wealth of Britain.

Differentiation, stratification and life chances

Activity

Look at the photographs of the characters in the three photographs above. Write down any thoughts or ideas you have about them – who they are, what they do, perhaps what they think, and any obvious differences. Afterwards, as a group compare notes.

You will probably find that you are able to write down some thoughts about them and their lives, and how you feel about them. This is the process of *differentiation*, which is central to social life.

Differentiation

On meeting someone for the first time, you will make a number of things about them. Almost certainly you will be aware of their sex, their age, their ethnicity or skin colour, how they talk or act, and if they are disabled this will also figure strongly in your consciousness. (You might also be interested in how attractive they are, but that is another story!)

The resulting way you categorise people (for example, young, white, disabled) will very strongly influence how you behave towards them. Whether we like it or not, all of us carry in our heads these and other categories which very much influence our behaviour. The classification of people into categories occurs in virtually all societies, today and in the past, and tells us many things about the society.

Definition

Differentiation – the different ways people are treated according to the social group they are believed to belong to

The process by which people are placed into different social categories is known as social **differentiation**. It is important to remember that this categorisation, or differentiation, is based upon differences which are socially created rather than natural. So, for example, skin colour takes on significance in our society and really does impact upon the way those of African-Caribbean origin are treated, but eye colour or hair colour is not seen as having any great importance.

Differentiation, then, is the process by which we treat people differently according to the social group they belong to. Examples of differentiation today and in history include:

- age
- gender
- ethnic origin
- disability.

Stratification

The next term we need to explore is that of **stratification**. The word comes from the Latin term *strata* which means 'layers'. The term is often used interchangeably with differentiation and it has some similar meaning. However, there is a crucial difference. Stratification refers to the inequalities suffered (or enjoyed) by people as a result of the socially constructed differences between them. If you think of the word 'layers' it actually means one on top of another.

But if stratification means the situation whereby some groups of people are above others, then we need to know *how* we measure some as being higher than others.

> **Definition**
>
> **Stratification** – the division of people into groups based upon how much wealth, social prestige and power they have

Sociologists have suggested that there are three absolutely key elements which either individually, or more likely all together, form the basis of stratification. These are:

- *power* – the ability of some people to have their wishes override those of others. Powerful people can therefore organise society so that they are more likely to benefit from it than others
- *economic differences* – some people are richer than others. They can use this money to live a particular lifestyle so that others are excluded. They can also influence the actions of others through their ability to pay
- *social prestige* – the basis of social prestige or social status is complex. For the time being, we can say that most societies value certain abilities or attributes more than others. Those fortunate or able enough to have these attributes may be given high levels of prestige by others. A society could, for example, value holiness more than anything else, or footballing ability, or intelligence.

So, stratification refers to the way that inequalities are organised and distributed in any society.

Examples of stratification today and in history include:

- social class
- estates (the feudal system)
- caste
- slavery.

Life chances

> **Definition**
>
> **Life chances** – the advantages or disadvantages people have which can affect them doing well or badly in society

We have said that most of us differentiate between people and that groups of people are stratified into layers which reflect the inequalities of society. Another way of looking at this, especially from the viewpoint of individuals in the different strata is to talk about **life chances**. The term was first used by Max Weber, a sociologist writing at the beginning of the twentieth century.

Life chances refer to the different opportunities that are presented to people and which they have the opportunity of grasping, depending upon which social stratum (stratum is the singular of strata) they belong to. It is not too difficult to understand that a rich, public-school educated person is more likely (that is, will have higher life chances) to be financially successful than someone from a council housing estate who attended a local 'failing' comprehensive school.

Life chances vary depending on your starting point.

The relationship between stratification, differentiation and life chances

Stratification, differentiation and life chances are not separate, but tend to overlap and complement each other. For example, British society has for a long time been stratified by the social class system. However, differentiation, based on ethnicity, age, gender and disability, occurs within social class.

Although the bulk of sociological research has, in the past, been on social class, and although it still remains a very important influence on our lives, sociologists have increasingly turned their attention to the other forms of differentiation and how they affect our lives. For example, *within* each social class, people of different sexes, different ages and from different ethnic backgrounds have quite distinctive experiences. Women are more likely to be found in routine office employment and are less likely than men to achieve senior management positions. People from African-Caribbean, Bangladeshi and Pakistani backgrounds are more likely to be in lower paid work. Young people and those over 55 are more likely to be unemployed.

Social stratification over time and place

Ascription and achievement

Stratification and differentiation have occurred throughout history. However, as we are going to see, the form they take varies quite considerably. Sometimes for example, the system of stratification is quite open. People may be born into one group and over time may move up or down (this is known as social mobility, see page 68). If the stratification system is 'open' in this way, it is known as an *achievement*-based system, because people's position may well be based on their achievements. An example of this form of stratification system is social class, which has characterised Britain in the nineteenth and twentieth centuries.

On the other hand, some stratification systems do not allow people to move up or down – they are fixed. The position you are born into is where you stay. These are known as *ascriptive* systems because they are based on some quality which people are born with (this is what **ascription** means). An example of an ascriptive society is the Hindu-based caste system in India.

There have been two particularly important forms of ascription-based systems in history:

* estates
* castes.

Estates

In feudal societies, which existed in Europe until the late sixteenth century, people were divided into estates, which were based upon ownership of land. Individuals swore allegiance to the king, who rewarded them with land. In turn, followers of these landholders swore allegiance to them and were rewarded with portions the land. The distribution of land ended with tiny plots being given to peasants, who swore allegiance in exchange for giving a portion of the produce from their land, plus occasional military service. Each level was known as an *estate*. The divisions between the estates were very marked, with great stress laid on the lower estates giving the higher estates higher status. It would have been unthinkable for a person from one estate to marry a person from a higher estate.

Caste

The caste system developed in India. It is based upon the Hindu religion, which preaches that people have more than one life and that they are born into a particular caste in a life according to their behaviour in their previous lives. Someone who has been extremely wicked will be born into the lowest caste and a good person into the highest caste. The fact that one's caste is determined by God means in essence that it is extremely difficult to change caste and move upwards, no matter how much money or land a person acquires. There are rigid lines between the castes and no form of social mixing is allowed, indeed a person of a higher caste who touches a person of a lower caste regards himself as being contaminated.

The caste system

Brahmins – priests
Kshatriyas – soldiers
Vaishyas – traders
Harijan (untouchables) – outcasts who have to do the worst work rejected by others

A person is born into a jati [a division of a caste] and this is the only way of acquiring membership. The Hindu doctrine of 'karma' teaches young Hindus that they are born into a particular sub-caste because of what they did in their previous life. Amongst the 500 million Hindu people, the higher castes contain about 20 per cent of the population and the middle and lower castes just under 60 per cent. The 'untouchables', now called Scheduled Castes (SC), contain about 15 per cent. The widely scattered and culturally backward tribal communities, now called Scheduled Tribes (ST), comprise 7.5 per cent.

Caste: a living division

It all started at a crowded cinema in southern India when an Untouchable boy accidentally brushed his leg against an upper-caste youth sitting next to him. [As a result] … a fight broke out.

After the brawl in the cinema, an upper-caste clan known as the Reddis kidnapped the father of the Untouchable boy and forced the son to turn himself over to them. According to press reports, the higher-caste Indians thrashed the boy badly but left him alive.

The Untouchables hit back. When the time came for the Reddis to plant rice in the paddies after the monsoon rains, Untouchables would not work for them.

A human rights organisation said that … police armed with clubs herded the Untouchables out of their mud-hut settlement. In the nearby rice fields, a mob of more than 500 upper-caste farmers awaited the fleeing Untouchables with swords and axes.

Survivors said that as many as 20 Untouchables were stabbed and beaten to death in the four-hour carnage.

Source: Adapted from *The Independent*, 10 August 1991

1 Which is:

a) the lowest layer?

b) the highest layer of the caste system?

2 How does a person enter a particular caste?

3 Would it be possible for members of different castes to be friends, do you think?

4 How would people recognise those from a different caste?

5 Can you think of any other form of differentiation in Britain which might be considered to have the characteristics of caste (born into group/cannot change/beliefs by some about inferiority and superiority, etc.)?

Main points ▶ All societies have ways in which people are classified by others – this process is known as differentiation.

▶ Some of the main forms of differentiation in society are age, gender, ethnic origin, disability, though there are others depending upon the type of society.

▶ Most, if not all, societies group people into different strata or layers and give them different levels of power, financial reward and social prestige. This process is known as stratification.

▶ Three examples of stratification are estates (the feudal system), caste, social class.

▶ Stratification and differentiation coincide, so that both influence each other. Within and across strata, people differentiate amongst the various groups.

▶ Systems of stratification in societies vary in the extent to which they allow movement between the strata.

▶ Sociologists call societies which are 'open', i.e. which allow movement, achievement-based societies.

▶ Sociologists call societies which are 'closed', i.e. which try to keep people in the categories in which they were born, ascription-based societies.

▶ Social mobility is the term used to describe movement up or the stratification system.

▶ The result of differentiation and stratification is that people have very different opportunities in life. These differences in opportunities are known as life chances in sociology.

The importance of social class

Social class remains one of the main forms of social stratification in British society. We still grade people, according to differences in income and wealth, as well as status differences, based on accent, ways of behaving and styles of life. However, most people would agree that social class is less important today than previously.

Although many people are in the same social class as their parents, this is not true for everyone. Social class is 'open' and people move up or down the social class 'ladder'. This movement is known as social mobility (see page 68).

In the rest of the chapter we will examine the continuing importance of social class, how it has changed over time and the way that sociologists explain the basis of social class and measure it.

The impact of social class

- *Birth* Children of unskilled working-class parents are three times more likely to die within a year of birth than the children of professionals. Working-class women are more likely to be single mothers. Mothers from working-class origins are likely to have children at an earlier age.
- *Health* Working-class people are three times more likely to have a serious illness than middle-class people. They are six times more likely to get arthritis and rheumatism.
- *Marriage and family life* Working-class couples tend to have children earlier in marriage, and tend to discipline their children in different ways from the middle class.
- *Income* The higher up the social class ladder you climb, the larger your income.
- *Education* Two-thirds of children from professional backgrounds (such as doctors or solicitors) achieve 5 or more GCSEs at grade C or above, compared to only one fifth from manual backgrounds (such as labourers/cleaners). The children of the middle classes are also more likely to go to a traditional university, as opposed to the newer, less prestigious ones.
- *Death* A man with a professional job can expect to live seven years longer on average than a man with a labouring job. (The difference is less pronounced for women.)

The structure of social class: a day in the life

Jacky and Martyn Atkinson. She is a scientist, he is a financial actuary. They have two daughters and employ three cleaners and two gardeners.

6.30am: Radio alarm goes off

6.45am: Out of bed. One person gets ready, while the other gets the kids up and down to breakfast.

7:45am: Martyn leaves for work, Jacky gets dressed.

8am: Before work, Jacky drops children off at school, which looks after them until lessons start at 8.30.

Noon: Two gardeners arrive (once a fortnight). They used just to do the flower beds and Martyn would mow the lawns. Now the gardeners do both.

1:30pm: Three cleaners come in (once a week) for two hours or so to dust, vacuum, clean all over the house and do the washing-up.

3.30pm: School ends. Children stay on at after-school club.

5pm: After-school club moves to a nearby church where the children are given tea.

6.15pm: Martyn collects children from club on the way home. Jacky gets home around the same time.

John Hirrel. Made redundant after privatisation of British Gas. Now works as domestic help in London

8am: Grab breakfast and jump on the Tube to Richmond

10am: Quick coffee with the clients, then unpack their shopping and put it all away.

10.30am: Make a start on the large main living room, all wooden floors and heavy wooden furniture. Polish everything then put it all back in its proper place.

1.30pm: Lunch break. If it's in summer, a glass of cider and a salad in the back garden, in winter something in the kitchen.

2.30pm: Clean up the dining room, do all the washing up and put everything away. Everything cleaned, including outside of the cupboards and the fridge. Put the rubbish out.

4.00pm: Start on the lounge and TV room. Clear it out, quick vacuum and a dust.

4.45pm: Move upstairs and the same for the two bedrooms.

6–7pm: Home, via the Tube. Walk through Richmond Park if weather nice. Take home pay: £35 for the day.

Source: *The Observer*, 19 January 1997

1 In what ways do the lives of people such as the Atkinsons and John Hirrell link with each other?

2 What differences can you see between the Atkinsons and John Hirrell?

3 What similarities can you find in their lives?

4 Could you imagine John Hirrell and his family being friends of Jacky and Martyn Atkinson? Explain your answer.

Explaining social class

Although it is agreed that social class influences our lives in many ways, there is less agreement about what social class actually is and what its origins are. The two sociologists who first discussed social class in the last century, Max Weber and Karl Marx, have left behind quite distinct sociological traditions. Marxists see society as fundamentally divided into two groups, while those influenced by Weber see society as consisting much more of a 'ladder' of different groups, with only small differences between them.

A third approach, developed by Talcott Parsons, called *functionalism*, saw social divisions as being helpful to society.

The Marxist view

Definitions

Bourgeoisie – the rich and powerful who own industry and commerce

Proletariat – all employees, no matter what grade, who work for the rich and powerful

The Marxist view of social class is that in every society one group emerges which gains control of the economy (in Britain today, industry and commerce; in pre-industrial Britain, it was the land). Marx calls these the **bourgeoisie**, and they arrange society to their own benefit using their enormous wealth and power. They are only a tiny fraction of the whole population, no more than 5 per cent. Everyone else in society works for these people, making them richer.

Of course, there are massive differences between those people who work for the bourgeoisie – some are managers earning very high salaries, others may be employees who earn very little. However, they all share one fundamental link. They do not own, in any significant way, the industry or the commercial institutions. These people are called the **proletariat**.

Marxists today stress that there are many superficial distinctions between the various groups in society, but point out the enormous concentration of wealth in the hands of very few people in contemporary Britain. In order to understand our society, with its social problems and great differences in wealth and quality of life, Marxists point to the power of the bourgeoisie to manipulate the rest of the population to work for them and to accept this situation as being quite correct.

Criticisms of the Marxist view

Critics of Marx have pointed out firstly that it is possible to be socially mobile and to become successful in 'capitalist' society. Secondly, they have pointed to the collapse of communist regimes, such as Russia, which claimed to follow Marxist ideas, where those in power actually controlled the population for their own benefit in a far more ruthless way than in capitalist Britain. Thirdly, they have also argued that modern society has developed in a more complex way than Marx foresaw, writing a hundred years ago, and the idea of there being only two classes bourgeoisie and proletariat, is simply inaccurate. There are lots of other important divisions (such as race and gender), and class is splintered into a number of complex groupings.

Weber's view

Max Weber's view of stratification comes from this last criticism. For him, to divide society into two groups, on the basis of ownership of the economy or not, was just too simple. He suggested instead that social class was based on three elements:

- *economic factors*, such as how much money a person earned or inherited from parents
- *status*, such as the prestige we give to a person, based on such things as accent, style of dress and level of education
- *power* – the amount of influence a person has to affect important social decisions.

It is by balancing these three elements that we arrive at our judgement of where a person belongs in society. A scrap yard dealer may earn far more than a doctor, yet it would generally be agreed that in some way the doctor is of a higher social class than the dealer.

Weber's view of social class is that it is constantly changing, depending on people's opinions of the worth of a particular occupation. Ownership of property is important, as Marxists argue, but it is only one of a number of elements that link together to form our life chances, by which Weber means the chances of being successful in life.

Weber's model of stratification

Weber says that our position in society depends upon where we stand in three different rankings – how well off we are (class), how much prestige people give us (status), and how much power we have to get things done (power). In the diagram below you can see how a nurse compares with a double-glazing salesperson. There are differences in class, status and power.

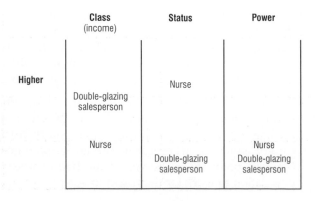

Question

How would you rank the following on the diagram opposite:
a) a director of a large international company?
b) a car mechanic?
c) a top civil servant?

The great advantage of Weber's model of stratification is that the three distinct elements (economic differences, status or prestige differences, and differences in power) allow a more flexible and detailed way of classifying people than Marx's model, which is based solely on economic differences.

The Functionalist explanation

A third explanation for differences in social status comes from the Functionalist 'school' of sociology. Functionalists argue that in every society, some jobs are more important for the continuing well-being of that society than others. In order to ensure that the best people are recruited to these crucial jobs, they need to be paid higher wages and to receive higher levels of social prestige. Supporters of this approach would give the example of paying a surgeon more than a secretary.

Critics of this approach argue that it merely *justifies* inequality, by saying that those at the top deserve their positions. Secondly, they ask how it is possible to judge which jobs are more important to society than others, apart perhaps from the more obvious ones. So, why should an advertising executive earn more than a nurse?

Activity

Copy and complete this table.

	Marxist	**Weberian**	**Functionalist**
Two of these approaches have a clear view on whether social class good or bad for society. Which are they and what opinion do they hold?			
What are the main causes of social stratification?			
What criticisms can you make of the approach?			
Which approach do you find most accurate?			

Main points ▸ Social class influences our lives in a considerable number of ways, including health, housing income and even politics.

▸ Sociologists disagree about the nature and importance of social class. There are three main 'theoretical' explanations:
   – Marxist
   – Weber's (known as Weberian)
   – Functionalist (originated by Talcott Parsons).

▸ Marxists say that there is a ruling class which controls and manipulates us.

▸ Weber says that there are three elements to social class based upon income, social status and how much power they have.

▸ Functionalists argue that class is based upon ability. There are some jobs which are more important to society than others, and the people who do these jobs should receive greater rewards.

Measuring social class

When sociologists are doing research and want to measure social class differences, they need a simple and clear way of dividing people into social class groupings. They have found that the simplest way to do this is grade people by their occupations.

There are a number of reasons for this – because information on people's occupations is simple and quick to obtain, but also because occupation is related to a number of very important social differences, such as differences in:

• earnings
• standard of education
• accent and styles of dress, because these in turn reflect differences in education and occupation
• values and patterns of behaviour, again reflecting education
• how people are ranked by others and given prestige, so the doctor receives greater prestige than the estate agent.

All these put together clearly reflect class differences.

How our occupations influence our social class

The diagram illustrates how occupations influence, and in turn are influenced by, other aspects of our lives.

Copy the diagram and add three more ways in which occupation influences us, and two ways in which occupation is influenced by other factors.

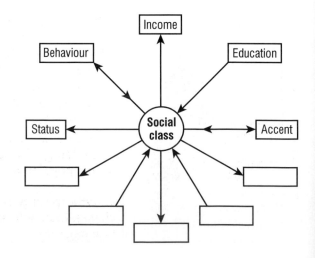

National statistics – socio-economic model (NS-SEC)

The official system of classification now used by the government, known as the National statistics – socio-economic (NS-SEC) model has eight categories, which are shown in the cartoon below.

Where you rate in the new social order

ILLUSTRATIONS by IAN JACKSON

1. Higher management and professional occupations		2. Lower managerial and professional occupations	3. Intermediate occupations	4. Small employers and own account workers	5. Lower supervisor, craft and related occupations	6. Semi-routine occupations	7. Routine occupations
1.1 Employers and managers in larger organisations	1.2 Higher Professionals	Nurses and midwives	Clerks Secretaries	Publicans	Printers	Shop assistants	Waiters
	Doctors	Journalists	Driving instructors	Play group leaders	Plumbers	Traffic wardens	Road sweepers
Company directors	Barristers and	Actors and musicians	Computer operators	Farmers	Butchers	Cooks	Cleaners
Corporate managers	solicitors	Prison officers	Telephone fitters	Taxi drivers	Bus inspectors	Bus drivers	Couriers
Police inspectors	Clergy	Police		Window cleaners	TV engineers	Hairdressers	Building labourers
Bank managers	Librarians	Soldiers (NCO)		Painters and	Train drivers	Postal workers	Refuse collectors
Senior civil servants	Social workers	and below)		decorators			
Military officers	Teachers						8. Never worked/long term unemployment

Source: *The Guardian*, 1 December 1998

In many studies, in this book and in others, you may find a six-point scale used. This is because it is only recently that the government has changed its classification and consequently much of the available information uses the older scale which was known as the *Registrar-General's classification*. The main difference between the old Registrar-General's model and the new NS–SEC model is that there is a increase in groupings in the 'middle class' occupations, which reflects the changes in British society that have taken place over the last 30 years.

Goldthorpe's classification

Another way of measuring social class was suggested by Goldthorpe when he did a famous study of social mobility (movement up and down the social classes). He simply divided people into three main social 'classes':

- the *service class*, which consisted of professionals and managers – about 14 per cent of the population
- the *intermediate class*, such as people in shops and offices doing routine work – comprising about 31 per cent the population
- the *working class*, which was most people who work with their hands in building, manufacturing and repairing – comprising about 55 per cent of the population.

Goldthorpe argues that though there are divisions within each of these three classes, those who comprise each class can be said to enjoy similar life chances (see page 46).

Women have criticised the traditional
ways of measuring class and have
created their own forms of classification.

Measuring the social class of women

Traditionally, one big problem with using occupation as a way of measuring
social class was that it gave an inaccurate picture of women's class position.
This is because women are clustered in certain types of jobs and usually in the
lower levels of companies. The new NS–SEC classification, which expanded
the middle range of jobs, seems to have overcome this.

Women, social class and employment

Population of working age[1], by gender and social class, Spring 1999, UK

What differences can you
spot in the sorts of jobs that
women are employed in
compared to men?

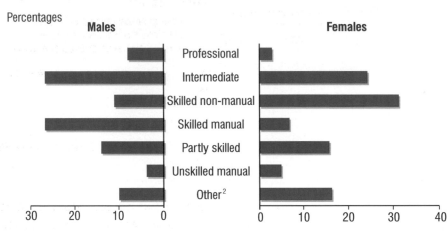

1 Males aged 16 to 64, females aged 16 to 59.
2 Includes members of the armed forces, those who did not state their current or last occupation, and those who
  had not worked in the last eight years.
Source: Labour Force Survey. Office for National Statistics

Source: *Social Trends 30* (The Stationery Office, 2000)

Social class and market research

A commonly used way of dividing people into groups is the classification A–E
devised by the advertising and market research industry:

* A – upper middle class, comprising top business people, high professionals
  and senior civil servants
* B – middle class, important people in management, professions and civil
  service, but not the top
* C1 – lower middle class, people in supervisory positions, clerical and sales
  staff
* C2 – skilled working class, people who are skilled working with their hands
* D – working class, people who work with their hands, but have no specific
  skills
* E – those at the lowest levels of subsistence, people without work on state
  benefits or pensioners with only the state pension to live off.

The changing social classes

Changing social class

Social Grade
Percentage of total population

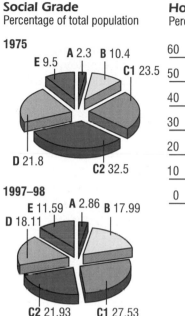

1975
E 9.5 A 2.3 B 10.4
C1 23.5
D 21.8
C2 32.5

1997–98
E 11.59 A 2.86 B 17.99
D 18.11
C2 21.93 C1 27.53

How we see ourselves
Percentage who describe themselves as...

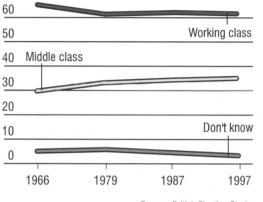

Source: British Election Study

Grade guide

A Upper Middle class: Higher managerial administrative or professional

B Middle class: Intermediate managerial administrative or professional

C1 Lower middle class: Supervisory or clerical and junior managerial, administrative or professional

C2 Skilled working class: Skilled manual workers

D Working class: Semi and unskilled manual workers

E Lowest subsistence level: State pensioners or widows (no other earner), casual or lowest grade workers

Source: NRS

Source: *The Guardian*, 15 January 1999

Look at the pie charts:

1 What percentage of the population were in C2 in 1997–8?

2 What percentage of the population were in D in 1995?

3 What changes have taken place over time?

Look at the diagram 'How we see ourselves', which shows how people describe themselves when asked what class they belong to.

4 What changes have taken place, if any, in how people describe themselves?

5 What conclusions would you draw from this?

General patterns of change

We have seen that social class exists in Britain and exerts considerable influence over our lives. However, social class, like all aspects of society, changes over time. In this section we will examine just what changes have taken place across and within the social classes. Before we look at each of the main social class groups in detail, however we need to note a few general trends which have taken place. These trends include:

- **fragmentation** within social classes
- **overlap** between the 'borders' of the social classes
- **value diffusion**.

Fragmentation

Whereas traditionally the divisions within social classes have been relatively small compared to differences between social classes, the end of the twentieth century saw the growth of many different interests, levels of income and styles of life *within* the social classes. This has been referred to as the fragmentation of social class.

Overlap

Traditionally, the three social classes – the working, middle and upper – had fairly clear boundaries, which were based upon type of employment. The working class worked with their hands in labouring occupations; the middle class worked mainly in offices; and the upper class either did not work or were in senior management positions or the traditional professions of the law and medicine.

However, four main changes in the occupational structure have taken place which have muddied the divisions between social classes:

- There has been a decline in manual work.
- There has been an increase in routine office work to replace it.
- There has been an increase in what is termed the 'new professions', such as teachers and social workers.
- There has been a large increase in the numbers of women working.

The result is that although we can definitely see how life chances are affected by social class, the exact boundaries (where each social class starts and finishes) are a matter of dispute.

Value diffusion

Traditionally each social class had very distinctive sets of values and these were illustrated by ways of life and leisure pursuits. However, the influence of the mass media, of advertising, of the travel and leisure industries have all brought about a change in the habits of the social classes, such that – although there are still differences – they are more subtle than before. All social classes go on holiday abroad, but the more successful middle class go to more 'exclusive' destinations. All social classes own a video, but they may hire different films, and so on.

Bearing these points in mind, we will now look at each social class in turn.

The working class

In the 1950s, the working class formed two-thirds of the workforce and consisted of manual workers in manufacturing industries. Wages were low and so were living standards. The working class had a set of attitudes and ideas which were distinctive and which reflected their struggle to achieve a decent quality of life. There were divisions between the working class, generally based on levels of skill. So the more skilled workers tended to be the leaders of the community and those who led and formed the trades unions, the Labour Party and most other working-class social and political organisations.

However, from the 1960s onwards, changes began to creep into the working class which began the process of fragmentation we described earlier. The first attempt to explain these changes became known as the *embourgeoisement* argument, which suggested that the better-off sections of the working class had been absorbed into the middle class.

Research has since showed this was untrue, but today sociologists now suggest that we can best understand the working class as consisting of two, or possibly three, groupings. These are:

- the traditional working class
- the new working class
- the underclass.

Before we look at each in detail, we need to note the *decline in **all** working-class employment*. In 2000, only 32 per cent of all employment was in manual work, and only 8 per cent of unskilled workers were employed in industrial work.

The traditional working class

This would appear to be the group most in decline. The traditional working class consists of those employed in the declining heavy engineering and manufacturing industries and those unskilled manual workers employed in construction. Technological innovations have replaced many of these unskilled jobs, and occupational change means that there are fewer of these types of industry in the UK to even provide this employment. The type of employment available to them is increasingly insecure, so that a 'job for life' is highly unlikely.

These people tend to be older, poorer and living in social ('council') housing.

The new working class

These are the growing portion of the working class. The males are more likely to be employed in a range of skilled or semi-skilled occupations in the newer light industries, domestic repairs or maintenance. The women are more likely to be employed in routine clerical work, shops or other services. Families, therefore, are likely to have two income earners, unlike the traditional working class where the male was the only or main breadwinner. This helps ensure a degree of affluence. The new working class are more likely to adopt a 'consumerist' lifestyle which means that they have money to buy a wide range of goods and services, as well as leisure activities.

An important point to note is that the new working class is partly based on the affluence caused by the employment of women and, in turn, this income has allowed women to demand a much greater say in the running of the household and in family decisions.

Members of the new working class are more likely to be in secure employment and to have decent pensions and assurance. They are also more likely to be buying their own homes.

The underclass

The existence of the underclass is a matter of great political debate and in some ways is linked to our discussion of the lone parent families on page 168.

The argument for the underclass comes from a group of writers who claim that a new 'class' has emerged which prefers to rely upon state benefits rather than to work. The level of state benefits are higher than the wages that the members of the underclass would earn, so there is no incentive to work.

According to the underclass argument, the 'class' is reproducing itself through relatively uncontrolled sexual activity, which accounts for the increase in never-married lone mothers. Furthermore, it is claimed that the children of these families are socialised into similar attitudes.

The members of the underclass are more likely to be found in large social (council) housing developments in areas of high unemployment.

Arguments against the existence of the underclass

Lack of evidence

Critics argue that there is no evidence to suggest a stable, sizeable group of people who have distinctive attitudes to employment and state benefits. They argue that most research indicates that the overwhelming majority of people who are supposed to be members of the underclass (young, unemployed) actually want a decent job.

Unemployment

The real cause of poverty amongst young people is lack of job opportunities. It is no coincidence that the underclass tend to be in areas of high unemployment. The young people are marginalised by lack of opportunity, which prevents them from getting decent jobs, obtaining their own home and forming stable relationships.

Education, training and investment

The critics claim that by attracting employment to the areas where the underclass are most likely to live, by investing in decent housing and community projects and finally, by improving the quality of education, there would be a much lower level of unemployment amongst young people.

Activity

Copy and complete this table summarising the arguments for and against the underclass

Arguments for the underclass	Arguments against the underclass

Main points ▶ Social class has changed very considerably over the last 20 years.
▶ Three main trends can be identified:
  - fragmentation – the breaking up of classes
  - overlap – the boundaries between them are not as clear as they once were
  - value diffusion – values and ideas are shared across the social classes much more than in the past.
▶ The working class has split into two main groups – the traditional working class and the new working class.
▶ The traditional working class is poorer and is in the declining industries and areas of unemployment.
▶ The new working class is more affluent and has higher levels of home ownership.
▶ There is a debate as to the existence of a third group called the underclass, consisting of people who live on state benefits, in large social housing developments and do not wish to work.

The middle class

The traditional middle class was sure of its place – above the working class and below the upper class. It consisted of a range of people from (usually male) clerical workers at the bottom to managers and professionals at the top. Middle-class people were more likely to own their own homes, to have regular holidays, to live in suburbs and to send their children to grammar schools or private schools.

Like the working class, the technological, gender and occupational changes also fragmented the middle class. But, unlike the working class which has shrunk, the middle class has grown considerably.

Goldthorpe has suggested that the fragmentation which took place resulted in the formation of two groups, or classes. These are:
- the intermediate 'class'
- the service 'class'.

The intermediate 'class'

Definitions

Service industries – commerce which does not actually make anything, but instead provides some service, for example banking insurance, shops, leisure activities

White-collar work – routine work in offices and shops which does not involve physical work (whether skilled or not)

Proletarianisation – the decline in working conditions, status and salary of the routine white-collar workers, to a level indistinguishable from the working class

The intermediate stratum or the 'lower middle class' has grown with the massive increase in **service industries**. These industries have, until very recently, required large numbers of semi-skilled routine employees, to work in offices, behind counters in banks or shops or provide the personnel in leisure activities. Today, approximately 28 per cent of the workforce are engaged in routine **white-collar work**.

However, the status attached to white-collar jobs and the way they are treated by employers is no longer different to the way manual workers are treated. Some sociologists have described this as a process of **proletarisation**.

Question Why is this called proletarianisation? Look at page 51, and suggest why.

There is some dispute amongst sociologists about the extent to which proletarianisation has taken place, but there is no doubt that for a considerable proportion of routine office workers, particularly women workers, the conditions are little different from those experienced by modern-day manual workers.

Work is largely repetitive, relatively low paid and with only limited prospects of promotion. But what has changed is that these workers are more likely to describe themselves as middle class. We could argue that the conditions are little different from the working class, but how the employees *see themselves* is different.

One planet, different world

It is generally agreed that many routine white-collar workers (especially women) now have rather similar conditions of work and remuneration to blue-collar [manual] workers, and cannot helpfully be seen as being in a higher class.

The rise in employment in the service sector confuses the division between manual and non-manual workers anyway, and it is possible to argue that many of the most extreme forms of 'proletarianisation' – in the sense of poor wages, irregular employment and bad working conditions – are found among service workers.

Furthermore, it can be argued that many forms of supposedly 'working class' activity such as trades union membership and industrial action are now as strong, possibly stronger, amongst white-collar workers as they are amongst manual workers. In short, the idea of a 'collar line' being used to distinguish the middle from the working class has now been largely discredited.

Source: M. Savage, 'The middle classes in modern Britain', *Sociology Review*, November 1995

1 Does the author agree with the concept of 'proletarianisation'?

2 What reasons does he give for his conclusions?

The service 'class'

The last 50 years has seen an enormous growth in the higher levels of the middle class. In order to distinguish these higher levels from the routine work of the 'lower middle class', Goldthorpe has coined the term **service 'class'**. By this, he means the professionals and managers who run the country on behalf of the upper class – they are 'servicing' the needs of the rich and powerful for someone to run the country on their behalf.

In 2000, over 30 per cent of the workforce was employed as a manager or professional, whereas in 1950 the figure was only 6 per cent. There have been some increases in the older established professions, such as law, but far more important has been the growth in the 'newer' professions of teaching and social work, for example. So, today, about 16 per cent of the workforce are classified as professionals. In industry, there has been a similar growth in the new levels of management, so that about 14 per cent are classified as managers.

A similar growth has taken place in the self-employed, working as consultants, advisers and sales personnel. In 2000, about 11 per cent of the workforce was self-employed.

Main points ▶ There has been a very large growth in the middle class.

▶ The growth has been the result of a change in the occupational structure, with office and service jobs taking over from manual industrial work.

▶ The traditional middle class has been divided into two groups:
  - the intermediate stratum, consisting of routine white-collar workers
  - the service stratum, consisting of managers and professionals.

▶ A debate has occurred about whether the routine white-collar workers have declined in status and financial benefits compared to the working class. The term 'proletarianisation' has been used to describe this process.

▶ There is clear evidence that with the boundaries between manual and routine white-collar employment becoming blurred there is considerable overlap.

▶ Gender changes are very important in understanding the intermediate 'class', as the majority of the routine white-collar jobs and service work is now undertaken by women, whereas before clerical work was done by men.

▶ One major area of expansion of the service 'class' has been in the new professions and managers.

▶ In the last few years, the security of service 'class' jobs has been replaced by much greater insecurity, though with better rewards for the successful.

▶ Age is an important factor, as older service 'class' employees have less job security than younger employees.

The upper class

According to John Scott, the 'upper class' in Britain has, for the last two hundred years, been a **coalition** of different groups. The groups have constructed a network of links through:

- inter-marriage
- public school education
- common business and commercial interests.

Membership of the upper class tends to include both financial wealth and political influence.

The different groups in the upper class consist of:
- *landowners and aristocracy* – who were the original ruling class and whose wealth derives (at least originally) from ownership of land and property
- *owners of industry and commerce* – these rose to power and wealth in the nineteenth and early twentieth centuries. They own, or have very significant share holdings in, many of our most famous companies
- *newcomers* – these are the rich who have entered the upper class in the last generation on the basis of business ability.

Are all rich people members of the upper class?

Being rich and being a member of the upper class is very different. For example, pop stars and sportsmen may have become millionaires, but they are not members of the upper class. They remain apart because of their cultural and social origins. It is possible, however, that over time their children will enter the network which ensures entry into the upper class.

The continuing existence of the upper class

In a society which is supposed to be based on a person's ability, the continuing existence of an upper class largely based on inheritance is puzzling. Two things seem important:

- *Power* It is important to remember that stratification (see page 46) is not just based upon wealth, but upon differences in status and political power. Whenever the interests of the upper class are threatened, they try as hard as possible to use this status and power to ensure that they overcome the threat.
- *Incorporation* This is the ability of the upper class to accept newcomers (or at least the second generation) and make them part of their network through the processes of education, inter-marriage and business interests.

The new social tribes

Old money
The Ffankly-Darlings were very annoyed to learn the class war is over. Giles Ffankly-Darling is descended from the Duke of Chippenham and still lives in the family pile, in what used to be the gamekeeper's cottage (the family pile was turned into a health spa in 1972). In his mid-50s, he has substantial private means but you'd never guess to look at his patched tweed jacket and well-worn corduroy trousers. Henrietta Ffankly-Darling is on the county council and a whiz at organising fetes and charity functions. She is known as "that ghastly woman

who smells like a wet labrador". Where are they found? Hunt Balls, Tatler, royal box at Ascot. They are: the Royal family, hereditary peers and people who buy Country Life to read about their friends.

New money
Two years ago Steve Rich had an idea: he decided to sell fresh fruit over the internet. So he left his computing course at Leeds University and set up a company, Interfruit. Six months ago, he sold it for £30m. Steve is now working on another project from his 14-bedroom home in Berkshire. He also has a flat in

Kensington and a ski chalet in Zermatt, but Berkshire is where he keeps his fleet of cars – a convertible Mercedes, a convertible BMW and a convertible E-type Jaguar. He toyed with the idea of a Lamborghini, but decided that would be vulgar.
Where are they found? Power breakfasts, power lunches board rooms, private yachts.
They are: Alan Sugar, Bill Gates and similar entrepreneurs. Also lottery winners.

The Celebs
Gail B was lead singer with The Pigtails, a girl band that burst on

to the scene between March 5 and September 19 last year. Now she has her own cable TV show and is chums with Zoe Ball and Jamie Theakston (or at least sees them from time to time in clubs). She drives a metallic blue BMW Z3. Her boyfriend, Dwight Neville, plays for a Premiership club whose name she can never remember.
Where are they found? Film premieres, OK! magazine.
They are: Spice Girls, Premiership footballers, Chris Evans, Mr and Mrs Zoe Ball.

Source: *The Sunday Times*, 3 October 1999

Main points ▶ The upper class has continued to exist because of:
- inter-marriage
- public school education
- common business and commercial interests.

▶ When they are challenged, they use their political influence to defend themselves and they attempt to incorporate those challenging them.

▶ Incorporation means to seek to get the people challenging them either to join them or to be to them.

▶ The upper class consists of a coalition of different groups, which include:
- landowners and aristocracy
- owners of commerce and industry
- the newly rich.

▶ Being rich is not enough to join the upper class, as a series of cultural barriers prevent instant access.

Ao

The dynamic class structure: a summary

Copy this table and complete the boxes to show the characteristics of each of the groupings within the social classes.

The working class	*The traditional working class* Characteristics
	The new working class Characteristics
	The underclass Characteristics

| **The middle class** | *Intermediate class*
Characteristics |
| | *Service class*
Characteristics |

The upper class	*Landowners* Characteristics
	Owners of business and commerce Characteristics
	Newcomers Characteristics

Social class: an outdated idea?

Ten years ago, to question the existence of social class might have seemed ridiculous to most sociologists. However, in recent years there has been a growing debate about whether social class has outlived its usefulness as a concept.

Those who argue that social class is outdated base their argument on the following points:

- *New social divisions* Divisions between people based upon their ethnic group, religion, sexuality and gender are now more important than social class.
- *Class identity* Whereas once people identified with a particular social class, nowadays they are less likely to do so.
- *Changing occupational structure* The occupational structure has changed so much that the old working class and middle class divisions based upon types of work are now outmoded.
- *Growth of affluence* By and large, most people have similar wages and standards of living. There are exceptions in that there are still the very poor (the underclass) and the very rich, but that does not affect the bulk of the population.

Those who argue for the continuing importance of social class base their argument on these points:

- *Inequality* The inequality of our society is still very clear cut. Income, job security and status of employment are very much better for some groups than for others, as is access to political power.
- *Class is dominant* These groups are not based on gender and ethnicity, but cut across them and are more important. Although gender, ethnicity and age are important they are simply less important than social class.

Definitions

Marginalised – people who forced out of normal social life by poverty and unemployment

Casual employment – insecure employment where the worker has no permanent job or job security

Deregulated labour market – where workers have very few legal rights in their jobs to such things as paid holidays, good pensions, maximum working hours, etc.

The 30/40/40 society

The extract below is an example of how other forms of analysis can be used instead of social class. The author does not use occupation alone, but also looks at issues of job security and job prospects. The result is a rather different series of strata.

Society is dividing before our eyes, opening up new social fissures in the working population. The first 30 per cent are the *disadvantaged*. These include those four million who are out of work, including those who do not receive benefit or have not looked for work within official definitions – and so do not count as officially unemployed. It also includes unemployed women, and women who cannot work because the loss of their husband's Income Support would more than offset their wage. This 30 per cent, under stress and with their children poorly fed, are the absolutely disadvantaged.

The second 30 per cent are made up of the **marginalised** and the insecure, a category defined not so much by income as by its relation to the labour market. People in this category have insecure working conditions and have been at the receiving end of the changes blowing through Britain's offices and factories. There are now more than five million people working part-time, 80 per cent of them women. Then there are those with insecure but full-time work, unprotected through the growth of **casual employment** and fixed-term contracts.

The last category is that of the *privileged* – the just over 40 per cent whose market power has increased since 1979. These are the full-time employees and the self-employed who have held their jobs for over two years, and the part-timers who have held theirs for more than five years. The 31 per cent of the workforce still represented by trade unions generally fall into this category.

It is this segmentation of the labour market that is sculpting the new and ugly shape of British society. The fact that more than half the people in Britain who are eligible to work are living either on poverty incomes or are in insecure work has had dreadful effects on the wider society. Britain has the highest divorce rate and the most **deregulated labour market** in Europe, and these two facts are closely related. The impact of inequality is pervasive [it is everywhere], affecting everything from the vitality of the housing market to the growth of social security spending.

Source: *The Guardian*, 21 January 1995

Copy and complete this table to summarise the characteristics of the three groups in society.

Characteristics of top 30%	Characteristics of middle 30%	Characteristics of bottom 40%

Divisions in Britain today: a summary

	Broad social class groupings	Groups within social classes	Divisions other than social class		
			Gender	Ethnic group	Region
The upper class	The rich	The 'establishment' or 'ruling class'	Women concentrated in the lowest-paid jobs in each class	Blacks concentrated in lowest-paid groups/unemployed	The worse-off found in the north and the inner cities
The middle class	• Managers and professionals (mainly men); high pay	The 'service class'			
	• Routine white-collar workers in offices, banks, shops and caring services (mainly women); low pay	The 'intermediate' groups			
The working class	• Better-paid manual workers in secure employment in newer light industries • The self-employed	The 'new working class'			
	• Less-skilled, less well-paid manual workers; job increasingly under threat as industry contracts	The 'traditional working class'			
	• The poor; the unemployed	The 'underclass'			

Main points ▶ There has been great debate in sociology concerning the importance of social class in contemporary society.

▶ Some sociologists point out how important it still is; others argue that other social divisions have become more important.

▶ Those who argue against social class say that:
  – gender and race are now more important than class
  – people no longer are so aware of social class, nor define their identities in terms of it
  – the occupational structure has changed
  – there is a spread of affluence amongst most of society so the social classes are largely indistinguishable.

▶ Supporters of social class as an important concept argue that:
  – differences between social groups are perfectly clear still and as sharp as ever
  – gender and race are less important than social class and exist *within* class divisions rather than *instead* of them.

Social mobility

What is social mobility?

Probably the major difference between social class and other forms of stratification, such as caste, is the ability to move up or down the 'ladder' of social class. This movement is known as **social mobility**.

Why is it important?

The amount and type of social mobility is a very useful and important piece of evidence for sociologists – it tells us whether Britain is an 'open', or **meritocratic,** society, that is whether or not people arrive in top positions depending mainly upon their ability.

High rates of social mobility tell us that anyone with talent can climb up the social class system and make it to the top.

How do we measure social mobility?

Definitions

Social mobility – the ability to move up or down the 'ladder' of social class

Meritocracy – a society where a person's social and financial position depends mostly upon their ability

Long-range mobility – movement up or down by two or more occupational groupings – the least common form of mobility

Short-range mobility – movement up or down by only one occupational group – this is very common and it usually consists of people moving upward, as there has been a growth of middle-class jobs and a decline in working-class jobs

Self-recruitment – where the a person is in the same occupational group as their parents – this is very common, especially for the children who come from social class 1 backgrounds

There are two measures of mobility:
- *Inter-generational mobility* is the comparison of a person's occupation with that of his or her father.
- *Intra-generational mobility* is the comparison of a person's present occupation with his or her first occupation. We normally call this a person's 'career'.

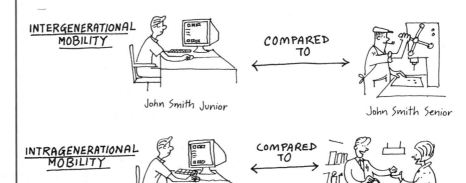

The extent of mobility in Britain

Inter-generational mobility

The Oxford Mobility Study was a major investigation of patterns of inter-generational social mobility in Britain. It was based on a survey of 10,000 males aged 20–64, who were divided into seven social classes.

Overall, the authors concluded that 30 per cent of the men had moved up and 18 per cent had moved down the class structure. However, most of the mobility was **short-range** (that is, no more than two occupational groups up or down), and only 7 per cent of those from social class 7 backgrounds (the lowest group) had reached class 1. On the other hand, almost half of those in social class 1 occupations had come from social class 1 backgrounds.

We can say that it is possible for people to move up the class structure, but it is a lot easier for those from the top to stay there.

Your chance of ending up in the service class

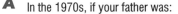

A In the 1970s, if your father was:

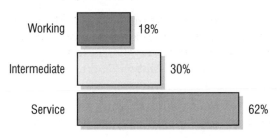

Working — 18%

Intermediate — 30%

Service — 62%

Source: Adapted from Haralambos et al., *Sociology: A New Approach* (Causeway Press) and *The Sunday Times*, 13 January 1980

B Female social mobility (compared to fathers' occupational class)

Fathers' occupational class	Respondents' occupational class			
	Service	**Intermediate**	**Manual**	**Total**
Service	82	114	47	243
Intermediate	68	134	137	339
Manual	64	211	347	622
Total	214	459	531	1204

Source: R.G. Burgess, *Investigating Society* (Longman), adapted from Goldthorpe and Payne (1986)

Look at A, which shows the inter-generational mobility for men.

1 Which group had the highest chance of entering the service class?

2 Which group had the lowest?

Look at B, which shows female inter-generational social mobility.

3 Which social class are the daughters of men working in service and intermediate occupations most likely to enter?

4 Are there any comments you can make about the mobility pattern of the daughters of manual workers?

Intra-generational mobility

This refers to a person's movement up or down the occupational structure in their own lifetime. Intra-generational mobility has declined over the last 50 years as fewer people are able to work their way up the promotional ladder from the lowest job to a senior position. Instead, people are more likely to be employed on the basis of their educational qualifications at higher or lower levels in companies. For those employed at the lower level of routine work, it is extremely difficult for them to break into management.

Women and social mobility

Women are split into two groups as regards their chances of upward mobility. Those women who have children appear to hit a barrier and have relatively low rates of mobility compared to men. This reflects the expectations on women to undertake the caring role for children. This pattern persists despite legislation to ensure that women do not lose out in career terms when they have children.

The second group of women, who do not have children and who pursue a career, appear to have rather higher chances than men of achieving upward mobility. However, the sorts of occupations in which they are successful tend to be different from those of men. Women tend to be concentrated in the higher positions in a range of caring, governmental and teaching roles compared to men.

Why is there movement up and down?

Sociologists have suggested four major reasons for social mobility:
- changes in the occupational structure
- education
- social background
- marriage.

Changes in the occupational structure

Over the last 40 years there has been a steady decline in the numbers of low-skilled jobs and a great increase in the numbers of professional and managerial positions. Quite simply, there are many more high status jobs around. This allows more people to move up, with relatively few moving down.

Education

The education system has been expanded and improved to give intelligent working-class children greater chance of success. Combined with the expansion in the numbers of top jobs, this has allowed considerable numbers of working-class children into higher status jobs. Thirty-five per cent of men in the professions are from working-class backgrounds of one sort or another.

Social background

A person's background, parental encouragement and peer group support can create a determination to succeed, as well as giving the individual the 'correct' social attributes. The child from a privileged background may have the right manners and accent to pluck a plum job. However, a determined, intelligent working-class child, given the right circumstances may well be equipped to succeed.

Marriage

Generally, people marry others from similar backgrounds to themselves. But movement up or down occurs when people marry someone from a different social class background.

Questions

1 A meritocracy is a society where people's jobs and incomes are a result of ability not friendship or family connections. Is Britain a meritocracy?
2 Find out and compare your parents' occupation with those of your grandparents. What social mobility (if any) has taken place?

Why is there such a high level of self-recruitment amongst higher groups?

- *Educational advantage* Families from the higher social groupings manage to provide their children with an education which ensures that they are more likely to succeed.
- *Contacts* in the world of work can often provide the younger generation with the chance of a 'good start'.
- *Social differentiation* plays an important role in that there is still discrimination on the grounds of sex and ethnic origin.

Activity

Copy and complete the diagram putting in the reasons for social mobility.

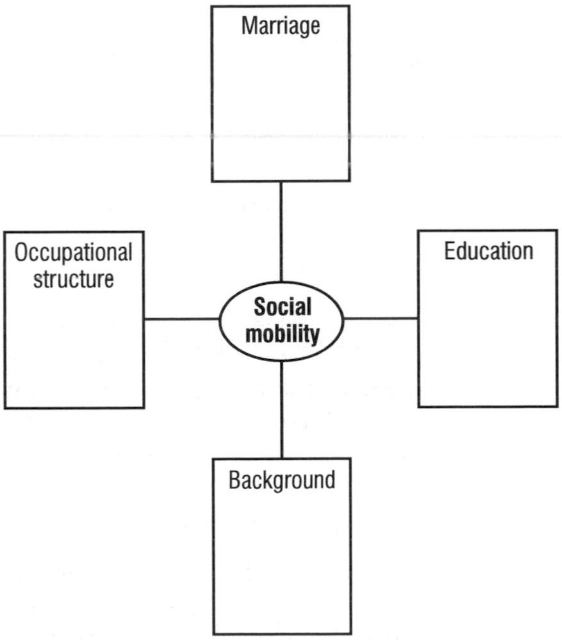

Marriage

Occupational structure

Social mobility

Education

Background

Main points
- Social mobility is the movement up or down the occupational structure.
- The greater the mobility, the more it shows that ability is the basis of social class.
- The term used to describe a society based on ability is a *meritocracy*.
- There are two types of social mobility:

- – inter-generational – across generations
- – intra-generational – one person's working career.

▶ The most common inter-generational movements are:
- – one occupational group up or down (short-range mobility)
- – to stay in the same occupational group as the parent (known as self-recruitment).

▶ There is decreasing intra-generational mobility as people enter companies at a level linked to their educational background.

▶ The main factors affecting the extent of mobility are:
- – changes in the occupational structure
- – educational change
- – social background
- – marriage.

▶ The highest groups are able to block movement into their 'class' and have the highest levels of self-recruitment. They do this by:
- – giving their children an elite education in private or public schools
- – social contacts to get top jobs
- – discriminating against certain categories of people, especially the ethnic minorities.

Wealth and income

One of the most obvious and taken-for-granted aspects of British society is the fact that some people have more possessions than others. Some people live in big houses, with smart cars and spend pleasant holidays in exotic places, while others scrape the barest existence from their work. What is not so obvious, however, is the scale of the inequalities in wealth and income, and the ways in which the rich obtain their money.

Wealth

The distribution of wealth

> **Definition**
>
> **Wealth** – the possession of things which, if sold, have great value. Wealth is often held in the form of stocks and shares, property and works of art

Official figures released by the government show that the most wealthy 10 per cent of the population own 51 per cent of all the marketable **wealth**. At the other end of the scale, the poorer half of the population own 4 per cent of the wealth. Many sociologists are doubtful about these figures, arguing that they understate the proportion of the wealth held by the rich.

Tax advisers help the rich to manipulate their assets in such a way as to appear less wealthy than they really are and so they avoid paying quite as much tax. These critics claim that the richest 10 per cent own as much as 70 per cent of the wealth, rather than 51 per cent.

How did the rich get their wealth?

According to a recent study, the chances of becoming rich from a working-class or lower middle-class background are increasing. Today, 20 per cent of millionaires are from less well-off backgrounds which is more than double the proportion 10 years ago. However, it is important to remember that 40 per cent of millionaires come from very wealthy backgrounds, and a further 30 per cent inherited considerable sums of money (from £10,000 to £100,000) which they used to start their businesses.

Who are the wealthy?

The wealthy are composed of:

- the British aristocracy, who own vast tracts of land – the Duke of Westminster, for instance, owns 300 acres of some of the richest parts of London in Belgravia, Mayfair and Westminster, amongst his total land ownership of 138,000 acres throughout Britain
- the owners of industry and commerce – only a small proportion of the population, about 10 per cent, own significant amounts of stocks and shares in companies
- the 'struck lucky' – these are the people who through good fortune (and, sometimes, talent) strike it rich. These include sports personalities, entertainers, those who win the National Lottery and those who had one good idea which was successful.

Wealth in Britain today

Distribution of wealth to the income groups

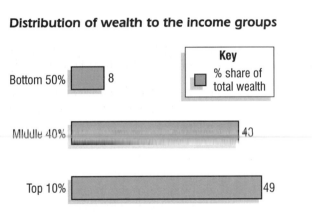

Key
% share of total wealth

Bottom 50%   8

Middle 40%   40

Top 10%   49

Source: Adapted from *The Guardian*, 13 February 1995

1 What percentage of total wealth is owned by the top 10 per cent?

2 What percentage is owned by the bottom 50 per cent?

Income

The distribution of income

Income is the flow of money people obtain for their work, from the state in benefits or from their investments. The top 10 per cent of earners take about 27 per cent of all income compared to 2.5 per cent earned by the poorest 10 per cent.

The figures are, however, more complex than this. Senior managers may well receive other benefits which are not obvious as 'income', but do benefit them. These 'perks' may include assistance with school fees, company car and cheap mortgage. On the other hand, they have to pay a higher proportion in tax and are not eligible for most state benefits.

Cutting the cake

The pie chart shows the distribution of income amongst the population of Britain. Each part of the pie chart represents the income levels of each fifth (or 20 per cent) of the population. You can see, for example, that the highest earning 5 per cent received 43 per cent of all income.

The share of incomes among the five household income groups

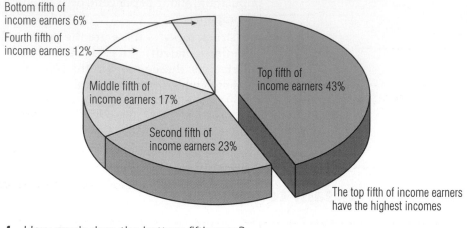

Bottom fifth of income earners 6%

Fourth fifth of income earners 12%

Middle fifth of income earners 17%

Top fifth of income earners 43%

Second fifth of income earners 23%

The top fifth of income earners have the highest incomes

1 How much does the bottom fifth earn?

2 What proportion of all income do the top two-fifths (40 per cent) of the population earn?

Income, wealth and differentiation

What we have seen is a great imbalance in the ownership of wealth and in the distribution of income. But which social groups are more likely to be high earners and to be wealthy? The answer by now is fairly predictable if you have read the rest of the chapter. The wealthy and the high earners are likeliest to be older, white and male. This does not mean, of course, that all the wealth and high earners are likely to have these characteristics, just that it is more likely.

In the next chapters we will explore issues of gender, race and age to see in more detail just why these patterns of income and wealth distribution have emerged.

Changes in the distribution of income and wealth

Definition

Disposable income – the money which someone has left to spend after the household bills and all other necessities have been paid for

During the twentieth century there was a very slow and limited decline in the proportion of wealth owned by the rich. There was also a limited redistribution in income.

During the 1980s to late 1990s, the redistribution of both was put into reverse. However, at the turn of the twenty-first century, the government has introduced a number of measures which have increased the income of the lowest groups by a small amount.

Since 1980, the **disposable incomes** of the richest tenth of the population have risen by 62 per cent and those of the poorest tenth have fallen by 17 per cent.

Questions

1 What is the difference between wealth and income?
2 Ought we to trust official statistics of income and wealth distribution? Explain your answer.
3 'Anybody can be rich if they work hard enough.' What comment do sociologists have to make on this statement?
4 What is your view on inherited wealth? Is it right that people should be able to leave all their wealth to their children or should no one be allowed to pass on their wealth, so that each generation could start off more or less equal?

Main points ▶ Wealth is property and investments which people own.
▶ Income is a person's inflow of money from whatever source – job, investments or pensions.
▶ There is a very great inequality of income and wealth in contemporary Britain.
▶ There has been a small amount of redistribution over the last 50 years.

---

3 CHAPTER SUMMARY

1 People distinguish other people in terms of social differentiation.

2 The result of social differentiation can be social stratification where people belonging to different groups will have different life chances.

3 Throughout history and society, there have been different forms of differentiation and stratification. Three important ones are caste, estates and social class.

4 Social class influences our lives in a considerable number of ways.

5 Sociologists disagree about the nature and importance of social class.

6 There are three main theoretical explanations – Marxist, Weberian and Functionalist.

7 Social class has changed very considerably over the last 20 years and three main trends have been identified – fragmentation, overlap and value diffusion.

8 The working class has split into two main groups – the traditional working class and the new working class.

9 There is a debate as to the existence of a third group called the underclass.

10 There has been a very large growth in the middle class, as a result of the change in the occupational structure, with office and service jobs taking over from manual industrial work.

11 The traditional middle class has been divided into two groups – the intermediate stratum and the service stratum.

12 The upper class has continued to exist because of inter-marriage, public school education and common business and commercial interests.

13 There has been great debate in sociology concerning the importance of social class in contemporary society.

14   Social mobility is the movement up or down the occupational structure.

15   There are two types of social mobility – inter-generational and intra-generational (within one person's working career).

16   The highest groups are able to block movement into their 'class' and have the highest levels of self-recruitment.

17   There is a very great inequality of income and wealth in contemporary Britain.

18   There has been a small amount of *redistribution* over the last 50 years.

Test Your Knowledge

1   Explain the meaning of the terms:
     a) social differentiation
     b) social class
     c) life chances.

2   Why is social class important in people's lives?

3   Identify and explain the three elements of social stratification according to Max Weber.

4   What three changes have taken place in the entire class structure of Britain?

5   What split has taken place in the working class?

6   How has the middle class changed in the last 30 years?

7   Is there such a thing as the upper class? If there is, who are members?

8   Why is occupation used to measure social class?

9   Some people argue that the old social class divisions are not as important as they used to be, and new divisions have started. One of these arguments is that a 40/30/30 society exists. Explain what this means.

10   What are the main reasons for social mobility?

11   What is the difference between wealth and income? Is wealth becoming more equally spread across society?

GENDER AND SEXUALITY

Chapter contents

Gender divisions in society

Gender images

1 Look carefully at the photo. What is their relationship, do you think? What do the poses of the two people in the photo suggest about how we see the roles of men and women?

2 This is the caption underneath the photo: 'Crown Prince Abdullah, heir to the Jordanian throne, with his wife Princess Rania Yassin' (they are now King and Queen). How does the language of the caption suggest that she is less important than him?

3 Look through newspapers and magazines for photos of men and women together. Is there any common pattern you can find?

4 What if the photo was of two men or two women and the caption referred to them as gay or lesbian – would it make you think about them differently?

Definitions

Sex – the physical characteristics based on genetic differences which distinguish males from females

Gender – the way society expects people to behave on the basis of their physical difference

Nowhere is the power of socialisation so clearly illustrated as in the creation of gender roles, that is in the different expectations we have of the proper behaviour for men and women. No one disputes that men and women are *physically* different (the division by **sex**), but sociologists argue that the differences in *behaviour* between men and women are not a result of these physical differences all, they are learned (the division by **gender**).

Learning the gender roles begins as a baby in the family, and every experience that a person has after that reinforces a few clear messages, that:

• males and females ought to act differently
• these differences in behaviour are the result of biology and are therefore natural
• those who do not wish to fit into the expected patterns of behaviour are 'deviants'.

The roles themselves are fairly clear: women are expected to be physically weaker, more emotional, have motherly and homely instincts, and do not have strong sexual desires. On the other hand, men are stronger, less emotional, more aggressive and have powerful sexual drives. To understand how these roles are learned and how they influence the lives of women in particular, we will explore a number of areas of women's lives, including childhood and education, work, motherhood, social life and leisure, and their experience of violence at the hands of men.

Are gender roles natural?

Sociologists argue that our expectations of males and females are not based on natural, biological differences, but are the result of different patterns of socialisation. But how can we prove this? Well, if gender roles are related solely to genetic characteristics, men and women should behave the same in all societies. Their natural, genetic characteristics will determine how they behave. If, however, they behave differently across time and cultures, it cannot be true that gender roles are 'natural'. (Finding out information by comparing cultures is known as the comparative method.)

In *Sex and Temperament in Three Primitive Societies*, Margaret Mead describes three New Guinea tribes: the Arapesh, the Mundugumor and the Tchambuli. Among the Arapesh, the ideal adult has a gentle passive, cherishing nature and resembles the feminine type in our culture. In relationships between the sexes, including the sexual, the Arapesh recognise no temperament between men and women. The main work of both adult men and women is child-bearing and child-rearing – indeed they call sexual intercourse 'work' when the object is to make the woman pregnant! The verb 'to give birth' is used for both of the sexes. Mead observed that if one comments on a middle-aged man as good looking, the people answer 'Good looking? Yes. But you should have seen him before he gave birth to all those children!'

Amongst the Mundugumor, the opposite of the Arapesh holds true, where both sexes follow our idea of the 'masculine' pattern. The women are as forceful and vigorous as the men, they detest bearing and rearing children, and men in turn detest pregnancy in their wives. Both sexes are reared to be independent and hostile and boys and girls have similar personalities.

In the third tribe, the Tchambuli, there was a great difference between the sexes. However, the males showed what we would say are 'female' characteristics and the women showed 'masculine' character-istics. Women are self-assertive, practical and manage all the affairs of the household. Men are 'skittish, wary of each other, interested in art, in theatre, in a thousand petty bits of insult and gossip. Hurt feelings are rampant … the pettishness of those who feel themselves weak and isolated, the men wear lovely ornaments (the women shave their heads and are unadorned), they do the shopping, they carve and paint and dance.'

A similar pattern of sex differences occurs in a South-West Pacific society studied by William Davenport.

'Only men wear flowers in their hair and scented leaves tucked into their belts or arm bands. At formal dances it is the man who dresses in the most elegant finery and … when these young men are fully made up and costumed for the dance they are not allowed to be alone even for a moment, for fear some women will seduce them.'

Source: A. Oakley, *Sex, Gender and Society* (M.T. Smith, 1972)

1 Describe the typical characteristics of males amongst:

a) the Arapesh
b) the Mundugumor
c) the Tchambuli.

2 What does the extract tell us about gender roles in our own society?

3 Provide three examples from your own experience when you have been treated differently solely on the basis of your sex.

Gender, differentiation and stratification

We have seen that gender roles are socially created. We will go on to explore in detail the implications for women of this 'social construction of gender'. However, before we do, it is important to remember the interconnections between stratification and gender.

Women have different life chances from men, and by the end of the chapter you will probably agree that women's life chances are poorer and more limited than those of many men. But remember that women are also divided by:

- social class
- age
- ethnic group.

Women *share* common life chances and experiences, but are also *divided* by social stratification and differentiation.

The life of a rich, upper-class woman is different from the life of a woman from the new working class. The life of a white woman is different from the life of a woman of Asian or African-Caribbean origin.

Divisions between women

Women across the world

When we discuss the situation of women, you could believe that all women share a common situation. This is not completely true, however, for there are many divisions between women based on race, religion, nationality and social class.

According to the United Nations, women grow more than half the food produced by developing nations. Women also collect most of the water needed to keep families and crops in these countries alive.

In some families, women are in charge of all the farming work because the men have migrated to towns in search of paid jobs.

The Food and Agriculture Organisation of the United Nations estimates that a third of rural households in developing countries are headed by women.

There is also a growing trend for women to migrate to towns in search of factory work. These factories produce goods for export to Britain and other western countries.

For example, much of the cheap clothing sold in British shops comes from countries such as the Philippines, Taiwan, Indonesia and Bangladesh. The clothes are made in factories which employ up to 90 per cent female labour.

The goods produced are cheap because rates of pay in countries such as the Philippines are lower than in Britain and because female labour is even cheaper than male.

Most women work for only two to three years in these factories, partly because the work is so wearing. For instance, many South Korean women are employed to put together the component parts of hi-fi stereos and other electrical goods. They have to spend long hours looking through microscopes, which can lead to eye problems.

Source: *The Guardian*, 26 March 1991

Race divisions

About 17 per cent of women from ethnic minorities are out of work, compared with 7 per cent among white females. The highest jobless rate is 28 per cent for Pakistani and Bangladeshi women.

Social class divisions

Jane Anderson, 24, is on an access course studying fashion and textiles at City and Islington College, north London. She was born in Linwood, near Glasgow, and left school at 16. Her parents are divorced. Both are unemployed.

I left school in 1987, age 16, with three GCSEs: My parents were divorcing, and school was hard. I went on to do a couple of … jobs, one as a dental assistant and one giving car insurance quotes. I stayed there for about three years but I was treated like a dog's-body; in the end, I resigned. When I was 20, I moved to London. I still had no job. I must have lived in about

six or seven places, with friends. What did I do all day? Not much. Sat around and watched telly. I became a bit of a soap addict. In the evenings we saw bands. I thought I was having fun.

Gradually, my attitude changed. I got bored; I was broke. Nothing was going on for me at all, but I couldn't find a way out. When you're out of work, you've no way of getting experience.

Because I'd been unemployed for so long, the employment office put me on a [skills training] course; out of 15 people on the course, I was the only one accepted into college.

I started at City and London last year. Next year, I'm intending to do a degree course in theatrical costume at the London College of Fashion.

I know what I want to do, and I'm going to do it. I have enormous drive, I want to better myself and I'm ambitious.

I'm still skint and I still wear clothes from charity shops, but I know I'll own a house one day, I know I'll be a success. I feel so proud of what I've achieved.

I'll show people how serious I am about my career. I'll have kids, but not until I'm established. Of course I want to make money. Who doesn't? … I

don't want to end up like all my girlfriends back in Linwood have ended up, pushing babies around.

Bryony Gibbins will be 20 next month. She was educated at Roedean, a girl's private boarding school in East Sussex. She has nine GCSEs, two A-levels and an A/S-level. She lives in her own flat in Kingston and attends St James's secretarial college in Kensington. Her parents are divorced. Her mother works for a travel PR agency; her father is a chartered accountant at KPMG.

I was at Roedean for seven years. I loved it. I suppose I

didn't know anything different. I wanted to teach primary science, so when I left Roedean I went straight on to study for a degree in education at Kingston University. I left after two weeks. It wasn't for me. It was all about how to teach kids English or geography. When I left, I was a bit worried about what my parents might say, particularly my father. He was fine about it.

… I didn't like being a student. I was lost. No one knew my name. I felt like I was simply a student identity number.

My father has bought me this flat in Kingston, where I live with my boyfriend and a tenant. It cost about £60,000. My father set up a trust fund for me when I was born, which gives me an allowance of £500 a month.

I know that's quite a lot, but I still have an overdraft. The fund pays for things like my car, which cost £6,000. It's a Renault Clio. I'm half way through my secretarial course in Kensington.

The fees are £2,000 a term, which my father also pays for. You learn shorthand and typing and word processing. It's quite a smart place. You have to wear skirts. I think it will give me a good start.

I don't worry about not having a degree. So many graduates can't find jobs anyway. I think secretarial skills will get me a good job.

Until then I can live off my trust fund. Hopefully, it'll go on until I can find a job. I can't get my hands on all the money until I'm 25 – my father knows me too well!

Ambitions? Well, I don't want to be the chairman of ICI. I'd be quite happy to plod along. …

Source: *The Independent*, 26 January 1995

You can see from reading the above extracts that there are big differences between women, as well as shared problems.

Some sociologists have suggested that the divisions of race, religion, nationality and social class, and even the place where they live, may be more important than their gender in affecting life chances. What do you think? Copy the grid below and complete it.

Gender	What do they share on the basis of gender?
Social class	How do they differ on basis of social class?
Nation/place	How does a woman's nationality or geographical position influence her life?
Race	How do they differ on basis of 'race'?

Main points
▶ Sex refers to the biological differences between people.
▶ Gender refers to the socially expected behaviour of men and women.
▶ Gender behaviour varies across time and society and cannot be said to be 'natural'.
▶ Gender forms another element of social stratification and strongly influences a person's life chances.
▶ There is a dispute between some feminist sociologists and others as to which is more important in determining life chances – a person's gender or his/her social class.

Childhood and education

Socialisation

Gender **socialisation** begins as soon as the baby is born. Many midwives ask 'Which would you prefer boy or girl?' Just asking the question suggests that the sex of a child is important to us. The answer is even more revealing as it shows the different expectations we have. The adjectives used to describe children of different sexes indicate just what these expectations are. Boys are described as strong, tough, 'a little rascal'. Girls are described as sweet, pretty or angelic.

Later on, as the child grows we have terms which are used to describe children who do not quite fit into the patterns of behaviour expected of their sex, for example 'tomboy' or 'cissy'.

Parents' expectations

Parents' expectations of children lead them to encourage different forms of behaviour from their children according to their gender. Although most parents are aware enough now of the problem of stereotyping children into strict conformity and may believe that they treat the children equally, differences still remain. Females are supposed to be more caring and to demonstrate this; they may also be expected to be tidier than their brothers and possibly to show more interest in helping around the house.

Certainly, despite the claims that children are treated the same, toys and games are very often linked to girls or boys.

Activity

Is it true that toys and games are used only by one sex? Visit local toyshops and ask the assistants their views. You could also ask children about their preferred toys and games.

How could you find out if boys and girls play different games. Do it!

Identity

In childhood we are gradually constructing our **identity**, that is our image of ourselves as a person and our place in the world. Adult identity is rather like a jigsaw, with our gender being one crucial element.

The processes of *imitation* and *identification* allow the growing child to insert this part of the jigsaw.

Imitation

Children imitate adults, and are encouraged to do so. So the son imitates his father, and in so doing learns traditional views of what manliness is. The girl imitates her mother, so games might involve dressing up in mum's clothes, wearing her high-heeled shoes and putting on her make-up.

Identification

Identification with adults also takes place, with children seeing themselves as their parents, or as heroes/heroines from comics and television.

Group pressure

This is applied to children by their friends (peer group) if they fail to act in the right way. Friendships develop along sex lines with separate groups of boys and groups of girls, playing different sorts of games.

Definition

Identity – a person's identity is composed of a mixture of personal experiences and wider images of the world and their place in it, provided by schools, the media and people who are important to the individual. It is usually linked to awareness of gender, race and social status, as well as an image of one's own body

Activity

Ask a small sample of young people aged 12–17 if, in their experience, there are differences in the ways that parents treat their sons and daughters concerning:

a) time to be in at night
b) places they can go
c) sorts of clothes they can wear
d) help around the home.

Why do they say they do this?

You might want to extend the survey and compare this with views of a small sample of parents.

Education

Choice and achievement

In terms of academic attainment, girls have significantly higher levels of achievement than boys, although about the same proportion of males and females eventually go to university. But success in education, as we will see later, is not necessarily linked to success in careers later in life.

As soon as males and females are given choices of subjects to study, they choose quite different ones. Girls are less likely to take Maths, Computing and the natural sciences, and are more likely to study English, Human Biology and foreign languages. This is even more pronounced at A-level.

There is some evidence that the intellectual abilities of girls and boys are slightly different, with girls being superior in the use of language, and in early adolescence boys develop greater ability in Maths. Even if these differences are natural, however, sociologists still argue that the more important influences on educational attainment of boys and girls are the social ones.

It has also been found that teachers, like parents, have different expectations of behaviour for boys and girls. Boys are expected to be more boisterous, girls to be quieter and more obedient. As a result, teachers are likely to treat the children differently according to their sex.

Definition

Hidden curriculum – the values which are taught to children in the school through the behaviour and expectations of teachers

The way that teachers act towards girls, and expect different behaviour and academic standards from them, has been called the **hidden curriculum** (a curriculum means the information taught at school). In effect, boys and girls are taught different things at school, although it is not officially organised that way.

Students' expectations

In education, one of the more important factors which motivates pupils and students is an idea of the future career prospects they may have. These ideas are a result of the wider culture, peer group influence, teachers' views and finally the individual's own desires.

There has been a very significant shift in attitudes over the last 30 years regarding the jobs which are seen as 'appropriate' for males and females. So females now stay on at school and enter higher education in equal numbers to males. They no longer see marriage and motherhood as the most important 'career' for them. It seems likely that, over the next 20 years, women will gradually move into a wide range of occupations, including those now dominated by men. However, today women are still concentrated in a narrow range of jobs which reflect the female role in our society. For large numbers of women, this is likely to continue as, when asked at school about future careers, they still choose this narrow band of jobs in the caring, secretarial and service industries.

> Twenty-one per cent of women are in science, engineering and technology occupations compared with 36 per cent of men. The one scientific occupation with more women than men is the relatively lowly job of laboratory technician.

Source: *The Guardian*, 19 October 1998

So, at school, males and females study different subjects, with females studying languages and social sciences, and males more likely to follow sciences. These choices of subjects relate to future careers, where women are concentrated in caring work (teaching, social work, nursing) or in a range of office jobs.

Choice of subjects and gender

How many (a) females and (b) males are studying sociology in your class? If you are studying in a mixed sex institution and you have chosen to study the subject voluntarily, why is there this balance?

The glass ceiling

Times have changed. Today women no longer expect to be a mother and housewife – they have aspirations. They can see just what they would like to achieve – not just a 'good job' but senior management – the very top jobs.

But although women can see where they want to go, they rarely seem to get there. Only 12 per cent of senior managers are women and more often than not, these jobs are in a narrow range of educational and caring occupations.

Women today face a glass ceiling – they can see the top jobs, but they just cannot get there.

1 Explain, in your own words, the meaning of the term 'the glass ceiling'.

2 From the main text, find explanations and examples for its existence.

Gender divisions: from school to work

Secondary and higher education

English, maths and history are fairly evenly studied by both sexes, but more girls than boys study biology, French, music and drama, whereas more boys study physics.

Females have a higher pass rate than males in virtually all GCSE subjects.

At university seven times more men than women study information technology (computing) and few young women are undergraduates in mathematics, physics and chemistry. Female students are much more likely to study social sciences and languages.

Training

The Equal Opportunities Commission says that more boys go into job-related youth training schemes. More than 60 per cent of trainees in Employment training are male.

> Young women leaving school are opting for 'traditional female occupations', according to a survey of inner-city schools by the Policy Studies Institute.
>
> It found that of 16-year-old girls who left school for work or training 40 per cent went into office work, 17 per cent into 'caring' jobs and 16 per cent into hairdressing.
>
> The survey looked at more than 2,500 young people from 34 schools in east and south London, Birmingham, Leeds, Manchester and Merseyside.
>
> Young men who left school went into a broader range of jobs. But more than half went into 'traditionally' male areas of construction, vehicle engineering and joinery or carpentry

Source: The Guardian, 12 September 1994

Work

More men than women go into these jobs: agriculture, forestry, fishing, engineering and construction.

More women than men go into these jobs: education, welfare, health services, clerical work, catering, and many service jobs.

Women are less likely to be promoted at work and less likely to be found in any senior management positions compared to men.

On average, women receive about 80 per cent of male salaries, reflecting the different occupations, and the lack of promotion.

Family

Women with young children tend to take a break from work or work part-time. But having children does not affect the working patterns of men so dramatically,.

Only 8 per cent of mothers with children aged 0–4 years are in full-time work and 21 per cent in part-time work.

However, over 80 per cent of fathers with young children are in full-time work and only 2 per cent in part-time work

Work

Definitions

Overt – people are open and obvious in their views and actions

Covert – where people hide their real views

Patriarchy – a society where the men hold more power than women

Women form about half the workforce today, yet they are seriously under-represented in management and the higher levels of the professions (such as medicine and the law). They earn on average about than 80 per cent of men's wages, and are far more likely to be in part-time work than men. This is despite the fact that is illegal to pay women less than men. And, as we saw earlier, they are more likely to be concentrated in a few areas of employment, particularly clerical and caring work, and the service industries.

The main reasons are as follows:

- A woman is still expected to be responsible for her children, unlike her husband/partner, who will be expected to help and support her in caring for the children and doing the housework, but she should *still be responsible* for it. You could say that society views a good father and partner as one who gladly helps look after the children and helps to run the household.
- Despite legislation which aims to:
  - give women equal rights with men
  - ensure that by taking time off from work to have children they do not lose out on their careers

  many women still do have significant career breaks to bear children and then to look after them. Even those who do not stay at home after the birth of their children have considerable stresses in organising childcare. This problem is becoming more serious with the growth of divorce and lone-parent families.
- It is still true that some men are prejudiced against women and do not accept their equality. This may be **overt**, where men state this is their view, or **covert**, where they do not actually realise their own prejudices, but dress them up under beliefs about the 'caring aspect of women' or their 'emotional nature'. Whichever is the case, the continuing oppression which results is known as **patriarchy**

Not equal yet: women's and men's pay

Now 30 years after equal pay legislation was introduced which made it illegal to pay men and women different wages for work of equal worth, one third of women workers (four million women) earn less than 80 per cent of men's average wage.

So why has this legislation and the legislation which followed failed?

Because women are concentrated in low paid and low status employment. Women fill 75 per cent of clerical and secretarial posts, but only 36 per cent of managerial and administrative posts.

Just under 50 per cent of all female workers are employed part-time and this means that they have less chance of promotion and career development.

Home and family responsibilities take their toll too. Women in full-time employment work fewer hours on average than men – the main reason is that they have to keep hours to a minimum because of caring for children.

1 In what ways does the photograph suggest that the nature of work and employment are changing?

2 In what ways would the photo have been different only 10–15 years ago?

A Employees:[1] by gender and occupation, 1991 and 1999, United Kingdom

Percentage

	Males		Females	
	1991	1999	1991	1999
Managers and administrators	16	19	8	11
Professional	10	11	8	10
Associate professional and technical	8	9	10	11
Clerical and secretarial	8	8	29	26
Craft and related	21	17	4	2
Personal and protective services	7	8	14	17
Selling	6	6	12	12
Plant and machine operatives	15	15	5	4
Other occupations	8	8	10	8
All employees[2] (=100%)(millions)	11.8	12.4	10.1	10.8

[1] At spring each year. Males aged 16 to 64, females aged 16 to 59.
[2] Includes a few people who did not state their occupation. Percentages are based on totals which exclude this group.

Source: Labour Force Survey, Office for National Statistics

B Full and part-time employment[1]: by gender, United Kingdom

C Weekly earnings gender differential[2], Great Britain

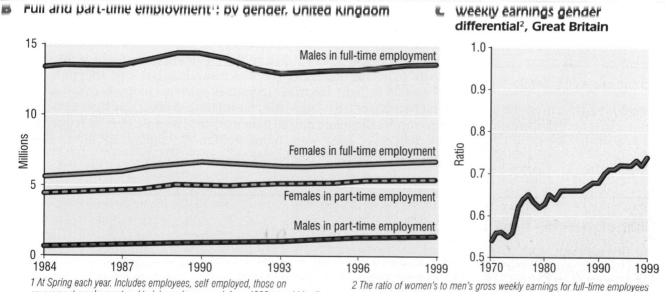

1 At Spring each year. Includes employees, self employed, those on government employment and training schemes and, from 1992, unpaid family workers. Full/part-time is based on respondents' self-assessment.
Source: Labour Force Survey, Office for National Statistics

2 The ratio of women's to men's gross weekly earnings for full-time employees at April each year. Until 1982, women aged 18 and over, men aged 21 and over. From 1983 onwards for employees on adult rates whose pay for the survey period was not affected by absence.
Source: New Earnings Survey, Office for National Statistics

Source: *Social Trends 30* (The Stationery Office, 2000)

Look at the main text and the tables and answer the following questions.

1 What proportion, on average, of men's wages do women earn?

2 Do men and women receive equal pay for equal work?

3 What reasons can you suggest for women earning less than men?

4 Why do you think women are more likely to accept low paid employment?

5 Why do women work fewer hours than men?

6 According to the chart:
   a) what is the most common type of occupation for women?
   b) what is the most common type of occupation for men?
   c) which sex has proportionately more jobs in management?

Women and the employment market

Definition

Employment market – the opportunities and constraints which a particular group face in obtaining work

Two hundred years ago, women were regarded very much as the equal of men – they worked alongside them in all sorts of labouring work, for instance. However, as the industrial revolution began to require fewer workers, gradually women were pushed out of the industrial workforce and the belief grew that the proper place for a woman was in the home. Feminist sociologists have argued that what was happening here was really a battle of the sexes and the males won, banishing women to the home.

At the turn of the twentieth century, less than 30 per cent of the workforce was female. However, the First World War (1914–18) took away the bulk of young men to fight. Women were recalled to the factories, where they did all the work men had done. But, with the war over, the jobs were returned to the men. The same thing occurred in the Second World War.

In the 1960s, however, the numbers of women in the workforce began to increase quite noticeably. This reflected the changing attitudes of women themselves. They began to fight against the idea that they ought not to return to work once they had children. Instead they began to seek work as soon as the youngest child began school. Allied to the changing attitudes of women was the growth in service industries (such as insurance, banking, shopping, etc.) and the growth in 'light' electronic industries (such as computer construction), which preferred women because they were cheaper to employ than men. They were also supposedly more nimble than men and, because they were prepared to work part-time, they were more flexible to employ. In short, female employees are attractive to employers.

Life chances and gender

Girls earn less than boys virtually from the day they leave school – and the gulf lasts the rest of their working lives.

Government statistics show that by the age of 20, women have a median [average] income of around £90 a week compared to £125 for men. By the mid-40s, the figure is £150 a week for females and £325 for males. Unusually, the figures count every penny in a woman's purse – from state benefit to salary, pensions and child maintenance. They exclude only housekeeping money given by men. Previous statistics compared only working women and men – but the new survey includes stay-at-home mothers and jobless men. This drags down the average. When full-time workers are counted, women are still behind in the pay stakes, earning £307 a week on average compared to £423 for men – power is becoming a mother

Even though two-thirds of women return to work after having children, most still pay a huge career price.

A woman's earnings are highest in her mid to late 20s, probably before she has children. Men reach a pay peak in their 40s, when they are usually reaping the rewards of long service and experience.

Source: *The Daily Mail*, 27 March 1999

1 What are the incomes of (a) males and (b) females at ages 20 and mid-40s?

2 Why does this survey give us a more accurate figure than comparing pay rates?

3 What is the main reason for women having lower incomes, according to the survey?

4 Why do you think that single mothers are one of the most financially disadvantaged groups in society?

5 What could the government do to alter the income of women?

Domestic labour

Definition

Domestic labour – work which is done in the house and which is not paid

Ask anyone what work is and they will probably reply with a description of paid employment, possibly giving the example of a clerk or manual worker. Few people would define housework as 'work'. Yet each day in Britain, millions of women spend a full day in the house, cooking, cleaning, washing and childminding. Each of these tasks by themselves if performed outside the home and paid would be considered a job. Studies of housework have shown that the amount of hours women work in the home is almost double that of people in offices and factories, and that women find the work very boring, physically exhausting and, worst of all, socially isolating, as they often have no one to talk to, except for young children, for long periods of the day. The biggest difference, however, was that at the end of the week, the housewife received no wage and her work was not even rewarded by others with the status of work.

The invisible work of caring

Most of Britain's six million carers are women. This form of work is known as 'invisible' as it is generally unpaid (although now there are some state benefits paid to carers) and does not appear in official statistics as economically productive work.

It could be argued that this is a 'choice' that women make. However, over one million of these women want to return to work but are prevented from doing so by the fact that there is no other way that the caring could be done.

Source: *The Daily Mail*, 27 March 1999

1 What do we mean by invisible work?

2 Why do women do this form of work?

3 The issue of caring work is becoming one of increasing concern to governments. This is because of the increase in lone parents, of the growing numbers of older people and the claimed weakening of the family. Why should governments (and possibly employers) be concerned?

Motherhood

Once married or in a long-term relationship with children, a woman finds that she is *expected* to do the bulk of the housework and childcare. Her husband/partner's career becomes the important one and her role is to combine work with being a good mother. A woman who wants a successful career rather than children is regarded as 'odd'. The modern ideal is to combine both work and motherhood. However, if the house is untidy or dirty, then comments are made concerning *her* laziness.

Maternal instinct

When a couple have children, it is expected that the woman ought to put the child first, and for the pre-school years she should give up work, or work part-time. This is because women are supposed to have a *maternal instinct*, which makes them put the needs of their children above their own needs. However, there is no absolute evidence to prove that this exists and sociologists argue instead that women are socialised into believing that they ought to put the needs of children before their own (unlike men?).

Some sociologists have argued that there is increasing equality in the family and that today men and women are equal. But feminists reply that men are still in control and that the family is really a trap for women.

(For a more detailed discussion on relationships in the family, see Chapter 7.)

Housework, image and reality

Source: *New Society*, 6 March 1987

1 Look at the cartoon. What images of women are portrayed?

2 Do you think that the cartoon presents an accurate picture?

3 Devise a cartoon to show what, in your opinion, are the husband or male partner's roles.

Social life and leisure

Leisure pursuits are also linked to gender roles and, although changes are happening, distinctive differences still remain between the leisure pursuits of males and females.

Though many sports have opened up for women, there is still a belief that the essential caring and emotional element to be found in most women prevents them from fully engaging in competitive sports. So, although women's football and rugby have increased greatly in participation levels, they still remain very small compared to male participation. Even when it comes to watching competitive sport, it remains true to say that far fewer women are interested than men.

Where wider gender roles do impact on sport is in the popularity of fitness and aerobics classes for women. The popularity of these classes is related to the fact that women believe they can achieve more attractive, slimmer figures. Men, however, are attracted to body building and fitness more because they wish make themselves more muscular. Both groups are seeking something from the activity, but what they want is a reflection of their gender roles.

In terms of going out, once again there have been changes. Women now talk about going out to 'pick up' men – suggesting how much more active they are now than the passive role they had 20 years ago. However, girls are still constrained by 'reputation' and have to be sure that they do not become labelled as 'easy' by men or other women. Women are not admired by other women because of the number of men they have had sex with, unlike many men.

The distinctions between the genders is maintained by the media, as certain images of men and women are promoted in film and print. These distinctions are sometimes very obvious, as in the case of the helpless female who stands to one side while the men fight, looking suitably horrified and frightened. But, more often, the images which are portrayed are more subtle. What these images do is to support the idea of how males and females ought to behave and also it reinforces the ideas that we already hold, perhaps even without being fully aware of them.

Activities

1 Choose any one of tonight's television programmes. Watch it carefully and write a brief description of the characters and roles of the main male and female characters.

In class, compare the types of parts females and males typically play.

2 Compare the contents and stories of comics/magazines intended for male and female readers. What happens to the stories if you change the sex of the main characters?

3 Find out the proportion of male to female teachers or lecturers in your school/college. Who are in the senior posts, such as heads of department and principal/headteacher?

4 In groups, discuss and devise a method of finding out:
a) the different academic subjects taken by males and females
b) the different careers that students intend to take.

The main issue you need to uncover is what differences, if any, emerge by gender.

Once you have decided a strategy, carry out your study and then report back your findings, and the difficulties you experienced in obtaining the information.

5 Write a paragraph, or sketch a diagram, to show how you see your future – but don't put your name on it. Put everyone's writing/diagrams in a mixed pile and look at them at random (or you could switch with another class). Can you tell which are written by males and which by females?

Women and violence

Sexual assaults

Most people believe that sexual attacks are performed by strangers at night in deserted streets, yet this is not the case. The majority of sexual attacks involve people who are known to each other, including family members, and about one third of rapes take place in the homes of the victims.

> **Definition**
>
> **Sexual bargaining** – the negotiations which men and women make over 'how far' they should go sexually

Carol Smart, in *Women, Crime and Criminology* (Routledge, 1976), suggests that rape should not be seen as being performed by disturbed men, but instead suggests that rape is merely an *extension* of normal **sexual bargaining** which occurs in UK society.

The socialisation of women stresses their allure to men. On the other hand, men are expected to initiate sexual encounters and women to at least make a show of 'resistance'. Therefore rape can be seen as an extension of the values of our society rather than being in opposition to them.

Domestic violence

> **Definition**
>
> **Domestic violence** – the use of violence by one member of the household against another (or others). Usually it is men who use violence against their partners and/or children

This is the use of violence against women by their partners within the home and, just like rape, there is assumed to be huge under-reporting in the official statistics. This seems to be caused partly by female partners feeling reluctant to report crime and, when there is a complaint, the police may be reluctant to arrest unless the violence seems to be quite 'serious'.

Domestic violence: the reality

Anyway, I was very tired that night and I went to bed early. Then he came to bed, and my little girl woke up, because she'd wet the bed. Anyway I went to see to her and I took the sheet and I moved it round so that I moved her off the wet part. And I went back to bed. Anyway she cried again and he went out to see to her. And I didn't know what had hit me.

He came in and he ripped the clothes off me and grabbed me by the feet, and dragged me out of bed. And he kicked me out into the hall and he called me all these names, and he said, "How dare you leave that child with a wet sheet on the bed." And he threw me into her bedroom. So I did the little girl, changed the bed all right round again, and then I went into the

bathroom and locked the door, because I was so upset. He came and knocked the bolt off and he dragged me back to our bedroom to make the bed. And I remember I had my dressing gown on and he threw me all the way down the hall and he ripped my dressing gown and then he threw me on the floor and he was kicking me and I was sitting there screaming.

And then he said he'd give me half an hour and then I was to go back into the bedroom and I was to apologise and he meant apologise properly. He put one arm round my throat, and he slapped me and punched me and he said, "How dare you look at me as if I'm repulsive to you. You're my wife, and I'll do what the bloody hell I like to you".

Source: Pahl, *Marital Violence and Public Policy* (Routledge & Kegan Paul, 1985)

Explanations for violence and sexual assaults

Sociologists have similar explanations for violence and sexual assault. Basically they argue that these are not performed by abnormal men as generally assumed, but that they are simple extremes of behaviour that occur very often. In the case of sexual assault (remember this is often between people who know each other), men are constantly exhorted to see women in sexual terms by the media and to believe that they know 'what women really want', and it is claimed that males may very often use forms of 'coercion' to obtain sex from partners.

When it comes to violence, sociologists argue that violence against female partners is deep in our culture. Historically, the use of a limited degree of violence by husbands has been culturally and legally acceptable, and it is only very slowly that this is being challenged.

Main points

▶ Socialisation is the process whereby people are taught to be members of society.

▶ Socialisation starts at infancy and is performed by the family and later by friends and the wider society. This process helps to form a person's identity.

▶ Females are more successful in the education system than males, but it does seem that teachers' expectations of the future careers of females are more limited and this may actually affect girls' beliefs in what they can achieve.

▶ A 'glass ceiling' seems to operate in Britain so that able women can progress up the promotion ladder at work and then seem to stop before their abilities are fully used.

▶ The reasons for the 'glass ceiling' include the fact that women are still expected to have greater responsibility for childcare and child-rearing than their partners and that there still remains some prejudice against them by employers.

▶ Although women are now as likely as men to be employed, they are concentrated in lower paid areas of employment, especially in caring and 'service' work (such as shops), and they are much more likely to be working part-time.

▶ At home, women still do more household tasks than males.

▶ Males and females still have different sorts of leisure pursuits.

▶ One of the most common forms of violence against women is domestic violence, which takes place in the home and is committed by husbands and partners.

▶ Sexual attacks are more likely to be committed by family members (and friends) than by strangers and more likely to take place in the home rather than outside.

Men: the new second sex

In the 1950s, a French women writer first used the term 'the second sex', referring to the unfair and patriarchal way in which women were treated. Today, some writers are arguing that as girls overtake boys at school and are slowly beginning to enter the higher jobs and break into areas of employment which were traditionally male, then it is men who are slowly becoming the second sex.

We are in a period of social change in which females are still earning less, undertaking more of the housework and taking the main responsibility for the children. However, many sociologists are now suggesting that as girls now outperform boys at school and have much greater belief in themselves and in the sorts of jobs they can do, so boys have entered a period of 'crisis'. Their traditional sense of superiority and their belief that they would have the top jobs is now being threatened. Furthermore, the values which were traditionally associated with men – toughness and physical strength, are increasingly out of tune, it is claimed, with the values of modern society. Young males are responsible for higher levels of crime, drug use and other forms of socially disapproved-of behaviour. What is necessary, it is argued, is that men start to change how they see themselves and how it is appropriate for them to act.

Gender and sexuality

Beauty

What is considered to be attractiveness varies across societies and time, with some societies stressing slimness, others weight. Sexual attraction is also attributed to different part of the body, so that the breasts can be regarded as highly sexual or as of no interest whatsoever, while other societies stress ankles, necks and ears.

Beauty is in the eye of the beholder

This is a computer image of what is defined as the perfectly beautiful face in the USA and Europe.

However, the idea of beauty has varied over time and society, as these photographs demonstrate.

Normality and abnormality

The traditional assumptions regarding the 'natural' nature of our **sexuality** have come to be questioned in recent years, and those who have different sexual orientations from heterosexuals, such as gays and lesbians, have used the successful feminist attack upon traditional male attitudes as their model of how to change our assumptions regarding the 'normality' of heterosexuality.

Gays and lesbians claim that anything up to about 10 per cent of the population share their sexual orientations. In a series of studies of sexuality in the USA during the 1950s, Kinsey found that 37 per cent of men had engaged in homosexual acts, and 15 per cent of women. The idea that there is any normal form of sexuality has been challenged by **cross-cultural studies**, with virtually any form of sexual activity being regarded as normal (or at least 'acceptable') in one society or another.

The idea that there are quite distinctive sexual 'types' of people, such as heterosexuals and homosexuals and lesbians, seems to be a relatively modern phenomenonm Europe. For, although various acts were condemned or thought of as illegal, it was the *acts* which were condemned. The term 'homosexual', for example, was not used until the mid-nineteenth century and it is only since then that the belief that people are *either* homosexual or heterosexual has developed. Today, in many non-Western cultures this clear-cut division does not exist. For example, among the Butak people of Sumatra, homosexual activity is seen as the normal form of sexuality for young males before they marry, when they take on a predominantly heterosexual role.

Gay and lesbian rights?

A lesbian who gave birth to a daughter after a do-it-yourself pregnancy said yesterday: 'It's time people stopped talking about traditional families. They are in the minority now.'

Natalie Wilson, 24, conceived her child after a gay man provided sperm which her lover implanted with an hypodermic needle.

In effect, this means the mother of a 6lb 10oz baby remains a virgin. She has changed her surname by deed poll so it is the same as her lover Denise Wilson, 26, and they plan to act as the baby's parents. ...

Natalie said: 'We just want people to accept us for what we are and leave us alone. They should give us a chance to give Ellesse a good life. Really, I am no different to a single mother – and there were more single mums at the hospital than married women.'

Natalie was 15 when she met Denise, then 17, as they socialised with friends. Natalie had fledgling relationships with a couple of boys 'but I never felt comfortable with them'.

Several months after they first met, Natalie and Denise kissed for the first time. Six months later, they were living together in a bedsit. Nearly a year later, Natalie told her parents of her true feelings. She said: 'They had probably guessed anyway.'

They plan to tell the infant her history when they think she is able to comprehend it. Natalie said:

'Frankly, I hope she grows up straight rather than gay. Gay people have too many problems but maybe people will be less prejudiced by the time she's an adult.

'Come back when she is 18. I'm sure people will be pleased.'

Source: *The Daily Mail*, 19 January 1995

1 Do you agree that the couple should have a child?

2 Do you think that their sexual orientation will influence the child's?

3 Do you think it matters anyway?

4 Why do you think Natalie said that she hoped her daughter would grow up to be 'straight'?

5 Is Natalie right when she says 'traditional families are in the minority now'?

Gay culture

In the last 20 years, gay men and lesbians have increasingly developed an alternative culture which rejects the negative images traditionally imposed upon them by the wider society.

Sexuality and life chances

Intolerance and harassment of homosexuals are rife, and most believe they receive less favourable treatment by the police and that the courts are biased against them.

Nearly half of the homosexual men and women questioned in the study, by Social & Community Planning Research, said insults had been shouted at them in public. One quarter had been physically threatened or attacked, and 21 per cent had been harassed at work.

Many were forced to hide their sexuality because of discrimination.

The report finds that society is more tolerant of lesbians than of male homosexuals. While 54 per cent of the lesbians had never encountered discrimination, only 38 per cent of male homosexuals could say that they had never experienced discrimination.

The researchers believe this is because lesbians are seen as less of a threat to society.

At work, 53 per cent of those surveyed said they kept their sexual identity secret from colleagues, and 44 per cent said they concealed it when applying for jobs.

Almost all of the 116 male homosexuals and lesbians believed employers would refuse job applications from gay candidates, and 96 per cent worried that they would lose their job if their employer discovered their sexual preference.

Although more than half of the heterosexual sample agreed that homosexuals made excellent teachers and youth leaders, one quarter thought they should be banned from working with children.

There was particular concern about homosexuals working with young children. More than 45 per cent thought it was never acceptable for a male homosexual to be a primary school teacher, and 34 per cent believed lesbians should never be allowed to teach in primary schools.

Source: *The Guardian*, 22 May 1995

1 What percentage of homosexual men and women had been:
   a) physically threatened?
   b) shouted at?

2 What percentage keep their sexual identity a secret at work? Why do they do so?

3 Who believed they had suffered more discrimination – males or females? Suggest a reason for this.

4 Of the heterosexuals interviewed, was any particular concern highlighted?

5 Do you agree or disagree with their concerns?

Sexuality, differentiation and stratification

An individual's life is affected very much by his or her sexuality, as we can seen in the extract above. If a person is gay or lesbian, it affects how he or she is treated by others, what jobs and careers are possible and whether they should be allowed to be parents. Gays and lesbians therefore can clearly be seen to have different life chances from heterosexuals. Sexuality forms another element of the complex inter-weaving of social strands which together form the pattern of stratification in British society.

Main points ▶ How people respond to homosexuality and lesbianism varies across time and societies.

▶ The term 'homosexual' has only been introduced into English fairly recently. It does not seem to have been used before the mid-nineteenth century.

▶ Gay and lesbian people have suffered discrimination because of their sexuality.

▶ Gays and lesbians have been able to challenge the discrimination they face and are seeking to obtain the same rights as heterosexuals in all areas of life.

▶ In some areas such as employment there is little opposition. But in other areas, such as the raising of children, there is considerable debate.

▶ Sexuality is another element of stratification.

---

4 CHAPTER SUMMARY

1 Sex refers to the biological differences between people.

2 Gender refers to the socially expected behaviour of men and women.

3 Gender behaviour various across time and society, and cannot be said to be 'natural'.

4 Gender forms another element of social stratification and strongly influences a person's life chances.

5 There is a dispute amongst some feminist sociologists and others about which is more important – a person's gender or his or her class.

6 Females are more successful in the education system than males, but female students are more limited in their aspirations. This may affect their future career prospects.

7 A 'glass ceiling' exists so that women rarely reach the highest positions in management or the professions.

8 The reasons for the 'glass ceiling' include the fact that women are still expected to have greater responsibility for childcare and that there still remains some prejudice against them by employers.

9 Although women are now as likely as men to be employed, they are concentrated in lower paid areas of employment, especially in caring and 'service' work (such as shops), and they are much more likely to be working part-time.

10 At home, women still do more household tasks than males.

11 Males and females still have different sorts of leisure pursuits.

12 Women suffer from domestic violence performed by husbands and partners.

13 Sexual attacks are more likely to be committed by family members to take place in the home.

14 How people respond to homosexuality and lesbianism varies across time and societies.

15 Gay and lesbian people have suffered discrimination because of their sexuality.

16 Gays and lesbians have been able to challenge the discrimination they face and are seeking to obtain the same rights as heterosexuals in all areas of life.

17 In some areas, such as employmnent, there is little opposition. But in other areas, such as the raising of children, there is considerable debate.

18 Sexuality is another element of stratification.

Test Your Knowledge

1   Explain, in your own words, the difference between sex and gender.

2   Are gender roles natural? Give examples to illustrate your answer.

3   How does family life affect gender differences?

4   In what way do the experiences of boys and girls differ at school?

5   Why are women less likely to do well in employment than men?

6   What do we mean by domestic violence?

7   Why is sexuality a 'social construction'?

Chapter 5

RACE AND ETHNICITY

Chapter contents

Race: myth and reality

Definitions

Race – a term which is rarely used in discussion but has its origins in the belief that there are biological distinctions between groups of people

Ethnic minority groups, Blacks and/or Asians – terms used where the writer wishes to compare the situation of all those members of these groups with the majority of British people

(People of) African-Caribbean/Pakistani/Bangladeshi (origin) – used when we wish to be more specific about the differences between groups. It also indicates that the people are most likely to be British born but of families who migrated here from those countries

The whole topic of **race** and immigration is a minefield of passions and prejudices, where even the language used is dangerous if not handled properly. The term 'race' has a long history of abuse. The idea that such a thing as a pure 'racial' group exists is dangerous nonsense. It has been claimed that one can divide people into three broad and overlapping groups – negroid, mongoloid and caucasoid. However, in practice it is very hard to distinguish these groups from one another, and anyway these divisions are meaningless. People from India, Pakistan and Bangladesh as well as most Europeans are all 'caucasoid', for example.

When the Nazis were in power in Germany during the 1930s and 1940s, they attempted to distinguish 'Aryan' people from others – but even they had great difficulty doing so.

Sociologists tend to use a variety of terms to discuss issues of 'race'. Perhaps the most common term is **ethnic groups** or **ethnic minority groups** to distinguish groups of people from each other. By these terms they mean groups of people who share distinctive cultures which are usually different from the culture of the majority of the people living in that society. If they use the term 'race', it has this meaning rather than any biological one.

In Britain there are very many ethnic groups, but some groups have drawn very little attention at all – the many thousands of Italians, for instance, who settled in Bedfordshire during the 1950s. While other groups, particularly people of African-Caribbean origin, Indians, Pakistanis and Bangladeshis, have been paid great attention. The common characteristic of those groups who have attracted much attention is skin colour. So some British sociologists, following the example of the leaders of these ethnic groups, commonly refer to all of them under the terms **Black people** and/or **Asian people**. In the USA the term 'people of colour' has been used, and you may find it in some textbooks. Clearly terms such as Asian people or Black people gloss over the large differences between different ethnic groups, but it does allow us to talk about the common problems resulting from the prejudice that they all face.

However, when we wish to look at the differences between groups, the terms **people of African-Caribbean origin** or **people of Pakistani origin** may be used.

Immigration

Historical background

Britain has always had a steady inflow (immigration) and outflow (emigration) of people (see the diagram on page 102). In the eighteenth century, Jewish people came here fleeing from the persecution they faced in central Europe, while the Irish began coming in the late 1840s and 1850s to escape from the terrible poverty and famines there. Incidentally, the single largest immigrant group in Britain today remains the Irish. However, most discussion about ethnicity centres around people of Chinese, African-Caribbean, Indian, Bangladeshi and Pakistani origin. Their patterns of migration into Britain can be divided into three main phases:

- from 1945 1961
- from 1961 to 1972
- from 1972 to the early 1990s.

From 1945 to 1961

African-Caribbean people were the first to come to Britain after the Second World War in 1945, and then from the mid-1950s they were joined in ever-increasing numbers by Indian, Bangladeshi and Pakistani people.

The reasons for immigration at this time was that Britain was experiencing a period of great prosperity in the 1950s; in fact, there were too many jobs for the workers available. First African-Caribbean people and then Asians were encouraged to come here to take the jobs that the British did not want. Usually these were the lowest paid or most unpleasant work.

It was not just chance that led these people to come to Britain. The immigration was the result of the British Empire which had led Britain to rule most of India and the Caribbean Islands. The people of African-Caribbean origin, in particular, thought of Britain as their 'motherland' where they would be very welcome. Many of them intended to stay in Britain for the rest of their lives. Those who came from India and Pakistan believed at the time that they would stay a few years, earn money and then return 'home'.

From 1961 to 1972

There was a sharp decrease in the numbers of immigrants from the West Indies, but the numbers of Indian and Pakistani immigrants remained fairly high. However, just to get the scale of immigration in proportion, by 1962 only 0.5 per cent of the population were 'non-white' immigrants.

The reasons for the change in the pattern of immigration was an Act of Parliament in 1962 which limited the numbers of immigrants allowed into Britain. Effectively only those with jobs and who had skills we wanted were allowed to enter Britain. Because a higher proportion of people from Indian had these skills and qualifications, a greater number of them continued to come. Also, the wives and dependants of migrants already settled here were allowed to join them. As the original Indian and Pakistani migrants were generally males, the period after 1961 was one of consolidation of families and of wives arriving to join their husbands.

From 1972 to the early 1990s

During this period, immigration from the Caribbean Islands was extremely low, whilst the numbers from India, Bangladesh (Bangladesh became an independent country in 1971) and Pakistan declined. However, there was an increase in the 1970s of people of Asian origin who lived in Africa. During the 1970s a process of 'Africanisation' took place in many of the newly independent countries as they sought to push Asians out of senior government, professional and commercial positions. These people were British passport holders, and the British government reluctantly accepted them.

The 1980s saw a low level of immigration, typically about 4,500 people a year, who were generally family members, or new spouses of people already living here.

Patterns of immigration

Below are some of the main inflows of people to Britain in the past.

40,000 years of migration to Britain

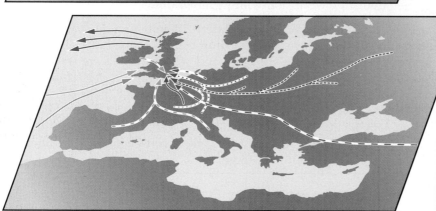

Since 1900

◄ ◼ ◼ From East Africa (British Asians) 1968–76
◄ •••• From Indian subcontinent 1950–71
◄ ▬ ▬ From West Africa 1950–71
◄ ◼ • ◼ From Hong Kong and SE Asia 1950–71
◄—— From the Caribbean 1948–71
◄—— To and from EU (ECC) 1972–
◄—► To and from Old Commonwealth 1900–
◄ – – Greek and Turkish Cypriots 1950–71
◄ • — • Displaced Persons and Cold War refugees 1945–68
◄ •••••• Refugees from the Third Reich 1933–45
◄ – – – Belgian refugees 1914–18
◄—— From Ireland 1900–

1066–1900

◄ ▬ ▬ Main wave of immigration from Ireland 1830–60
◄------ Political refugees 1789–1900
◄—— Servants and seafarers from India and China 1700–1900
◄—— Slaves from West Africa and West Indies 1555–1833
◄—— Huguenot and other Protestant refugees 1560–1720
◄ – – Gypsies c.1500
◄ – • – Weavers from the Low Countries 1337–1550
◄ •••••• Lombards, Hansa and other merchants 1250–1598
◄ ▬ ▬ Jews 1066–1290 and after 1656
——► Emigration to North America, South Africa, Australia and New Zeland 1560–1900

Before 1066 AD

◄—— Normans 1066
◄ – – Norwegians 800–1000 AD
◄ •••••• Danes 800–1000 AD
◄—— Frisians, Saxons, Angles, Jutes 400–600 AD
◄—— Romans 43–410 AD
◄—— Celts 1000–150 BC
◄ – – – Bronze Age, Neolithic and earlier migrations into NW Europe

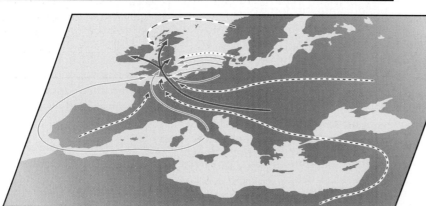

Source: Commission for Racial Equality, *Roots of the Future* (1996)

1 Do you think it is true to say that the British population has ever been one 'race'?

2 When we talk about immigrants or ethnic minorities, which groups do most people mean?

3 Is this accurate?

4 How best can we describe the composition of the British population throughout history?

Recent migration: the 1990s onwards

A very significant change in migration patterns occurred from the 1990s onwards. The migrants entering Britain were generally **asylum seekers**. Because of the changes in the law after 1971 the possibilities to enter Britain for employment were greatly reduced. Those who enter Britain now do so largely on the grounds of being in danger because of their political beliefs. The more recent arrivals in Britain include people from such diverse countries as the former Yugoslavia (for example Croatia, Bosnia, Serbia), from Turkey, from Somalia and from the Middle East.

Why did migrants want to come to Britain?

People who came to Britain did so for a combination of the following reasons.

Push reasons

They may have experienced dreadful poverty in their original country and hope to find a better life in Britain. This is the main reason for most Caribbean, Bangaldeshi and Pakistani immigration. They may have suffered persecution and been forced to leave, such as the Asians who were thrown out of Uganda, or more recently Kurds in Iraq and Turkey.

Pull reasons

Because of labour shortages in the 1950s, immigrants from the Commonwealth were encouraged to come to Britain. The British textile industry, for example, has relied upon cheap immigrant labour to survive. The strong family ties amongst Asian immigrants meant that close relatives have been brought to Britain wherever possible. Over two-thirds of Indian, Pakistani and Bangladeshi immigrants come to join relatives already settled here.

Citizens

It may have been useful once to examine the problems faced by the ethnic minorities in terms of them being immigrants, but this is no longer so. The majority of all Blacks and Asians living in Britain are British-born *citizens*; they are not immigrants, and indeed they are now second or third generation citizens.

Definitions

Racism – the belief in the idea of the existence of distinctive 'races' and that some races are superior to others

Racial prejudice – when people are disliked simply because they belong to a particular ethnic group

Attitudes close to home

In a recent survey, the majority of those questioned believed that there is **racism** in Britain today and 35 per cent admitted to being **prejudiced** themselves in some way.

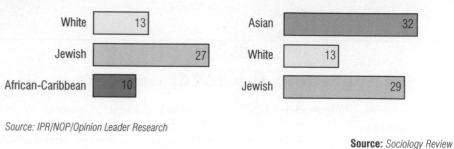

Would you mind if one of your close relatives were to marry a person of Asian origin? Mind a lot

White	13
Jewish	27
African-Caribbean	10

Would you mind if one of your close relatives were to marry a person of African-Caribbean origin? Mind a lot

Asian	32
White	13
Jewish	29

Source: IPR/NOP/Opinion Leader Research

Source: *Sociology Review*

Studying racism is a difficult and emotive issue. So, when we read statistics like this we have to be very careful.

1 Which group is least likely to want to marry an Asian or African-Caribbean person?

2 Which group is least likely to object to marrying those of Asian origin?

3 Which group is least likely to mind marrying a person of African-Caribbean origin?

4 What attitudes to ethnicity do the charts above indicate in your opinion?

5 In small groups devise two simple surveys to find out people's attitudes to:
a) racism
b) 'going out with' (or cohabiting/marrying if you prefer) people from different ethnic groups.

Ask a small sample of people outside your class these questions.

What results do you get? Did you notice any differences in answers depending upon the ethnic origin of the interviewer? Where there any other patterns you noticed?

Refugees and asylum seekers

Definitions

Refugee – a person who has been accepted for asylum

Political asylum – when a person flees one country because they are being persecuted for their political views and asks to live in safety in another country

As we saw earlier, there has been a very significant growth in the numbers of people who flee their countries because they claim they are being persecuted for their political beliefs. The growth has been so great that there are many who argue that the real reason for the increase in those asking for **political asylum** is that they want to improve their economic position. Whatever the real reasons, relatively few are given the right to settle in Britain permanently, with approximately 70 per cent of claims for **refugee** status being refused. In the mid 1990s about half of all those seeking political asylum were from Africa, with Nigeria heading the list.

Attitudes to asylum seekers

In 1999 there were 86,000 applications for asylum waiting to be considered, compared to 56,000 the previous year.

People are split into two groups concerning the motivations of asylum seekers. One group argues they are really 'economic migrants' who just use asylum-seeking as a way of getting into the country. Others argue that they are mainly genuine. Does the following information, drawn from a British government study, throw any light on the debate?

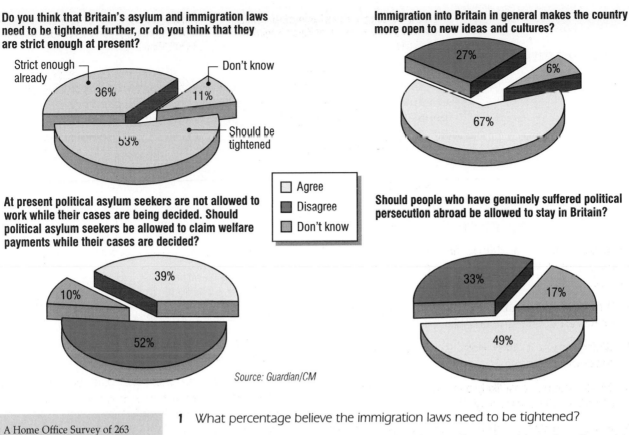

Do you think that Britain's asylum and immigration laws need to be tightened further, or do you think that they are strict enough at present?

Strict enough already — 36%
Don't know — 11%
53% — Should be tightened

Immigration into Britain in general makes the country more open to new ideas and cultures?

27%
6%
67%

Agree
Disagree
Don't know

At present political asylum seekers are not allowed to work while their cases are being decided. Should political asylum seekers be allowed to claim welfare payments while their cases are decided?

39%
10%
52%

Should people who have genuinely suffered political persecution abroad be allowed to stay in Britain?

33%
17%
49%

Source: Guardian/CM

A Home Office Survey of 263 refugees published in 1995 found that two-thirds had been employed in their home country, 76% had university degrees and 30% had professional backgrounds.

Source: *The Guardian*, 9 February 1999

1   What percentage believe the immigration laws need to be tightened?

2   What percentage think that political asylum seekers should not be allowed to claim welfare benefits?

3   What total percentage of people could not agree with the statement, 'Should people who have genuinely suffered persecution abroad be allowed to stay in Britain?'?

Main points ▶ The idea that biological races exist has been disproved.
▶ The term 'race' used by sociologists reflects discussion of social differences.
▶ Migrants first came to Britain in the 1950s and large-scale immigration largely finished in the 1970s as a result of a series of laws restricting immigration.
▶ Today a significant proportion of people entering Britain are claiming refugee status.
▶ Historically people have come to settle in Britain for the better quality of life here.
▶ People who have come here have experienced **discrimination**.
▶ The majority of ethnic minority people living in Britain were born here or have spent most their lives here.

Definitions

Racial discrimination – when people are treated unequally simply because they belong to a particular ethnic group

Direct discrimination – when people are treated less favourably because of their 'race'

Indirect discrimination – when a rule which appears to be equal for all actually discriminates against certain groups

Housing and settlement patterns

Settlement

The majority of Britain's ethnic minorities live in urban areas. In London, for example, 'non-white' ethnic minorities make up 20 per cent of London's population, and ethnic minorities of all kinds comprise 30 per cent of the London population.

Segregation by race

Although Black and Asian people form less than 7 per cent of the total British population, they are concentrated in a relatively few areas of a few major conurbations, in particular the Midlands, London and its surroundings, and West Yorkshire.

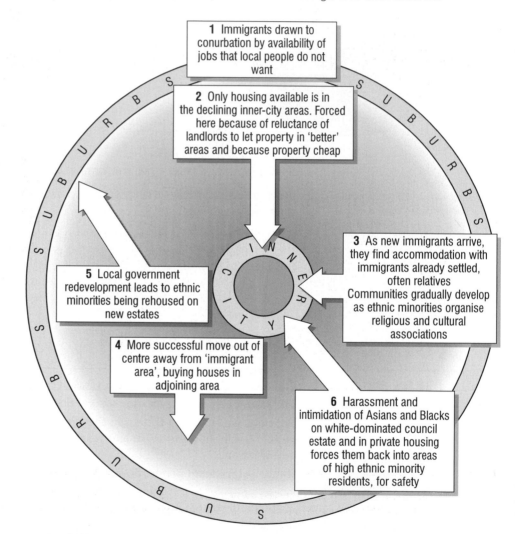

1 Immigrants drawn to conurbation by availability of jobs that local people do not want

2 Only housing available is in the declining inner-city areas. Forced here because of reluctance of landlords to let property in 'better' areas and because property cheap

3 As new immigrants arrive, they find accommodation with immigrants already settled, often relatives Communities gradually develop as ethnic minorities organise religious and cultural associations

4 More successful move out of centre away from 'immigrant area', buying houses in adjoining area

5 Local government redevelopment leads to ethnic minorities being rehoused on new estates

6 Harassment and intimidation of Asians and Blacks on white-dominated council estate and in private housing forces them back into areas of high ethnic minority residents, for safety

Look at the diagram.

1 What influenced the patterns of settlement of ethnic minorities in Britain?

2 How would you summarise the settlement patterns of ethnic minorities in Britain?

3 What possible benefits/disadvantages might this pattern leave for:

(a) the lives of ethnic minority members?

(b) the development and continuation of racism?

Settlement patterns of some ethnic minority groups

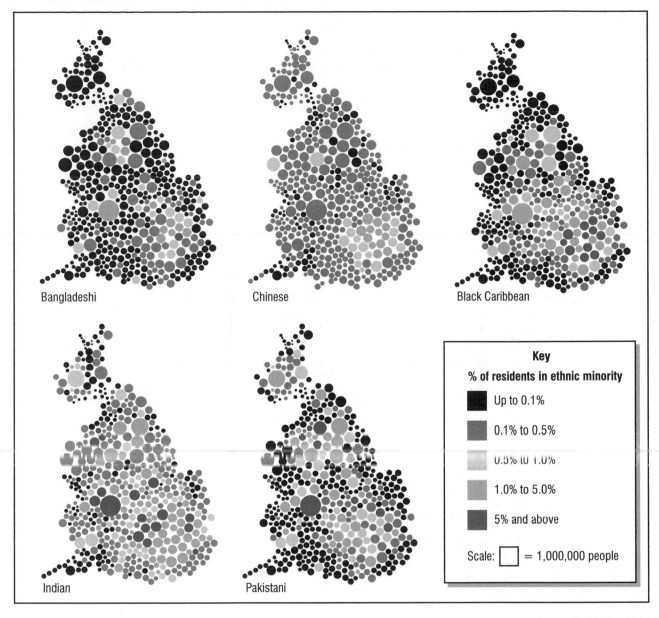

Bangladeshi

Chinese

Black Caribbean

Key

% of residents in ethnic minority

Up to 0.1%

0.1% to 0.5%

0.5% to 1.0%

1.0% to 5.0%

5% and above

Scale: ☐ = 1,000,000 people

Indian

Pakistani

Source: *Social Atlas of Britain*

Look at the maps.

1 What differences can you find in the areas of settlement by the different ethnic groups?

2 Why do you think that migrants tend to settle in one area and not another? (Imagine you are arriving for the first time – what would influence you in your choice of place to live?)

About 3 million people, or 5.5 per cent of the population, do not classify themselves as 'white'. About 30 per cent of these are from African or African-Caribbean backgrounds and approximately 50 per cent from 'South Asia', that is of Indian, Pakistani or Bangladeshi origins.

Housing

Census figures indicate that there are differences in housing between those of ethnic minority backgrounds and the majority population. Although the picture is complicated, one can say that, overall, those from ethnic minority backgrounds are less likely to live in the better accommodation. However, those of Indian and Pakistani backgrounds were more likely to own their own property than the majority of the population, whilst those of African-Caribbean backgrounds were more likely to live in local authority housing.

In terms of homelessness, people from ethnic minorities formed a disproportionate number of those who were officially defined as homeless. For example, in London ethnic minorities form 45 per cent of all the official homeless, and overall ethnic minority members are three times more likely to be homeless.

Housing and ethnicity

Housing tenure in Britain, by ethnic group, 1991

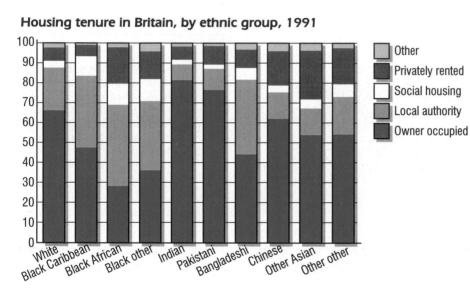

Source: Commission for Racial Equality, *Housing and Homelessness* (1999)

1 Which two groups are most likely to be owner occupiers?

2 Which two groups are most likely to live in local authority housing?

3 Which group is most likely to be in privately rented accommodation?

Race and life chances

Racial harassment and violence

Attitudes to racial violence

Over half the **racial attacks** against South Asians and more than one in three against Black Caribbeans are committed by 16–25 year olds. In nine out of ten cases, the perpetrators are White.

Definitions

Racial harassment – actions and language which are intended to cause the victim, at the very least, to feel upset or uncomfortable in some way and, at worst, to lead to direct or indirect harm

Racial attacks – use of violence against members of ethnic minorities motivated by racist beliefs

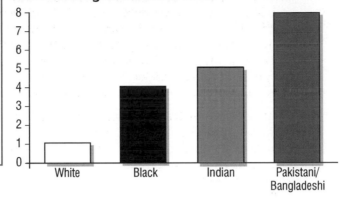

Percentage of each ethnic group who thought that race was a motive in one or more of the offences committed against them in 1995

Source: Commission for Racial Equality, *Racial Attacks and Harassment* (1999)

1 Which ethnic group were most likely to believe that the motive for the offence was 'racial'. What was the percentage?

2 Which group was least likely to believe that the motive was 'racial'? What was the percentage?

3 Can you see any weakness in these statistics?

The reality of racial harassment and violence

Mal Hussein and Linda Livingstone run a corner shop in Lancaster – but their lives are filled with terror. Over the last eight years they have had over 2,000 racist-inspired attacks. Hussein has borne the brunt of these attacks – he has been shot at, stoned and racially abused. The store and their flat above it have been fire-bombed six times while they were inside.

Despite constant complaints to the police, the only time arrests were made was when a television crew filmed a night attack. According to Mal Hussein, 'For twenty-four hours a day, seven days a week, we have lived under siege. The police have failed us'.

Source: quoted words taken from *The Guardian*, 2 March 1999

1 What example of harassment, as opposed to violence, is given in the extract?

2 How would you combat this?

3 Check back copies of your local paper. Are there any incidences locally of racial harassment and violence?

Employment and unemployment

Overall, there are differences in the types and levels of employment that people from ethnic minorities perform compared to the majority population. Generally, the members of the ethnic minorities are less likely to be in professional and managerial positions, and more often in lower paid and routine work. This is an overall picture though, as people from Indian backgrounds (in particular those from families who came here from ex-British colonies) are more likely than the majority population to be in professional positions. So, we can see very clear differences between the ethnic minority population and the majority population, and we can also see differences between minority ethnic groups.

Occupational distribution, by ethnic group, averages for June 95–May 96

	Mgmt admin prof & tech %	Clerical/ secretarial %	Craft, plant & machines %	Personal & protective servs %	Sales %	Other %
All groups	36	15	22	11	8	8
White	36	15	23	11	8	8
Non-White	36	14	21	11	9	9
Black	30	16	18	15	6	11
Indian	38	14	27	4	11	6
Pak/Bangla	29	9	30	15	10	5
Other	47	14	10	14	8	8

Labour Force Survey, Summer 1995–Spring 1996

Source: Commission for Racial Equality factsheet (1997)

For the groups other than those of Indian origin, there are quite a number of shared work characteristics:

- They are all under-represented in the professions (such as law) and in senior management positions.
- They are less likely to be promoted.
- They are more likely to be engaged in employment involving shift work.
- They have higher unemployment rates than the average and they tend to have lower incomes.

The reasons for these conditions of employment vary across groups and their specific history of immigration. For example:

- Older workers from Bangladesh and Pakistan, who are first-generation immigrants, will have been recruited for poorer paid work, often in declining industries (such as textiles). Those who came from the Caribbean were more likely to be in semi-skilled work and those from African-Asian backgrounds to be in professional positions and self-employed.
- Differences occur in terms of generation, so that the children of the first-generation immigrants are far less likely to accept these levels of employment.
- Differences occur between the sexes as well, so that females from African-Caribbean backgrounds are actually successful in education and employment, whilst males are less successful at school and also are less likely to be in higher status employment.

All groups, however, share the fact that they suffer from racial discrimination in employment.

Race and the criminal justice system

We have seen in an earlier section that members of the ethnic minorities are more likely than the majority of the population to be subjected to attacks and harassment. But there is some evidence that not only are they victims of violence from the general public, but also that they are not treated equally by the criminal justice system. In particular, it is claimed that young males of

African-Caribbean origin are 'picked on' by the police. The evidence is complex and very much in dispute, but it is true that this group of males are more likely to be stopped by police, to be arrested, and that a higher proportion of them are in prison compared to their numbers in the general population.

The police argue that this simply reflects the fact that they do have a higher crime rate, which is not surprising given that the typical profile of an offender, of whatever ethnic group, is young and with low income. Critics argue that policing styles (stopping and searching young African-Caribbean males) will:

- uncover higher levels of crime
- cause a perception of unjust treatment
- lead to a dislike of the police amongst those of African-Caribbean origin.

People of Asian origin have put forward different criticisms of the police concerning their failure to prevent racist violence.

Definition

Institutional racism – where an organisation (such as a college or company) has procedures and regulations which, by their very nature, discriminate against certain groups in the population

Sociological research tends to support criticisms of the police attitudes and dealings with young males of African-Caribbean origin. Sociologists have uncovered what they call a 'canteen culture' amongst the lower ranks of the police in which racist language and beliefs are freely expressed. Furthermore, despite attempts by police forces to counteract racism in the police it appears that this has had only limited effects. In 1999, an official inquiry (headed by a High Court judge) was held into the racist murder of a black youth, Stephen Lawrence (see below). The inquiry accused the Metropolitan Police (the London police force) of being **institutionally racist**, meaning that racist ideas and attitudes exist throughout the police force and influence the way the way the police operate.

All English and Welsh police forces have since implemented anti-racist campaigns amongst police officers and the Home Office has insisted that all police forces must employ a similar proportion of ethnic minority police officers as there are in the local population.

The murder of Stephen Lawrence

Stephen Lawrence, an 18-year-old A-level student, was stabbed to death one evening in 1993 – because he was black. The police response was heavily criticised six years later in an official inquiry.

Stephen Lawrence was a gifted and extrovert 18-year-old with a close family and a wide circle of friends. He was studying for A-levels and wanted to become an architect. He was killed as he waited for a bus home in April 1993 with a friend, Duwayne Brooks, with whom he had spent the evening.

The murder took place in Eltham, a mainly white suburb of south-east London that is regarded by many residents as the 'frontline' against the migration of black people from the inner city. There had been two racist killings there in recent years.

The first police officers arrived on the scene to find Stephen, who had been stabbed twice in the chest, bleeding to death on the pavement, and Duwayne pacing up and down in an agitated state.

None of the officers administered first aid; nor, despite Duwayne pointing out the direction in which the gang had fled, did they launch a proper search for Stephen's assailants.

Although it seemed likely that the killers lived locally, officers did not conduct house-to-house inquiries because they thought it was too late to wake people up. The only people seen behaving suspiciously that night were five white youths who drove past the murder scene twice,

laughing and jeering. But although a call was put out on the police radio, they did not check the car for a week.

It was later established that its occupants had included two violent racists convicted in connection with the murder in 1991 of a black boy, Rolan Adams. Perhaps it was coincidence that drew them to the spot where Stephen was knifed. Perhaps not.

Source: *The Independent*, 25 February 1999

Look up the reports surrounding the McPherson Inquiry on the Internet by searching newspapers such as **The Times, The Guardian, The Daily Express.**

Racism in the police force

In the early 1980s the Metropolitan Police asked a group of researchers to investigate policing practices 'on the beat'. The results were often rather shocking.

On one occasion 'DJS' was with two officers who were dealing with a suspected bomb in a mailbag. Of the two postmen who noticed a sound coming from the bag in the back of their van, one was black and the other white. The black man was the driver, and the white man saw him as the boss; if for example he was asked a question, he often said 'I don't know about that, you'll have to ask my driver'. Later the police questioned the black man in a friendly manner and the answers were given with clarity, common sense and courtesy.

As they got back into the car afterwards, one of the officers, checking through his notes, said to the other, 'Was it the coon who called us out?' The other replied 'Yes, believe it or not, it was the coon that was the driver.'

Source: D. Smith and J. Gray, *Police and People in London* (Gower, 1985)

Since this research was published, the police report that they have been tackling racism in the force.

1   What does the extract tell you about the taken-for-granted attitudes of the police officers about black people? Give an example to illustrate your answer.

2   Do you think the police officers were deliberately being racist in the language they used referring to black people?

3   Some people have argued that passing laws against racial discrimination has little effect in combating racism. How does this extract illustrate this argument?

4   Some sociologists have argued that 'racism is deep our culture' and that our language contains many words and phrases we commonly use, which strengthen this racism. Explain how language can lead to discrimination.

Institutional racism and the legal system

The Law Society denies its profession is institutionally racist – 16 per cent of trainees and 5 per cent of practising solicitors are from ethnic minorities. But it agrees with the Society of Black Lawyers that Black and Asian solicitors tend to be concentrated in the profession's lower ranks.

There are no ethnic minority judges among the 98 High Court judges, four among the 562 circuit judges, five among the 360 district judges and one among the 93 stipendiary (senior) magistrates in England and Wales.

Source: Based on *The Daily Telegraph*, 23 February 1999

Education

The ethnic minority population in Britain is relatively young compared to the population in general and 22 per cent of them are of compulsory school age. Approximately 40 per cent of Asians and 25 per cent of those of African-Caribbean origin get five or more higher grade GCSEs, compared to 45 per cent of white students.

However, these differences between ethnic groups hide the fact that females of Indian origin are particularly successful compared to all groups, and that girls of African-Caribbean origin are also noticeably successful. On the other hand, males of Bangladeshi origin are more likely than most groups to achieve low grades.

After finishing compulsory education, it is noticeable that ethnic minority young people are more likely to be studying for vocational qualifications which lead directly to employment, rather than academic qualifications which are not specific to an area of employment.

Explanations for the variations in school attainment

- These variations in educational attainment reflect gender differences in education in general (see pages 271–6).
- Educational attainment reflects social status – and we know that members of the ethnic minorities are, overall, more likely to be poorer.
- The language used in the home. A survey of school students in London showed that over 25 per cent spoke a language other than English in their homes, and although most young people speak and write English fluently, their parents may struggle with English. For example, only 4 per cent of Bangladeshi women and 28 per cent of Pakistani women over the age of 45 are fluent in English.
- The British educational system largely reflects a European, white view of the world, its history and its literature. This may disadvantage certain ethnic groups.

Race and education

The chairman of the Commission for Racial Equality ... accused the Qualifications and Curriculum Authority which oversees the curriculum of alienating black children by promoting a notion of Britishness that reflected "the values and culture of the white, English middle class" instead of the diversity of modern Britain. ... The Anglo- and Euro-centrism at the centre of the curriculum meant that pupils were being denied information about famous people from other cultures.

Source: Based on *The Daily Telegraph*, 6 January 1998

1 What does Euro-centrism mean?

2 What does the extract mean when it talks about the curriculum (that is, the subjects being taught) 'alienating' black children?

3 Choose any one history textbook or comment on any novels you have read recently. Check through the index and see what image is portrayed of Asian or African-Caribbean people.

This is part of a letter written to a newspaper in reply to a previous letter, claiming that schools are institutionally racist and so contribute very heavily towards the lesser educational achievements of many children from certain ethnic minority backgrounds.

If institutional racism is responsible for Pakistani, Bangladeshi and Black-Caribbean children doing worse than their white equivalents, then what is responsible for Indian and Chinese children doing so much better?

Source: *The Daily Telegraph*

1 Explain, in your own words, the argument put forward by the letter writer.

2 As sociologists, what does this tell us about making generalisations based on 'race'?

Race and stratification

It is clear from what we have learned so far that people do have distinctive experiences on the basis of their ethnic group membership. Overall, people from African-Caribbean, Pakistani and Bangladeshi backgrounds, and rather fewer of Indian origins, are more likely to be found in lower paid, lower status employment and to live in poorer housing conditions than the majority of the British population. But it is not simply that they face worse conditions, they also suffer from specific discrimination which is directed at them because of their skin colour. So, 'race' is an important element in understanding their lives.

However, it is also important to remember that there are very great cultural and economic differences *between* the various ethnic minority groups. Although people of African-Caribbean origin and those of Pakistani origin may share discrimination, they have little else in common – different family structures, different religions, different cultural beliefs and behaviour.

As well as these differences there are distinctive differences in the economic and social positions of the various ethnic minorities. Although Asian, Indians who came here during the 1970s from Africa, and later their children, have been one of the outstanding success stories in British commerce, professions and business, the Bangladeshi population have remained concentrated in some of the worst jobs.

To summarise this, we need to understand that race is useful for understanding shared discrimination, but it can gloss over the very great differences between the various ethnic groups.

Which is more important 'race' or social class?

The differences between the various ethnic groups in Britain have led a number of sociologists to argue that using the term 'race' or 'ethnic minorities' draws attention away from the fact that, in terms of employment, income and housing standards, these groups are simply members of an exploited working class and that they share these conditions with white people. These sociologists point out that professional doctors of Indian origin have much more in common with other white professionals than with other Asians. For these sociologists, social class is more important than race.

Race and social class

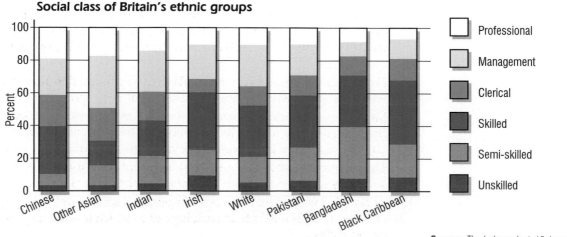

Social class of Britain's ethnic groups

Legend: Professional, Management, Clerical, Skilled, Semi-skilled, Unskilled

Ethnic groups: Chinese, Other Asian, Indian, Irish, White, Pakistani, Bangladeshi, Black Caribbean

Source: *The Independent,* 12 June 1996

1 Which ethnic minority has the highest rates of semi-skilled workers?

2 Which group has the lowest?

3 Which group has the lowest percentage of professional workers?

4 Which group has the highest proportion of managers?

5 Looking carefully at the chart, if you were asked to choose the two groups with (a) the highest percentage of high status jobs, and (b) the highest percentage of low status jobs, what would they be?

6 Does the chart help you to work out whether 'race' or social class is more important in understanding a person's life?

Race, gender and stratification

Before leaving the issue of stratification, we need to mention the impact upon the role of women that ethnicity creates. Some of the ethnic minority cultures, more notably the Muslim religion, have a different view of the role of women. The result is that Muslim women are strongly discouraged from working outside the home or for having an independent life outside their family commitments. This can be contrasted very strongly with the great stress placed upon personal independence and the importance of work for women of African-Caribbean origin. The exact impact of ethnic origin and culture upon the role of women is a matter of great dispute, but certainly it does have some degree of impact and when discussing what affects a person's life chances we need to realise that women are divided by ethnicity as well as by social class.

Main points ▶ Overall, there are clear differences in the life chances of members of ethnic minority groups, compared to the population in general. However it is equally important to remember that there are very great differences *between* ethnic minority groups.

▶ Ethnic minority groups tend to live in larger urban areas, particularly in London, Bristol, parts of Lancashire and Yorkshire, and the Midlands.

▶ Overall, members of the ethnic minorities have worse housing conditions than the general population. However, those of African-Caribbean origin are more likely to live in local authority housing and those of Indian and Pakistani origin are more likely than the majority of the population to own their homes.

▶ Ethnic minority groups are more likely to be subjected to attacks than would be expected given their proportion of the population.

▶ Members of the ethnic minorities overall perform less well than the population in general. However, some groups particularly African-Caribbean females and those of Indian origin are particularly successful.

▶ There is considerable evidence that people of African-Caribbean origin are less likely to be treated fairly than the population in general.

▶ Although it is clear that race is an important factor in determining life chances, there is a debate in sociology as to which is more important – race or social class.

Explanations for racism

There are two basic explanations for racism. The first type stresses the *individual* and the second stresses *cultural* reasons.

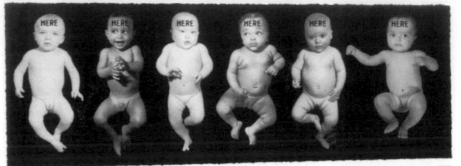

THERE ARE LOTS OF PLACES IN BRITAIN WHERE RACISM DOESN'T EXIST.

COMMISSION FOR RACIAL EQUALITY

Source: Commission for Racial Equality

The individual

Individuals who tend to 'bottle up' their frustrations and problems find an outlet for them in hostility against certain easily identifiable groups, such as those of different skin colour, different nationalities, different religions or anyone who does not 'fit in', such as gay people. This is often linked to an 'authoritarian personality' which is very rigid and conventional.

Critics of this explanation argue that if 35 per cent of the population admit to being racially prejudiced in some way, can so many people be unable to express their feelings, and suffer from an authoritarian personality? These critics argue that the answer must lie in the British culture.

Challenging perceptions of race

What if?

Royalty, it is claimed, embody the values of British society. Yet the idea that one of the royals might marry a black or Asian citizen has never even been suggested.

Not amused ... Benetton's computer-altered image of the Queen, which makes her appear black

Buckingham Palace yesterday expressed its disapproval at the latest in a series of controversial advertising campaigns by the Italian clothing manufacturer Benetton, which shows a photograph of the Queen depicted as a black woman in its April catalogue.

Her Majesty's nose and lips have been broadened in the computer-aided photograph, which will appear with the words 'What if?' A spokesman for Buckingham Palace said: 'We don't like members of the Royal Family being used in this way. Specific guidelines have been laid down to prevent them from being used for commercial purposes. They shouldn't be be used to promote any product.'

The black queen, in a formal pose wearing a frown, is part of an advertising campaign designed to challenge perceptions on race. Other photographs due to appear in Colours, the monthly Benetton catalogue, will depict the Pope as Chinese, Arnold Schwarzenegger as black and Michael Jackson and Spike Lee as white.

Source: *The Guardian,* 27 March 1993

Cultural explanations

Definitions

Ethnocentric – a way of looking at things from a particular cultural viewpoint and ignoring other possible ways of seeing the world. For example, seeing the history of the world only from a 'white' British viewpoint

Scapegoating – blaming certain groups of poorer or less powerful people for problems in society, instead of seeking out the real causes

Stereotype – to exaggerate differences between one group and another so that these differences are made to seem more important than the similarities. A problem with all research on social class and ethnicity

This second approach, taken by most sociologists today, argues that prejudice against certain ethnic minorities is part and parcel of our culture. People are socialised into thinking in racial terms, through the **ethnocentric** history we learn at school, through the media and in some cases through the family.

The reason why culture contains so much prejudice is explained in two main ways:

* scapegoating
* stereotyping.

Scapegoating

The real explanations for social problems such as unemployment, poverty or poor housing may be too complex for many people to understand. A simple, easily understood explanation is that it is the fault of 'outsiders', such as the ethnic minorities who are taking the jobs or the housing. The fact that this is not true is simply ignored.

For example, the Nazi regime in Germany blamed Jews for the economic problems which the country had faced, even though this was totally untrue. The resulting scapegoating of the Jews led to millions being murdered.

More radical sociologists have gone further and argued that blaming ethnic minorities for society's problems draws attention away from the real cause – the enormous inequality in wealth and income in our society. By blaming ethnic minorities for social problems, people are blinded to this inequality.

Explaining racism

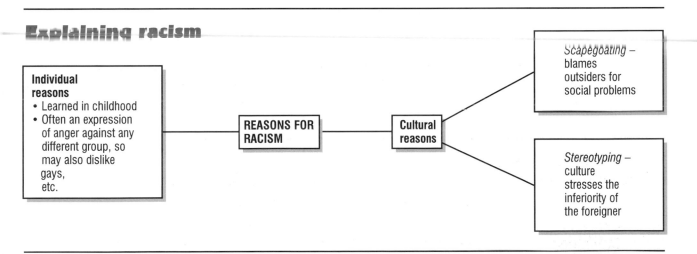

Stereotyping

This explanation goes hand in hand with scapegoating. When Britain was a colonial power, invading other countries (or 'tribes') and then exploiting them for its own good, it was necessary to depersonalise the people being oppressed – to make people believe that the conquered are somehow inferior to the conquerers. How else would it be possible to justify slavery? Africans, for example, were portrayed as 'children' who needed white people to keep control over them.

People from African and Asian origins came to be seen as inferior and this view of them entered into our culture. Today, these beliefs have been challenged as clearly untrue. However, once ideas enter cultures they may take a long time to disappear, no matter how false they are.

Stereotyping?

The Home Secretary (the government minister responsible for law enforcement) said on Radio West Midlands:

"There are relatively few real Romany gypsies left, who seem to mind their own business and do not cause trouble to other people. And then there are a lot more people who masquerade as travellers or gypsies, who trade on the sentiment of people but who seem to think because they label themselves as travellers that they have a licence to commit crimes."

Chris Johnson, a lawyer for the Travellers' Advice Team, said: "He made racist assumptions about a whole community and showed enormous ignorance of travellers' issues."

Source: Based on *The Daily Telegraph*, 19 August 1999

1 Do you think the Home Secretary's remarks were racist?

2 Do you think the terms 'stereotyping' or 'scapegoating' could be applied? Or do you think that what he said was true?

Racism in action

I GET ON FINE WITH ASIANS —THERE'S ONE IN THE SHOP DOWN THE ROAD AND HE'S ALWAYS CHARMING TO ME.

I'D BE ALL IN FAVOUR OF MY DAUGHTER GETTING MARRIED TO A BLACK MAN IF IT WEREN'T FOR THE PROBLEMS THE CHILDREN WOULD FACE.

NEGROES HAVE A ROUGH TIME OF IT. BUT THEY DO SEEM TO GET A CHIP ON THEIR SHOULDERS SO EASILY AND IT DOESN'T DO THEM ANY GOOD AT ALL.

OF COURSE I THINK THEY SHOULD BE TAUGHT SOMETHING ABOUT THEIR OWN CULTURES. BUT BY THE SAME TOKEN THEY OUGHT TO BE MAKING MORE OF AN EFFORT TO LEARN ENGLISH AND FIT IN HERE.

Source: *New Internationalist*, March 1985

1 The statements above are frequently heard. Do you agree, or disagree, with them?

2 What, do you think, are the real feelings of each speaker? Explain each one separately.

3 In each case, what would you do, or say, if you were the person being addressed?

4 The young man on the right says '… they should be taught something about their own cultures.' What do schools teach about Africa or India? What attitude does this create?

5 Change the words in the bubbles so they make four positive true statements about ethnic minorities and their contribution to the life of Britain.

And what these attitudes mean in daily life

Sukhjit Parma, 34, described how he had suffered almost four years of systematic racial abuse at the hand of his foreman and group leader while working at the Ford East London engine plant. Mr Parma said that senior staff ignored his complaints as he was subjected to racist graffiti including the word "Paki" daubed across his payslip and death threats accompanied by Klu Klux Klan symbols scrawled on a lavatory wall.

After complaining, he said he was made to work in an oil spraying booth without protective clothing until he was sick and was threatened with broken legs if he persisted with his allegations. His lunch was also kicked out his hand by a colleague who objected to Indian food.

Source: Based on *The Daily Telegraph*, 24 September 1999

Racism in the NHS

A five-year research project by Dr Sam Everington, a London GP found that white applicants to medical school were twice as likely to get a place as Blacks or Asians. Black doctors were six times more likely to be disciplined by the General Medical Council and consultants were 3.33 times more likely to be given a merit award (higher pay because of their exceptional ability) if they were white.

Activity

Copy the diagram and write one paragraph in each box to summarise each issue.

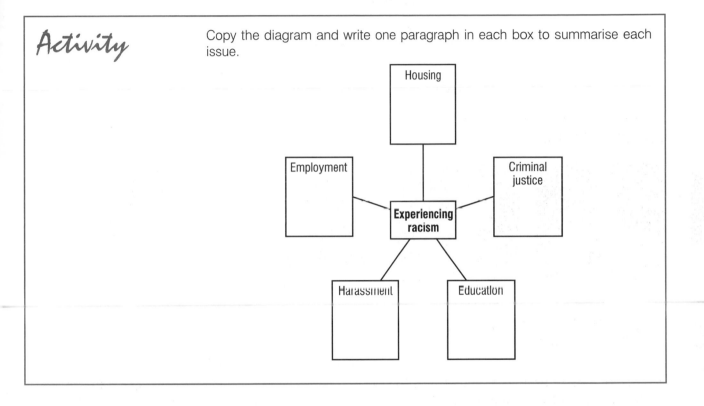

Assimilation, integration and diversity: the changing nature of ethnicity in Britain

Discussions about immigration and immigrants are now irrelevant. Britain is a multi-cultural society.

But if we can no longer look at the relationship in terms of immigrants entering a society, how best can we understand the relationships between different ethnic groups, and between them and the majority population? Furthermore, what is going to happen in the future?

A number of possible 'models' have been suggested, which help to explain current relationships and make predictions about the future. These include:

- **assimilation**
- **integration**
- **self-segregation**
- **diversity**.

Assimilation

Definition

Assimiliation – when ethnic minority groups are absorbed into the majority culture, adopting mainstream values and behaviour

This is where the immigrant group gradually adopts the values and culture of the majority of the population, over a period of two or three generations, and effectively becomes part of the main culture. When migrants first arrived in Britain from the Caribbean in the 1950s, they believed they would be accepted by the British and they expected to be assimilated. This meant that the rejection and racism which they encountered was even more hurtful.

It seems that because the white British were not prepared to fully accept the new migrants from the Caribbean, the succeeding generations of black British were less keen to be fully assimilated.

Self-segregation

Definition

Self-segregation – when an ethnic minority group largely cuts itself off from the majority culture

This is the opposite of assimilation and is where a group cuts itself off from the host country and tries to keep all of its customs intact in the new country. This was a model which had been used by the British when they had colonies and which largely characterises the approach of British people who retire to Spain. These people gather in groups together, do not learn the Spanish language and try to retain as much of their 'Britishness', whilst living in Spain. This is relatively rare in Britain and although a small proportion of Pakistani and Bangladeshi minorities may have attempted this, it seems not to have happened once the second generation has attended British schools.

Integration

Definition

Integration – when ethnic minority groups remain distinctive, but adapt and conform to the majority values and behaviour

People who arrived from India, Pakistan and Bangladesh did not have the self-segregation approach to their settlement in Britain. They were aware of their own identity and religions and wished to maintain them, as Jewish immigrants in the nineteenth century had done. They wanted to adapt and be integrated in certain limited areas, such as commerce and the British legal system, but to retain their own culture and identity.

This model characterises the majority of first generation Asian immigration to Britain.

Diversity

Definition

Diversity – an acceptance of a range of different cultures which share some common features, but also value the differences

Over time a significant proportion of people who have been born or lived most of their lives in Britain have extended their participation in most British customs and styles of life. So they will be full members of all aspects of the dominant culture, but have also maintained a commitment to their own customs. In turn, their customs and style of life has had an impact on the wider British culture. This two-way sharing of values and customs is known as diversity. This would appear to be what is happening in Britain today.

Relationships between majority and minority ethnic groups

Assimilation

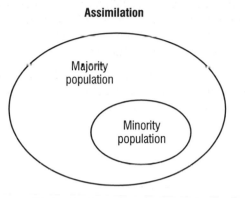

Ethnic minority groups are absorbed into the majority culture, adopting mainstream values and behaviour, e.g. the Irish.

Integration

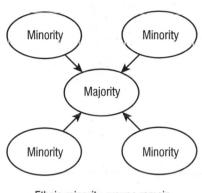

Ethnic minority groups remain distinctive, but adopt and largely conform to majority values and behaviour, e.g. Jews.

Self-segregation

Diversity

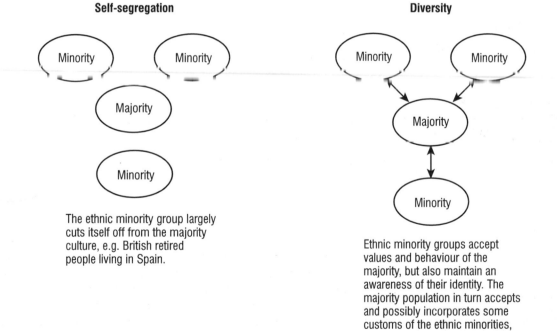

The ethnic minority group largely cuts itself off from the majority culture, e.g. British retired people living in Spain.

Ethnic minority groups accept values and behaviour of the majority, but also maintain an awareness of their identity. The majority population in turn accepts and possibly incorporates some customs of the ethnic minorities, e.g. Hindus and Muslims in Britain.

The future? According to Census data:

- Out of a total of 13 million marriages, about half a million were mixed marriages, consisting of people from different ethnic groups.

- 40 per cent of black Caribbean-origin men between 16 and 34 and 20 per cent of black Caribbean-origin women of the same age were living with a white partner.

- 7 per cent of Indian men and 4 per cent of Indian women aged 16–34 were living with a white partner

1 What does this suggest about the relationships between the different ethnic groups?

2 What implications might this have for British society in the future?

Ethnic minority success: rejecting stereotypes

The majority of this chapter has been taken up with an exploration of how the life chances of members of British ethnic minorities are more likely to be limited than for the majority of the population. But this is an overall picture. Overall, what we have seen *is* true, but we must not fall into a stereotypical view that this limiting of opportunity is the experience for all and that it will necessarily continue.

There has been a very marked change in the possibilities for younger members of the ethnic minorities. In most spheres, such as employment, house purchase, harassment and leisure pursuits, laws have been passed which protect their rights and convey the message that they are full and equal citizens in Britain. The police have finally accepted that there is institutional racism and are under great pressure to eradicate this. Opinion polls suggest that racist attitudes have declined, although they still exist. But whereas open racism was once acceptable in Britain, it is now largely seen as wrong. As we saw before, diversity characterises contemporary Britain and most people welcome this.

So, the contemporary situation is one of change. Members of ethnic minority groups are now visible in the arts, on television and in film, in sport and in business. But they are outnumbered in these areas, and they are less likely to be found in any senior management positions.

A success story: one of many

Perween Warsi came to Britain from India in 1975. She started by supplying snacks to local pubs and restaurants, before setting up S&A Foods in Derby. In 1986, she won contracts to supply Asda and Safeway with S&A Foods' own Shahi brand of ready-to-cook chilled meals. In 1994, the *Independent on Sunday* reported that S&A Foods was the fifth fastest growing private company in Britain, with a £20 million turnover and 350 employees. In 1996, S&A foods, with TV chef Ken Hom, launched a new range of dishes. Perween Warsi was the Midlands Businesswoman of the Year in 1994. Her ambition is to make S&A Foods the first British multinational to be run by a woman.

Source: Commission for Racial Equality, *Roots to the Future* (1996)

Combating discrimination

The **Race Relations Act** makes it unlawful to discriminate against anyone on the grounds of race, colour or nationality.

It applies to housing, education, goods and services (ranging from buying insurance to having a drink in a pub) and advertising.

Under the 1986 **Public Order Act**, it is an offence to behave in anyway which can incite racial hatred.

The **Crime and Disorder Act** introduced 'racially aggravated offences', which is where a more severe punishment is given by the courts if an act of violence occurs for racial motives.

Main points

▶ There are two categories of explanations for racial prejudice – individual and cultural.

▶ Individual explanations argue that a person has something in their personality which makes them hate those who are different from them.

▶ Cultural explanations argue that racism is 'in the culture' and people are merely reflecting that when they express racist ideas.

▶ There are two types of cultural explanations:
  – scapegoating, when ethnic minorities are blamed for problems
  – stereotyping, when people are taught to view ethnic minorities as inferior.

▶ Sociologists have tried to understand how different ethnic groups will act towards each other and the majority population. In different countries, different patterns have emerged.

▶ In Britain they suggest that it is increasingly being explained by diversity – an acceptance of a range of different cultures which share some common features, but also value the differences.

▶ There is a danger of stereotyping discussions of ethnicity by always seeing race as a problem and with all members of the ethnic minorities being oppressed. This is not true. Gradually members of ethnic minority groups are entering higher status positions in society and being accepted as having a right to be there.

5 CHAPTER SUMMARY

1 The idea that biological races exist has been disproved.

2 The term 'race' as used by sociologists reflects discussion of social differences.

3 Migrants first came to Britain in the 1950s and large-scale immigration largely finished in the 1970s, as a result of a series of laws restricting immigration.

4 Today a significant proportion of people entering Britain are claiming refugee status.

5 Historically people have come to settle in Britain for the better quality of life.

6 People who have come to Britain have experienced discrimination.

7   The majority of ethnic minority people living in Britain were born here or have spent most their lives here.

8   Overall, there are clear differences in the life chances of members of ethnic minority groups, compared to the population in general. However, it is equally important to remember that there are very great differences *between* ethnic minority groups.

9   Ethnic minority groups tend to live in larger urban areas, particularly in London, Bristol, parts of Lancashire and Yorkshire, and the Midlands.

10 Overall, members of the ethnic minorities have worse housing conditions than the general population. However, those of African-Caribbean origin are more likely to live in local authority housing and those of Indian and Pakistani origin are more likely than the majority of the population to own their homes.

11 Ethnic minority groups are more likely to be subjected to attacks than would be expected, given their proportion of the population.

12 Members of the ethnic minorities overall perform less well than the population in general. However, some groups particularly African-Caribbean females and those of Indian origin are particularly successful.

13 There is considerable evidence that people of African-Caribbean origin are less likely to be treated fairly than the population in general.

14 Although it is clear that race is an important factor in determining life chances, there is a debate in sociology as to which is more important – race or social class.

15 There are two categories of explanations for racial prejudice – individual and cultural.

16 Individual explanations argue that a person has something in their personality which makes them hate those who are different from them.

17 Cultural explanations argue that racism is 'in the culture' and people are merely reflecting that when they express racist ideas. There are two types of cultural explanations:
    – scapegoating, when ethnic minorities are blamed for problems
    – stereotyping, when people are taught to view ethnic minorities as inferior.

18 Sociologists have tried to understand how different ethnic groups will act towards each other and the majority population. In different countries, different patterns have emerged.

19 In Britain they suggest that it is increasingly being explained by diversity – an acceptance of a range of different cultures which share some common features, but also value the differences.

20 There is a danger of stereotyping discussions of ethnicity by always seeing race as a problem and with all members of the ethnic minorities being oppressed. This is not true. Gradually members of ethnic minority groups are entering higher status positions in society and being accepted as having a right to be there.

Test Your Knowledge

1   Why did people migrate to Britain after the Second World War?

2   Where did migrants settle? Why?

3   Give two examples of how the life chances of members of the ethnic minorities tends to be worse than that of the majority of the population.

4   How are race and social class linked?

5   What cultural reasons for racism are there?

6   What possible relationships are there between different ethnic groups? Which one do you think typifies Britain today?

Information source for project work:
Commission for Racial Equality
Elliot House
10–12 Allington Street
London SW1E 5EH

http://www.cre.gov.uk

AGE

Chapter contents

- ### Ageing as a social process
  Sociologists see age as a socially important thing. They argue that attitudes to age are more important than physical age.

- ### Rites of passage and age divisions
  Age is socially divided into the various stages from childhood to old age and we take on the identity of each age by going through a rite of passage.

- ### Childhood
  Although we tend to think of children as innocent creatures in need of care and protection, this has not always been the case, and attitudes to children have varied over time. Even today, for example, there are 300,000 young people fighting in wars all over the world.

- ### Youth
  Youth represents a period of transition from childhood to adulthood, but has become so important that it is now regarded as a stage of life itself. We explore what happened in the 1950s to launch the the idea that youth are a distinctive group in society. Today, youth culture underpins most of the music recording sales and a large proportion of magazines, television and cinema output. We examine the wide variations in youth culture, often ignored when people talk about young people as if they were all the same. We also look at the question of what youth culture does for young people – does it help them in a period of great social and personal change, or is it really created by the media to make money?

- ### Adulthood
  For most people, the period of adulthood is when they 'make it' or not. However, it represents the most affluent and socially prestigious period of their lives. We ask the simple question – why? Is it a natural thing or are there social forces at work? By now, any reader will have guessed that sociologists rarely accept the natural and obvious explanations.

- ### Old age
  In recent years, the numbers of older people has grown massively in society, and it may just be that we are in a period in which our views of older people are slowly changing. However, for most people over retirement age, old age means that their income and social status declines to a low point. This has not always been the case and in many societies in the past, older people were treated with a degree of respect. We explore the reasons why the status of old people changes over time.

Good time girl?

Margi to wed lover the same age as her son

He is less than half her age and his background is a far cry from the world of showbusiness.

Yet Philip Rubin, who celebrated his 21st birthday a fortnight ago, is to become the second Mr Margi Clarke.

The 44-year-old former *Coronation Street* actress and *Good Sex Guide* presenter announced her plans to marry unemployed Mr Rubin, who is the same age as her son, at a soap fans' convention in Blackpool.

Source: *The Daily Mail*, 9 June 1999

1 What is your view about the marriage? Do you think she is acting sensibly? Is he a fool to marry someone so much older?

2 Does age matter when it comes to love?

Ageing as a social process

Ageing is, of course, a natural process that happens to us all and it can be seen in the physical changes that occur.

But ageing also has a social element to it, so for sociologists the fascination with age comes from the fact that we *treat people differently* according to their age, and have very *different expectations* of what people ought to do at different ages in their lives. A 40-year-old woman skipping along a high street, amongst the shoppers on a Saturday afternoon would be a ridiculous sight. She would be told to 'act her age', and onlookers would think she was mad, drugged or drunk. But what if a four-year-old boy was skipping along? There would be absolutely no comment – it would be seen as natural. What about a man and a woman aged over 60 who are kissing passionately one evening outside the pub. Disgusting? Admirable? Normal?

I am fairly sure what your reaction would be! Age has a social as well as a biological element, in that we judge people according to how we expect people of a certain age to behave.

Ageing: also a question of identity

What's your inner age?

That face in the mirror. It's not really you, is it? Inside, you're forever young. Aren't we all, says JOANNA BRISCOE.

You're 35 but there's been some terrible mistake. Because inside your head, you're 16. Admit it. You still pretend you're on *Top of the Pops* while lamely jigging around to music when the house is empty. Your world-weariness is threaded with dreams of searing romance and stardom. You half-suspect that you might still be famous. You sometimes can't believe you're sufficiently grown-up to drive a car, bring up children or understand tax returns. And you simply can't comprehend those lines on your face. Whatever happened to the space between acne and wrinkles?

There's a phenomenon that defies demographics. It is widespread, potent and rarely talked about. It's called the inner age. The existence of the inner age is a bit of a secret but it runs like this: most of the population is roughly 17. A sizeable minority is 12. Then there are nine year-olds, 22-year-olds and the odd 30-year-old.

Facts are irrelevant. Chronological age bears little relation to the internal conviction that we are secretly and magically a different age altogether.

Our internal age is usually younger than the figure 50 callously indicated by our passports. It's the age with which we most identify and to which we somehow subconsciously assume a right.

Source: *The Daily Express*, 26 June 1999, Internet edition

1 What does the author mean when she says that 'chronological age bears little resemblance to the internal conviction that we are secretly and magically a different age altogether'?

2 Do you think this is true?

3 Do you think there are adults who try to act 'too young'? Give examples?

4 Show this extract to a small sample of older people (your relatives, perhaps) and ask for them to comment. How true do they think the extract is? Does it apply to them?

5 What does the extract and the text tell us about the relationship between chronological age, socially expected behaviour of age, and the identity a person has of themselves?

6 Do you think this article has any relevance to the news item we looked at earlier – 'Margi to wed lover the same age as her son'?

Rites of passage and age divisions

Age divisions

The major age divisions which sociologists suggest are socially important are:

- childhood
- youth
- adulthood
- old age.

Definitions

Age status – the way that people receive different amounts of income and social prestige depending upon their age

Rite of passage – the ceremony that signifies leaving one stage of life and entering another

As we progress through each of these to our deaths, we are regarded by others in very different ways, and of course we also look at ourselves differently. These different stages often reflect real differences in our quality of life too, as most people get progressively better off and receive higher status, until old age when they enter a decline. Sociologists refer to each different stages of life as an **age status**.

We will use these stages or age statuses to discuss the social nature of age, bearing in mind the fact that age divisions are both natural and socially constructed.

However, before we do that, we need to look at *how* people move from one age status to another, and this is the idea of **rite of passage**.

Rites of passage

Definition

Transition – in sociology this means the period of change from being one age status to another; for example, the period of change from being a child to being a youth

Societies are based upon predictability and clarity, and when these are not obvious, people seek out ways of creating clarity and predictability. Some sociologists suggest this is one of the roles of religion for example – to make sense of our place in the world and provide clear answers to the point of life.

The **transition** from one age to another – childhood to youth, youth to adulthood and adulthood to old age – is indicated in most societies by *social markers* which spell out in no uncertain terms to other people what a person's status is. For example, in Jewish society there is the *bar mitzvah*, which is a ceremony that marks the end of boyhood, and for girls there is the *bat mitzvah*. Today, these are largely ceremonial, but they once signalled an important change in a person's life, which told others to treat them seriously and to accept them as full adults, with all those responsibilities and rights.

Ceremonies which act as social markers of status are known as rites of passage and, although less common than they were, we still have some left. Soon after birth, for instance, we celebrate with baptism, and our countdown to death begins with our retirement.

In Britain today, the change from one stage of life to another is confused and unclear, and the rites of passage have lost some of their meaning . There still are eighteenth birthday parties to celebrate adulthood, but then the majority of young people continue to depend on their parents either by living at home and working, or by having their parents support them financially at university or college. Marriage, which used to signify that a person was fully adult, has been partially replaced with co-habitation, and many people retire early, so the traditional retirement function has lost much of its meaning in these situations.

Rites of passage are not, strictly speaking, only to do with the change from one age to another. They are also about moving from one social status to another.

So, there is a formal ceremony when a ☐
university to celebrate and tell everyone that
the negative side of things, a criminal trial
person is found guilty, told they are evil and

A rite of passage

The bar mitzvah is a ceremony [a rite of passage] which each boy goes through in the Jewish religion at the age of 13. It means that a boy has entered the adult Jewish community: has become a man, ready to fulfil the commandments gleaned from the Talmud, the book that codifies ancient Jewish laws and traditions. Many girls now participate in a parallel ceremony at the age of 12 called a bat mitzvah ('bat' means daughter).

Traditionally, the first public declaration of a child's new acceptance into adulthood takes plac☐ thirteenth birthday. This ceremony closes with the boy's father reciting the Hebrew blessing, 'Blessed are you who releases us from the responsibility of this child'. The blessing makes clear the boy's new responsibility to himself and the community's recognition of their altered responsibility to him.

So the social impact of the bar mitzvah is profound. It draws into consciousness a clear line between childhood and adulthood.

Source: *New Internationalist*, August 1984

But rites of passage are not just for youth

Rites of passage continue throughout people's lives and are not solely restricted to the transition from youth to adulthood. At the other end of the spectrum of age are the rites of passage into old age and even death. Here is an example about my own Dad. Incidentally, he cried when he got home.

Everybody working in the offices came over to the Special Features Room as work finished that day. Even the Managing Director, a rarely-seen figure, turned up (late) especially for the ceremony. At exactly 4.30 p.m. one bitter February day, my father became the centre of interest. Speeches were made on his 35 years of service, broken only by time in the armed forces. ... 'Never missed a day's work in all that time.' ... 'An example of hard work and commitment to the interests of Oakalls newspapers.' ... 'a popular figure in the office'. My mum looked on proudly, her hair specially permed for the occasion, dressed in a brand new outfit. The office presents were given – a set of silver plated goblets and a copy of the front page of the paper on the day my dad first started work. For an hour the drink flowed and photographs were taken. Then my mum and dad caught the bus home, just like he had done for 35 years ('broken only by time in the armed forces'). And when he arrived home he was a pensioner.

1 In your own words, explain the meaning of the term 'rite of passage'.

2 In both extracts the person had a new social status after the rite of passage. What was this new status?

3 Compare the different levels of status for both individuals before and after the two ceremonies.

4 Give three examples of rites of passage which people go through today. For each example, explain how the status of the person had changed.

5 Rites of passage may be much less dramatic than the examples in the text. For example, they could be about having your ears pierced or being allowed to 'hang around' on the corner. Give two examples of rites of passage you have been through and explain why they were important to you.

6 What purpose does a rite of passage serve for the individual and society?

7 Many sociologists say that a trial in court is really a great ceremony that often ends in a rite of passage. Can you explain why they would say this?

8 Is there a clear rite of passage in modern society to indicate the move from childhood to adulthood? How might this possibly affect young people's lives?

Today, we think of children as being 'precious', delicate creatures who are in need of protection, and indeed we have special laws to protect them. These laws prevent such things as sexual relationships with adults, full-time employment and being exposed to drugs or alcohol.

Boys and girls go out to kill

It has not always been this way. It was only with the coming of industrialisation with its increase in wealth for the middle classes and the greater chances of children surviving at birth, that the idea of the 'precious' modern child was born.

Before that (and amongst the working class, long after that) the child was seen as a miniature adult as soon as he or she emerged from infancy. So children worked for long hours in agriculture and then in factories, until the reforms of the 1820s.

In the nineteenth century, children were divided into two groups: those of the middle and upper classes who were regarded as delicate creatures in need of protection, and the children of the working class who were seen as far tougher and capable of looking after themselves. Both groups of children were strictly controlled by parents and, if they were disobedient, they were harshly punished.

Throughout the twentieth century, however, there grew a general acceptance that children of all kinds are in need of protection and guidance, and that blind obedience reinforced by violence is wrong.

Routine 'beatings' by parents, common at the beginning of the twentieth century, would now be regarded as a crime. In the contemporary family, the views of children are generally regarded as being worth taking into account and the relationship between the majority of parents and children is (ideally) one of partnership.

We ought to note though, that there is still much violence against children and the fact that social workers and the National Society for the Prevention of Cruelty to Children (NSPCC) still exist, indicates just how great the problem is.

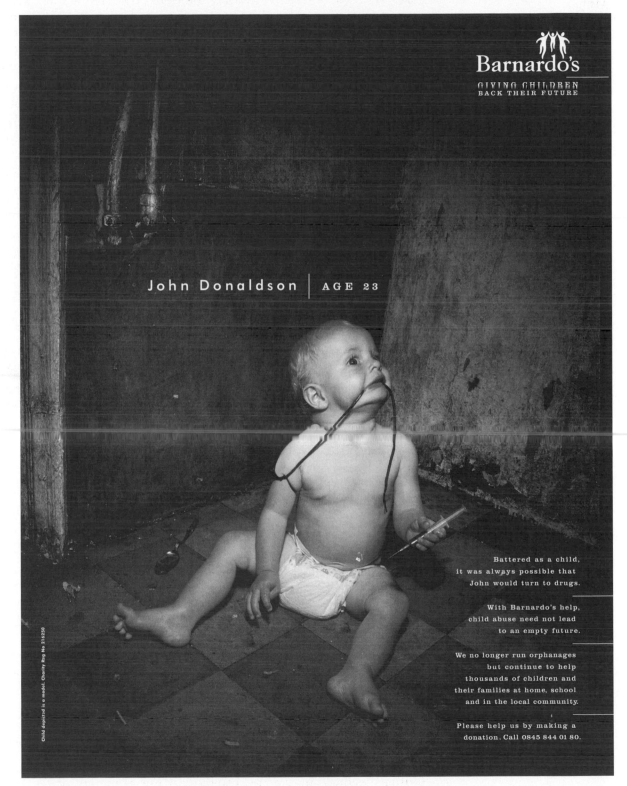

John Donaldson | AGE 23

Battered as a child, it was always possible that John would turn to drugs.

With Barnardo's help, child abuse need not lead to an empty future.

We no longer run orphanages but continue to help thousands of children and their families at home, school and in the local community.

Please help us by making a donation. Call 0845 844 01 80.

Barnardo's
GIVING CHILDREN
BACK THEIR FUTURE

Child depicted is a model. Charity Reg No 216250

Questions

1 Why does the picture above shock us?
2 Does it tell us anything about our attitudes to childhood?

The changing attitudes towards childhood

**Up to the
eighteenth century**

ARISTOCRACY

Boys were treated as 'little men', trained in the art of war, and possibly learned some reading and writing

Girls were educated to be mothers and wives; no formal schooling; household skills learned

PEASANTS

Boys were expected to work in the fields as soon as able; no such thing as childhood; treated roughly

Girls had no childhood; worked from earliest age; trained to be a farm-worker first and a mother/wife second

**Industrialisation
1700**

RICH

Boys were treated as little creatures who were to be strictly brought up to learn how to be 'gentlemen'; often attended public schools; children wore special clothes and were regarded as inferior to adults

Girls were seen as being less important than boys; taught that they had to make perfect wives and run the household while men got on with business; rarely attended school; treated strictly; special clothes for girls introduced

WORKING CLASS

Boys worked from very early age in factories; very often treated with brutality by parents; little time for childhood, never had time to play; strict discipline; no special clothes

Girls treated as boys; worked from a very early age; no special clothes; not regarded as being very different from boys; treated strictly and punished with violence

**Twentieth century
1900–49**

MIDDLE CLASS

Boys began to be treated with love and affection; encouraged to do well at school and in sports; children seen as in need of care and protection; if parents fail, state takes over; higher expectation of boys than girls

Girls treated with love and affection; stress on being pretty and learning to be a successful wife and mother; as century progresses increasing stress on education and career
For boys and girls: close family life

WORKING CLASS

Boys By middle of century, the working class had adopted idea of the innocence of children and it was normal to treat children with love and affection. Diminishing use of violence in discipline

Girls As boys above, but less stress on educational achievement and career prospects; close family life

1950s onward

DEVELOPED/AFFLUENT WORLD

Differences in social classes have declined, though divisions in income remain, which lead to different opportunities for sport, leisure and education. Ethos of parenting is now strongly on love and affection, and the importance of encouraging success. Smaller families allow deeper relationships with parents. Gender differences remain, but are becoming less important as education is seen as equally important for females as well as for males. Main differences lie in the shortening of childhood and the extension of youth

DEVELOPING NATIONS/POORER COUNTRIES

Childhood at best resembles the conditions of peasantry in Britain before 1800 (see above). Children may work long hours, be used for sexual exploitation, have little, if any educational opportunity, and a short expectation of life.

A moving image of young people

Late 19th century: society strove to impose strict moral and religious codes. The use of children as wage-earners was seen as wrong; children and young people were considered at risk of delinquency if not given care and protection. Their inability to survive independently of parents was regarded as further proof of their 'moral weakness'. Education was a rememdy for this; it became compulsory from 1870.

Mid-19th century: children and young people were increasingly seen as delinquents. Many adults felt that precocious children needed curbing.

1890s: young people were seen as worthy of academic study with the birth of the Child Study movement.

1900s: Children and young people were seen as innocent, incompetent, undisciplined things to be acted upon and 'improved' by adults. The start of the Edwardian social-service state ensured children were given new prominence – for instance, they were provided with school meals. The welfare of the child began to be seen as vital to the welfare of the state.

1930s–40s: understanding children's relationship to the family and their environment was seen as an important factor in creating a socially stable individual.

1960s to present: children and young people are still viewed with some ambivalence; adults see them representing both innocence and corruption. New teenage affluence has led to new kinds of youth sub-culture – such as mods and rockers, teddy boys, punks and, more recently, ravers. Many adults disapprove of these trends.

Source: *The Guardian*, (Education section), 30 March 1993

Damned kids!

What has happened to traditional British good-manners and sensible parenting?

No matter where my wife and I go to eat, drink or rest we seem to be engulfed in an army of small children running around screaming, shouting, and generally getting in the way of those of us who just want to get on with a quiet drink or a meal. And if a polite comment is made to parents, all that you receive is some lame excuse about 'children being children'. It's about time that children learned respect, like I had for adults when I was child.

Source: Based on a letter to a local paper

1 What does the letter tell us about attitudes of some people to children in Britain?

2 Do you agree with the letter writer, or any part of what he is saying?

3 The writer refers to parents saying that 'children will be children'. When you have read the next extract 'Childhood amongst the Ik', what comment can you make about this phrase?

Childhood amongst the Ik

The Ik were a small tribe who lived in northern Uganda. The Ik regarded children as a great nuisance. So much so, that they were thrown out by their mothers at the age of three and expected to look after themselves. In this environment, a child stands no chance of survival on his own until he is about 13 years old, so children form themselves into two age bands, the first from 3 to 7.

For the most part they ate figs that had been partially eaten by baboons, a few cherries, bark from trees, and when they were really hungry they swallowed earth or even pebbles.

Source: Adapted from C. Turnbull, *The Mountain People* (Picador, 1974)

1 At what age does the mother regard the child as old enough to care for itself?

2 Would a child in Britain be capable of looking after him or herself at this age?

3 Some people argue that our abilities are completely controlled by our age and that our development is 'natural'. Does this extract tell us anything about our ideas of what children are capable of?

4 What does the extract tell us of the relationship between mother and child?

Main points

▸ Age divisions are a mixture of both physical and social differences.

▸ People are expected to behave in certain ways, according to their age.

▸ Sociologists usually distinguish between childhood, youth, adulthood and old age.

▸ Childhood (as opposed to being physically young) is socially constructed and is a relatively new idea.

▸ In different societies there are very great differences in the expectations of what children should and can do.

▶ Over time in Britain we have come to see children as being innocent and in need of protection, but this was not always the case. For example, in the seventeenth–nineteenth centuries children were often believed to be naturally wicked.

▶ There are differences in the ways that children are treated, depending upon such things as their ethnic background, their sex and their social class.

▶ Today, many children in the poorer nations of the world live and work in conditions which resemble those endured by European children almost 200 years ago.

▶ A rite of passage is when a person moves from one social status to another.

▶ Rites of passage are much less important today than they used to be. However, they still remain.

Youth

Definitions

Culture – a whole way of life that guides our way of thinking and acting. People within a culture regard it as somehow natural; for example, the difference between British values and Italian values

Subculture – exists within a culture and is a distinctive set of values that marks off the members of the subculture from the rest of society; for example, youth (sub)culture

Contraculture – a form of subculture which actively opposes the dominant culture of society; for example, terrorist groups

We use the term 'youth' in normal conversation without a very precise notion of the age at which we enter and leave it. Does youth finish at 16 when you can leave school? Or 17 when you can drive a car? Or maybe at 18 when you can vote and legally purchase alcohol? Perhaps youth is not directly restricted to any age, but is over when you marry?

Clearly the notion of youth is confused and unclear. But perhaps this very lack of clarity provides us with a clue to the meaning of youth – it can best be understood as a period of transition between childhood, when we are bossed around and regarded as having little to contribute to discussions on matters of importance, and adulthood, when we are weighed down with domestic concerns, the mortgage and the rearing of children.

This period of change from childhood to adulthood is elastic in length, and is lengthening as the time spent in education increases, so that relatively few people now work full-time before 18 years of age. Indeed, with increasing numbers of young people going onto university, youth may well be stretching to 21.

The term 'youth' then refers to the period of transition, however long that may be, between childhood and adulthood, which has gradually developed from just a brief time of change into being a stage of life itself.

Youth culture

The development of the age of youth has been associated with the growth of distinctive values which young people hold. These values serve to distinguish them from the older generation. **Subculture** is the correct term to describe these noticeably different sets of values. However, instead **youth culture** has become the most commonly used term.

Youth transition and the origins of youth culture

Youth and youth culture are relatively new concepts which began to emerge in the 1950s and since then have grown massively and developed into many different types of youth culture.

Historically young people in Britain followed a clear transition from childhood and education, to employment, to marriage, to parenthood and – eventually –

to grandparenthood and death. This was normal and expected and very clearly marked through various rites of passage. There were clear differences between males and females within this overall pattern, with women concentrating on child-rearing and putting employment second to this. Young people generally followed both their parents' values and their parents' pattern of employment.

The transition from each stage to the next was very clearly marked out in this traditional way of life. However, from the 1950s onward, and at an ever-increasing pace, these traditional forms of transition were put under pressure, and from the 1970s onward the youth transition from childhood to adulthood had become one of the most dramatic and important phases in people's lives.

However, the transition points have become vaguer and vaguer and certainly for youth the length of the transition has increased greatly.

Three 'points of pressure' on the traditional transition gave birth to youth culture:

- affluence
- speed of social change
- the development of age-specific media.

The growth in affluence

Young people have much lower incomes than adults, they are generally in full-time education and their income comes from allowances from parents and part-time employment. Those who are in employment earn much lower wages than older workers. However, the income they do have is usually available for spending on leisure activities and clothes. So, their **disposable income** is quite high, as they are not weighed down with mortgages and heavy household bills. This **relative affluence** of the majority of British youth has increased since the late 1950s, so that young people are now recognised by manufacturers as a key 'market' to sell goods to.

Social change

Technology is changing at an increasingly rapid rate and is bringing about great changes in social behaviour, but it does this at different speeds with different generations. Computer games, for instance, were unknown to parents whose children (or mainly boys to be more accurate!) now grow up with them as a normal pastime. Mobile phones and the Internet are used by all age groups, but are a normal part of many young people's lives.

So, the expectations and behaviour of previous generations do not seem so relevant to each generation over the last 40 years. This means that youth has increasingly developed its own ways of acting and its own codes of behaviour – as the ideas and values of the older generations may not 'fit' new social and technological situations.

As a result of these factors, amongst others, the experiences of young people are very different, and they will have different experiences of growing up and very different youth cultures.

The development of age-specific media

One hundred years ago, there were no radios, televisions or computers, and recorded music was virtually unknown. Today, life would be almost unimaginable without film, television, radio, recorded music, magazines and papers, and the Internet. The majority of the media is commercial, so that they have to make money to stay in business. The most profitable activity is to target recorded music, magazines, radio stations and programmes and so on, to specific audiences. One of the major target audiences is young people, because they are relatively affluent and they have a large disposable income. Over the last 40 years, this has led to an explosion of types of media which are directed at young people and which help them to identify themselves more clearly as 'youth', as opposed to older people or children.

Activities

1   Look through old photos of your parents or relatives when they were young. Do they have any old records with pictures of the artists on the covers? Go to the library or second-hand book shops and look for books on fashions or pop music history.

From all this evidence, collect information on fashion and music styles. Copy and complete the table below for two styles (you can add more if you wish).

Name of youth style	Name of youth style
Music:	Music:
Hair-style:	Hair-style:
Make-up (if appropriate):	Make-up (if appropriate):
Clothes style:	Clothes style:
Examples of language used:	Examples of language used:

2   Interview your parents or relatives about their views and behaviour when they were younger. Did they have a clear and identifiable style and youth culture?

Contemporary youth cultures: differentiation and stratification

Youth now has been broken up, or fragmented, into a number of different styles, which are distinguishable from one another by differences in clothes, use of language, musical tastes, hair and make-up styles.

It is not possible to provide a simple explanation of what the differences are based on, for example, why somebody chooses one particular youth culture and not another. It seems that all we can say is that youth both *share* similar experiences and are also *divided* by their different experiences, which are linked to such things as differences in ethnicity, gender, sexuality, social class, region and religion.

Why do we have youth cultures?

We now know why youth culture developed in Britain. But sociologists have asked what, if anything, does youth culture actually do for youth? Two very different answers have been suggested:

- Youth cultures help solve the specific problems faced by young people, as opposed to other age groups.
- Youth cultures are largely the result of manipulation by the media.

Youth cultures as solutions to problems

As we have just said, some sociologists argue that youth cultures offer a possible solution for young people during their transition between childhood and adulthood. However, although these sociologists agree about the idea of youth culture as a solution to problems, they disagree about what those problems are and just how youth culture resolves them.

Similar problems face all youth

One group of sociologists, known as functionalists (see page 53), argue that all young people face *similar problems*. Young people are unsure of themselves in the difficult period of transition from childhood to adulthood.

In order to cope with this period of uncertainty and transition, young people develop a culture which provides them with a clear way of behaving and style of dress, so that the *whole peer group acts in a particular way* and young people can feel safe in the secure in their group. Everyone has similar difficulties in this period of transition and everyone feels similarly reassured.

According to this approach, any differences between young people are not seen as being very important.

Different problems faced by youth

This approach claims that young people face *very different problems and opportunities* according to class, gender and ethnic background. The approach argues that the different problems faced by different sections of youth are so great that they develop their own responses, which include clothing styles, attitudes to music and forms of language or 'argot'. Each group devises its own image in such a way as to reflect the differences between them and their own particular problems.

Manipulation by the media

This approach disagrees with the other two approaches. It accepts that there a number of different youth cultural styles, but does not agree that they represent some form of response. The 'post-modern' approach is that youth culture is best understood as a messy mixture of original ideas by young people and the ability of large music and fashion companies to manipulate young people to buy their goods. The result is that youth culture is partly the result of manipulation by those who want to make money out of them, and partly some real creativity by young people.

An evaluation of the 'what are youth cultures for?' arguments

Functionalists argued that youth culture and, more specifically, a young person's own peer group provided a much needed sense of security in that frightening transition from childhood, home and security to adulthood, the world outside and employment. Certainly, it is true that a sense of security is needed, but the approach simply does not explain *why there are so many different forms of youth culture*. So, 3 out of 10 for this explanation.

The argument that youth subcultures represent some form of rebellion by working-class youth is very interesting. There is the belief that working-class youth cultures represent a genuine attempt by the oppressed working class to solve their problems by dressing in certain ways or by using drugs for instance. But really, it just doesn't add up. So, working-class kids just sit down and decide how they are going to dress and talk and what music they want to hear, so that will help them

through being poor and powerless? I don't think so! But, it does provide an interesting explanation for the wide variety of different youth cultures, and certainly young people are trying to rebel. So, 6 out of 10.

The post modern approach is very different – it suggests that youth culture is shallow, essentially meaningless and is constructed from a wide selection of different influences, some of them the result of manipulation by large media and fashion organisations, some of them reflecting the originality of young people and some from traditional values. Well, this is a bit hard to understand, but if it is saying that modern youth culture is just a mix of lots of different influences and that it is pretty meaningless (despite what the 'stars' say), it seems fairly true to commonsense explanations and it does help explain the variety of different youth cultures. I'll give it a score of 7 out of 10.

1 According to the extract, what three approaches are there to explain youth culture?

2 Which is the highest scoring?

The peer group

Definition

Peer group – a group of a person's own age who are important to them; the group exerts influence over individual members; most often used when referring to young people

Before we go on to look at the different sorts of youth styles, we must briefly glance at a key group for young people – the **peer group**.

As children, most of us are brought up in families which, ideally, provide us with protection, emotional security and a sense of belonging. As we grow up, the constraining bonds of the family prove too tight, we need more freedom, but without losing that sense of security. It seems that the role of the peer group is to do just that; it gives independence and security. The peer group consists of other people of the same age who are seen as the correct people to judge our behaviour against.

The peer group can be a decisive influence on a young person's lifestyle. We have all heard of someone in trouble with the law having 'got in with the wrong crowd', and it is true that status within the peer group partially comes to replace loyalties outside.

The influence of the peer group

Attitudes to school

Attitudes to work

Attitudes to crime

Social and political views

Attitudes to drugs

Leisure choices

1 Would you say that you belong to a peer group? What term would you use for your friends?

2 Do you think that they influence you in any way?

3 Do you think your peer group help you get on with your parents and family?

Varieties of youth cultures in Britain

There is a wide variety of youth cultures which reflect the range of youth who live in contemporary Britain. As we discussed earlier, it is pretty obvious that black inner-city youths have very different experiences of life than do, for example, white, suburban youth, or Asian youth. These differences are often reflected in the styles of clothes, the choice of music and the forms of expression of the different groups.

Before we examine these different forms of youth culture, it is important to remember that there are many shared elements to youth culture. Above all else, youth culture in all its forms stresses leisure and enjoyment. So, the vast majority of young people seek as much enjoyment as possible from life, and they are less concerned with long-term planning than adults would like. This, combined with the fact that most adolescents are free from major worries over household bills and family responsibilities, means that they are more likely to have an active leisure life and that their leisure is more important to them than it is to many adults.

Middle-class youth culture

Middle-class youth are more likely to stay in the education system to take A-levels or a degree, so their form of youth culture is more likely to be based on student life. They are aware of the expectation to be successful in education and the pressure to study. For these young people, the youth culture is more restricted when they are young, but they are more likely to go to university later, with its isolation from the 'real world' in tolerant academic surroundings. They are more likely, therefore, in the longer term to have the opportunity to explore new lifestyles and attitudes without the possibility of being disciplined.

The situation for many working-class young people is different in that living at home may lead them into conflict with parents.

Working-class youth culture

Working-class youth has developed a number of **styles** which sociologists have linked to the changes which have taken place in the working class over the last 30 years. They point out the different extremes which reflect the splintering of the working class into the poorer, usually inner city or large social housing estates on the fringes of towns, and the more affluent children of those who benefited from the increase in affluence in the 1980s and 1990s. The poorer groups have appeared to move more to use of drugs and are more likely to engage in aggressive behaviour. On the other hand, the affluent are more likely to purchase their leisure in terms of clubs and sports, and through relatively expensive clothes.

The future of youth cultural styles amongst the working class will depend very largely upon the chances of getting work. Clearly, if there are no jobs, then the opportunity to buy 'named' clothes, mobile phones, CD players and cars will be limited. Yet against this, there are now very firmly established expectations that youth have concerning possessions; they think it is only fair that they have decent clothes and possessions. What seems to have happened is that not only has there been a widening of divisions amongst the working class, but also that these divisions are made even wider by regional differences, with higher rates of youth unemployment in parts of the north of England and Scotland.

What causes the differences in subcultural styles?

Youth   Youth culture occurs in the period of relative freedom from childhood constraint and adult responsibilties.

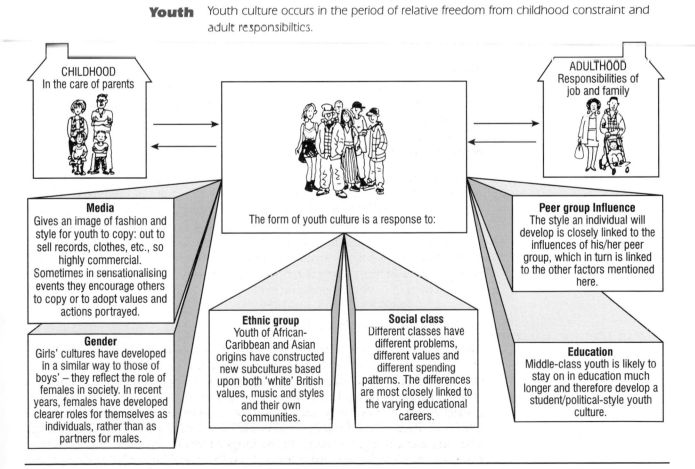

CHILDHOOD
In the care of parents

ADULTHOOD
Responsibilities of job and family

The form of youth culture is a response to:

Media
Gives an image of fashion and style for youth to copy: out to sell records, clothes, etc., so highly commercial. Sometimes in sensationalising events they encourage others to copy or to adopt values and actions portrayed.

Peer group Influence
The style an individual will develop is closely linked to the influences of his/her peer group, which in turn is linked to the other factors mentioned here.

Gender
Girls' cultures have developed in a similar way to those of boys' – they reflect the role of females in society. In recent years, females have developed clearer roles for themselves as individuals, rather than as partners for males.

Ethnic group
Youth of African-Caribbean and Asian origins have constructed new subcultures based upon both 'white' British values, music and styles and their own communities.

Social class
Different classes have different problems, different values and different spending patterns. The differences are most closely linked to the varying educational careers.

Education
Middle-class youth is likely to stay on in education much longer and therefore develop a student/political-style youth culture.

Ethnicity and youth cultures

Youth of African-Caribbean origin

The youth cultural styles of this group is possibly the most dynamic and influential of all youth cultures. Music and dress styles have been borrowed from the black music artists in the United States and adapted and re-invented in a British 'black' style.

Some sociologists have suggested that music and style has been a very effective way for British black youth to gain status.

Youth culture: Asian perspectives

Until the 1980s, Asian youth had been 'hidden', with no clear identity as far as the wider white and black youth cultures were concerned.

However, the second generation, British-born Asians began to construct their own identity during the late 1980s and began to develop a British Asian identity. This has involved a process of keeping their own sense of identity as Asians, but incorporating large elements of British culture so that what emerges is a something unique to them – a hybrid subculture.

This new subculture involves western-style clothes, plus their own styles of music which overlap with mainstream music, which allows them to keep many traditional values, for example towards the appropriate behaviour of females and commitment to the wider family.

But it is not possible to talk about one Asian youth culture – there are a number and these are based upon differences in places of origin of parents (Bangladesh, Pakistan, India, Africa) on the one hand and differences between religions, on the other (Muslim, Hindu, Sikh).

The youth culture jigsaw

Young British Asians found themselves in the position of having to reconcile the starkly opposing cultures, lifestyles and moral codes ... on the one hand ... of their inherited Asian-ness, ... and on the other ... with their new Britishness. They ... learned to put on ... 'white masks' that allowed them to participate in the activities and ethos of their white peers at school and college and also, whenever necessary, to concentrate and highlight their cultural difference in order to identify themselves as different from the majority group ... which ... involves them adopting the music and songs of popular [Hindi] films, ... which they have used to create ... a popular and meaningful subculture of their own ... this has produced dynamic, contemporary, bhangra/rap/reggae musical cross-overs ... .

Source: Adapted from S. Johal, 'Brimful of Brasia', *Sociology Review*, Vol. 8, No. 1, September 1998

1 What does the author mean when he says that young British Asians put on a 'white mask'?

2 What does their youth culture allow them to do?

3 Find examples of distinctive music which reflect Asian and African-Caribbean identities. What about the music of other ethnic groups? Bring some to school/college and after playing it, swap your views on them. Which do you prefer? Why?

Youth culture: female perspectives

Studies of female youth cultures show they have changed very considerably over the last 20 years. Early research had shown that youth cultures were very much based on the activities and ideas of males, and females were ignored – largely because they were more likely to be kept at home and more closely controlled by parents.

Although parents still tend to control females more than males, young women are now far more assertive and have created more 'space' for themselves. Role models on television have reflected this, with a much greater emphasis on the right of young women to engage in sexual activity and to express sexual ideas.

Young women now play a central role in youth culture and are as active as males in leisure activities. Even at the 'extremes' of youth behaviour, young women play an active part – although far less likely to be involved in criminal or anti-social acts, they are as likely to 'do drugs' and to go out at weekends for example.

Being a teenage girl

The questionnaire below was taken from a girls' magazine. This is how one 14-year-old girl filled it in. Compare your answers to hers.

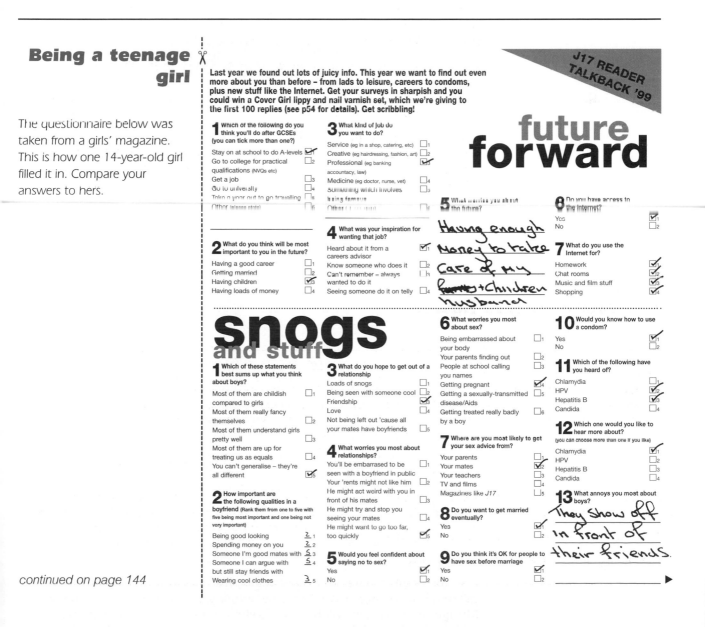

continued on page 144

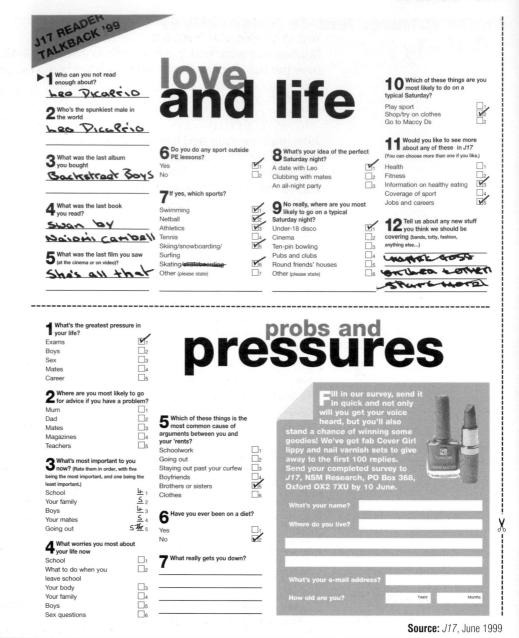

Source: *J17*, June 1999

Activity	Sociologists often use a method known as observation (see page 34) to observe very closely the actions of a particular group, pretending they are seeing behaviour for the first time, as if they are from another planet. Often this makes 'normal' behaviour' seem fresh and more puzzling, requiring explanations.
	Choose one or more of the following places: school, college, pub, club, MacDonalds, hanging around the shops. Conduct some observational research, noting the different behaviour of males and females.
	What differences do you observe? Suggest why they might be behaving differently. Are there any differences in behaviour between different groups, ages or types of females and between different males?

It is important to remember that females, like males, are going to behave very differently according to social class and ethnic group. For example, working-class Muslim Asian females will be more likely to conform to traditional values than middle-class Hindi Asian females, whose parents came to Britain from East Africa.

Activity

Young people and freedom

Choose a specific age group – I would suggest 16–17-year-olds. Conduct a survey which will provide the information to complete the table below.

Devise a series of questions, using anonymous questionnaires. Use the categories shown in the table, and add in any other factors you find useful. Also ask the person what ethnic group and religion they would categorise themselves as, and add these to your table.
Do any differences emerge?

The habits of 16–17-year-olds

	All %	Females %	Males %
Drank alcohol in the last week			
Smokes cigarettes regularly			
Smoked cannabis in the last month			
Girl/Boyfriend allowed to stay the night by parents			
Stayed out all night in the last month.			
None of these things			

Music and meaning

Music is a tremendously important site of common culture, for individual and collective symbolic work and creativity ... young people's central cultural life interest.
Source: P. Willis, *Common Culture* (Oxford University Press, 1993)

1 Explain in your own words what the quote above means.

2 Draw a diagram which illustrates the sorts of music associated with different styles, ethnic groups and ages. Suggest an explanation of why and how that music might have become associated with any/all of them.

Youth stratification and generation

Some sociologists have suggested that the division between the various age groups, and particularly young people and older people has become as important as social class. However, when it comes to agreement on fundamental values, there seems to be quite a strong sense of agreement between the different generations.

Most surveys of young people indicate not how radical they are, but just how conformist they tend to be. Attitudes to drugs and even sex are quite conservative. Most young people are not really interested in politics and look forward to a decent job, a settled relationship and a decent income.

But at the same time, it still needs to be accepted that there are differences in the generations in terms of different levels of power and of income. Children are powerless, young people have greater power over their decisions, and more income – but not as much as middle-aged people, who dominate the better jobs in employment, the media and in politics. Finally, old age is a time of decline, poverty and low status.

So, it is clear that age, or to be more precise 'generation' does divide people to some extent, but that there are considerable bonds between them too.

Finally, whilst we are discussing divisions of power and income, we need to be aware of the fact that within each generation the experiences of power, employment and status are very different for men and women, ethnic groups and social classes.

Main points

▸ Youth is a relatively new period of age.

▸ It represents a period of transition from childhood to adulthood.

▸ A youth culture has developed since the 1950s which reflects distinctive youth values.

▸ The origins of youth culture were caused by – affluence, speed of social change, the development of an age-specific media.

▸ There are many different varieties of youth culture, including those based on class, ethnicity and gender.

▸ Sociologists disagree on the purpose of youth culture.
   – One group say that it exists to solve the specific problems faced by young people.
   – Another group of sociologists argue that youth culture is largely the result of manipulation by the media.

Adulthood

Adulthood is the period of maximum power and social prestige for the majority of the population. It is the time of life when earning power and disposable income are usually at their highest. Like the other periods of life, adulthood is as much a social as a physical period of life and some sociologists have argued that it was 'created' by a process of exclusion. This means that each generation has 'battled' against each other for the rights to the highest status and the best income. Adults won; old people and children lost. Perhaps youth is the new challenger.

At first it does seem a bizzare idea, but it does seem to fit the facts as we have seen them in this chapter, with the emergence of the power of youth and (as we shall soon see) the decline in the power of old people.

What we need to remember is that there is no natural reason why adults should have higher status, greater income and more power than the other age groups. The answer may just lie in the fact that they have imposed this on the other groups over time, because they are stronger.

Just one proviso though: the differences we have spoken about – gender, ethnicity and social class – are just as strong in adulthood compared to the other ages. It is just that within each of these groups adults are the best off.

Income and age

Mean individual income¹: by gender and age, 1996–97, Great Britain

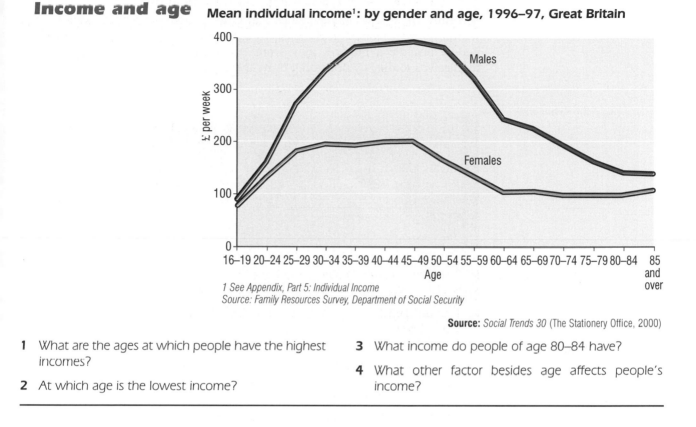

1 See Appendix, Part 5: Individual Income
Source: Family Resources Survey, Department of Social Security

Source: *Social Trends 30* (The Stationery Office, 2000)

1 What are the ages at which people have the highest incomes?

2 At which age is the lowest income?

3 What income do people of age 80–84 have?

4 What other factor besides age affects people's income?

Old age

Today, well over 20 per cent of the population is above retirement age and that figure is going to continue increasing. Improvements in standards of living, better housing, better diets and improved medical care have all helped cause this rapid expansion in life expectation. Much of this is discussed in Chapter 9. In this chapter, we will concentrate on the changing attitudes to older people and the problems they face.

Never before in history have there been so many older people. A time traveller from the seventeenth century would be just as shocked to see all the old faces around as by the changes in technology. Indeed she or he would be shocked by the number of people over the age of 40, never mind 60!

In most societies in history, old people would be of enough rarity to guarantee them some degree of status. Furthermore, in traditional societies based on agriculture, where there was little technological or social change, each generation learned from the previous one. In these societies older people may well have had relevant advice to give to younger generations. However, the situation is entirely different in modern complex societies where technology and culture change so rapidly that the experience of one generation is not really useful to the next. The result is that the older people in our society have low status and many have low incomes. Old age is portrayed as a time to be feared, a time of decline preceding death.

But it is not all bad. First of all, people do not just live longer, they remain active and healthy longer. It is claimed that for many, the most affluent and relaxed period of people's lives is now the first eight years after retirement.

Secondly, there is no real evidence that older people were necessarily treated with any great respect in the past. In many traditional societies, when older people became a burden, they were encouraged via the culture to 'allow themselves to die', by not eating or by leaving the tribe to die.

Should older people use Mick Jagger as a role model, do you think?

Stratification and older people

The underlying assumption is that the elderly are a *problem* for society. The growing proportion of the population who are elderly is emphasised, and particularly the burden of the 'old' elderly (i.e. over seventy-five years old) and the 'very old' elderly (over eight-five) who are seen as a *burden* on the State because they are high users of health and welfare services.

This 'social problem' focus leads to a more general image of older people as poor, disabled, dependent and passive.

They are also seen as a burden on younger women because most care of the elderly is done by women. The elderly are primarily seen as a **homogeneous** group and attention is given to *age relations*, rather than *class* or *gender differences* among the elderly. But how does social class influence these age relations? We have only to consider the Queen and the rest of the older royalty, the many elderly judges and politicians and the old rich men who dominate the economy to realise the sharp contrast they provide to the more general image of the old.

Source: Adapted from S. Arber, 'Class and the elderly', *Social Studies Review*, 1989

Definition

Homogeneous – a single group with similar characteristics

1 What is the assumption when talking about 'the elderly'?

2 Why is it wrong to talk about 'the elderly' as a homogeneous group?

3 What does the extract suggest is the relationship between social class and age?

4 Suggest other forms of differentiation within older people.

5 Make a list of the costs and benefits of older people in your family and your community.

6 In your opinion, who should be responsible for older people when they need to be cared for?

Images of old age

A big house used to be a good idea with a family.

But now that you are alone again it may seem more of a burden than an asset.

The upkeep of a large, near empty home can be an expensive liability, as well as a quiet and lonely place. The rooms you rarely use, repairs that are never done, and a garden which seems to grow bigger by the year. Isn't it time you took a closer look at *Countryside's* exciting range of luxurious apartments.

Created with you in mind, the care and dedication applied to the design and construction of these exclusive apartments is the hallmark of *Countryside's* reputation for building quality homes of

character and elegance.

Any essential repair and maintenance jobs are taken care of, and with a residential housekeeper, it's nice to know someone is there to cope with any emergencies.

Strolling in the beautifully landscaped garden, relaxing in the

Countryside

friendly atmosphere of the residents lounge, or the comfort of your own apartment. Whichever you choose, you can be sure that *Countryside's* unique blend of complete privacy when you want it, or a shared environment when you don't, allows you the privilege of enjoying the retirement you deserve.

If you live in Essex or East Anglia and would like to visit one of our luxury retirement apartments but find it difficult to do so, we will be happy to collect you, show you round and take you home again.

For further details please complete the coupon or telephone **Eve Bayley** on **(0277) 234136.**

Read the text.

1. What image do you think is portrayed about the social role of older people?

2. What does the text suggest about the health and future health prospects of older people?

3. How does the advert suggest that the future will be one of 'dependence'?

4. The advert refers to 'enjoying the privilege of enjoying the retirement you deserve'. What does this mean? Does it convey any message about a person's working life and its value?

5. In the illustration there is a husband and wife (at least I presume they are!) sitting together. Look at page 229 in Chapter 9. Check the statistics on mortality. What do you think the truth is?

6. Compare the 'message' about older people in this advertisement with the extract 'The supercentanarians of Abkhazistan' on page 150. What conclusions do you reach?

The supercentenarians of Abkhazistan

In Britain the number of supercentenarians [people over 100] is estimated at 1 in 4000 of the population. In Abkhazistan to the South of Russia, the number is 204 in 4000.

Perhaps the most important reason for long life is the attitude of these people to growing old and in the way their society is organised. At an age when most people in this country are thinking of drawing their pension, Abkhazians think of themselves as in their prime. They are not obsessed by age as we are. No one is forced to retire at 60 or 65 and older people go on working in the fields, caring for the flocks of sheep, doing housework and looking after their (great) grandchildren.

Source: *People not Pensioners* (Help the Aged, 1978)

1 What is the main reason for the long life span?

2 What are the main differences between the way old people in Abkhazistan act and the way old people act in our society?

3 What makes older people act differently in Abkhazistan?

The third age

In spite of the "halo" effect of nostalgia, 38 per cent of the over-50s now think that life is more satisfying than when they were younger. ... Among those aged 50–54, the figure rises to 47 per cent, much higher than for people aged 15–34. Even among the over-70s, satisfaction levels are rising – from 24 per cent in 1988 to 28 per cent now. ...

During the 1990s the number of over-50s increased by 9 per cent, compared with a 3 per cent growth in total population. ...

"Third-agers" ... have more surplus income and leisure time. They spend it on holidays, visits, pets, gardening, reading books and newspapers, eating out and watching videos.

Change in self-image

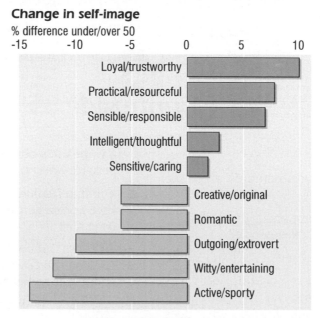

Source: Adapted from *The Independent*, 9 November 1993

1 Explain what the term 'third age' means.

2 The general belief is that the older you get, the less happy you are. What does this extract suggest?

3 Is the number of over 50s declining or increasing, in proportion to the population as a whole? What social effects do you think this might have?

4 Think of any effects this might have on society (patterns of consumption. holidays, the media, etc.).

5 Look at the chart showing changes in self-image. Which self-images decline?

6 What self-images increase?

7 Design a simple questionnaire to ask a sample of three 'third-agers' how they would rank these attributes gained and lost.

Main points ▸ Adulthood is a socially constructed age period.

▸ Adults have managed to make other age groups less powerful and be dependent upon them.

▸ They have done this largely by 'squeezing them out' of employment.

▸ Adulthood is the period in most people's lives of greatest wealth and prestige.

▸ Adults are stratified by age, social class and gender.

▸ Old age is a socially constructed period of life.

▸ Older people have low status in modern western societies.

▸ Older people have higher status in some societies – usually where they are able to continue working and having some power.

▸ Older people, like the other age groups, are distinguished by differences of social class, gender and ethnicity.

---

6 CHAPTER SUMMARY

1 Ageing is both a social and a natural process.

2 People are treated differently and are expected to behave in different ways according to their age.

3 Our lifespans are divided into a series of age statuses – childhood, youth, adulthood and old age.

4 The transition from one age status to another is marked by rites of passage. In modern society, the transitions are not as clear as they were historically.

5 Childhood has changed over the last few hundred years in a number of ways – mainly that we now see children as more in need of care and protection.

6 Differences still exist between the different social classes, ethnic groups and sexes in their experiences of childhood. Perhaps the greatest differences are between children in richer and poorer countries.

7 Youth is a relatively new age status, which emerged from the 1950s onward.

8   A youth culture has emerged which is distinctive.

9   The origins of youth culture seem to lie in the growth of affluence of young people, the speed of social change and the development of media aimed specifically at them.

10   Sociologists disagree about what youth culture does for young people. Some argue that it helps them solve their problems, others that it is mainly the result of the media.

11   There are many different youth cultures in Britain, linked to gender, social class and ethnicity, amongst other things.

12   Adulthood is the period of greatest power and income for most people, though great differences exist between adults.

13   There are increasing numbers of older people.

14   Older people are regarded as a problem and with very limited respect. This may not have been true in traditional societies.

15   However, because there are increasing numbers of older people and because they are more likely to be in good health and to have better incomes than in the past, the quality of life for many older people is increasing.

Test Your Knowledge

1   Describe how our attitude towards children has changed over time.

2   What do we mean when we say that age has a social element to it?

3   What is a rite of passage? Give two examples.

4   What three reasons have been suggested for the development of youth culture from the 1950s onward?

5   What do we mean when we say that youth culture helps to solve problems? What criticism has been made of this?

6   Choose two varieties of youth culture (for example, by social class or ethnicity) and explain why they are different.

7   How have adults gained their power and income compared to other age groups?

8   Why is the meaning and experience of old age changing?

FAMILIES, PARTNERSHIPS AND MARRIAGE

Chapter contents

- **Defining families**

  We begin with what appears to be the simplest of tasks, defining the family. As always in sociology, this 'simple task' becomes ever more complex the more we investigate it. In the end, we arrive at a rather cumbersome definition which points to the fact that we need to carry the discussion further into two areas – structures and diversity.

- **Family structure**

  There are lots of different family types, or structures. These include the extended family, the nuclear family, the lone-parent family and the reconstituted family. Although each one is a 'family', each type (or structure) is quite distinct.

- **Family diversity**

  Our studies so far have demonstrated the complexity of the family and this section takes us one step further by exploring how influences from outside impose themselves on the family and bring about yet greater variety. These influences include social status, ethnicity, location and sexual orientation.

- **Changing family forms**

  Continuing this theme of dynamism and complexity, we look at the way the family has changed over time and the factors which have helped bring about the changes. Perhaps the most important influence historically has been industrialisation and the consequent changes in social life which industrial societies require. Over time society has also changed economically, technologically and socially, and these changes have had an impact on the family.

- **The role of the family in society**

  Every so often a debate breaks out in the media about the breakdown of the family (which we explore in the next few sections), but the underlying assumption is always that the family is a good thing – good for the family members and good for society. We debate the truth of this.

- **The lone-parent family**

  Of all the types of family, the lone-parent family has been has been singled out for attack. Some people have accused it of creating 'an underclass' of lazy, immoral people who commit crime and 'sponge' off the state. We look at the reality of lone or single parenthood, what causes it and what the impact is on society and its members.

- **Alternatives to the family**

  The assumption of most people is that the family forms the basis of social life, and although it has a number of weaknesses, there is no alternative. However, a few people have suggested that society could be organised in different and, they would claim, better ways, which would involve replacing the family. We look at two example of possible replacements – communes and kibutzim.

- **Marriage and cohabitation**

  This section examines some issues surrounding marriage, including the debate over the decline in marriage and its apparent replacement by cohabitation. Has marriage had its day? Is there any value to being married in Britain today? These questions lead us to examine the meaning of marriage in other times and other societies and an interesting variety of views on the usefulness of marriage as an institution for both society and individuals emerge, including the argument that marrying for love is not such a good thing.

- **Divorce**

  We examine the legal changes making divorces easier to obtain and the reasons why so many marriages now end in divorce.

- **Family relationships**

  This section provides an overview to the changing relationships between family members and reminds us that life within families is experienced differently by the different genders and generations.

With this ring … lesbians symbolically 'marry' in San Francisco. Should gays and lesbians be allowed to marry?

Defining families

Some definitions

Here are some definitions of a family given by young people in a recent research report.

'A family is a group of people which all care about each other. They can all cry together, laugh together, argue together and go through all the emotions together. Some live together as well. Families are for helping each other through life.' (Tara, 13)

'My mum is important to me because she feeds me and clothes me and loves me very much. My dad is important to me because he pays for the food I eat and the clothes I wear. He cares for me and loves me very much.' (Nadia, 9)

'Families are for help, mental and physical stability, love, support.' (Alvin, 14)

Which definition do you think is the most accurate? Try to write your own definition of the family, in your own words. Compare it with the sociologist's definition below.

Source: V. Morrow, *Understanding Families: Children's Perspectives* (National Children's Bureau, 1999)

A family is best described as a group of people most often consisting of adults and their offspring, living with or near each other. The adults in the relationship are typically closely related in some way either through marriage or cohabitation.

If this sound a very clumsy definition to you – it is! One of the key issues of this chapter will be to explore the variety of family types which exist. As you will see, there has been such a change in what is considered as 'the family' that it is very difficult to define it simply.

We can flesh out this vague definition by saying that families vary in two ways:
- by structure
- by social diversity.

Family structures

The different types of family structure are:
- the extended family
- the nuclear family
- the lone-parent family
- the reconstituted family.

Household and family

In the discussion which follows we will also be referring to **households** quite frequently. It is important to realise that families and households are different things, with a household simply meaning one or more people living in the same dwelling. Whereas a family, however we define it, will as a minimum be a group of people related by ceremonial and/or blood ties, living together or in frequent contact.

The extended family

The **extended family** generally consists of three generations of people, that is grandparents, parents and children, who all live close to each other and maintain regular contact.

This type of family is usually found in societies where a large group of people living together can be of real use. For example, in society based on farming, a large family can sow, reap and care for animals more efficiently than just parents and a couple of children. Or, in the early industrial society of the nineteenth century in Britain, where there was terrible poverty, a large family could provide a form of mutual aid, especially in times of crisis, such as high unemployment. The greater the number of possible workers, the greater the chance of someone bringing home a wage. In Britain today, the extended family in the traditional sense is not common, although it is quite normal amongst people of Asian origin.

The nuclear family

The **nuclear family** is much smaller than the extended family and generally consists of only parents and their children, of which there are generally two. Contact with wider **kin** is weaker and less frequent than amongst members of the extended family.

This type of family is usually found where a large group would be more of a hindrance than a help. In some 'simple' societies based on constant movement and the hunting of animals (as occurred in large parts of Africa, South-East Asia and South America until early in the twentieth century), food can be in short supply and a small, fast-moving group is more likely to survive.

Nuclear families are also found in advanced industrial societies, such as Britain and Germany where there is less need to rely upon the family for help. The nuclear family appears to be the most common form in Britain today.

But it is in decline, with the 'traditional' nuclear family of a couple with dependent children comprising approximately 23 per cent of all households, a drop of 15 per cent compared to 30 years ago. Indeed, this model actually only represents about 1 in every 20 households in Britain at any one time.

However, the idea that this means the majority of families are 'isolated' from their wider kin is not true, In a study by Finch, 72 per cent of (adult) respondents lived within one hour of their mother, and around half saw their mother at least once a week.

The lone-parent family

<table>
<tr><td>

Definition

Lone- or single-parent family – only one parent living with the children. Ninety per cent of lone-parent families are headed by women

</td><td>

The **lone-parent family** consists of a single parent, plus his or her dependent children. It is usually headed by a female. In Britain, the growth of the lone-parent family is a result of the rise in the number of divorces and the increased number of pregnancies amongst never-married women.

In 2000, there were over 1.5 million lone-parent families in Britain, with more than 2.8 million children living in such families, an increase of one third since 1990.

</td></tr>
</table>

The reconstituted family

<table>
<tr><td>

Definition

Reconstituted family – a family which has at least one step-parent

</td><td>

This **reconstituted family** term refers to families which are composed of individuals forming new relationships and bringing with them dependent children from a previous relationship. Reconstituted families may be formed by divorce or the break-up of a previous relationship or where a lone parent forms a new relationship. The result is an increase in the numbers of families which are headed by step-mothers and step-fathers.

</td></tr>
</table>

The family situation may be further complicated when the couple have their own, 'joint' children. About six million people live in reconstituted families in Britain today, and about 1 in 10 children live with step-parents.

As soon as a 'nuclear family' mould is broken, the nature of the relationships that constitute 'family' are opened to question. If a man comes to live with a divorced woman who has three children, does his mother become their grandmother? Can he, himself, be their stepfather if there is no marriage? If so, how long must he be in residence before he graduates into that role from being the mother's lover? And if there is a marriage, does he, the step-father, remain part of the children's family if their mother divorces him? Policies based on the old, neat categories of 'marriage' and 'divorce' simply do not fit today's world.

Source: P. Hewitt and P. Leach, *Social Justice, Children and Families* (Commission on Social Justice, 1993)

Family diversity

We can see then that over time a range of family types or structures have emerged and declined. However, these main types are made more complicated by the fact that variations have emerged within them. For example, the experience of extended families may vary greatly depending upon such things as social class background, ethnic and cultural influences, how and where people live and what their sexual orientation is.

This is complicated to explain, but easier to give examples of, so we will simply move on to look at these forms of family diversity.

The main factors influencing the diversity of family forms are:

- social status
- ethnicity or culture
- sexual orientation
- location.

Social status

Although social class is arguably in decline, it is still true that there is a wide variety of values and financial differences between people in contemporary Britain. These will have a strong influence on the experiences of families. So, Young and Willmott found, in their 1950s study, a vibrant extended working-class family but, by the late 1980s, Willmott showed how this had changed to a more flexible, looser arrangement. The middle-class family is still more likely to take the nuclear form with less direct contact between members.

These social class differences seem partially caused by rather greater emphasis on geographical mobility (prepared to move house away from their origin) amongst the middle class in their search for career advancement.

Ethnicity and cultural belief

<table>
<tr><td>

Definition

Stereotype – to exaggerate differences between one group and another so that these differences are made to seem more important than the similarities. A problem with all research into social class and ethnicity
</td></tr>
</table>

It is important not to **stereotype** families and individuals by ethnic background. However, there are differences by ethnic background. For example:

- South Asian families (those of Indian, Pakistani or Bangladeshi origin) tend to be larger than average and live in households of two or more families.
- They are also less likely to live in lone-parent households than those classified by the Government's Office for National Statistics as 'White' or 'Black'. Whereas 22 per cent of white families are lone parents, the figure is only 9 per cent for Indians and 17 per cent for Pakistani/Bangladeshi families. The figures for those classified as 'Black' indicate that 55 per cent of these families are headed by lone parents.

Whatever views are held about morality or whether lone parents are a social problem, the point emerges that there are cultural differences which impact upon the structure and life experiences of families.

Sexual orientation

In many ways this is one of the most challenging aspects of changing ideas of the family. Gay and lesbian partners have increasingly demanded the right to undergo 'marriage' ceremonies, claiming that the law ought to be altered to enable them to do so. Gay and lesbian couples are also seeking to have their own families through adoption and artificial insemination. Whatever society's views on these changes, they do represent a strong challenge to the traditional heterosexual view of marriage and the family.

Location

Relatively little research has been carried out to examine the significance of location for the family, but where a person lives is an important influence on their lives and family types do vary by region, depending partially upon ethnic mix, social class and regional values. Some examples of this are the larger size of families in the Midlands; the higher proportion of lone parents in London and the lower proportion of cohabitation in the north of England.

Varieties of family in Britain

Immigration has brought a number of family forms to Britain that are clearly different from traditional patterns. Such families put a much greater emphasis on the demands and duties of kinship.

Asian families are a clear example of this. Ballard argues that the basic pattern of a south Asian family consists of a man, his son and grandsons, together with their wives and unmarried daughters. This family has been transferred into a British setting. The man is clearly the head of the household, controlling the family finances and negotiating the major family decisions.

The male dominated nature of family life creates a very different experience for women within the ethnic minorities. In the early years of immigration, many women found themselves cut off from outside society.

Social and language barriers kept them trapped in the home. Some Asian families created a state of Purdah [the woman must keep herself covered and is allowed no contact with men outside the family].

The reason for the attempt by (these) ethnic minorities to control the lives of women is the need to maintain family honour. Every member should be seen to behave properly.

Serious problems have been created with the second generation, the immigrants' children who were born and have been brought up in the United Kingdom. School teaches these children to want more independence, as opposed to the family stress on loyalty and obedience. It must also be remembered that many of the first generation immigrants grew up in societies where there was no such thing as adolescence or youth culture, so conflict is inevitable when their children act like British teenagers.

Families of African-Caribbean origin in Britain present a further distinct family pattern that reflects their culture of origin. The colonial system based on slavery weakened the bonds between men and women. The lack of stable employment later left the man unable to support a family by his own efforts. The mother–child relationship became the central structure of the family. Driver suggests that there are two types of black family structure in Britain. There is the nuclear family, where both partners share the full range of domestic tasks. But there is also the mother-centred family. The black mother is left to bring up the children, run the home and provide income. She must do this in England without the range of support that she could have obtained from female relatives in the West Indies. This is caused by the lack of stable employment for men.

Source: A. Wilson, *The Family* (Tavistock, 1985)

1 From the description of the South Asian family, would you call it nuclear or extended?

2 Who is the clear head of the South Asian family? Give two reasons for your answer.

3 Describe the situation of women in the more traditional South Asian family.

4 Why should there be 'serious problems' for the Asian family 'created with the second generation'?

5 The extract suggests that there are two patterns of families from African-Caribbean origins in Britain. What are they?

6 What reasons does the extract suggest for the growth of the two different types of African-Caribbean origin family?

Main points ▶ It is difficult to talk about 'the family' as it varies so greatly.

▶ To help us understand this, it is useful to look at the family as having a number of *structural forms*, which vary according to how many people are considered family members and what their relationships are. These forms are
   – extended
   – nuclear
   – lone parent
   – reconstituted.

▶ But these in turn vary in diverse ways – affected by a range of social factors which include
   – social status
   – ethnic background
   – cultural and religious beliefs
   – the place where people live.

Changing family forms

Before **industrialisation**, when most people obtained their living from the land, people lived for a relatively short time – a typical person in seventeenth-century England would expect to die in their early 40s. They apparently married and had children fairly late in their lives. The result was that it was unusual for a family of three generations (children, parents and grandparents) to live together, simply because the chances of people surviving to the age of being grandparents were slim.

What was common was that families of parents, children and their spouses often lived close to one another and had frequent contact. Households were often large, not because there were extended families living together, but because it was common practice in pre-industrial Britain for the better-off to take the children of the poor as servants, or helpers. When they grew up, they left their adopted 'home' to look for better employment. So for most people, the nuclear family was normal, but people lived nearer to one another and had greater contact than today.

The better-off were more likely to live in extended families because:

- they had longer life expectancies, caused by better diets and less work
- family members were more likely to stay at home as their parents could provide for them, with land and jobs.

The pre-industrial family

Two famous studies overturned the belief, held by most sociologists, that most families in Britain were of the extended type before industrialisation, as was normal throughout most of Europe.

Laslett, in *The World We Have Lost*, studied the parish records of births, marriages and deaths of 100 English villages from the sixteenth century to the nineteenth century. He found that most households throughout this period had an average size of 4.75 persons (for example, parents and three children). In other words, the normal family type throughout this period appears to be the nuclear family.

Anderson, in *Family Structure in Nineteenth-Century Lancashire*, studied the Census material for Preston, Lancashire in 1851. He found that there was an increase in the size of the family at about this time and explains this by saying that the increase in jobs provided by industrialisation meant that more distant relatives were attracted to the town and came to live with the families already there. Some stayed at home to look after the children and some worked in factories. The result was a type of community and family structure similar to that found in East London in the early 1950s, which has now died out.

Questions

1 What was the most common family type in pre-industrial England – extended or nuclear?
2 Why did the studies by Laslett and Anderson change sociologists' ideas about the family before industrialisation?
3 What happened to working-class families and communities with the growth of industrialisation?
4 What type of family was most common in Europe before industrialisation?

The effects of industrialisation on family form in Britain

For the poor, the effects of industrialisation on the family structure were considerable. Jobs in agriculture declined and those in factories expanded rapidly so that people were forced to move into towns. Long hours of work, in dreadful conditions, with low pay and no form of welfare state meant that the extended family became a very useful way of pooling resources in times of need or illness. Also, after the early stages of industrialisation were over, life expectancy increased. So, by the middle of the nineteenth century, the extended family had become common amongst the working class and this form of 'self-help' continued well into the twentieth century.

Gradually, better conditions of life and the activities of the Welfare State eroded the mutual need that had created the industrial extended family and there has been a move towards the nuclear family. Contact with wider kin is maintained though, through the use of telephones and cars. This means that a family does not have to live together to keep in contact.

For the middle class, the extended family was normal in the nineteenth century. The main reason for this was nepotism, that is jobs and income were obtained through the father. The younger generation stayed at home because it was in their financial interests to do so, and middle-class women were trapped at home because it was not considered right for them to work.

Early in the twentieth century, there was a move towards the nuclear family, as the younger generation were able to find their own jobs. Cultural stress on the close relationship between husband, wife and children increased, to the exclusion of the wider kin. So small nuclear families developed. The increase in geographical mobility has also been an influence on both the middle and working classes, leading to nuclear-style families. To find work in modern societies, it is necessary to move. The smaller, nuclear family, with its looser ties to kin, allows people to move more easily.

The extended family: alive and well in Britain

In the mid-1980s Peter Willmott studied family life in North London. He expected to find isolated families, but in fact he found the extended family to have altered in form, but still to be vibrant. He concluded that there were three types of extended family which encompassed most kinship arrangements in Britain.

The first type is the *local extended family*. Typically two or perhaps three nuclear families in separate households – parents and their married children, typically daughters, with their own children – live near each other. They see each other every day or nearly every day, and they provide mutual aid on a continuing basis. This kind of arrangement probably still applies to something like one in eight of the adult population of Britain. It is more common among working-class families than middle class, in stable communities than in those marked by residential mobility or redevelopment, and in the north of England, the Midlands, Scotland and Wales rather than in southern England.

The second type, and the one that is now becoming dominant, is the *dispersed extended family*. Like the local extended family, this is composed of two or more nuclear families, again typically made up of parents and their married children, with their children. The big difference is that it is not localised and the meetings are consequently less frequent. Nonetheless, there is still fairly frequent contact, say once a week or once a fortnight, and support is still provided both in emergency and on a regular basis. Such an arrangement depends on cars (or a good public transport service) and on telephones. This pattern is probably more common in middle-class circles than in working-class ones. The evidence on contacts suggests that this second type probably operates for about half the adult population.

On these estimates, this leaves under half the population for whom kinship is less important. Their type of arrangement might be called the *attenuated extended family*. The people concerned include students and other young people, both those who are single and young couples before they have any children of their own. They are at a stage when they are, as they need to be, breaking away from their family of origin – when kinship matters less, and their age peers more, than at any other phase in life.

Source: P. Willmott, 'Urban kinship past and present', *Social Studies Review*, November 1988

Using information from the extract, copy and complete this table.

Types of extended family	Proportion of population	Characteristics	Differences from traditional extended families

Two views of the contemporary extended family

Small families are only one reason for the lack of support networks. Even where exceptionally large families exist and have extensive kin-networks intact, they are often too geographically dispersed [spread out over the country] to be useful to each other on a day to day basis.

And even where relatives do still live closely together, the adults of both generations [may be working] so that the presence of a grandmother, aunt or sister just down the street is no guarantee of help, and parents may not even seek it.

Source: Adapted from P. Hewitt and P. Leach, *Social Justice, Children and Families* (Commission on Social Justice, 1993)

1 What three reasons are there for a lack of support between people today?

2 Do you think this lack of support is true for your family? Read the next extract and see whether it reflects your experience more.

But that is not the end of the story. If one looks, in the 1980s, not at the proximity [closeness] of relatives, but at contacts between them, a different picture comes into focus. A number of recent surveys have shown that between about two-thirds and three-quarters of people – people of all ages, not just the elderly – still see at least one relative at least once a week. I recently completed a study of married people with young children in a North London suburb, a district where as many as a third of the couples had moved in within the previous five years. There, the proportion seeing relatives at least weekly was precisely two-thirds. Of those with parents alive, one in ten saw their mother or father or both every day, and nearly two-thirds of living parents and parents-in-law were seen at least once a month. Working-class people saw rather more of their parents and other relatives than middle-class people did, but the differences were not large.

The evidence from that and other recent studies also shows that relatives continue to be the main source of informal support and care, and that again the class differences are not marked. In my North London research, nearly two-thirds of people were helped by relatives, particularly mothers or mothers-in-law, when one of the children was ill; nearly three-quarters were helped with babysitting, again mainly by mothers or mothers-in-law. Four-fifths looked to relatives, mainly parents or parents-in-law, when they needed to borrow money. Surveys of elderly people show that most of the informal help and care they receive comes from relatives, particularly their children or children-in-law.

So, despite a decline in the proportions of people living with or very near to relatives, kinship remains an important force in the lives of most people.

Source: P. Willmott, 'Urban kinship past and present', *Social Studies Review*, November 1988

This extract, describing research in the mid-1980s, tells a different story from the first extract.

1 Does Willmott see the family as being actively helpful?

2 Give three examples of the help he mentions.

3 In your opinion, which extract describes life in Britain today?

The family and technological change: a summary

	The pre-industrial family	Industrialisation and the family	The family today
Structure	Mainly nuclear families, but the better-off had larger households, as people came to stay with them; late marriage; small families because of the high death-rate of children	Working-class families – became extended as numbers of children increased because of higher child survival rates (results of medical improvements) and people crowded into limited housing available in towns Middle-class families – became extended, as younger generation remained at home until they were economically free to leave and set up own house	Nuclear families, with connections by telephone/car to wider kin (although) Asian families are extended)
Relationships	Not very close or warm; marriage and child-rearing mainly for economic reasons; idea of 'love' is unusual	Working-class – children close to mother; father and mother not close at all; women oppressed by men Middle-class – children not close to parent; father–mother, cold relationship; women oppressed by men	Close family relationships, the 'privatised' family; husband and wife fairly equal, 'symmetrical'; but women still expected to be responsible for domestic matters; children are seen as extremely important
Functions	Family very important as all worked together in the home or on the farm; family looked after its members if they survived to old age	Working-class – family very important to survival; pooling of economic resources; helped each other where possible in all matters; older generation looked after by younger generation	Mainly emotional, but still practical and financial help (loans, etc.) when needed; state and voluntary services assist or replace the family in many of its functions
Wider setting	Agricultural society, people living in the countryside in small villages 	Industrialised society, people living in large towns 	A mobile family moving for promotion and to take job opportunities; people living in suburbs; light industry and offices are places of work

Main points ▸ The family has changed over time.

▸ The influence of industrialisation has been particularly important.

▸ This helped to create extended families and later helped to break up the traditional form of extended family.

▸ Today the nuclear family dominates, but people still keep in touch with other family members.

▸ There are variations in closeness, according to social class.

The role of the family in society

It is not that absurd to claim that the family forms the cornerstone of our society. Indeed, a world without the family would seem strange to us. However, there is considerable disagreement between sociologists about whether the family is a good thing (the beneficial view) or actually harmful (the critical view).

The functions of the family

Isaac Shapera studied the life of the Kgatla tribe in South Africa in the early 1930s.

The household usually consists of a man with his wife, or wives, and dependent children, but often includes other people as well. ... They live, eat, work and play together, consult and help one another in all personal difficulties and share in one another's good fortune. They produce most of their own food and material needs; ... they are the group within which children are born, reared and trained in conduct and methods of work and they perform the ceremonies connected with birth, marriage, death and other ritual occasions.

The family gets its food by growing corn, breeding animals and collecting wild plants which can be eaten ... [and] it builds its own huts. In all these activities everybody except the infants take part, men, women and children having special jobs according to sex and age. The women and girls till the fields, build and repair the walls of the huts, prepare food and beer, look after the chickens and fetch water, wood (for fires) and collect wild plants. The men and boys herd the cattle, hunt and do all the building.

Source: Adapted from I. Shapera, *Married Life in an African Tribe* (Penguin, 1971)

1 Who lives in the household?

2 Name four things that the family does together.

3 Amongst the Kgatla, being invited to certain ceremonies indicates who is regarded as most important to the person involved in the ceremony. What does this tell us about the family?

4 Some people have described the pre-industrial family as an 'economic unit'. What do you think they mean by this? Use the extract to illustrate your answer.

5 Write a brief description, or draw a diagram, to indicate the tasks of the family in Britain today. Would you say it is as important today, as in the past?

The beneficial view of the family

The role of the family in small-scale agricultural or hunting societies was absolutely central. Indeed, in many cases the tribe was really a few extended families joined together. Individuals were taught the skills necessary to survive, were given work and received status and authority in the wider tribe according to their position in the family.

Industrialisation, urbanisation (the growth of cities) and the sheer numbers of people in society have altered the position of the family in modern society. But it still remains an extremely important social institution which fundamentally influences the course of our lives. The family acts as the link between the individual and society and, according to the beneficial view, it benefits both.

The analysis of the role of the family outlined below is generally associated with the functionalist school of thought in sociology. This approach usually examines any social institution, such as the family or education system, by asking the question: What function does this social institution perform for society?

Asking this sort of question usually leads these sociologists to stress the beneficial aspects of the institution under question, and to underplay the harmful aspects, so the family is seen as giving such things as love and affection.

The functions of the family in the beneficial view are:

- socialisation
- emotional stability
- economic provision
- reproduction and sexual activity
- identity.

Socialisation

The individual

In order for a person to become truly 'human', that is to act in socially acceptable ways, an individual must be socialised (see Chapter 1). This is the basic role a family performs for individuals, moulding them to the expectations of society. Only through this can a person a play a full part in social life.

Society

Society cannot exist without rules and expectations of behaviour. A society full of unpredictable individuals would simply collapse in chaos. The family socialises children into correct forms of behaviour. If children (or adults) fall out of step with society in some way, the family is usually the first place where punishment takes place, so the family not only socialises, but also acts as an agent of social control.

Emotional stability

The individual

Young children need to be shown care and affection to become stable adults. The family is ideally the place where this affection is freely given. Even for adults, there is a need for people to discuss their problems and to feel needed. At its best, the family can keep a person emotionally fulfilled and stable.

Society

If society is to continue, then people must be motivated to carry on and not to drop out. By giving people a reason to work, to uphold the rules of society and to conform, the family effectively ensures the continuation of society.

Economic provision

The individual

Young children need to be supported until they reach the age of self-sufficiency. The family provides for them and for adults who are not working through incapacity or unemployment. All aid from the state is channelled through the family to individuals.

Society

The modern family does not work together producing goods as in pre-industrial times, but today families do consume as a unit. Clothing, food and household items all make the family a major agency of spending in our society and, therefore, it is still very important economically.

Reproduction and sexual activity

The individual

Although sexual activity is common outside marriage, for most people regular sexual activity is limited to their husband/wife, or the person they intend to marry. As a result of this pattern of sexual activity, most of us are born into families.

Society

A society can only exist if there are people. Quite simply families produce the people who compose each generation. If unregulated, sexual activity causes problems of jealousy and conflict. By having a culture which stresses that the correct place for sex is within permanent relationships, much conflict is eliminated.

Identity

The individual

Being born into a family gives an individual identity – a name, a background and a social class position.

Society

Families promote social order by locating people along class and status lines. Individuals know where they belong, where others are in terms of social status, and their own position with regard to them.

Activity

Copy the diagram below and write a summary of each issue in the boxes.

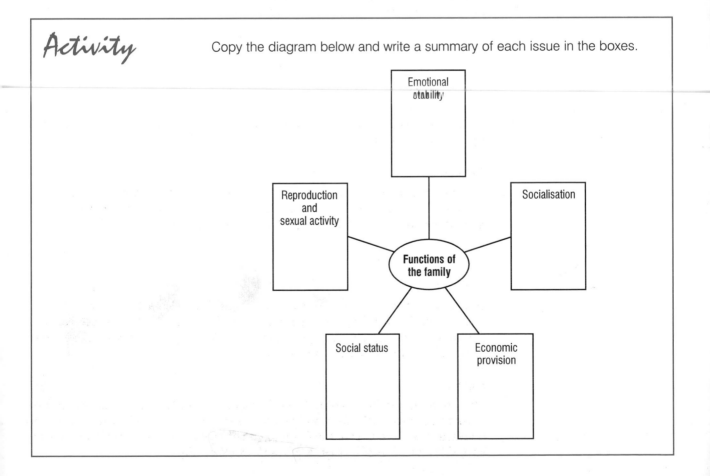

The critical view

Definition

Feminist approach to sociology – a perspective which argues that much traditional sociology is the study of society from the man's point of view and by looking at it from a woman's viewpoint a whole range of findings of traditional sociology are brought into question, and a set of new questions also emerge

Other sociologists, particularly **feminist** writers, have argued that the functionalist view of the family is mistaken. Instead, they claim, the family has many aspects which are harmful to its members – particularly women and children. They list a number of unpleasant elements of family life which are ignored by functionalist sociologists. These include:

- domestic violence
- child abuse
- emotional harm
- the exploitation of women.

Domestic violence

Home is where the ~~heart~~ ... violence is

The home is, in fact, the most dangerous place in modern society. In statistical terms, a person of any age or of either sex is far more likely to be subject to physical attack in the home than on the street at night. One in four murders in the UK is committed by one family member against another.

Source: A. Giddens, *Sociology* (Polity Press, 1993)

Domestic violence is almost always violence by the male partner on the female. The extent of domestic violence is not known for certain, but one accurate piece of research by Mooney of violence in North London suggests that as many as 10 per cent of women had been assaulted in their homes by their partners. Over their lifetime, Mooney also claimed that about 25 per cent of women were subjected to some form of violence by other family members. The British Crime Survey (a government study of crime levels) suggests that only about 50 per cent of those attacked ever report it to the police because of:

- fear of their partner
- embarrassment
- the belief that they may be partly to blame for their partner's violence.

'Sometimes he gets in a real rage and just lashes out if he finds me "cheeking" him. I really should learn to hold my tongue – after all he's not a bad bloke really.'

Victim of violence, explaining her decision to stay with violent partner.

Child abuse

Abuse against children takes four main forms – physical, emotional, sexual and neglect. Clearly they overlap, as any one can accompany the others. The NSPCC has suggested that there may be as many as 1.5 million children in Britain suffering from one or more types of abuse.

Violence and changing views of parenting

What constitutes 'abuse' varies over time, with no fixed standard. The 1998 Human Rights Act, for example, may well be interpreted as banning all physical punishment, including slapping children. In 1999 a Scottish sheriff's court ruled that a father used 'excessive' force when he slapped his daughter after she refused to be injected at a dentist's surgery.

What do you think? Are there occasions when you regard it as acceptable for parents to smack their children?

Emotional harm

The intense emotional ties of the nuclear family can lead to forms of psychological damage and emotional hurt. Constant conflict between parents has been linked to later psychological problems in the children and, in turn, they are more likely to have higher rates of divorce later in life.

Unhappy families

Children of divorced or separated parents run twice the risk of suffering problems ranging from poor performance at school to psychiatric disorder later in life, a definitive assessment of all available research today concludes.

But many such problems will stem not from parental separation but from the conflict preceding it, according to [the] experts. ...

The experts' conclusion is that deeply unhappy couples should stay together 'for the sake of the children' only if they can protect them from the effects of the misery and feuding. Otherwise separation may be the better option.

Source: *The Guardian*, 24 June 1998

According to the extract, what effect does parents arguing have on the children?

The exploitation of women

Finally, feminist writers have constantly pointed out the unfairness of family life to women. It is women who have their careers interrupted by childbirth and women who carry the main responsibility for childcare. Women are therefore more likely to be financially dependent on their partners, which gives them less power over decision-making in family matters.

The loving family?

At least 750,000 children in Britain may suffer long-term trauma because they are exposed to domestic violence, a survey published yesterday suggests.

Many develop sleeping problems, become anxious, aggressive or withdrawn, and find it difficult to form close relationships as a result, the researchers say.

The survey, by NCH Action for Children, is based on a poll of 108 mothers with 246 children, who had suffered domestic violence. It is the first to examine the effects of domestic violence on youngsters. It found that:

- Three out of four women questioned said their children had seen violent incidents, and almost two-thirds of the children had seen their mothers beaten.
- One in 10 women reported having been raped in front of her children.
- All claimed their children were aware of violence.
- Almost three in 10 mothers said their violent partner had also beaten their children.
- One in three said their children had developed bed-wetting problems, while nearly one in three said the youngsters had become violent and aggressive. Three in 10 had problems at school.

The survey also shows that children witness violence over long periods. On average, the relationships the study described as violent lasted seven years.

Tom White, director of NCH Action for Children, said domestic violence was the second most common violent crime reported to police in Britain, and made up more than 25 per cent of all reported violent crime.

The researchers estimate one in 100 marriages is characterised by severe and repeated violence, affecting at least 750,000 children each year.

Source: *The Guardian*, 6 December 1994

1 Domestic violence is usually viewed only as a feminist issue. How does this extract broaden the problem?

2 How many marriages are estimated to be characterised by severe violence?

3 How many children does this affect?

4 What other problems does the research show up?

5 Look carefully at the statistics given in the article and the size of the sample. What comments can you make?

Main points ▶ There are two views on the role of the family in society.

▶ The first of these views, associated with the functionalist perspective is that the family is beneficial to all its members. The family provides a number of functions including socialisation, emotional stability, economic security, reproduction of the species (and a controlled sexual outlet), identity.

▶ An opposing stance is taken by feminists and other critics who argue the family can be harmful to some of its members. They point out that these harmful aspects include domestic violence, child abuse, emotional harm, the exploitation of women.

The lone-parent family

One of the most biggest changes in the family in the last 25 years has been the steady growth in the number of lone-parent (or single-parent) families. In the last ten years alone, there has been an increase of 30 per cent in their number. Today, almost one quarter of all families with children are headed by a lone parent – almost always a women.

In 2000, there were over 1.5 million lone-parent families in Britain, with about 2.8 million children living in such families. About 14 per cent of lone mothers had never married nor lived with a partner. A further 14 per cent had cohabited once, and 48 per cent had been married once.

Lone parents: a moral debate

Definition

New Right – a political and academic approach to understanding society which stresses that the government (which is paid for by hard-working tax payers) should not have to support people who have through their own decisions either chosen not to work or made themselves unemployable

Since the 1990s there has been very considerable debate over the effects of lone-parent families on society. There are two quite distinct approaches to the lone-parent family.

- One approach is associated with the academic and political movement of the **New Right**. These writers are very critical of the growth of one type of lone-parent family – where the mother has never married – and argue that it has been directly responsible for a range of social problems. Never married mothers are seen as a good example of people who have chosen to make themselves unemployable by their own actions. Why should the government look after them by taxing other people?

- On the other hand, liberal and feminist writers have leapt to the defence of lone mothers.

Source: *The Sunday Times*, 11 July 1993

Question What image does the cartoon on the left give of single mothers? In your opinion, is this true?

The New Right attack on lone mothers

The New Right argues that (never married) lone mothers who are reliant upon the government for financial aid bear a strong responsibility for helping to undermine the values of society. In particular, they argue that children are harmed because there is no father to provide financial support and to help socialise the child into the normal values of society.

Furthermore, the reliance upon state aid means that the traditional responsibilities of the male have been taken away. This has led to a generation of young men in inner cities and large-scale social housing developments who have no responsibilities and who are therefore more likely to turn to anti-social behaviour. With no family to support and the availability of social security payments, they see no need to work. Similarly, the mothers have no incentive to work as they too receive government support and very often receive priority for housing.

Some writers have suggested that this has helped form an **underclass** of people who simply do not want to work, and who bring up their children to think in the same way.

Families with dependent children

Families with dependent children: an analysis, Great Britain 1998–9

	Percentages
Lone mother	
Single (never married)	9
Widowed	1
Divorced	8
Separated	5
All lone mothers	22
Lone father	2
Married/cohabiting couple	75
All families with dependent children	100

Source: Adapted from *Social Trends 30* (The Stationery Office, 2000)

1 What percentage of all families are headed by lone mothers?

2 What is the largest group of lone mothers?

3 What percentage of all lone parent families are headed by a father?

Reasons for growth in the number of lone-parent families:
- divorce, separation, death of partner
- women not wishing to marry when pregnant.

Definition

Scapegoating – blaming certain
groups of poorer or less powerful
people for problems in society,
instead of seeking out the real
cause

Defence of the lone-parent family

Feminists defend the lone-parent family by pointing out that:

- the huge majority of lone mothers (92 per cent) claim not to have become pregnant deliberately and it is an unforgiving society which punishes them and their children by refusing to give them state benefits
- for many young women, the lone-parent family was more likely to provide safety and security than the two-parent household, given rates of violence and abuse by men against women and children
- there is no real evidence for the existence of a separate 'underclass' with people intent upon avoiding work. This is a myth which **scapegoats** young people for the problems of society.

Main points ▸ There is a bitter debate over the never-married lone parents.

▸ The New Right argue that the growth of the lone-parent family is a bad thing which has helped to undermine social values and costs taxpayers an unfair amount in benefit payments.

▸ Feminist and liberal writers disagree and argue that the lone-parent family is better than the violence and abuse of many two-parent families. They also point out that if benefits were not paid to the lone-parent families, it would be the children who would suffer.

Alternatives to the family

Critics of the family have long sought an alternative that would provide the beneficial aspects of economic and emotional security, without the restrictions on freedom that the family normally imposes.

Abolition of the family

The first, and obvious, solution is to abolish the family completely. The two best known attempts to abolish family life were in Russia after the communist revolution of 1917, and the activities of the revolutionary Khmer Rouge which took over in Cambodia in the 1970s.

In both cases, the family was seen as the link that perpetuated the values of the old society. If the new communist society was to succeed, the younger generation had to be brought up with a new set of values. Family life and marriage were weakened and children encouraged to see the state as their 'family', rather than their own kin.

In Russia, the abolition of the family resulted in chaos, with an increase in crime, in deserted children and social problems in general. The state simply could not cope with people as individuals. It needed the organisational unit of the family. Soon, the family was re-introduced in Russia and even promoted as the ideal way to live.

The Khmer Rouge regime collapsed and has been replaced by a society which stresses family life.

Communes

The second alternative to the family is the commune, that is a group of people living together who generally share their possessions and treat children as 'belonging' to the whole commune, not just to their parents. A number of communes exist in Britain today, usually based on religious ideals. However, probably the most famous form of commune is the *kibbutz* of Israel, although only 2 per cent of the population actually live in these communes. *Kibbutzim* are generally agricultural-based, with some element of industry. Jobs are allocated on a rota (so everybody does 'good' and 'bad' work) and, rather than wages, each *kibbutz* provides for all the wants of its members. Marriage is not regarded as important; couples can simply share rooms if they wish. Children themselves do not usually live with their parents but with others of their own age group in dormitories, simply sharing the evening meal with their parents if they want. According to the *kibbutz* philosophy, children should not see themselves as possessions of their parents but as independent members of the *kibbutz*.

Questions

1 What do you think about the idea of a commune?
2 Would you live in one with your friends?
3 What would your attitudes be to sexual relationships?
4 Who would look after the children?
5 What would happen if you had a difference of opinion? How would you sort it out?
6 How would you organise the finances?
7 Do you see any other problems?

Main points ▸ Alternatives to the family have been tried.
▸ These include abolishing the family completely and communes.
▸ However, there remains some doubt over how effective or long-lasting these alternatives are.

Marriage and cohabitation

A comparison of marriage types

In Britain, we regard marriage as the 'union of a man and a woman'. However this is not the only type of marriage in the world. Below are some of the varieties of marriage that exist.

General types	Name	Description		Where?	Why?
Monogamy	Monogamy		One man married to one woman	Europe today Japan	A balance between males and females, with a cultural stress on the relative equality of male and female; Christian culture
	Serial Monogamy		Couples marry, divorce, then re-marry different partners	USA Britain Europe	Decline in the sanctity of marriage: not seen as lasting a lifetime: associated with increase in divorce; secular culture
Polygamy	Polyandry	or more	One woman married to a number of men	Parts of Tibet	Restricts numbers of children so keeps population low; useful in agricultural societies with limited amount of land
	Polygyny	or more	One man married to a number of women	Acceptable amongst Mormons of Utah, USA. Some Muslim local societies	Maximises possible number of children: important in societies with a high death-rate; possibly linked to imbalance of sexes (too many females): Muslim and Mormon cultures

Polygyny

It is widely believed that polygyny (having more than one wife) originated in response to the social and economic needs of rural African societies. It provided as many hands as possible to cultivate the land, and fight against high infant mortality. Children in Africa are believed to increase the prestige, wealth and social status of the family, and are thus always welcome. Yet polygyny was transferred almost intact to the cities among rich and poor, workers and intellectuals alike. … In Senegal, 32 per cent of men had two or more wives. However, urban polygyny is difficult to justify in terms of salaries and costs. Salaries are low, families are large and few individuals within families are breadwinners (because of unemployment).

Marianne Diop is 56; she works as a secretary in a hospital. Her husband is a retired postman. Mr Diop has married four wives in all, fathered 22 children and divorced twice. He now shares his life with second and third wives, Marianne and Anjinata. They live in different houses but within walking distance.

Mr Diop only involves himself in crises, like the birth of an illegitimate child to his daughter. The everyday needs of the children are the mother's concern.

It would be unfair to portray Mr Diop as a selfish indifferent man. But with two wives, two households and 22 children, it is not difficult to understand why he does not find enough time for all. Some children are neglected, while others are favoured; some receive enough support and guidance, others very little. It is the institution of polygyny which creates these conditions.

Source: Adapted from D. Topouzis, 'The men with many wives', *New Society*, 4 October 1985

1 What does polygyny mean?

2 What reasons does the author suggest for its origins?

3 Have people in cities abandoned polygyny?

4 Who do you think benefits more from polygynous marriage?

5 What is the relationship between Mr Diop and his children?

6 What comparisons can you make between the typical British family and the polygynous one of Senegal?

7 How does the extract illustrate the way that culture changes more slowly than technological and economic situations?

And in Britain

A 'cad' who was married to three women at the same time was jailed for eight months yesterday after being convicted of bigamy.

Passing sentence on Michael Thomas, aged 44 at Reading crown court, Assistant Recorder Humphrey Malins told him: "A civilised society must not permit men to treat women in this way.

This is an affront to the institution of marriage.

"To use an old fashioned and perhaps underused phrase, you were a cad."

The crime came to light when Mr Thomas's latest wife found a set of incomplete divorce papers. She approached the police, who found he was already married – not once, but twice.

Source: *The Guardian*, 10 September 1994

1 Compare the two extracts above. What do they tell you about culture and ideas on marriage?

2 Do you think that it is right for a person to have two partners at the same time?

The importance of marriage in pre-industrial societies

The anthropologist, Levi-Strauss, met, among the Bororo of Central Brazil,

– a man about thirty years old … unclean, ill-fed, sad and lonesome. When asked if the man was seriously ill the natives' answer came as a shock: What was wrong with him? – nothing at all, he was just a bachelor, and true enough, in a society where labour is … shared between men and women and where

only the married status permits the man to benefit from the fruits of woman's work, including delousing, body painting, and hair plucking as well as vegetable food and cooked food (since the Bororo woman tills the soil and makes pots), a bachelor is really only half a human being.

Source: G. Hurd *et al.*, *Human Societies: An Introduction to Sociology* (Routledge & Kegan Paul, 1986)

1 Describe the man Levi-Strauss met amongst the Bororo.

2 What was 'wrong' with him?

3 What is the advantage of 'married status'?

4 What are our attitudes to unmarried middle-aged men? Give reasons for your reply.

5 What does your reply to question 4 tell you about the importance of marriage and attitudes to sexuality in our society today?

Why arranged marriages can suit modern women

The rules of arranged marriage have changed. Samina Saeed, editor of the newly launched *Asian Woman and Bride*, explains how.

There's a whole new form of arranged marriages emerging for today's young people. In many families, the couple will be introduced at the girl's home, then they will go out as a couple and arrange to meet up again if they get on. Married friends I know have played Cupid by setting up a date between a younger sister and a man they think she would be interested in. Then all the family meet in a dinner party type situation. It's a sort of combination of arranged marriage and westernised blind date – but I have known it to work.

Of course, arranged marriages aren't for everyone. But I think there's a lot to be said for them, especially the modern ones where there is a great deal of choice. Where else would you be introduced to a man your parents had specifically selected, someone with a similar background and family situation? Most people would argue that marriages stand a better chance of working if both people are from similar backgrounds, have similar outlooks and whose families get on with each other. Arranged marriages are a way of ensuring that.

Your family will also be checking that the man they have chosen has a good education, a job and reasonable prospects. But that's just what happens in non-Asian families all the time – your parents will always want to weed out partners they think are not right.

Source: *The Daily Express*, 15 June 2000, Internet edition

1 What are the advantages of an arranged marriage compared to the 'falling in love' marriage?

2 Which do you think is likely to be more stable?

3 Which type of marriage would you prefer?

Male inmates at a prison in Sao Paulo kiss their new wives during Brazil's first mass prison wedding. The 120 brides had to arrive two hours early so they could be thorougly searched.

The decline of marriage?

There is a widely-held belief that the institution of marriage is crumbling in Britain. People who support this argument point to:

- the numbers of lone-parent families, usually headed by a woman who, we have seen, compose almost 25 per cent of all families with dependent children
- the increasing numbers of people preferring to **cohabit**
- the continual decline in people marrying, with 85,000 fewer couples marrying compared to 25 years ago
- the most damning piece of evidence, the large increase in divorce which began to take place in the early 1970s and which continues today.

However, there is evidence to suggest that there still some life left in the institution of marriage. As we shall see in the next section on cohabitation, it appears that although people cohabit in much greater numbers than previously, they are still likely to marry at some stage in their relationship, particularly after the birth of children.

Fewer women and men are marrying and when they do marry, it tends to be when they are older. However, the majority of the British population will marry at some point (on current trends it is likely to be between 75 and 80 per cent), and at present 60 per cent of all adults are married (the rest are single, cohabiting, widowed or divorced).

> **Definitions**
>
> **Cohabitation** – partners with or without children, who are sharing a household but not married to each other

Marriages and divorces

Marriages and divorces, United Kingdom

1 For both partners.   2 Includes annulments.   3 For one or both partners.
Source: Office for National Statistics; General Register Office for Scotland;
Northern Ireland Statistics and Research Agency

Source: *Social Trends 30* (The Stationery Office, 2000)

1 In what year were first marriages at their highest?

2 What has happened since then?

3 How many thousand remarriages were there in 1997?

4 What has happened to the numbers of remarriages?

5 What pattern of divorce has emerged since 1961?

Reasons for the decrease in marriage

There appear to be two, linked factors affecting the decrease in marriage. The first of these is the increase in the age of first marriage – since 1971, the average age of first marriage has increased by approximately 5 years. Today the average age of marriage is 28 for men and 26 for women. The delay is partially linked to longer partici-pation in education and consequently later entry into work, but much more important has been the increase in cohabi-tation amongst the British population.

Of those couples involved in remarriage (for at least one partner), there does not seem to be a rejection of marriage, as approximately 22 per cent of individuals who separate from their partners marry again within three years (General Household Survey). This popularity may not be as high for the never-married. At present in the UK cohabitation appears to be a stage before marriage, but if the trends in the Scandinavian countries are followed here, it may well develop into an alternative to marriage itself.

1 What two reasons are causing the decline in marriage?

2 What alternative to marriage is increasing? What might happen in the future?

Cohabitation

What's the point of getting married to someone if you haven't lived with them? You don't know what they're like, do you.

Source: Quoted in P. Abbott and C. Wallace, *An Introduction to Sociology: Feminist Perspectives* (Routledge, 1997)

In your view, which is better, marriage or cohabitation?

Cohabitation has increased greatly in the last 25 years. Today, just under 10 per cent of British adults are cohabiting, but for those under 35 it is as high as 30 per cent. In 1979, just 3 per cent of all women aged 18–49 were cohabiting. Cohabitation has not yet replaced marriage as the normal form of permanent relationship, but it is normal for cohabitation to happen before marriage.

Cohabitation: an alternative to marriage?

Percentage of British adults who are not married, but who are cohabiting, 1998–9

	Percentages	
	Males	**Females**
16–19	1	8
20–24	18	27
25–29	39	39
30–34	44	35
35–39	36	29
40–44	31	26
45–49	28	16
50–54	17	16
55–59	18	12
All non-married aged 16 to 59	26	25

Source: General Household Survey, Office for National Statistics

Births outside marriage as a percentage of all live births, Great Britain

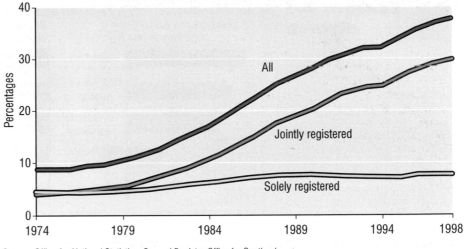

Source: Office for National Statistics; General Register Office for Scotland

Source: *Social Trends 30* (The Stationery Office, 2000)

Look at the table.

1 At what age are non-married people most likely to be cohabiting?

2 Why do you think this is?

Look at the graph. It shows us how many babies are registered legally in the names of either both parents (joint registration) or just one parent (sole registration).

3 What has happened to the numbers of jointly registered babies?

4 What has happened to the numbers of solely registered babies?

5 What do you think the changes in the figures might suggest about relationships?

But it does seem that cohabitation as a permanent form of relationship is increasing in popularity and there is a possibility that it may eventually challenge marriage.

Cohabiting couples are also an old phenomenon as it is estimated that between the mid-18th and mid-19th centuries as much as one fifth of the population in England and Wales may have lived together unlawfully for some time.

Source: Information drawn from S. McRae, *Changing Britain: Families and Households in the 1990s* (ESRC, 1999)

Divorce

It is generally agreed that marriages are increasingly likely to end in divorce, and that marriage for life is disappearing. The evidence for this argument exists, but it is not totally convincing. In 1999 there were 170,000 divorces, a rate of approximately 13 per 1,000 married population and for every divorce in 1999, two marriages took place. We also know that approximately 40 per cent of marriages will end in divorce, which is extremely high compared to 30 years ago. On the other hand, this means that 60 per cent of marriages will not end in divorce!

Reasons for divorce

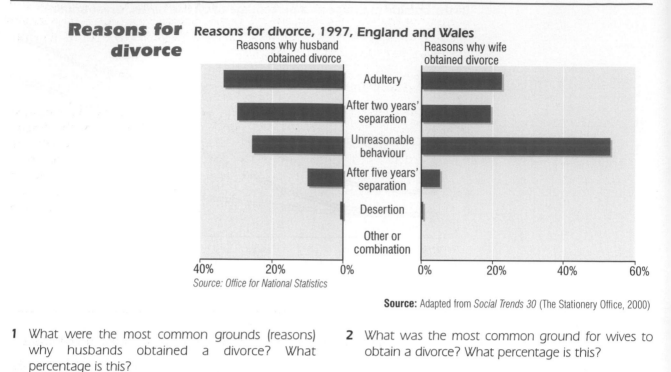

Reasons for divorce, 1997, England and Wales

Source: Office for National Statistics

Source: Adapted from *Social Trends 30* (The Stationery Office, 2000)

1 What were the most common grounds (reasons) why husbands obtained a divorce? What percentage is this?

2 What was the most common ground for wives to obtain a divorce? What percentage is this?

What is undeniable, however, is the steadily increasing divorce rate – between 1970 and 1999, the number of divorces more than doubled.

The rise in the divorce rate in Britain is not unusual, and it reflects a trend in most European countries.

The social implications of divorce

Divorce is not just the splitting up of a relationship between two people, it also has implications for society. Divorce has implications for:

- the role of caring
- social security
- children
- cohesion of society.

Role of caring

Traditionally, family members cared for each other. In particular, help flowed in different directions depending upon age, financial resources and health (see pages 190–1 for a discussion of the family life cycle). When divorce occurs, however, the wider family of in-laws is split up and becomes fragmented. The situation becomes even more complicated when the ex-partners remarry and new family members are added.

Social security

Divorce can often lead to financial problems for family members as assets are divided. Usually the mother is left with care of the children, but her income may well be inadequate to cope with caring for them. The man may not be able or may not wish to contribute enough money to achieve an adequate standard of living for his ex-wife and children. The result is generally that the state has to step in, providing social benefits for the wife and children

Impact on children

Approximately one in four of all children will experience the divorce of their parents before reaching the age of 16. A report published by the Joseph Rowntree Foundation concluded that the children of divorced parents run twice the risk of suffering a range of social problems, from poor performance at school to psychiatric disorders in later life. They are more likely to drink and smoke more heavily and to take drugs. The authors claim that it is not necessarily divorce itself which leads to these problems, but the arguments and family tensions which may lead up to it.

One interesting point is that children whose parents divorce have a significantly higher chance of themselves divorcing.

Children and divorce

Children in families of couples divorced: by age of child, England and Wales

Thousands

	1971	1981	1991	1998
Under 5	21	40	53	40
Age 5–10	41	68	68	68
Aged 11–15	21	52	40	43
All aged under 16	82	159	161	150
All couples divorcing	74	146	159	145

Source: Office for National Statistics

Source: *Social Trends 30* (The Stationery Office, 2000)

1 How many children aged under 16 had parents who divorced in 1998?

2 What increase was this on 1971?

3 What percentage were aged under five?

4 At what age do you think that it is most difficult for children to cope with parents divorcing?

Cohesion of society

Throughout this chapter we have seen just how important the family is to society. It (ideally) holds people together in caring relationships; it provides a home and financial support; it socialises them and provides them with a sense of identity. The family is hard to substitute as those who have introduced communes or have sought to abolish the family altogether have found. Divorce, it could be argued, weakens these bonds and disturbs the provision of the functions we discussed on page 164.

Changes in the law and the divorce rate

Year	Number of divorces	Major changes in the law
1857		Divorce available through the court for the first time. This law allowed men to obtain divorces if their wives were unfaithful. However, this reason was not sufficient for women to obtain divorces; they had to prove cruelty against them, as well. The law reflected the Victorian attitudes towards women.
		No divorce available for the working class, only a 'legal separation'.
1921	3,000	
1923		Women received equality with men under the law, regarding grounds for divorce. They began to get custody of the children.
1931	4,200	
1937		The law extended grounds for divorce to include adultery, cruelty (mental and physical) and desertion. Divorce became easier to obtain.
1941	7,500	
1945		End of the Second World War – great social disruption.
1949		People could apply for legal aid to obtain divorces. This was particularly helpful for housewives who had no income of their own.
1951	39,000	
1961	32,000	
1969		The irretrievable breakdown of marriage became the only ground for divorce, no proof of 'misconduct' was necessary. Two years' mutually agreed separation, or five years' if only one partner wanted divorce, was all that was necessary.
1971	80,000	
1981	157,000	
1991	169,000	
1996		Divorce possible after one-year separation – 'no fault' basis
1999	170,000	

Source for divorce figures: *Social Trends* (HMSO, 1986 and 1994)

1   What is the clear trend in divorce statistics?

2   What do the changes in the law tell you about attitudes to marriage?

3   Do the legal changes tell us anything about the position of women in society?

4   Give one legal reason why there has been an increase in the divorce rate since 1971.

5   If a person marries today, what chance is there of them remaining married, according to the information above?

Reasons for the rise in divorce rates

Legal changes

Quite simply, it is much easier to obtain a divorce today than ever before. Since 1969 the only reason needed to obtain a divorce has been the 'irretrievable breakdown of the marriage'. So, if two people feel they cannot stay together any longer, they can divorce. This contrasts very strongly with the previous situation where one partner had to prove that the other partner had done something wrong, such as being unfaithful or using violence against them.

It would be wrong, however, to see changes in the law as the cause of the increase in the divorce rate. The law changed as a *response* to changes in the attitudes of people towards marriage and the family.

Changing values

Divorce until the 1950s was regarded as morally wrong and people looked upon divorcees as having somehow failed. These attitudes were deeply ingrained and were closely linked to religious beliefs about the permanence of marriage, as a holy institution created by God. The general decline in the influence of the Christian churches has meant that there has been a consequent weakening of the view that marriage is for life. In line with this, the stigma (disgrace) attached to divorce which prevented many people from separating has weakened.

The attitude of women

There is general agreement that it is women who are the 'losers' in many marriages. They give up their work, their financial independence, in return for the role of housewife and mother. The rising status of women in society and their increasing refusal to accept the traditional 'inferior' roles of housewife and mother, with the man in charge of the household, has meant that 70 per cent of divorces are now started by wives.

Splitting up: causes and costs

FACT: In 75 per cent of all divorces, it is the wife who starts proceedings.
FACT: When questioned, the majority of divorced and separated single mothers felt better off alone because of their increased independence and control over their own lives and resources.

Source: Based on information in A. Garnham and E. Knights, *Putting the Treasury First: The Truth About Child Support* (CPAG, 1994)

According to research by Bradshaw and Millar for the Department of Social Security, the following reasons were given by respondents for separating from their partners:

- 31 per cent of total responses gave infidelity or one person finding a new partner as the main reason;
- 33 per cent gave 'not getting on';
- 20 per cent of respondents gave violence as a reason
- 16 per cent gave financial reasons;
- 16 per cent said their partner did not give enough time to the family;

- 15 per cent cited alcohol or drugs
- 26 per cent of respondents gave 'lack of communication';
- 7 per cent that a partner was lesbian or gay.

(These percentages do not add up to 100 as more than one response was possible.)

Source: A. Garnham and E. Knights, Putting the Treasury First: The Truth About Child Support (CPAG, 1994)

1 What are the three most common reasons for getting divorced?

2 Who is more likely to start divorce proceedings – husbands or wives? Drawing from the information contained above, can you suggest any reasons for this?

The clash of backgrounds

The sheer size and complexity of modern urban society (large towns and cities) means that it is likely that couples from very different social and ethnic backgrounds will meet and marry. Clearly the potential for trouble between the couple will be increased by their different expectations and attitudes. Alongside this problem of **cultural diversity** is the fact that the community in most cities has been weakened and traditional pressures imposed on a couple with a faltering marriage, by the local community and by the extended family, no longer exist.

Definition

Arranged marriage – where the decision about whom to marry is made by the families, not only the individuals concerned

The romantic marriage

Traditionally, and even in Asian **arranged marriages** in Britain today, love was not the most important element of marriage. It was more important that there was a stable union between two well-matched people, linking two families. By contrast, the cultural stress in contemporary Britain is on 'falling in love'. Indeed, a recent survey of people under 25 found that romance was regarded as the most important quality in a good marriage. But if the couple 'fall out of love', there is little to hold them together. By contrast, where love is not so important but the maintenance of the family is, the bonds holding the family together are far tougher.

Traditional marriage relationships

Divorce is one mechanism for dealing with the pressures and problems caused by marriage. However, there have traditionally been other ways of reducing marital conflict.

Traditional marriages in China

In pre-1948 China, the roles of husband and wife were clearly defined. Respect and not romantic love was demanded between husband and wife. There was an extended family system, so that intimate emotional contact between husband and wife was less intense than in our own system. Incorrect marital behaviour was prevented in part by supervision by older relatives. If the wife built up a reservoir of hatred and fear, it was more likely to be aimed at the mother-in-law, rather than the husband.

Source: Adapted from W.J. Goode, *World Revolution and Family Patterns* (Free Press, 1970)

Looking for love in Britain today

1 Why were there fewer disputes between husbands and wives in traditional Chinese marriages?

2 How does this differ from the views of marriage/relationships illustrated in the 'heartline' adverts?

3 What does this tell us about culture, marriage and the family?

Divorce and the reconstituted family

The term 'reconstituted family' refers to families composed of individuals forming new relationships and bringing with them dependent children from a previous relationship. The family situation may be further complicated when they have their own 'joint' children. About six million people live in reconstituted families in Britain today, and about 1 in 10 children live with their step-parents. The growth in divorce rates means that of all marriages in Britain today, approximately 15 per cent were second or subsequent.

The National Child Development Programme, a longitudinal study of young people, reported in 1998 that step-families were likely to be poorer than average, and the parents were found to express greater unhappiness over relationships than those in first families. The highest levels of unhappiness (18 per cent of step-fathers and 20 per cent of partners) occurred when they had both step-children and their own joint offspring.

Question	Having read all the evidence regarding marriage and divorce, what do you think? Is the increase in divorce a bad thing (not just for the individuals but for society)? Or should we continue to make divorce easier to obtain?

Main points ▶ The number of marriages have declined over the last thirty years.

▶ The number of people divorcing has increased. Today approximately 40 per cent of marriages will end in divorce.

▶ The increase in divorce rates is related to:
  – legal changes
  – changes in attitudes towards marriage as an institution for life
  – the changing status of women
  – the increasing complexity and fragmentation of society
  – the very high 'romantic' expectations of marriage.

▶ Cohabitation has increased greatly and now represents a normal activity for people. The majority of those who cohabit will eventually marry. In the future this may not be the case.

Family relationships

In essence, the family is no more than a special relationship between a group of people. These relationships are never static; they change over time. The relationships between husbands and wives, and between parents and children are vastly different today from a hundred years ago. To understand the changes fully, we need to divide them into three categories. These are relationships between:

• partners
• children and parents
• the older generation and the family.

Relationships between partners

Sociologists have divided the changing relationships between partners into three phases.

Phase 1: pre-industrial societies

Before Britain became a society almost totally based on industry, about 150 years ago, most people lived in the country and worked in agriculture. At this time, husband and wife were generally equal in their dealings with one another. Both of them worked to earn income and they relied heavily upon each other. However, most sociologists agree that the relationship between them was not very close.

Phase 2: industrial family

In the second phase of the development of the modern family, during the last century, women lost their independence and equality. The result of laws restricting the working hours for women, and the Victorian beliefs concerning the purity and fragility of women meant that they withdrew from the workplace and increasingly the role of housewife and mother became the norm. Men became the breadwinners and, as they were the ones with the money, they also took charge inside the family.

It is important here to distinguish between the working class and the middle class, as there were considerable differences between them. The wife in the middle-class family was not expected to work either in or out of the home. Instead, she supervised the work of the cleaning lady and the nanny. The husband's role was to go out to business and to provide for the family.

Life in the working-class family was different in that the household chores and child-rearing were seen as exclusively the wife's tasks. Husbands spent long hours at work and they preferred to pass their leisure in the pub, in the company of male companions. In these circumstances, women turned to each other for assistance, in particular to mothers and daughters. Help was freely given and very powerful bonds developed, which were much stronger than those between husband and wife. The father, although the head of the household, was also a bit of an outsider because of his long absences. Violence against wives and children was quite common.

Phase 3: the contemporary family

Between the 1930s and the 1950s, a change took place in the relationships between husbands and wives in middle-class families. A warmer, closer relationship began to be accepted as normal. A slow move towards equality began too, with joint decision-making and an increase in shared leisure activities. The wife remained responsible for the home and the children (now with no nanny to help her), but increasingly the husband would see it as his duty to help her. Because of this move towards equality in husband/wife roles, the sociologists Young and Willmott used the term **symmetrical family** to describe the new form of family relationship.

Gradually, these ideas spread to the working class, so that by the 1960s many younger working-class couples shared their household chores and their leisure activities, with the husband replacing the mother as the main helper to the wife.

When a husband and wife share housework and their leisure, sociologists call this a **joint conjugal role relationship**. However, when they perform separate tasks and have different leisure pursuits, sociologists describe their relationship as a **segregated role relationship**.

Definitions

Symmetrical family – a family where the adults share household tasks, and see themselves as equals

Joint conjugal role relationship – where the partners share all household tasks and have leisure activities in common

Segregated role relationship – where the partners have separate tasks and leisure interests

---

Question

How would you describe the relationship in:

a) the phase 2 family?
b) the phase 3 family?

Reasons for the move towards the symmetrical family

Women began to reject the housewife role. They demanded a greater say in decision-making in the home and to be considered equal to their husbands. Further, they insisted that men ought to become involved in tasks about the home. Contraception allowed them to limit the number of children they had and gave them the freedom to obtain paid employment. Financial independence from husbands in turn strengthened their position of equality in the family.

The resettlement of many working-class people from the inner cities in the 1950s into overspill estates and the increasing affluence of others who bought their own homes led to a much greater interest in home improvements and home life generally. Men preferred to stay in, improving their homes, watching television or playing with the children than going to the pub. This new form of leisure pattern amongst working-class men led to the term *privatised worker* being used (indicating that the worker was interested in his private family life).

Symmetry or patriarchy?

Feminists have bitterly criticised this symmetrical family/privatised worker description of modern family life. They argue that husbands benefit far more from marriage than wives. It is still regarded as the woman's task to look after the children, to cook and to do the housework. Husbands 'help' their wives and are regarded as being good husbands if they occasionally relieve their wives from childminding, or wash the dishes.

Women, too, give up their careers far more often than men in order to look after the children. Staying at home with young children is often lonely and frustrating, as well as being exhausting. The term **patriarchy** has been used by sociologists to describe this situation of continuing male dominance of the family.

Definitions

Patriarchy – a society where the men hold more power than women

Patriarchal family – a description of the family often used by feminist sociologists which suggests that the wishes of the husband/male partner are dominant and there is no sense of equality

The changing relationships within the family

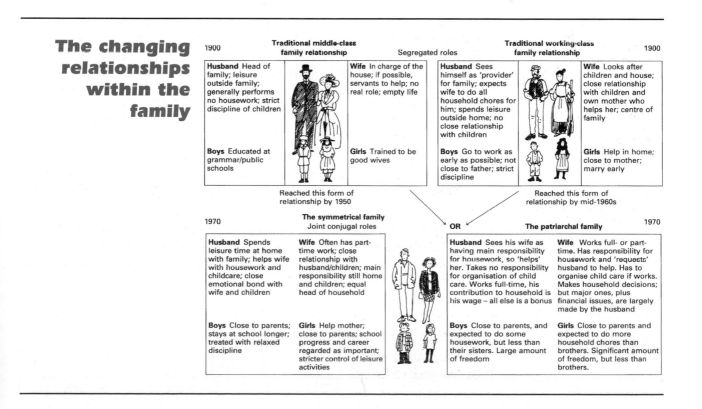

1900	Traditional middle-class family relationship		Segregated roles	Traditional working-class family relationship		1900
	Husband Head of family; leisure outside family; generally performs no housework; strict discipline of children	**Wife** In charge of the house; if possible, servants to help; no real role; empty life		**Husband** Sees himself as 'provider' for family; expects wife to do all household chores for him; spends leisure outside home; no close relationship with children	**Wife** Looks after children and house; close relationship with children and own mother who helps her; centre of family	
	Boys Educated at grammar/public schools	**Girls** Trained to be good wives		**Boys** Go to work as early as possible; not close to father; strict discipline	**Girls** Help in home; close to mother; marry early	

Reached this form of relationship by 1950

Reached this form of relationship by mid-1960s

1970	The symmetrical family		OR	The patriarchal family		1970
	Joint conjugal roles					
	Husband Spends leisure time at home with family; helps wife with housework and childcare; close emotional bond with wife and children	**Wife** Often has part-time work; close relationship with husband/children; main responsibility still home and children; equal head of household		**Husband** Sees his wife as having main responsibility for housework, so 'helps' her. Takes no responsibility for organisation of child care. Works full-time, his contribution to household is his wage – all else is a bonus	**Wife** Works full- or part-time. Has responsibility for housework and 'requests' husband to help. Has to organise child care if works. Makes household decisions; but major ones, plus financial issues, are largely made by the husband	
	Boys Close to parents; stays at school longer; treated with relaxed discipline	**Girls** Help mother; close to parents; school progress and career regarded as important; stricter control of leisure activities		**Boys** Close to parents, and expected to do some housework, but less than their sisters. Large amount of freedom	**Girls** Close to parents and expected to do more household chores than brothers. Significant amount of freedom, but less than brothers.	

Changing relationships between husbands and wives

Traditional relationships This extract comes from a 1950 study of a working-class mining community in north-east England.

The comedian who defined home as the place where you fill the pools in on a Wednesday night was something of a sociologist. With the exception of a small minority of men ... the husbands of Ashton for preference come home for a meal after finishing work and, as soon as they can feel clean and rested, they look for the companionship of their mates.

The wife's position is very different. In a very consciously accepted division of labour, she must keep in good order the household provided for by the money handed to her each Friday by her husband. While he is at work, she should complete her day's work washing, ironing, cleaning or whatever it may be – and she must have ready for him a good meal.

The wife's confinement to the household, together with the acceptance of the idea that the house and the children are primarily her responsibility, emphasise the absence of any joint activities and interests for husband and wife.

Source: N. Dennis, F. Henriques and C. Slaugher, *Coal is Our Life* (Eyre & Spottiswoode, 1956)

Symmetrical family In a study of middle-class households in the late 1950s it appeared that a change was taking place in relationships between husbands and wives. Young and Willmott later decided on this evidence and further research that the family in Britain today is best described as 'symmetrical', meaning that husbands and wives regarded each other as equal and shared domestic tasks.

Most Woodford men are emphatically not absentee husbands. It is their work, especially if rather tedious which takes second place in their thoughts. ... 'In the old days,' as one wife said, 'the husband was the husband and the wife was the wife and they each had their own way of going on. Her job was to look after him. The wife wouldn't stand it for it nowadays. Husbands help with the children now. They stay more in the home and have more interest in the home.'

The couple share the work, worry and pleasure of the children. 'We have the same routine every night,' said Mrs Foster, 'I'd put one child to bed and my husband puts the other. We take it in turns to tell them stories too'.

Husbands usually have their own specific tasks within the family economy, particularly in decorating and repairing the home.

Source: P. Willmott and M. Young, *Family and Class in a London Suburb* (Routledge & Kegan Paul, 1960)

1 How would you describe the husband/wife relationship in Ashton – segregated or conjugal? Why?

2 Do you think the husbands and wives in Ashton spent much leisure time in each other's company?

3 In what way has the middle-class relationship changed between husband and wife?

4 By the 1970s Young and Willmott described most families in Britain as 'symmetrical'. What did they mean by this?

Activity

The view that there has been a move towards greater equality in marriage between husband and wire has been challenged by feminists.

If you come from, or have access to, a two-parent household, devise a simple chart like the one below to show which activities/tasks are done in your household in one week by:

a) your mother; b) your father.

Tasks	Mon Time	Tues Time	Wed Time	Thur Time	Fri Time	Sat Time	Sun Time
e.g. cook							

Sharing household tasks

Household division of labour in Britain

% saying always or usually the woman –

Washing and ironing	79
Looking after sick family member	48

% saying always or usually the man –

Makes small repairs around the house	75

Household division of labour among dual-earning couples in Britain

% 'always' or 'usually' done by woman

Washing and ironing

Man earns more than woman	83
Woman earns more or same	63

Looking after sick family member

Man earns more than woman	48
Woman earns more or same	40

% 'always' or usually done by man

Makes sall repairs around the house

Man earns more than woman	74
Woman earns more or same	79

Source: *British and European Social Attitudes: The 15th Report* (Ashgate, 1998)

Eight out of 10 women say they prepare every meal in their household, according to a government survey yesterday that casts doubt on the reality of "new man" culture [where men are supposed to be caring fathers and to share equally in the household tasks].

Just over half of men believe boys should be taught how to cook whether or not they want to learn, says the survey of more than 2,000 adults commissioned by the Department of Health's nutrition task force.

It found that while views on cooking were generally positive, there was a contrast between attitudes and behaviour. Eighty per cent of women said they cooked every meal, 12 per cent cooked once or twice a week, 5 per cent less than twice and 3 per cent never.

Only 22 per cent of men said they cooked every meal, 39 per cent cooked once or twice, 20 per cent less than this and 18 per cent never. The Office of Population Censuses and Surveys, which carried out the survey, acknowledges that the figures do not add up but says they should not be taken literally. Women who prepared most meals would have chosen the "every" category rather than "once or twice". However, it concludes: "The traditional model still predominates."

Source: *The Guardian*, 25 January 1995

Look at the tables.

1 What percentage say women always or usually do the washing and ironing?

2 How does this change when both men and women are in employment?

3 What do men do instead?

According to the text:

4 What proportion of wives cook every meal in the household?

5 What does the extract mean when it says that there is a 'contrast between attitudes and behaviour'?

6 The extract refers to the 'new man' culture? What does this mean? What evidence is there for it in the information given above?

The relationship between children and parents

The twentieth century, and particularly the last 40 years, saw a revolution in the way that children are treated by parents. Before this the father was the undisputed head of the family, with children expected to accept his orders without question. There were no benefits from the state, little protection against the violence in the home, and it was generally agreed that children were inferior creatures whose opinions were not worth listening to.

There were, however, social class differences. The sons of the middle class were likely to attend a grammar or public school and be groomed for a career in the professions. The girls were not educated for a career, but to be good wives. Because the children were often sent away from home for their schooling, the relationship between parents and children would often be rather cool.

Parents and children in a simple society

But the pygmies have learned from the animals around them to doze with one eye open and a sleepy midday camp can become filled in a minute with shouts and yells and tearful protestations as some baby, crawling around this warm friendly world, crawls into a bed of hot ashes or over a column of army ants. In a moment he will be surrounded by angry adults and given a sound slapping, then carried unceremoniously back to the safety of a hut. It does not matter much which hut because as far as the child is concerned all adults are his parents or grandparents, they are all equally likely to slap him for doing wrong, or fondle and feed him with delicacies if he is quiet and gives them no trouble. He knows his real father and mother of course and has a special affection for them and they for him, but from an early age he learns he is the child of them all.

The pygmies have no special words to indicate their own parents, like 'mum' and 'dad'. For them all adults in the group are given the same name.

Source: C. Turnbull, *The Forest People* (Picador, 1976)

In Britain, children are extremely close to their parents, rather than any other people. Parents' love is focused almost exclusively on their own children, not on other people's.

1 Who has the 'right' to discipline children in pygmy society?

2 From your own experience, who has this right in Britain today?

3 What does the passage mean when it says 'he learns he is the child of them all'?

4 Why do you think the pygmies have no separate word for 'mum' or 'dad'?

5 What does the extract show us about the belief in our society that the only 'proper' way to bring up a child is to have an extremely close relationship between parents and children to the exclusion of everybody else? (In your answer you might find it helpful to think about the idea of 'culture'.)

Among the working class, children were expected to contribute financially to the family at the earliest possible opportunity, leaving school and assuming adult responsibilities at a very early age. Although the relationship between father and children was cool, that between mother and daughter was usually strong.

In the last 40 years, attitudes towards children have gradually changed. The newer attitudes occurred first amongst the middle class and then were taken up by working-class families. These attitudes stress emotional warmth towards children, greater tolerance of their views and attitudes, greater freedom from parental control after the age of 14. However, children are subjected to greater control when younger as there is a belief that they are at risk from a wide range of dangers including such things as sexual assault or traffic accidents.

The reasons for the changes in child/parent relationships are connected with the smaller size of families, so that children are treated more as individuals, with higher educational standards and maturity of children, and with a change in views on the correct way to bring up children. Psychologists and other experts now tell us to bring up children with love and affection in order to create an emotionally stable adult.

However, it would be wrong to say that all parents now bring up children with love and affection. Cruelty to children is still widespread, and the National Society for the Prevention of Cruelty to Children (NSPCC) estimate that about 600 children are deliberately injured by their parents each year.

Gender differences

Although the very distinctive differences in the ways that girls and boys have been socialised in the past have gradually been eroded, there still are some more subtle – differences. Despite claiming that children are treated equally, girls are still more likely to be expected to help in the home, they are still more likely to be bought different games and to be expected to behave in a more caring manner. Language used to describe boys and girls is different, with boys being 'handsome' and girls 'pretty', for example.

Girls too are more likely than boys to be more strictly controlled in their movements as they are considered to be more likely to be 'in danger' – particularly of sexual assault or harassment.

However, one significant change is that career expectations are now higher for both males and females, and the idea that a girl should expect to be a housewife has been replaced by the expectation to be a mother, a partner and in employment.

Main points

▶ The relationships between family members has changed over time.
▶ Historically, women were responsible for most of the housework and caring for the children.
▶ Men were expected to provide an income and to be the 'head of the family'.
▶ This has changed, but the extent of the changes is in dispute.
▶ One group of writers believe that there is now a symmetrical or more equal relationship between husband and wife.
▶ Feminist writers argue that men still have greater power than women.
▶ The status of children has risen considerably, so that today parents are more likely to listen to them.
▶ Gender differences remain, however, as girls and boys are brought up differently. The extent of the different socialisation is less than in the past.
▶ Older people still help the younger generation with financial aid and child-minding.

Relationships between the older generation and the family

For the first time in history, a person can now reasonably expect to live into his or her seventies. This means that there has been a huge growth in the number of three generation families (grandparents, parents, children).

It is often claimed that old people were held in high esteem in pre-industrial societies, though it is difficult to prove this. It is likely that, since so few people lived to any great age, there was a degree of status in simply having survived. As the oldest male in each family usually owned the land (in agricultural societies land equals wealth), he clearly remained powerful until his death.

In modern society, old age is normal and, as the older generation have little economic power over the young, the status of old people generally is low. This affects relationships within the family. Some writers have gone so far as to claim that old people are often abandoned in our society and are not wanted by their children when they become a burden. To support this argument they point to the growth of residential and nursing homes for older people. However, the evidence does not seem to support this extreme argument. It is true that over half of those aged 75+ live alone, but this seems to be because they choose to do so.

Children or, more accurately, daughters still look after their parents, and maintain close contact by telephone and visits.

Family contacts

Family contact, Great Britain, 1995

	Percentages	
	Mother	**Father**
Daily	8	6
Less than daily but at least once a week	40	33
Les than once a week but at least once a month	21	20
Less often	27	29
Never	3	9
Not answered	1	3
All	100	100

Source: British Social Attitudes Survey, Social & Community Planning Research

Source: Adapted from *Social Trends* 29 (The Stationery Office, 1999)

1 What percentage of adults see (a) their mothers and (b) their fathers at least once a week?

2 What is the total percentage of adults who see their mother less than once a month?

3 What reasons can you suggest for the patterns of visiting which are demonstrated in the table?

4 What other important form of contact is not mentioned in the table?

5 Do you think that the table suggests that parents are isolated from their adult offspring?

Definition

Family life cycle – the changing relationships between the different generations of the family as they grow older

The family life cycle

One useful way of understanding the importance of older people in the family is to look at the **family life cycle**. By this, sociologists mean that as people move through the various stages of life from young married couple with dependent children through to old age, help, both physical (baby-sitting) and financial (loans), flows from one age group to the other. Where grandparents are healthy and possibly financially sound, they give help to their children who are in the phase of setting up home and family and therefore in need of help. As the older generation become infirm, it is their turn to be helped.

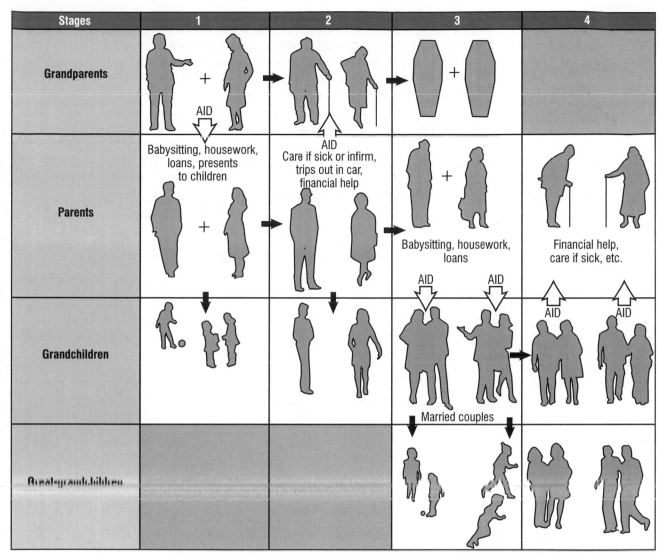

The family life cycle

7 CHAPTER SUMMARY

1   It is difficult to talk about 'the family' as it varies so greatly.

2   To help us understand this, it is useful to look at the family as having a
    number of different forms or structures (for example, extended, nuclear,
    lone parent) which in turn vary in diverse ways which include such
    things as social status, ethnic background, cultural and religious beliefs,
    and the place where people live.

3   The family has changed over time and particularly important has been
    the the influence of industrialisation.

4   There are two views on the role of the family in society.
    – The first of these views, associated with the functionalist perspective, is that the family is beneficial to all its members.
    – An opposing stance is taken by feminists and other critics who argue the family can be harmful to some of its members.

5   There is a bitter debate over the never-married lone parents.
    – The New Right argue that the growth of the lone-parent family is a bad thing which has helped to undermine social values and costs taxpayers an unfair amount in benefit payments.
    – Feminist and liberal writers disagree and argue that the lone-parent family is better than the violence and abuse of many two-parent families.

6   Alternatives to the family have been tried, which include legally abolishing the family and communes.

7   The number of marriages has declined over the last 30 years.

8   The number of people divorcing has increased. Today approximately 40 per cent of marriages end in divorce.

9   Cohabitation has increased greatly and now represents a normal activity for many young people. Although, at present, the majority of those who cohabit will eventually marry, in the future this may not be the case.

10 The relationships between family members has changed over time.

11 One group of writers believe that there is now a symmetrical or more equal relationship between husband and wife, whilst feminist writers argue that men still have greater power than women.

12 The status of children has risen considerably, so that today parents are more likely to listen to them.

13 Gender differences remain, however, as girls and boys are brought up differently. The extent of the different socialisation is less than in the past.

14 Older people still help the younger generation with financial aid and child-minding.

Test Your Knowledge

1   Identify and define three structural forms of the family.

2   What do we mean by the term 'family diversity'. Give two examples of ways in which the contemporary family is diverse.

3   Explain, in your own words, how industrialisation and changes in the economy have influenced the family.

4   Has the extended family disappeared in contemporary society?

5   What are the functions of the family?

6   What criticisms have the New Right made of the lone-parent family? What responses have been made by critics of the New Right?

7   What are the social implications of divorce?

8   Explain the meaning of the terms 'symmetry' and 'patriarchy'. Which term best describes the family in society today?

THE MEDIA

Chapter contents

- ## The changing media

  We start the chapter by looking at the what we mean by the term 'the media'. We then explore just how much the media have changed during the twentieth century. This leads us to a brief exploration of why the media are important in our lives and likely to become ever more significant to us and to society.

- ## The media and social control

  Newspapers, film and television have a very important role to play in passing on values and ensuring that what we see and read reinforces the dominant values in society. The increase in the amount and variety of media should have provided us with greater challenges to accepted values, but this does not seem to have taken place. It is relatively rare that the media challenges accepted values.

- ## The impact of the media on our behaviour

  This section takes us into a detailed discussion of how the media affect our behaviour. What we find is that people make sense of the media in very different ways and, above all else, they are 'selective' in what they take in. It would appear that the media tend to reinforce values which we already have. This is important for a range of debates about the media, for example just how do the media influence people to commit violent or sexual crimes. The answer seems to be, only if the perpetrator was interested in committing the crime anyway.

- ## Ownership and control

  We uncover the patterns of ownership and control of the media. What emerges is that the entire range of media output is gradually coming under the control of fewer owners, linking television, film, newspapers, books and the Internet into a few enormous conglomerates dominating the world. What are the implications for freedom of information?

- ## Content of the media

  We take up that question of freedom of information here, with a discussion of which factors influence the content of the media. There seem a number of important factors, in particular the role of owners who clearly wish to protect their interests. However, owners are constrained by the need to make a profit, so they will not wish to offend advertisers nor the public whom they rely upon to buy their magazines or watch their films. Another factor which affects newspapers and the news on television is just what journalists think makes a 'good story'.

- ## Women and the media

  Most of the rest of the chapter looks at the relationship between the media and various groups in society. In the first of these discussions, we see that the traditional portrayal on the media of women has not changed substantially – women are still measured by their looks. When it comes to women's magazines, an extremely lucrative market for publishers, it seems that they choose a narrow range of themes which consist primarily of relationships, parenthood and the home, and combining these with a career.

- ## 'Race' and the media

  Issues linked with ethnic minorities have always been predominantly linked to 'social problems' and this seems to have changed little. However, in recent years, the emphasis on ethnic minorities living in Britain has shifted to a scapegoating of asylum seekers.

- ## Crime and the media

  The media have consistently exaggerated the extent of crime in Britain and its seriousness. This has created a climate of fear for many women and older people. The news media have exaggerated crime because it sells newspapers and because crimes usually fit the 'news values' we looked at earlier.

- ## Advertising and the media

  Finally, we look at the impact of advertising on the audience. What we find is that it is extremely difficult to prove that advertising actually has any impact on increasing the sales of a particular product. What seems to happen is that people who are interested in a particular product might well be influenced, but not others. This is interesting as it throws some light on the issue of what should be allowed to be advertised and whether we need ban any advertising – presumably not?

The changing media

The **media** (or the **mass media**) refers to all forms of written communication to the public, such as newspapers, magazines and books and to all forms of transmitted communication, such as radio, television, cinema and the Internet. The term now includes the new generation of mobile phones, linked to the Internet. (Incidentally, the word 'media' is the plural of 'medium' and so we say 'the media are …'.)

The first medium was the printing press which was developed on a large scale in the seventeenth century, but as most people could not read, it only assumed great importance in the twentieth century.

Development of the broadcasting media in the twentieth century

1926	BBC begin radio broadcasting
1936	BBC begin television broadcasting
1955	Commercial companies begin television broadcasting
1972	Commercial companies begin radio broadcasting
1984	Beginning of cable television
	Beginning of satellite broadcasting
1990s	Widespread growth of personal computers and access to the Internet
2000	New generation of mobile phones connected to the Internet begin to be sold

The real growth in the media took place, at an ever increasing pace, during the twentieth century. Film, radio and recorded music began to change people's leisure habits and even their understanding of the world. It was no longer necessary to actually see people act or hear them play music 'in the flesh' – these could be reproduced through film or recording. We take these recordings for granted today, but it was an amazing culture shock initially. When one of the first films ever made – of a train coming into a station – was shown in a 'cinema', the crowd simply could not grasp that it was not actually happening, and serious injuries occurred as the audience stampeded for the exits in a desperate effort to escape being run over by the train! Today, the media surround us, providing us with a window on the world, but also bombarding us with messages about how we ought to behave and what we ought to buy.

The new technology and the media

In the last 20 years, there have been enormous changes in broadcasting and printing, brought about mainly by the power of new technology.

Broadcasting

Three developments have affected broadcasting in recent years:
- cable
- satellites
- digital broadcasting.

These technologies mean that it now is possible for many more television stations to broadcast. The potential exists for a massive increase in stations to cater for all tastes and interests, but two things limit this:
- First, the increased competition for advertising means that there is a greater inclination to go for the most popular, if not necessarily the best, programmes.

Different aspects of the media

The media as...

a window on the world – TV and print show us a much wider world than previous generations

an interactive link – mobile phones and the Internet allow us to communicate much more widely and quickly

a provider of information – the media educate us on a huge range of topics, so we are much better informed than ever before

a filter – however the media don't tell us everything; they choose what they want us to see

an interpreter – the media interpret the world and make sense of it for us

a mirror – we see our own society through the media and our place in it

a controller – the media make it clear which values are correct and which deviant

Source: Adapted from P. Trowler, *Investigating Mass Media*, 2nd edition (Collins Educational, 1996)

- Secondly, the enormous costs of setting up broadcasting networks by cable or satellite mean that only the richest and biggest companies can enter the market.

What has emerged therefore has not been a growth in minority interests, but a battle to attract mass audiences. Digital TV will increasingly allow TV sets to become interactive, with viewers responding to information from the broadcaster.

Ninety-eight per cent of British households have a television.

Computer games

Computer games have developed into one of the most common pastimes of younger people, particularly boys, and have pushed out more traditional sports. The global market is dominated by only three companies Sony, Sega and Nintendo.

A rare sight – computer games, usually based on violent action, are generally played by boys.

Video and DVD

These have provided a completely new outlet for film since the mid-1980s. The video does not seem to have lowered attendance at cinemas, but quite the opposite, in fact, it seems to have generated greater interest in films. DVDs seem likely to replace video as CDs replaced cassettes and records.

Currently, 85 per cent of British households have a video or DVD.

Print

The developments in information technology allow newspapers and books to be produced with fewer staff, at lower costs and in a shorter time. The result has been an explosion of publications with more books, magazines and newspaper articles published today than ever before.

The Internet

This has been the single biggest area of growth since the late 1990s in any medium. The Internet offers access to a huge range of sites and information. A wide variety of companies have now started to provide services directly to people via the Internet and potentially it has the power to enable people to purchase all their goods and services from home, as well as receiving up-to-date information on virtually any area they wish.

Mobile phones

Mobile phones themselves are not part of the mass media, but the new technology which links them to the Internet allows communication in a way unimagined in the 1990s. In 2004, there will be 700 million mobile phones worldwide, allowing advertisers and possibly broadcasters to communicate directly to them.

Access to the Internet

UK home access to the internet

By household composition (%)

Retired households

One adult	1
Couple	5

Non-retired households

One adult	15
Couple	25
One adult, one child	7
One adult, two or more children	11
Couple, one child	31
Couple, two or more children	35
All other households	19
All households	19

By region
(previous year's figures in brackets)

Scotland 14% (8%)
N Ireland 11% (5%)
North-east 14% (7%)
North-west 18% (9%)
Yorkshire & Humberside 15% (8%)
East Midlands 19% (9%)
West Midlands 20% (8%)
Wales 15% (7%)
East Anglia 22% (11%)
London 25% (16%)
South-west 19% (9%)
South-east 24% (13%)

By percentage

1998   1999   2000

Source: ONS

Britain's poorest households are being left behind in the digital revolution because they cannot afford access to the internet. Figures released yesterday reveal that a "digital divide" has opened up between the poorest households and the better off. While the number of households with access to the internet has doubled in 12 months to 6.5 million – around one in four homes – levels of access vary greatly depending on income.

As few as 3% of poorer households are online, compared with 48% of more affluent households.

Claire Shearman, co-chairwoman of Communities Online commented: "There is a growing belief that dot.coms are the future of the economy. But if you don't have access to the skills and the knowledge to thrive in that economy because of where you live, or how much money you earn, you won't be included."

Source: *The Guardian*, 11 July 2000

Look at the diagram

1 What percentage of households had access to the Internet at the end of 1998?

2 What percentage of households had access by the end of 2000?

3 Which two household types were most likely to have access to the Internet? Why?

4 Of non-retired households, which household type had the lowest access to the Internet? Suggest reasons for this.

5 Which three areas had the highest percentage of households with access to the Internet? Suggest why this might be.

6 What does the article mean when it refers to a 'digital divide'?

7 Why will that become more important in the future?

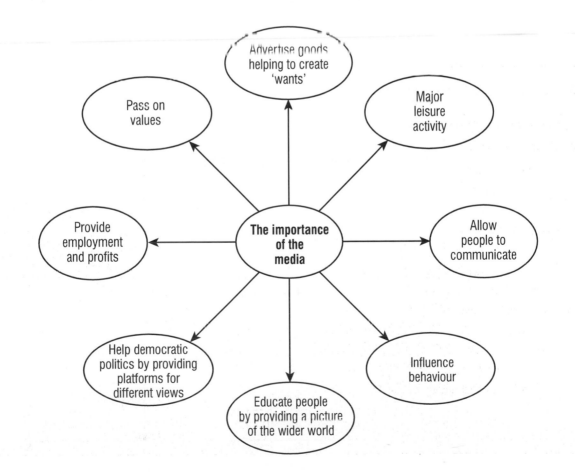

Main points ▶ The media include all forms or written and transmitted communication to the public.

▶ The growth of the media has been extremely fast, with most of it occurring in the twentieth century.

▶ The media have had an enormous impact upon society.

▶ In the future, the Internet appears to be the single most important form of medium, as it will allow people almost unlimited access information and entertainment.

▶ However, access to the Internet is not equal, and there are clear social class divisions emerging.

The media and social control

Definition

Social control – people learn the expectations and values of society (culture) through socialisation and if they do not follow the guidelines of society, then they are punished in some way (social control)

Every society needs order and predictability. This involves persuading people to behave in certain socially-acceptable ways, and punishing those who refuse to do so. This is the process known as **social control**. As the media are one of the main sources of information about the world for most people (virtually all of us watch television, read newspapers and magazines, for instance), they play an important part in making people conform. They give us correct models of behaviour to follow, at the same time criticising anti-social behaviour.

Of course, the media are not always acting to promote social control. They also act as critics of current and emerging trends in society. Newspapers and magazines can promote alternative values just as much as they do traditional conservative ones. But the range of magazines, television programmes and newspaper stories do give us a clear indication of the range of acceptable behaviour. This can also flag up the changes in the values of society. Nowadays, explicitly sexual magazines, for example, are hidden away on the top shelves of shops, whereas 20 years ago they were displayed prominently in most newspaper shops.

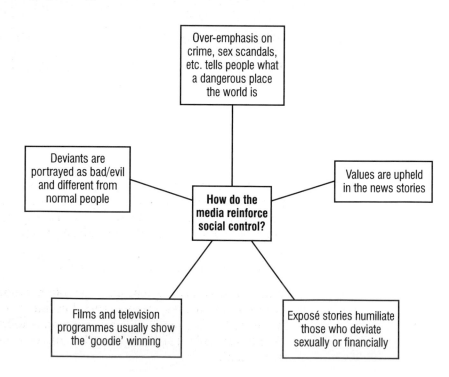

The impact of the media on our behaviour

In the first section, we read about how sociologists argue that the media play an important part in socialisation and social control. They teach us values and then reinforce these values by criticisms of those who 'deviate'.

But we also need to explore the process of *how* the media affect individuals. Sociologists have suggested four ways of understanding the effects of the media on individuals:

- the personal (or behaviourist) approach
- the opinion leader approach
- the audience selection approach
- the cultural approach.

Can seeing violence cause people to commit violence?

The personal approach

This approach stresses that the media have a very direct effect on the individual. People are said to respond to the 'stimulus' (message) of the media. For instance, a child watching a television programme containing violence is likely to be influenced into committing a similar violent act.

The opinion leader approach

This approach argues that most people have one or a number of individuals whose opinion they respect, and they are more likely to be swayed in their opinions by the views of these 'opinion leaders' than directly by the media. People are only influenced by the media when the opinion leaders are in agreement.

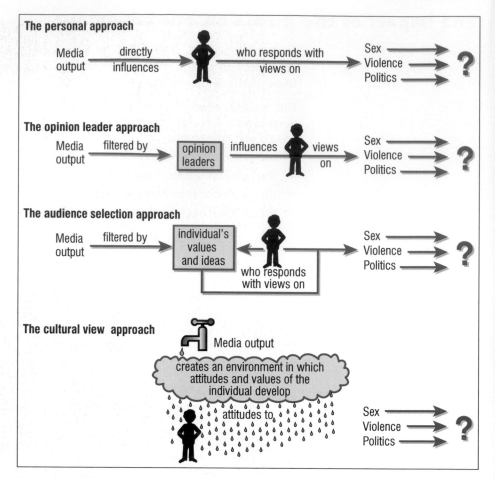

The personal approach

Media output — directly influences — who responds with views on — Sex / Violence / Politics — **?**

The opinion leader approach

Media output — filtered by — opinion leaders — influences — views on — Sex / Violence / Politics — **?**

The audience selection approach

Media output — filtered by — individual's values and ideas — who responds with views on — Sex / Violence / Politics — **?**

The cultural view approach

Media output — creates an environment in which attitudes and values of the individual develop — attitudes to — Sex / Violence / Politics — **?**

How the media influence people

The audience selection approach

This approach starts from the fact that the audience chooses which films and programmes to watch and which newspapers to buy. Depending upon why they have bought it, or are watching it, the newspaper or film will influence them. Therefore, someone who likes the idea of committing violence may watch a violent film and enjoy it for that. Another person may simply enjoy the elements of suspense in the same film, and may see the violence as of no importance or even irritating. The content is therefore understood in different ways by the viewer or reader.

Question

Look at the section of a page from a newspaper opposite.

When you looked at the page, what was the first thing to catch your attention?

Source: *The Sun*, 13 December 1998

People are selective. If you were interested in buying things for the home, the advert would attract your attention and you might even ignore the story about the flats collapsing. If you were 'reading' the paper for the news, then you might not even notice the advert.

The cultural approach

This approach follows on from the personal approach, but goes further in exploring the culture within which the media exist and influence people. The media are not seen as having an immediate effect on individuals, but they have instead a very slow effect, building up a climate of opinion and expectations about society.

Attitudes towards women, for instance, are strongly influenced by the way they are portrayed in the media. 'Sexy' photographs in magazines and sensual images in films do not directly drive men into raping women, but it does strengthen the way in which they see women as sexual figures whose looks count more than their personalities.

The effects of the media

In so far as there is a consensus about the effect of television, it involves the following.

First, television does not have a strong independent effect. It is too easily ignored, talked over or switched off. Furthermore, people perceive selectively. They see and hear those things which tend to confirm their present world-view; they pass over or filter out information which does not have a place in their mental cupboards.

Consequently, the main impact of television is confirmatory [strengthens views already held]. If it presents images which fit with what people already believe, it bolsters those views; if what it presents clashes with views already held, it is ignored or explained away. Second, television messages influence only the sympathetic. Only those disposed to see some issue in a particular light respond positively to attempts to influence them in that direction.

Source: Adapted from S. Bruce, 'Pray TV: Observations on Mass Media Religion', *Sociology Review*, November 1991

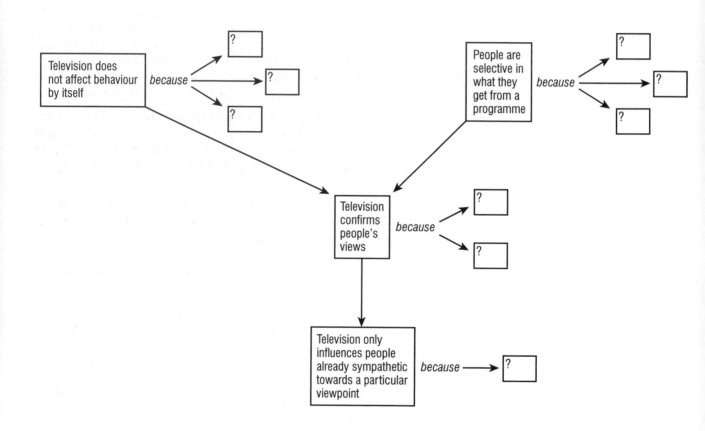

Of course, this model also applies to newspapers, films, books and the Internet.

Using the information in the extract and the main text, copy the diagram above and complete the blank boxes

Main points ▶ The media play an important role in maintaining social control in society by transmitting values and demonstrating correct ways of behaving.

▶ The extent of media influence on our behaviour is the subject of considerable debate.

▶ There are four different approaches to understanding the influence of the media. These are – the behaviourist approach, the opinion leader approach, the audience selection approach and the cultural approach.

▶ It is important to understand that viewers and readers have a complex relationship with the media. When people watch or read, they are selective in what they take in.

Ownership and control

How do we get our views about the world which exists beyond our own day-to-day experience? Partly through stories from friends, but probably more often by watching television, seeing films, reading magazines and newspapers, listening to the radio – and for the more adventurous – scouring the Internet. If anyone can get control over these and make sure that you read and see what they want you to read, then your view of the world is likely to be influenced by their views.

Your freedom to read, listen to and see a range of different opinions is very important in a democracy, where people choose a government and where, if we feel that there are issues which we are concerned about, we can try to persuade the government to do something about it. The greater the range of views, the more effective the democracy.

In recent years, as the media have increasingly become owned by fewer companies, there has been a lot of concern expressed over the fact that these companies are limiting the range of views on offer.

Two views of the media

The media give a free airing of social and political issues where opinions differ. Not only that but they also act as watchdogs, criticising politicians and the powerful when they override the interests of ordinary people.

versus

The media are in the hands of a few powerful companies who impose their views on us. The role of the media is to distort reality, justifying the deep inequalities of wealth that exist, at the same time keeping the masses happy with pictures of attractive women and stories on sex and sport.

To find out the truth we need to look at two key issues:

- Who own the media today?
- What are the contents of the media and how are they chosen?

Ownership of the media

Trends in media ownership

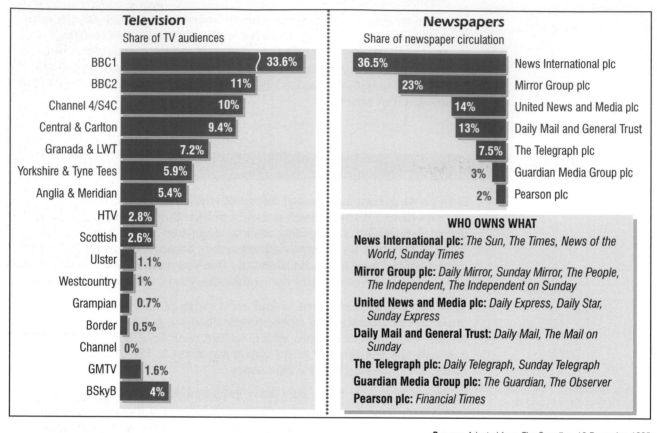

Television
Share of TV audiences

BBC1	33.6%
BBC2	11%
Channel 4/S4C	10%
Central & Carlton	9.4%
Granada & LWT	7.2%
Yorkshire & Tyne Tees	5.9%
Anglia & Meridian	5.4%
HTV	2.8%
Scottish	2.6%
Ulster	1.1%
Westcountry	1%
Grampian	0.7%
Border	0.5%
Channel	0%
GMTV	1.6%
BSkyB	4%

Newspapers
Share of newspaper circulation

36.5%	News International plc
23%	Mirror Group plc
14%	United News and Media plc
13%	Daily Mail and General Trust
7.5%	The Telegraph plc
3%	Guardian Media Group plc
2%	Pearson plc

WHO OWNS WHAT

News International plc: *The Sun, The Times, News of the World, Sunday Times*

Mirror Group plc: *Daily Mirror, Sunday Mirror, The People, The Independent, The Independent on Sunday*

United News and Media plc: *Daily Express, Daily Star, Sunday Express*

Daily Mail and General Trust: *Daily Mail, The Mail on Sunday*

The Telegraph plc: *Daily Telegraph, Sunday Telegraph*

Guardian Media Group plc: *The Guardian, The Observer*

Pearson plc: *Financial Times*

Source: Adapted from *The Guardian*, 16 December 1995

1 The diagram shows the share of newspaper circulation statistics in 1995. Which two companies dominated the press in Britain in that year?

2 What proportion of the television audiences did the BBC hold in 1995?

Three trends emerge when looking at media ownership:

- *concentration* – the media of all types are coming under the ownership of fewer and larger companies
- *globalisation* – the companies owning the media are global companies which span the world, so there will be fewer independent sources of information in the entire world. Satellite television transmission means that one company can now broadcast to whole continents
- *diversification* – companies now cover a range of linked media, so they own television, radio, magazines and newspapers and even Internet providers.

Globalisation: the world connections of News International owned by Rupert Murdoch

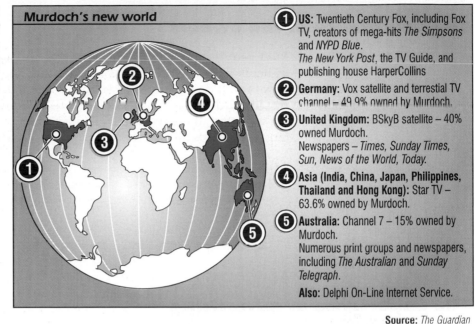

Murdoch's new world

① **US:** Twentieth Century Fox, including Fox TV, creators of mega-hits *The Simpsons* and *NYPD Blue*.
The New York Post, the TV Guide, and publishing house HarperCollins

② **Germany:** Vox satellite and terrestial TV channel – 49.9% owned by Murdoch.

③ **United Kingdom:** BSkyB satellite – 40% owned Murdoch.
Newspapers – *Times, Sunday Times, Sun, News of the World, Today.*

④ **Asia (India, China, Japan, Philippines, Thailand and Hong Kong):** Star TV – 63.6% owned by Murdoch.

⑤ **Australia:** Channel 7 – 15% owned by Murdoch.
Numerous print groups and newspapers, including *The Australian* and *Sunday Telegraph.*

Also: Delphi On-Line Internet Service.

Source: *The Guardian*

Globalisation, diversification and concentration

Synergy has been the buzzword of the week. The marriage between Time Warner and America Online was said to be full of it – synergy between the old media of solid newspaper journalism and glamorous celluloid films combined with the new media of the world wide web.

The breathless coverage of the merger marvelled at its enormity – the biggest of all time, worth up to $180bn, "bigger than Mexico" [its economy, that is].

Consumers would have a vast array of choice at their fingertips, cyber-surfing effortlessly between their favourite Warner movies and the latest news on CNN.com, picking up their AOL messages along the way, before

browsing through online articles from Time, Fortune or Sports Illustrated, or watching Bugs Bunny cartoons.

... questions have arisen about what the corporate mega-merger means, for example, is the new synergy really just old-fashioned cross-promotion? Will it amount to anything more than Time magazine and CNN pumping out worshipful reportage on AOL, with AOL returning the favour by playing Peter Pan to tens of millions of internet users, leading them down a familiar path to Time magazine, CNN and Warner movies?

What will be the future of journalistic integrity in a world where newspapers, magazines,

television news channels and cartoon characters are all part of the same sprawling corporate monolith?

According to Mark Crispin Miller, the director of the Project on Media Ownership at New York University, medical evidence unearthed in 1935 about the dangers of smoking was suppressed for decades in the mainstream press because the tobacco companies were the biggest advertisers in the newspaper business.

Reporters have to be careful not merely about offending some group of local advertisers, they have to be aware of a whole range of corporations, including the one that owns the newspaper or network or

television station they work for.

There really isn't anything like the same amount of relative independence that the big media had 20 years ago.

Thus, when Time published a cover story about tornadoes a few years ago, the critics were quick to point out the resemblance between the picture on the front and the advertising poster for a newly released Warner Bros film, Twister. Late last year, the toy phenomenon Pokemon appeared on Time's cover – reasonably enough perhaps in view of its grip on children around the world, except that the cover appeared just as Warner launched Pokemon, the movie.

Source: Adapted from *The Guardian*, 17 January 2000

1 Explain how the extract illustrates:
a) globalisation
b) diversification
c) concentration.

2 Give two examples of how the contents of Time magazine (one of the biggest selling magazines in the world) was influenced by the process of diversification.

Content of the media

The importance of the owners

Most people think that the owners of the media have direct control over the contents of the magazines, newspapers, films and television productions which they own. It does seem sensible to note that it is unlikely that anything which would attack the owners or their interests would be broadcast. However, for the most part, there seems only limited direct control placed on the output of large companies by the proprietors.

> 'Usually it isn't necessary for the boss to interfere. The culture of the newsroom in this corporate system tacitly requires you to learn the ropes. You learn what to do and what not to do. You've got to make a living.'

Source: Mark Crispin Miller, the director of the Project on Media Ownership at New York University, quoted in *The Guardian*, 17 January 2000

The importance of advertising

It is clear that the media are owned by very few people, but this does not mean that the companies or owners necessarily control their contents. Publishers and broadcasting companies have to take into account that the medium, whether television or newspapers, must be commercial; that is, that it attracts a large (or at least affluent) audience and that the medium attracts advertising. Although the personal views of the owner are important, these can be overridden by the need to make money.

Broadcasters and publishers need to ensure a large audience with the sort of interests and income to afford the products of advertisers. On the other hand, they must be careful not to offend advertisers. An exposé on the dubious practices of a travel firm is unlikely to attract advertising from that firm!

> ... medical evidence unearthed in 1935 about the dangers of smoking was suppressed for decades in the mainstream press because the tobacco companies were the biggest advertisers in the newspaper business.

Source: Mark Crispin Miller, the director of the Project on Media Ownership at New York University, quoted in *The Guardian*, 17 January 2000

The importance of marketing

Having to balance advertising revenue and commercial interests tends to lead media companies to follow one of two paths.
* *the specialist approach* – to appeal to a smaller audience with proven attractiveness to an advertiser (such as specialist car magazines)
* *the mass market approach* – to appeal to as many people as possible. Media which do not rely solely on advertising revenue, such as recording companies and film companies, tend to follow this approach.

The contents of the news

When journalists set up a news story for television or for the newspapers, they are clearly influenced by ensuring they do not offend the proprietor and by having to ensure that what they write or broadcast is commercial. But of all of the millions of events going on in the world, why do they choose only a few for publication or broadcast. The answer seems to be that journalists share an idea of what components a 'good story' must have. These components are known as *news values* or *journalist values*, and include the following elements.

- *Limited period of time* The time period of the event should be short and self-contained. A good story is one where there is a clear beginning and end. A terrible famine one year in Africa is news, but the long-term malnutrition of Africans from poverty is not a good story.

- *Importance* A good story must be fairly important to the person watching or reading. Often this means that the item of news must be national or local. Few British people would be interested in seeing a news item about a major car crash in Venezuala, but it would interesting if it was an important person locally.

- *Understandable* Complex events do not make good stories, so the simpler an event is the better.

- *Unexpected* There should always be an element of surprise, otherwise why is it noteworthy?

- *Composition* For newspapers and general news programmes on television, there has to be a mix of news, such as sport, human interest stories, politics, humour, and so on. News is covered if it is needed for that 'slot'.

- *Personalities* Stories are far more interesting if they are about people, not about issues or events. The media always try to include a 'human angle' in their stories.

- *Political and legal pressures* Finally, there are 'outside' pressures on journalists from such things as the laws of libel (you are not allowed to print or broadcast untrue statements about people).

Media content: the influence of the owners and influences on the owners

GLOBAL MEDIA plc.
owner: H. Jones
PROFITS

The power of an owner to influence people ultimately depends upon the profits.

... normally, editors and journalists have understood the sorts of news items and ways of presenting them that would be acceptable to the owners, which has made heavy-handed interference by them unnecessary (in other words that the paper is generally conservative and supports the views of big business, the law and the police – with only slight criticism of these institutions allowed). Owners have usually had a power over the appointment of senior managers too.

Source: Adapted from M. Grant, *The British Media* Comedia, 1984

1 In what way do owners influence the content of the media?

2 What influences owners?

Main points ▶ The media are extremely important in providing us with information, particularly in a democracy where people choose their leaders on the basis of information provided by newspapers.

▶ There appear to be three trends happening regarding the ownership of the media:
  – concentration – a few large companies are buying all the media
  – globalisation – these companies cover the world
  – diversification – the companies cover the entire range of media including film, the Internet, television, magazines and newspapers.

▶ There is a great debate over the extent that these trends are having on the content of the media.

▶ The content of the media is partially influenced by who controls it, but also important are the profits that a company makes and the need to keep advertisers content.

▶ Media try to attract a specialist audience and thereby attract considerable targeted advertising, or they opt for a mass market approach aiming to be popular to a broad spectrum of the population. Usually sales are higher and advertising lower.

▶ When journalists write news stories, they are influenced by news values, which consist of what journalists think a good story ought to be based upon.

Media and audiences

As we have seen, the media tend to aim their output at different audiences. This enables them to sell advertising, or to capture a mass market. The content of the media varies mainly according to the audience that they are aimed at. For example, whereas BBC Radio 1 aims at young people, Classic FM aims for an older, middle-class audience which is attractive to advertisers.

The newspapers, too, reflect these divisions and in some ways mirror the social and economic differences in British society, with the 'quality' papers (such as *The Guardian* and *The Independent*) and the popular or 'tabloid' newspapers (such as *The Mirror* or *The Sun*). The content, style of writing and presentation of these papers vary considerably, with the information in the 'quality' papers being more detailed and less sensational than that in the tabloids. The focus of the quality papers tends to be on politics and economics, while the stress on the popular papers is on sensational stories often involving some sexual or criminal element.

The same sort of analysis can be made of television broadcasting, with specialist channels such as Sky Sport, and populist channels such as Channel 5.

Activities

1 Design a newspaper.

a) As a group, obtain copies of as many daily and weekly newspapers as you can, both national and local.

b) Do they have different sorts of story in them? Classify the differences in terms of content, style of language, layout, etc.

c) What explanations can you give for the differences?

d) Design your own front page, with imaginary headlines, layout and content.

2 Listen to Radio 1, Radio 5 and Radio 4. What different audiences are they going for? Choose any one 'story'. How would it be presented on each of the stations?

Media audiences

Reading of national daily newspapers: by gender, Great Britain, 1998–9

A

	Percentages	
	Males	**Females**
The Sun	24	17
The Mirror	15	12
Daily Mail	12	12
Daily Express	6	5
The Daily Telegraph	6	5
Daily Star	5	2
The Times	5	3
The Guardian	3	2
The Independent	2	1
Financial Times	2	1
Any national daily newspaper	60	51

B **Television viewing: by gender and age, 1998, United Kingdom**

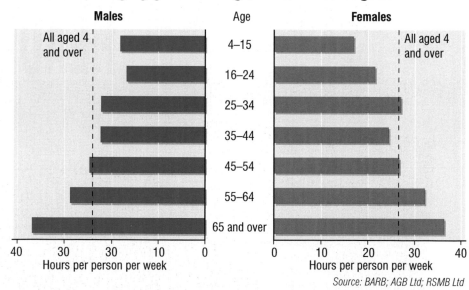

Source: BARB; AGB Ltd; RSMB Ltd

C Subscriptions to satellite and cable television: by social class of the head of the household, 1998-99, United Kingdom

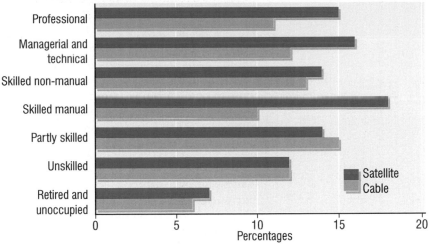

Professional
Managerial and technical
Skilled non-manual
Skilled manual
Partly skilled
Unskilled
Retired and unoccupied

■ Satellite
□ Cable

Percentages

Source: Adapted from *Social Trends 30* (The Stationery Office, 2000)

Look at A.

1 The **Financial Times** and **The Daily Telegraph** are two of the most profitable newspapers. How can this be?

2 Are there any differences in how many males and females read newspapers?

Look at B.

3 Which age group watches most television? Which watches least? Suggest some reasons for this.

Look at C.

4 Which social class has the highest percentage of subscribers to satellite television? How do you think this might influence programmes, if at all?

Women and the media

The media both reflect and help maintain the main roles of women which are to combine being attractive, having a good job and being 'caring' mothers and partners.

We are so accustomed to descriptions of women which describe them as 'attractive blond, 25, etc.' and to comments on their clothes, as well as 'sexy' photographs that we think little of it. As for the caring role, this is catered for by the large number of women's magazines on sale. Those aimed at the 'older' women deal with household problems, house design and decorating, cooking, and romance stories. Those aimed at younger women are more concerned with attractiveness to men (and problems with men) and, to a lesser extent, careers.

Ferguson in *Forever Feminine* found that there were certain themes which could be found in all women's magazines. These included the value of youth and beauty, female unpredictability and the importance of love in women's lives. But women buy these magazines in large numbers, spending £230 million a year on specialist women's magazines. Advertisers too are prepared to pay £190 million each year to gain access to women.

Media messages

Source: Based on M. Ferguson, *Forever Feminine: The Cult of Women's Magazines* (Heinemann, 1983)

As a group look through a cross-section of women's magazines.

1 What themes in the diagram can you find in the magazines?

2 Are there any other themes you could add to the diagram?

3 Do the themes vary depending upon whom the magazine is aimed at?

As a group look through a cross-section of men's magazines.

4 What themes can you find? Are they different from those in women's magazines?

5 Draw your a diagram of 'Themes in men's magazines', similar to the one above.

This process of analysing the contents of the media known as content analysis (see page 33).

'Race' and the media

The attitude of the media towards issues of race and of migration is to portray them as social problems. The general position of the media has been to report on the negative aspects of ethnic minority British people. Prominence is given in the 'tabloid' press to an association between 'race' and crime.

However, sometimes the positive activities of a few ethnic minority Britons are celebrated and are portrayed as having overcome adversity to be successful. This is good in one way, as it presents them in a good light, but the downside of this is that it also implicitly suggests that the reason why so many members of the ethnic minorities suffer from lower standards of living than the majority is their lack of effort or ability.

Portrayal of ethnic minority groups by headines

The table below shows an analysis of headlines of a selection of daily newspapers and how they refer to minority ethnic groups.

	The Times	Sun	Telegraph	Mail	Guardian
MEC: neutral	22	11	20	15	26
MEC: negative	19	25	32	16	14
MEC: positive	4	1	4	4	5

MEC = minority ethnic group

Source: Adapted from P. Trowler, *Investigating Mass Media*, 2nd edition (Collins Educational, 1996); figures originally from T. Van Dijk, *Racism and the Press* (Routledge, 1991)

1 Overall, what is the most common 'tone' adopted – neutral, negative or positive?

2 Were there any differences between newspapers? Explain your answer.

Crime and the media

False impression of the patterns of crime

Press and broadcasting coverage of crime tends to concentrate on certain areas and gives the impression that these sorts of crime are far more common than they realise. In order to give exciting headlines, or dramatic images, the media concentrate on violent crime and sex cases, which are over-reported by a minimum of 20 times their actual occurrence. This creates stereotypes of crime and criminals in people's minds, so that older people, for instance, may be too frightened to go out.

Over and under-reporting of crime by the media

Over reported	Under-reported
Drugs	**Drugs**
Cocaine abuse	Alcohol abuse
Marijuana abuse	Tobacco abuse
Glue sniffing	Food additives
Crime	**Crime**
Sex crime	Fraud and general white-collar crime
Violent crime	Theft and handling stolen goods

Source: P. Trowler, *Investigating Mass Media*, 2nd edition (Collins Educational, 1996)

What other activities do you think are:

a) over-reported?

b) under-reported?

Women, crime and fear

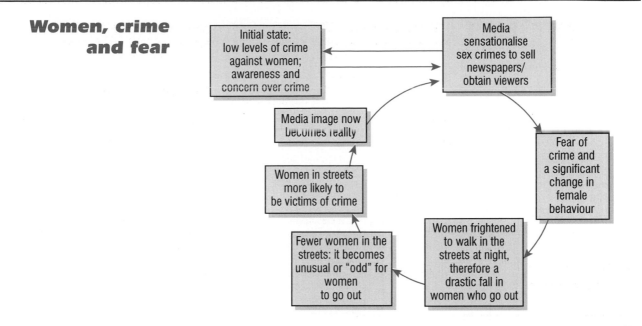

Initial state: low levels of crime against women; awareness and concern over crime

Media sensationalise sex crimes to sell newspapers/ obtain viewers

Media image now becomes reality

Fear of crime and a significant change in female behaviour

Women in streets more likely to be victims of crime

Women frightened to walk in the streets at night, therefore a drastic fall in women who go out

Fewer women in the streets: it becomes unusual or "odd" for women to go out

Source: S. Moore, *Investigating Deviance* (Collins Educational, 1995)

1 Do the media give a true impression of the extent of crime?

2 Why is this so?

3 How can the media actually help create crime?

Media, the police and crime

Because the bulk of the information about crime and police activities comes from the police, reporters have to be careful to be sympathetic to the police. If they were to be too critical in their writing and broadcasting, they might well lose their sources of information. This is important when it comes to complaints against the police by people who feel they have been treated badly, as journalists are hesitant to write about the accusations. Consequently, some sociologists suggest that alternative views are not fairly treated in the press.

Scapegoating: the creation of 'folk devils' and moral panics

Definitions

Moral panic – when a social problem is hugely exaggerated by the media leading to a great public concern completely out of proportion to the real problem

Scapegoating – blaming certain groups of poorer or less powerful people for problems in society, instead of seeking out the real causes

Certain groups in society are often seen as posing a particular threat to the social order, for instance football 'hooligans'. The media exploit the possibilities of a good story and sensationalise the issue. They focus so much on the area that public anxiety is whipped up and strong police action demanded. This results in a severe crackdown on the groups perceived to be dangerous, even if much of the material written and broadcast about them is not true.

Moral panics occur fairly regularly, and studies have been done on gangs of youths, on young black men and on homeless people begging in the streets. At the time of writing there was great media scare about asylum seekers 'abusing' the system of entry into Britain in order to 'scrounge' off the state. Although each case I have mentioned was very different, what each moral panic had in common was that the group causing the panic were relatively powerless. This why sociologists argue that these people are **scapegoats** who attract our attention and annoyance.

A moral panic

The media can help to create a moral panic by labelling a group of people as deviant/bad and then creating a stereotype image of this group. The public are concerned and demand action by the police. Anyone who fits the public stereotype of this type of troublemaker is then under suspicion.

There is usually at least one moral panic each year. In the past they have concerned football supporters, inner-city black youths, drug-takers and asylum seekers.

Using the model below, follow the history of any one moral panic.

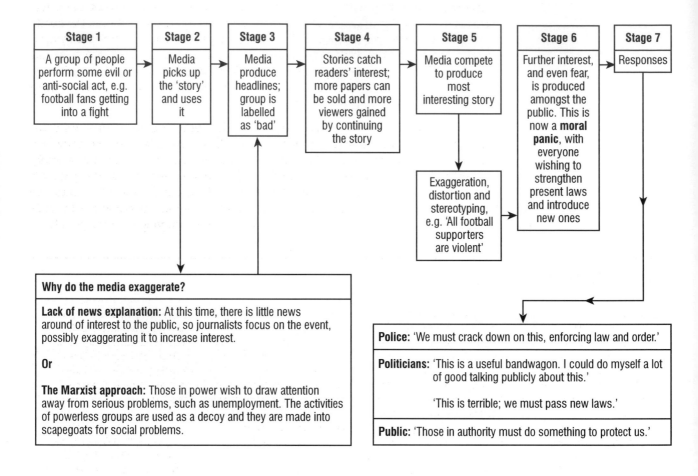

Why do the media exaggerate?

Lack of news explanation: At this time, there is little news around of interest to the public, so journalists focus on the event, possibly exaggerating it to increase interest.

Or

The Marxist approach: Those in power wish to draw attention away from serious problems, such as unemployment. The activities of powerless groups are used as a decoy and they are made into scapegoats for social problems.

Police: 'We must crack down on this, enforcing law and order.'

Politicians: 'This is a useful bandwagon. I could do myself a lot of good talking publicly about this.'

'This is terrible; we must pass new laws.'

Public: 'Those in authority must do something to protect us.'

Main points

▶ Within each medium (for example, newspapers, television) there are different audiences. This affects the content of the broadcast or published work.

▶ Women are a major market for magazines and there is a small range of themes which seem to reflect and reinforce the role of women in society.

▶ Overall, newspapers and the media in general seem to treat women differently from men.

▶ Issues surrounding ethnic minorities in Britain tend to be linked to social problems. Recently this has extended to asylum seekers.

▶ False impressions are given of the extent and seriousness of crime in Britain.

▶ Sociologists say that this has helped create fear amongst women.

▶ Certain groups in society are scapegoated and their activities are made to seem much worse than they are through moral panics.

Advertising and the media

As we have seen in the chapter, advertising is a crucial financial ingredient for most media – without the income from it, most private television companies, for example, simply couldn't continue in their present form. Instead there would only be subscription-based television.

The first question is whether advertising actually works. And the answer seems to be that sometimes it does and sometimes it doesn't. This is a surprisingly vague answer when you consider that for as basic a thing as a bar of soap, the advertising and marketing costs can account for about one third of the price. However, it is often difficult to *prove* that advertising actually works, for goods might have sold well without advertising, or people may continue buying a particular product instead of switching to another brand (reinforcing 'brand loyalty'). Finally, people may stop buying a product, despite excellent publicity, for reasons which have nothing to do with the advertising, for example a drop in spare cash if mortgage rates rise.

It is, however, generally agreed that advertising only reaches people who are sympathetic to the message anyway. People 'read' adverts, just like they pay attention to or ignore other articles in the media. So, adverts have to be carefully targeted to attract people who would be likely to be interested in the product. Therefore, advertisers must place their adverts in the right sort of medium to reach their audience, and must create an advert which is attractive to their particular audience, even it is uninteresting or even annoying to other people.

Does advertising work?

In *The Hidden Persuaders*, Vance Packard exposed how advertisers were trying to 'ferret out' and then exploit our deepest needs – emotional security, 'reassurance of worth', status, sex and so on in attempts to sell products.

Market researchers are still using nearly all the strategies Vance Packard described, and new ones have been added. Peter Cooper, a psychologist who founded the Cooper Research and Marketing Agency, says, 'We want to attach meanings to brands, ones appropriate to those different groups in society, to get people to buy those brands rather than other similar objects', for example Lux lather on the face of a beautiful, mature women – soft skin, fewer wrinkles, youth, beauty, sexual attraction, or a Renault 5 ... youthful, fun-loving, stylish.

Is the advertising expertise of decades now doing its deadly work and manipulating us unawares? ...

But, research seems to show that we are not that gullible. ... whether or not ads are successful depends on many other factors including, surprise, the quality of the brand. Price is also important, packaging, distribution, competition and so on.

Second, if advertising could really 'dictate how our society must think, act and dream' as some critics claim, then heavily advertised products should grab an ever increasing share of the market at the expense of less heavily promoted products – 'but such trends cannot be identified'.

Third, if advertising were such a powerful manipulator, the report says, the failure rate for new products backed by heavy advertising would not be anything like the estimated nine out of ten.

Source: Adapted from M. Tysoe, 'Never give a sucker an even break', *New Society*, 2 May 1985

1 Briefly explain how advertisers try to make us buy products.

2 What sort of 'meanings' do advertisers create concerning:
   a) perfume?
   b) beer?
   c) jeans?
   d) cars (there could be more than one meaning here depending upon the 'market')?
   e) Coca-Cola?

3 According to the extract, are advertisers wholly successful in selling things? Give two reasons for your answer.

4 What other important factors are there?

5 What are the two most effective advertisements which have influenced you? Explain why they did so.

Main points ▶ Advertising is very important financially for much of the media.

▶ It is unclear whether advertising is particularly effective in getting people to purchase the advertised goods.

▶ It seems that only people who would be tempted to buy anyway are influenced.

---

8 CHAPTER SUMMARY

1 The media include all forms or written and transmitted communication to the public.

2 The growth of the media has been extremely fast, with most of it occurring in the twentieth century and it has had an enormous impact upon society

3 In the future, the Internet appears to be the single most important form of medium, as it will allow people almost unlimited access information and entertainment.

4 However, access to the Internet is not equal, and there are clear social class divisions emerging

5 The media play an important role in maintaining social control in society by transmitting values and demonstrating correct ways of behaving.

6 There are four different approaches to understanding the influence of the media on its audience. These are the behaviourist approach, the opinion leader approach, the audience selection approach and the cultural approach.

7 It is important to understand that viewers and readers have a complex relationship with the media. When people watch or read, they are selective in what they take in.

8 The media are extremely important in providing us with information, particularly in a democracy where people choose their leaders on the basis of information provided by newspapers.

9 There appear to be three trends happening regarding the ownership of the media:
   – concentration – a few large companies are buying all the media
   – globalisation – these companies cover the world
   – diversification – the companies cover the entire range of media including film, the Internet, television, magazines and newspapers.

10 The content of the media is partially influenced by who controls it, but also important are the profits that a company makes and the need to keep advertisers content.

11 The media try to attract a specialist audience and thereby attract considerable targeted advertising, or they opt for a mass market approach aiming to be popular to a broad spectrum of the population, where sales are higher and advertising lower.

12 When journalists write news stories, they are influenced by news values, which consist of what journalists think a good story ought to be based upon.

13 Within each medium (for example, newspapers, television) there are different audiences. This affects the content of the broadcast or published work.

14 Women are a major market for magazines and there are a small range of themes which seem to reflect and reinforce the role of women in society.

15 Issues surrounding ethnic minorities in Britain tend to be linked to social problems. Recently this has extended to asylum seekers.

16 False impressions are given of the extent and seriousness of crime in Britain.

17 Certain groups in society are scapegoated and their activities are made to seem much worse than they are through moral panics.

18 It is unclear whether advertising is particularly effective in getting people to purchase the advertised gods, as it seems that only people who would be tempted to buy anyway are influenced.

Test Your Knowledge

1 Why can it be argued that the Internet might actually disadvantage poorer people in employment and education?

2 Name the four approaches to explain the ways in which the media can affect behaviour. Take one of these approaches and explain how it works in your own words.

3 What do the following terms mean:
a) globalisation?
b) diversification?
c) concentration?

4 Identify and explain any three factors influencing the content of newspapers

5 What do we mean by news values? Give two examples.

6 What themes run through women's magazines?

7 Explain the term 'moral panic'.

POPULATION, PLACES AND COMMUNITIES

Chapter contents

- ### Demography
  The subject of demography is important to government planners and sociologists. This chapter examines the reasons for this. We see that the key factors of births, deaths and migration determine the size of the population.

- ### Births
  We learn the meaning of the terms 'birth rate' and 'fertility rate', and examine the reasons for changes in the birth rate over time.

- ### Family size
  Family size has altered over time, and it varies according to social class and ethnicity. This section examines the reasons for this.

- ### Deaths
  We explore the changes in the death rate over time. In particular, we look at the explanations of why the death rate is lower for some groups compared to others. This leads us to discuss the reasons for the great increase in life expectancy which took place over the twentieth century.

- ### Migration
  This section looks first at international migration and examines the reasons why people wish to come into Britain. Then we examine the movement in the population within Britan and the social consequences of the move from north to south. We learn the meaning of the key terms 'immigration' and 'emigration'.

- ### Urban and rural changes
  We look at the reasons for the growth of the cities in Britain, and for their subsequent decline in population. We explore the reality of life in the urban and rural areas and examine in some detail the idea of community. We learn the terms 'urban', 'rural', 'urbanisation' and 'deurbanisation'.

- ### Community and place
  We explore the idea of what a community is and why people have a sense of belonging when living in one place, but not in another. It is often argued that living in the countryside seems to be an important reason for having a sense of community – but is this really true? We will find out.

Demography

> **Definition**
>
> **Demography** – the study of the changes in the composition (size, age, distribution, sex balance) of the population

The study of population concentrates on:

- the changing size of the population
- changes in the age structure of the population
- the changing patterns of where in the country people live
- the proportions of one sex compared to the other.

The correct term for the study of the population is **demography**.

The government does most of the fact-finding about the size and composition of the population. For example, every birth, marriage, divorce and death has to be notified to the local government registrar. The information is then sent on to the government's Office for National Statistics. A second crucial source of information is the Census, which is the national survey of every household in Britain carried out every ten years by the government. The government's

Office for National Statistics also carries out more specialised studies, such as the Family Expenditure Survey, and the General Household Survey.

For up-to-date information on population statistics, go to your college/school library or to the local public library and ask for *Social Trends* (published by the Office for National Statistics) which will be kept in the Reference Section. This contains virtually all the statistical information you want.

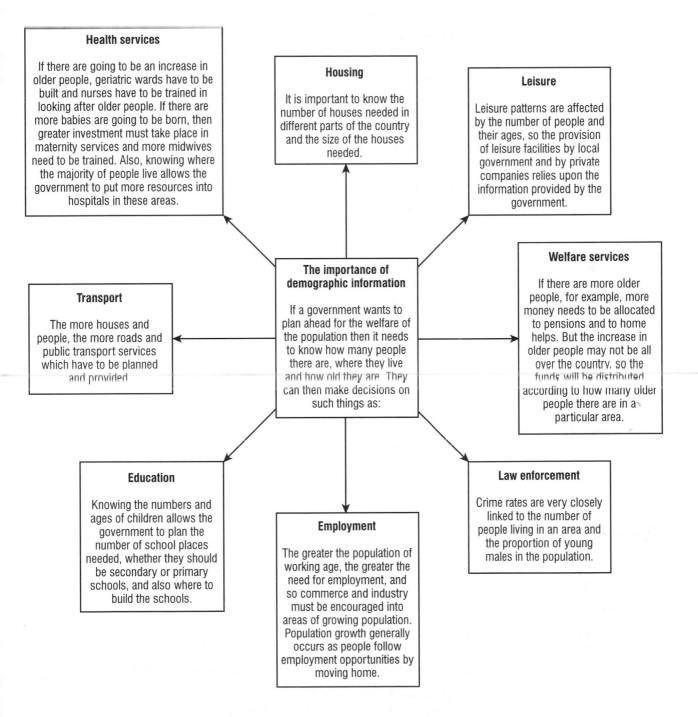

Health services

If there are going to be an increase in older people, geriatric wards have to be built and nurses have to be trained in looking after older people. If there are more babies are going to be born, then greater investment must take place in maternity services and more midwives need to be trained. Also, knowing where the majority of people live allows the government to put more resources into hospitals in these areas.

Housing

It is important to know the number of houses needed in different parts of the country and the size of the houses needed.

Leisure

Leisure patterns are affected by the number of people and their ages, so the provision of leisure facilities by local government and by private companies relies upon the information provided by the government.

Transport

The more houses and people, the more roads and public transport services which have to be planned and provided

The importance of demographic information

If a government wants to plan ahead for the welfare of the population then it needs to know how many people there are, where they live and how old they are. They can then make decisions on such things as:

Welfare services

If there are more older people, for example, more money needs to be allocated to pensions and to home helps. But the increase in older people may not be all over the country, so the funds will be distributed according to how many older people there are in a particular area.

Education

Knowing the numbers and ages of children allows the government to plan the number of school places needed, whether they should be secondary or primary schools, and also where to build the schools.

Employment

The greater the population of working age, the greater the need for employment, and so commerce and industry must be encouraged into areas of growing population. Population growth generally occurs as people follow employment opportunities by moving home.

Law enforcement

Crime rates are very closely linked to the number of people living in an area and the proportion of young males in the population.

What determines the size of the population?

The population of Great Britain is 59.5 million. It increased by over 20 million people during the twentieth century.

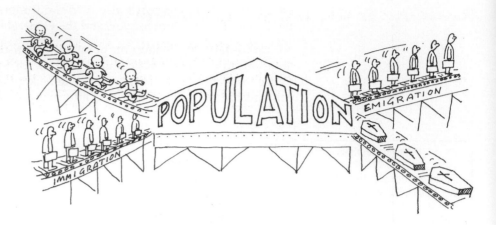

Population growth or decline is decided by people entering through birth and migration and leaving by death and emigration.

At any one time the size of the country's population is the result of:
- the number of births
- the number of deaths
- the number of people entering or leaving the country.

The population of Britain grew fastest in the first decade of the twentieth century when it grew by an estimated 385,000 a year. Today the population is 59.5 million – the eighteenth largest in the world. However, it is an ageing population: in 1901 one person in 20 was aged 65 or over, but by 1998 the figure was one in six. One in 15 of the population is from an ethnic minority.

Main points ▶ Demography is the study of changes in the population of a place.

▶ Information on population change is crucial for the government if it wishes to plan a range of public services including health, education, transport, housing and social services.

▶ The main source of information is the Census – a national study carried out every ten years by the government.

▶ The population size is determined by the number of people born, the number of people who die and the difference left between the numbers entering and leaving the country.

Births

Changes in the birth rate

Generally in the twentieth century the **birth rate** fell. In 1901, for example, the birth rate was 28.6, by 1951 it had fallen to 15.7, and in 2000 it was only 12.00, under half that 1901. To look at it another way, in terms of family size, women born in the 1930s had an average of 2.45 children, compared to 1.8 for women born in the years since 1975.

The decline in the birth rate has not been regular, however. In certain periods, the birth rate has actually increased, for example, in the period immediately after the Second World War, then again from the middle of the 1950s to 1964, and finally since 1978 there has been a slight recovery in the numbers of births from the lowest point in 1977.

Definitions

Birth rate – the number of babies born in a year for every 1,000 people in the population. The higher the birth rate, the more babies are born

Fertility rate – the number of children born for every 1,000 women of child-bearing age (approximately 15–40 years of age)

Reasons for the fall in the birth rate

The most obvious reason for the fall in the birth rate during the twentieth century, and continuing into the twenty-first century, is that methods of birth control have become increasingly available and more widely used. However, to know that something exists does not mean that it will be used. People choose to use birth control methods to limit their family size. The following reasons have been suggested for limiting family size:

- the costs of children
- standards of living and childcare
- changing values
- changing attitudes of women
- cultural expectations.

The costs of children

In the past when there was no state pension and private pensions were beyond most people's reach, the best investment for old age was a large family to look after you. But today, the costs of keeping children until they leave education at 16 or 18 (or increasingly 21) are very high and the need for them to provide support in old age has declined. People therefore do not want large families.

Standards of living and childcare

Closely linked to the first point is the fact that couples prefer to have a higher standard of living than spend their lives and their money rearing children. Couples prefer one or two children as they can then enjoy a high standard of living, and give their children a higher standard of living.

Changing values

Churches have generally looked with disapproval on the use of birth control. The decline in the influence of the churches has meant that fewer people now regard birth control as wrong. Termination too has become acceptable as a means of preventing 'unwanted' preganancies.

Changing attitudes of women

This is probably the most important influence on the birth rate. Over the last century, women changed their views on their role. Traditionally women were expected to stay at home for most of their adult lives, to be housewives and mothers. Today, women want careers of their own and see being a mother as just one part of their lives. The result has been that:

- women want fewer children
- women want children later in life (so they can start a career first)
- childbearing is contained within a shorter period (so that they can go back to work more quickly).

Childbearing now occurs much later in life, commonly around 30 years of age and women return to work on average only 3.5 years after the birth of their last child.

Cultural expectations

All the explanations above combine together to lower the birth rate and, as a result, it has become regarded as normal to have only two children. People are now coming to expect this from marriage and to regard larger families as slightly abnormal

Reasons for the periodic rises in the birth rate

There have been three periods when the birth rate has risen: in the late 1940s/early 1950s, in the early 1960s, and a smaller increase in the 1980s. People born in the 1950 and 1960 increases are often referred to as the 'baby-boomers', despite the fact that they are now in their forties or fifties.

The 1950s increase

The reason for the rise in births in the late 1940s/early 1950s was that the Second World War (1939–45) had separated many couples and, on being reunited, they wished to start, or complete, their families. Six years of births were compressed into only a few years after the war.

The 1960s increase

The rise in the birth rate in the late 1950s and early 1960s was due to very low unemployment and high wages. Young couples were particularly well-off and married young. Early marriages plus affluence led to large families.

The 1980s increase

The most recent rise in the birth rate, in the 1980s (although it is still very low compared to the 1950s), was caused by two things.

- Women who had delayed having children, as we saw earlier, now began to have them.
- People born in the 1950s expansion were now old enough to have their own children.

Family size

Family size and social class

The result of the decline in the birth rate has been smaller families. In 1900, for example, an average family had 3.4 children. Today, the size of family has almost halved, with the average number of children in a family down to 1.85 children.

However, the decline in family size has not always been at the same pace across all social groups. Professional groups have always been ahead of the working class by about 20 years in reducing average family size. This seems to be because they first saw the advantages of smaller families and were more likely to know about, and want to use, contraceptives. Today, however, the differences in family size are very small across the social classes with two children being the most common choice.

Family size and ethnicity

The average family size for the range of ethnic groups which make up the British population varies considerably. There are two main factors which influence the size of families across ethnic groups:

- culture
- age composition of the ethnic group.

Culture

We have already seen how the culture of the majority, white population has shifted to a stress on having no more than two children. However, for Asian groups in the population there is still a great importance in having larger families. The family has a particularly important place in the culture of Asian groups in Britain and a successful marriage is one which includes a number of children. Children are expected to look after their parents in their old age and to provide financial and emotional support for brothers and sisters. This cultural stress is also supported by the disapproval of birth control by the Muslim and Hindu religions.

There is evidence, however, that over time the influence of British culture and its stress upon family limitation has had some effect, so that the birth rates of second and third generation British Muslims and Hindus appears to be moving towards the fewer children.

For those of African Asian origins, there appears to be very little difference from the majority population in completed family size.

Age composition

The greater the number of younger people in a society, the higher the birth rate. As a result of historical patterns of immigration, there is a higher proportion of younger people amongst those of Asian origin than amongst the population as a whole. This partially explains the higher birth rates for this group.

Main points

▸ Birth rate refers to the numbers born for every 1,000 people in the population.

▸ Throughout the twentieth century and into the twenty-first century the birth rate has declined.

▸ The main reason for the decline has been that women no longer wish to have large families and that people generally want higher standards of living for themselves and their children. By working and having fewer children, this can be achieved.

▸ There have been three periods in the twentieth century when birth rates rose for specific historical reasons.

▸ Linked to the decline in the birth rate has been a decrease in family size.

▸ There are differences between ethnic groups in terms of family size, with those of Pakistani and Bangladeshi origin having larger families on average.

Deaths

The **death rate** declined very rapidly in the nineteenth century and in the early part of the twentieth century. But since the 1920s there has only been only a slight fall. At present, the death rate is 10.0 for males and 11.0 for females.

Reasons for the decline in the death rate

In the nineteenth century there was a massive programme of public health improvements – decent drainage and guaranteed supplies of pure water, for example. This eliminated many of the killer diseases, such as cholera and typhoid. In the twentieth century, programmes of immunisation began to combat other diseases, such as polio and diphtheria, and the introduction of the National Health Service improved health care standards.

However, it has been argued that the improvements in the standards of living have been more important than medical advances in lowering the death rates. Improved diets, better quality housing and shorter working hours have all led to a much stronger resistance to diseases than ever before.

Definition

Death or mortality rate – the number of deaths each year for every 1,000 people in the population

Social class differences in death rates

In the table below, the figure 100 represents the average number of deaths (under 65). Any social class above 100, has a higher than average number of early deaths, and any figure below has a lower than average number of deaths.

The 'highest' social class is I, comprising top professionals and managers, and the 'lowest' social class is V, comprising unskilled labourers.

Social Class	I	II	III (non-manual)	III (manual)	IV	V
	66	72	100	117	116	189

Source: I. Reid, *Class in Britain* (Polity Press, 1998)

1 Which groups has the lowest number of early deaths?

2 Which social class has the highest number of early deaths?

3 Is there a pattern which emerges in the table?

Infant mortality

Definition

Infant mortality rate – the number of children under one year of age dying for every 1,000 children born

A very important element of the declining death rate has been the fall in the number of infants dying.

The fall in **infant mortality** was very marked in the twentieth century, with big reductions even in the last 40 years. In 1961, for example, the infant mortality rate was still about 26, whereas today the male infant mortality rate has fallen to 6.0 and females to 5.0. Compare this with a figure of 72 per thousand in 1921!

The reasons for the decline in the infant mortality rate are much the same as for the death rate in general, but also reflect the greatly improved midwife and maternity services provided by the NHS. However, even today, there are differences between the richer and poorer groups in society, and between different ethnic groups. This is partly a reflection of the better standards of housing and diet of the more affluent.

Research on social class and health inequalities

Fox conducted a longitudinal study of health differences between civil servants and found that the 'higher up the ladder' the greater the life expectancy. Those at the lowest civil servant grade were three times more likely to die before pensionable age than those in the highest grades.

Births and deaths

Births and deaths, United Kingdom

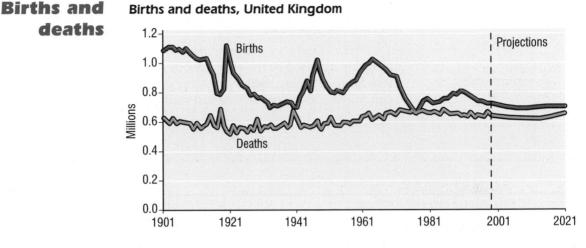

Thousands

	Population at start of period	Live births	Deaths	Net natural change (live births minus deaths)	Net migration (those entering UK minus those leaving)	Overall change
Mid-year projections[1]						
1998–2001	59,237	714	630	84	155	239
2001–2011	59,954	701	614	87	95	187
2011–2021	61,773	712	620	92	95	187

[1]1998-based projections.

Source: *Social Trends 30* (The Stationery Office, 2000)

Look at the graph.

1 How many (a) births and (b) deaths were there in 1901?

2 How many (a) projected births and (b) projected deaths were there in 2000?

3 When did the numbers of births increase? Suggest reasons.

4 When did the numbers of deaths increase? Suggest reasons.

5 Overall, what happened to the numbers of births in the twentieth century?

Look at the table.

6 Overall, from 1998 onwards, is the population going to increase or decrease?

7 Will there be more births than deaths, or more deaths than births? Support your answer with figures.

8 What will be the single biggest factor in the growth of the population?

Life expectancy

The number of people aged over 65 is nearly five times greater now than in 1901. Today, almost 20 per cent of the population are in this age group, and this will continue to increase. Indeed, by 2050 this age group will comprise more than 30 per cent of the population.

At birth a male can expect to live to 75 and a female to 80. People live longer lives than they have ever done before, and an increasingly large number of people can expect to have longer lives. This affects how people behave when they are younger as they have to plan for old age, thinking about pensions, about their health and also what sort of life they might like to lead after retirement.

Long life is caused by the very reasons that lowered the death rate; that is, high standards of living, better housing conditions, better diets, better working conditions and shorter hours, and medical advances.

Factors influencing population size

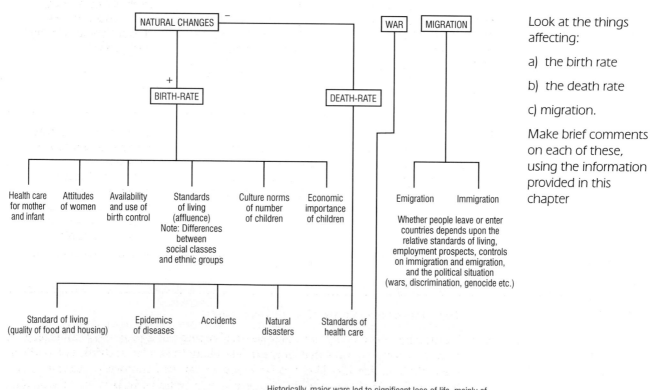

Look at the things affecting:

a) the birth rate

b) the death rate

c) migration.

Make brief comments on each of these, using the information provided in this chapter

Explanations for the differences in life expectancy and health between different social groups

	Sex	Social class	Ethnicity
Lifestyles	Males are more likely to engage in risk lifestyles, such as dangerous car driving/motorbikes and are more likely to drink alcohol and smoke. Women more health conscious.	Professional and managerial groups least likely to work in dangerous occupations to have lower stress jobs and less likely to smoke or drink excessive alcohol. Tend to be more health conscious.	
Use of health services	Females more likely to use health services than males. The NHS provides wider range of specialist services for females.	Professional groups more likely to use the complete range of health services.	Ethnic minorities are less likely to use health services, especially older people, possibly explained by language difficulties
Deprivation	Women are actually more deprived than men, but tend to have better diets and to be more aware of health issues. This seems to overcome the influence of deprivation and they have longer expectation of life.	Working-class people have lower incomes/poorer diets/worse living conditions and worse jobs. These all take their toll over a lifetime.	Most ethnic minority groups share similar low levels of income, diet, living conditions and stressful jobs as working-class people.
Biological	Higher death rates of infant males suggest that females are physically tougher than males.	Life expectancy differences caused by social and economic conditions – **not** biological differences.	Overall differences in life expectancy and health caused by social conditions. Though evidence of some differences in likelihood of diseases (for example, sickle cell anaemia).

Sex differences in life expectancy

Women are more likely than men to survive into old age. Apart from biological factors, the reasons are that they are less likely to smoke or drink as heavily as men. Women are less likely to be killed in car and motorbike accidents and they are less likely to work in dangerous occupations. In periods of war, men are also more likely to die as they will be in the armed forces.

By the age of 75, women outnumber men by almost two to one.

	Age	Under 1	1–15	16–34	35–54	55–64	65–74
Death rates per 1,000 of the population in 2011	Males	3.7	0.2	0.9	2.4	9.5	24.6
	Females	3.1	0.1	0.3	1.8	6.2	15.7

Source: *Social Trends 30* (The Stationery Office, 2000)

1 Which sex has the highest infant mortality rate?

2 Which sex has less chance of dying under the age of 74?

The ageing population: a social problem?

There is a great discussion over whether we should see the increased numbers of people who live to an old age as a burden to society or not.

For society as a whole, the **burden of dependency** increases. By this, we mean the costs of supporting older people, for example in pensions and additional health care costs, which are partially paid for by extra taxation. For families, the problem is the need to care for an increasing number of older people at home. The task of caring for older people is much more likely to fall on wives and daughters.

For older people, there will be some cases of loneliness, of poverty and of slow physical decline before death.

The burden of dependency

The dependent population of the UK, by age

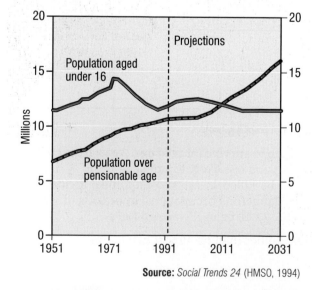

Source: *Social Trends 24* (HMSO, 1994)

1 How many people over pensionable age were there in 1951?

2 How many will there be in 2031?

3 What are the comparable figures for the under-16s?

4 People live longer. Why?

5 Do you think this is a good or bad thing for society? Explain your answers.

Or an opportunity?

People are now fitter and healthier much later in life, and most people can expect an active and relatively healthy retirement of ten years or more. Of course, older people do not necessarily stop working and many take on part-time work. There has been an increase in the affluence of older people too, so that private pensions provide them with a moderate standard of living. Within the family, older people can provide free child minding and support. The majority of older people do not need care for the bulk of their retirement and even when they do, this is more likely to be provided by the husband or wife than by the younger generation.

Finally, the decision on whether older people are a burden is mainly a political decision. Early retirement and high state pensions cost the state money, while later retirement and low pensions with limited health care costs the state a lot less.

Consequences of the growing numbers of older people

FOR INDIVIDUALS
Positive consequences: Escape from the drudgery of work; more time for leisure interests, education, learning new skills, Involvement with family
Negative consequences: Loss of income, status and sense of purpose with loss of jobs (especially if it is professional/managerial); loss of social contacts and deterioration in health.

FOR THE FAMILY
Positive consequences: Older people can provide help and companionship for the younger generations, babysitting, childcare, etc. (depends on their stage in the 'family life cycle').
Negative consequences: Infirm, older people place a great burden in terms of care on the younger generation. It is usually women who have to look after them, some having to give up their jobs and social lives.

FOR SOCIETY
Health and social services demands are very heavy and costly, with over 35 per cent of welfare costs for older people and pensions for the retired, involve heavy insurance burden on those working – known as the 'burden of dependency'.

The rapidly changing nature of society means that the experience of the old is no longer valued by the young. This leads to a loss of status of older people in society.

But much of the so-called burden of dependency is really a reflection of *political* decisions to make people retire at 60/65, causing poverty and loss of status. Retirement creates jobs for the young.

To find out more about older people, record an interview about their lives and their family. Compare your information with what is here.

You might want to question your own grandparents (if over 60) and some people in retirement homes.

More information can be obtained from the charity 'Help the Aged'

Main points ▶ The death rate refers to the numbers of people dying each year for every 1,000 people in the population.

▶ The mortality rate has been declining over the last 200 years.

▶ The main reasons for the decline appears to be an increasingly high standards of living, of nutrition and of health provision.

▶ Infant mortality (children dying under the age of one) has declined very markedly.

▶ People live longer now than at any point in history. The reasons for this are the same as those which affect the mortality rate – improved quality of life, food and health provision.

▶ Class and sex differences still exist between groups in terms of death rates and life expectatancy.

▶ The population of Britain is growing older on average and some people argue that this is causing a 'burden of dependency', as older people cost more in terms of pensions and health care costs. Others see it as an opportunity for grandparents to help in child care and for older people to contribute more to society with the spare time they have on their hands.

Migration

International migration

Definitions

Migration – the movement of people to live in a different place

Immigration – the movement of people into a country (or area)

Emigration – the movement of people out of a country (or area)

At the turn of the twenty-first century, about 70,000 people each year from other countries were being accepted to live in Britain – the single largest group accepted come from Asia. Very few people now **emigrate** from Britain. The difference between **immigration** totals and **emigration** totals is known as net **migration**.

In the 1950s immigrants began to arrive first from the West Indies and then from the Indian sub-continent. They came because of poverty at home and because there were not enough workers in Britain to fill all the job vacancies. From 1962 onward there was a series of laws restricting the numbers of new immigrants. Today, most accepted for settlement are coming to join their partners or have been accepted as in need of asylum.

Asylum seekers and refugees

During the late 1990s and the early part of this century, a very significant change took place in the reason for people arriving in Britain. People have increasingly come to Britain because they claim that they are being oppressed by their government and will suffer if they stay there. The majority of people who apply for asylum come from central and eastern Europe.

Internal migration

The move to the south-east

The distribution of Britain's population is increasingly becoming unbalanced. More people are emigrating to the south-east (excluding London, which is actually losing population) from other parts of Britain – most particularly from the north-west and West Midlands. In these areas, in particular, the birth rate cannot match the numbers leaving.

Internal migration: some statistics

The table gives the percentage change in the numbers leaving or entering (+ or −) the regions of the UK, according to age groups.

Thousands

	North East	North West	Yorkshire and the Humber	East Midlands	West Midlands	East	London	South East	South West	England	Wales	Scotland	Northern Ireland
Age													
15–24	0.1	−4.1	−0.7	−0.9	−3.1	−3.0	22.7	−1.2	−3.9	5.9	−0.8	−1.8	−3.5
25–34	−2.2	−3.2	−3.0	1.9	−2.2	6.4	−6.2	7.5	4.1	3.2	−1.1	−2.6	0.5
65–74	−0.1	−0.6	−0.1	0.7	−0.4	1.5	−5.2	1.2	2.4	−0.6	0.3	0.2	0.1

1 Which area:

a) gains most 15–24-year-olds?

b) loses most 15–24-year-olds?

2 Which area loses most people overall? Suggest possible reasons.

3 Draw up a table to show which regions are the overall gainers and losers in population. Put your lists in order. Suggest reasons for each region's place in the table.

4 Which area of the country has the highest migration of older people? Suggest reasons for this. What implications do you think this might have for:

a) housing?

b) health services?

c) social services?

d) local employment?

Reasons for internal migration

The main force driving people to move is the lack of jobs and, as most of the jobs are now in the south-east, that is where people have to go.

Population movement and social problems

A growing population shift from the north is creating greater pressure for more homes in the already overcrowded south-east of England, according to research by Joseph Rowntree Foundation and the Chartered Institute of Housing. The analysis does not dispute official government projections showing that England will need an extra 3.8m new homes between 1996 and 2021. But it argues that many more than anticipated might have to be sited in the south-east. Serplan, the consortium of south-east planning authorities, has scaled down earlier government guideline building targets from 1.4m to 914,000 homes early next century. It says any more would create "difficult environmental choices" – although planners still say a string of second generation new towns may be needed.

Official figures ... have underestimated the level of migration from England's less favoured regions. The population of the south-east has been rising by almost 70,000 annually.

At the same time, an increasing number of homes are being abandoned in the north, with departures from council housing alone put at over 116,000 annually.

Local authorities are now demolishing entire estates, including modern blocks of flats, because there is no demand.

Last month the full scale of the northern jobs crisis was revealed with the publication of a report showing that 500,000 jobs have been lost in the big cities since 1981 – compared with a net gain of 1.7m elsewhere, often in the south-east.

The report's authors warned that the "urban jobs gap" posed a threat to social cohesion, as well as the functioning of the labour market "which policy-makers would be foolish to ignore".

Source: Adapted from *The Guardian*, 25 June 1999

1   In which direction is the population shift?

2   What does this mean in terms of housing demand?

3   Why is Serplan concerned?

4   What is happening to housing in the north?

5   Can you suggest other problems that the shift of population may be causing?

Main points ▶ Migration refers to the movement of people; emigration means moving out and immigration means moving in.

▶ International migration: more people immigrate than emigrate.

▶ Internal migration: people are leaving the north of Britain to move to the south-east.

▶ The result of this is that there is increasing pressure on housing social services, health services and transport in the south-east, and a decline in the population of the north of Britain.

Urban and rural changes

The movement of the population from Scotland, the north and the West Midlands to the south-east has not been the only major population change. Over time there have also been changes in the balance between the number of people living in the larger towns and cities compared to those choosing to live in the countryside. These changes in the distribution of the population in Britain have many social consequences

Urbanisation

The growth of cities in Britain really begins with industrialisation, around the end of the eighteenth century. Before 1800, only about 15 per cent of the population lived in towns and cities; 100 years later, 75 per cent of the population lived in them.

The original growth of the cities was because people moved there from the countryside in order to get jobs. This happened because changes in methods of farming in the eighteenth century meant that there were fewer jobs in the countryside, while the process of industrialisation was creating more and more jobs in cities and larger towns. Until the middle of the twentieth century, the numbers of people living in the countryside continued to decline and those living in towns increased.

Urban areas today

Today, the majority of the population live in towns and cities, but their experiences of life in these places are very different. Towns and cities are divided by levels of affluence, cultural differences and ethnicity.

City centres

City centres are the focus for commercial activities, entertainment and shopping and have few people living there. The problems of the city centre include traffic and pollution, and crime and violence late at night when people leave bars and clubs.

Inner cities

The inner-city was originally the place where the wealthy lived. As they moved out to the better suburbs, the houses decayed and were turned into poor quality, rented accommodation. Alongside these are the inner-city developments built by local councils for the less well off.

In the last 25 years, a process of redevelopment, or *gentrification*, has taken place, with wealthy people moving back into the inner cities. But still the inner cities have some of the greatest problems of poverty and crime.

The suburbs

Suburbs vary from cheaper housing developments to very expensive areas. However, they tend to be full of houses which are privately owned and tend to have fewer social problems than either the inner cities or the social housing estates.

Social housing estates

These are large developments which are usually out of town centres which have been built by local authorities for rent by people on lower incomes. These tend to have the poorest quality housing, and some of the highest rates of crime and social problems. Some estates have such great problems that people refuse to live there and they become known as problem estates.

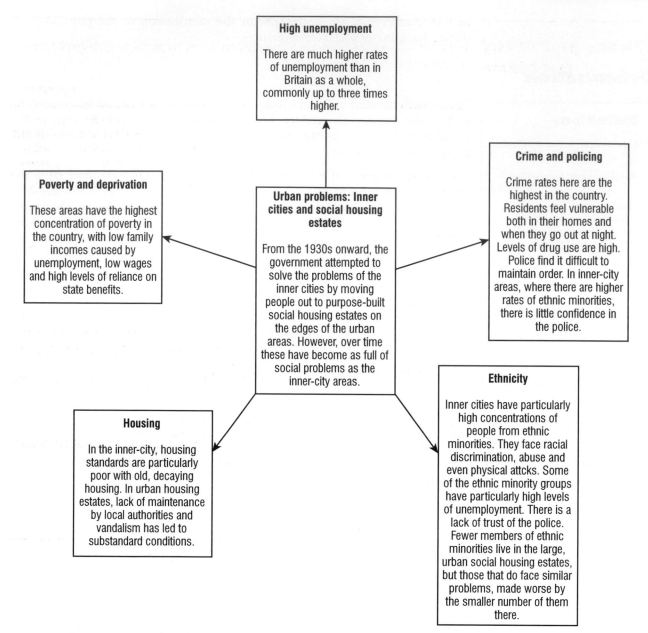

High unemployment

There are much higher rates of unemployment than in Britain as a whole, commonly up to three times higher.

Poverty and deprivation

These areas have the highest concentration of poverty in the country, with low family incomes caused by unemployment, low wages and high levels of reliance on state benefits.

Urban problems: Inner cities and social housing estates

From the 1930s onward, the government attempted to solve the problems of the inner cities by moving people out to purpose-built social housing estates on the edges of the urban areas. However, over time these have become as full of social problems as the inner-city areas.

Crime and policing

Crime rates here are the highest in the country. Residents feel vulnerable both in their homes and when they go out at night. Levels of drug use are high. Police find it difficult to maintain order. In inner-city areas, where there are higher rates of ethnic minorities, there is little confidence in the police.

Ethnicity

Inner cities have particularly high concentrations of people from ethnic minorities. They face racial discrimination, abuse and even physical attcks. Some of the ethnic minority groups have particularly high levels of unemployment. There is a lack of trust of the police. Fewer members of ethnic minorities live in the large, urban social housing estates, but those that do face similar problems, made worse by the smaller number of them there.

Housing

In the inner-city, housing standards are particularly poor with old, decaying housing. In urban housing estates, lack of maintenance by local authorities and vandalism has led to substandard conditions.

De-urbanisation: the move out of the cities

Definition

De-urbanisation – the process of people moving out of larger towns and cities

Although over 87 per cent of the population live in urban areas, certain important changes have been taking place.

There has been a move away from the cities, towards the outer suburbs, small towns and the countryside over the last 25 years. During this period, for example, London has lost 10 per cent of its population and has actually declined by two million people from its peak.

People prefer the better standard of housing available and the cleaner, less polluted environment of the suburbs and countryside. Cars and trains make travel into the big cities for work fairly quick and easy, although there are increasing problems of congestion. Companies too are moving out of the big cities, preferring the lower costs and higher quality of life for their employees in the smaller towns. This speed of this process has increased with developments in communications technology which means that people do not have to be near each other to communicate.

Areas and social problems

The table shows the percentage of people concerned about issues in different types of neighbourhoods in England.

Percentages

	Affluent suburban and rural areas	New home-owning areas	Council estates and low income areas	Affluent urban areas
Crime	52	60	68	63
Traffic	40	42	39	59
Vandalism and hooliganism	33	50	64	50
Litter and rubbish	23	44	54	50
Noise	17	26	35	41
Dogs	24	33	35	29

Source: Adapted from *Social Trends 30* (The Stationery Office, 2000)

1 What percentage of people living in affluent urban areas were worried about crime?

2 Was this the highest level of concern?

3 What least concerned people living in new home-owning estates?

4 Which area had a lower percentage of people concerned about issues – affluent suburban and rural areas or affluent urban areas?

5 Which area had the highest level of problems overall?

6 Which had the lowest?

7 Does the table tell us anything useful about urban, suburban and rural life?

The changing countryside

The view that life has always been pleasant in the countryside compared to the squalid life of the cities is a myth. Life has almost always been just as hard in the countryside and poverty was just as common. Unemployment, homelessness and disease were facts of life.

In the twentieth and into the twenty-first century, there remain large amounts of poverty in the countryside; one of the lowest paid occupations is that of agricultural worker and there is a lack of hospitals and clinics, local public transport and social services, as well as shops. Nevertheless, for those people who are able to commute to relatively well-paid jobs in the towns and cities, there are considerable attractions to life in the countryside and the last 30 years have seen a move away from the city to life in the small towns and villages.

One important reason for the move has been the fact that more affluent people can afford the high price of public transport into the cities, or can commute by car. A second reason which is growing in importance is the development of new technology, particularly e-mail and the Internet, which means that many professionals have less need to go into an office each day.

The effects on the countryside have been quite dramatic. There has been a decline in agricultural land as more housing developments are created – in the first 20 years of the twenty-first century, more than one million houses are needed to cope with the people who move away from city centres to the countryside. These houses will, of course, actually help to destroy the rural lifestyle which the people want.

Rural truths

An official government sponsored report on the rural environment [*The State of the Countryside 2000* by the Countryside Agency] found that:

... farm labourers face low wages and unaffordable housing – often having been priced out of the market by former city-dwellers. Unemployment is higher in the countryside and more workers depend upon part-time, seasonal or casual jobs.

Shops are closing in many villages and small towns – with devastating impact on those too old or too poor to drive. The typical village food shop is now 'only marginally viable' and rural post offices are fast becoming things of the past ... Country pubs are also closing at the rate of three per year.

Mr Cameron [Head of the Countryside Agency] issues a personal warning. 'Behind the rosy image of the rural idyll lie some very real problems; problems of rural isolation, a declining environment, pressurised and declining services and a vulnerable rural economy'.

Source: Adapted from *The Daily Mail*, 27 April 2000

1 Explain the meaning of 'part-time, seasonal or casual' types of work. What is the result of this for local people?

2 Why do you think the shops and post offices are closing? Why is it of particular importance to old people and those who cannot drive?

3 In your own words, explain what the extract means when it says that the countryside is not a 'rural idyll'.

4 Conduct a small survey. Individually, ask a small sample of people to name the first five words which come into their minds when you say the words 'Living in the country'. Pool your words. What images are shared by your respondents? Are they true or false, according to the information you have?

House prices in the more attractive parts of the countryside have risen to the point where local people cannot afford to buy, leaving the way clear for commuters to buy up the properties. The small, local communities have been altered by an influx of new people, bringing new attitudes and ideas. Often this may lead to conflict between the new arrivals from towns and cities and the population who live there already.

Some small communities have been completely swamped by huge new developments and new towns, such as Milton Keynes, Basildon and Peterborough, which were built on the site of a few small villages and now are complete towns.

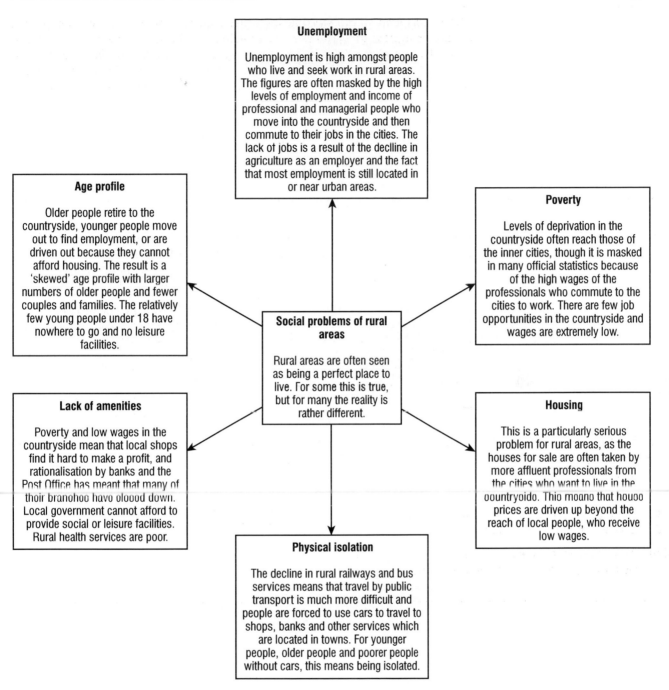

Unemployment

Unemployment is high amongst people who live and seek work in rural areas. The figures are often masked by the high levels of employment and income of professional and managerial people who move into the countryside and then commute to their jobs in the cities. The lack of jobs is a result of the decline in agriculture as an employer and the fact that most employment is still located in or near urban areas.

Age profile

Older people retire to the countryside, younger people move out to find employment, or are driven out because they cannot afford housing. The result is a 'skewed' age profile with larger numbers of older people and fewer couples and families. The relatively few young people under 18 have nowhere to go and no leisure facilities.

Poverty

Levels of deprivation in the countryside often reach those of the inner cities, though it is masked in many official statistics because of the high wages of the professionals who commute to the cities to work. There are few job opportunities in the countryside and wages are extremely low.

Social problems of rural areas

Rural areas are often seen as being a perfect place to live. For some this is true, but for many the reality is rather different.

Lack of amenities

Poverty and low wages in the countryside mean that local shops find it hard to make a profit, and rationalisation by banks and the Post Office has meant that many of their branches have closed down. Local government cannot afford to provide social or leisure facilities. Rural health services are poor.

Housing

This is a particularly serious problem for rural areas, as the houses for sale are often taken by more affluent professionals from the cities who want to live in the countryside. This means that house prices are driven up beyond the reach of local people, who receive low wages.

Physical isolation

The decline in rural railways and bus services means that travel by public transport is much more difficult and people are forced to use cars to travel to shops, banks and other services which are located in towns. For younger people, older people and poorer people without cars, this means being isolated.

Community and place

Definition

Community – a sense of belonging to a particular place and having something in common with other people who live there

As societies moved from being predominantly rural and agricultural, to being urban and industrial, the changes that took place were not just physical, such as the growth of roads, houses and factories, they were also changes in the way people behaved and thought.

Tonnies, a sociologist writing at the end of the nineteenth century, said that it was possible to distinguish quite clearly between:

- the social life of the traditional rural society, which he called *community* life (or *Gemeinschaft*), and
- the social life of the fast moving cities, which he called *association* (or *Gesellschaft*).

Community

This type of society is one where people have close contact with others, forming a tight social network, and where there is a sense of 'belonging'. People hold very similar values, and in general are very similar to one another. Individuals know each other not just in one role, but in many, for instance as sister-in-law, employer, next-door neighbour, friend.

OAKINGTON & WESTWICK COMMUNITY NEWSLETTER – MARCH 2000

THE HUMPTY DUMPTY PLAYGROUP. All the money from these events will go towards re-fitting the kitchen at the Playgroup hut. Please do come along and bring your friends:

➤ **On Thursday 16 March, 7.45pm** in Oakington School Hall we are holding a **Fashion Show**. Did you come to our other Shows? Weren't they fun? This is a great evening out. Models from the village parade the Zoom Fashion clothes along the catwalk and there is plenty of time to try on and purchase. Over 1000 brand new, high street boutique and store garments, most from £4 to £15. Cash, cheques (with card), Visa/Mastercard. Tickets available from Lis Warboys (**234365**), the shop or bakery, £2.50 including a glass of wine.

➤ **On Tuesday 4 April 7.00 for 7.30pm** we are having a **Fundraising Dinner.** This is a 5 course dinner at Cambridge Regional College, £15 per person. The College donates £8 from every ticket to Playgroup, so this is a brilliant fundraiser for us. Tickets are available from Sarah Welch (**235850**) with a £5 deposit please; numbers are limited so book early. There will also be a bar and a raffle.

➤ **On Saturday 8 April from 2-4pm** there will be a **Table Top Sale at Oakington School.** This is like an indoor car boot sale; you book a table for £5 and keep the proceeds of whatever you sell. There will also be a cake stall and refreshments. There are 20 tables available so please book early through Claire Edwards on **233682**. Entrance to the sale will be 20p.

OAKINGTON & WESTWICK LADIES SOCIETY. On Wednesday 16 February Honor Ridout visited the club and gave us a very interesting talk and slide show entitled "Extremes in Fashion: A History of Costume". We were shown slides of clothes and accessories of our ancestors from the middle ages up to date. It was obvious that nowadays the clothes we wear are much simpler and don't involve the metres of material they used in the Middle Ages nor the elaborate decorations like jewels etc that were used in the Victorian years.

Our next meeting, on **Wednesday 15 March,** will include a talk by Beryl Sealy entitled "The Clan that I Married: New Zealand Pioneer Family". The meeting starts at **7.30pm** in the Methodist Chapel.

Trisha Haws.

HISTON DISTRICT GUIDES. Are you an adult aged between 18 – 60 and have an interest in working with young people, maybe you have worked with Brownies or Guides before – then Histon District Guides would like to hear from you. Please call Elaine Bailey on **232962**.

VILLAGE MILLENNIUM EVENTS: Continuing our series of talks at The School – 7.30pm:

❖ *Tuesday 14 March*
"Archaeological Excavation in Oakington" by Stephen Macaulay.

❖ **Wednesday 19 April**
"History of Oakington Airfield" by John Hamlyn, (author of several books and a local historian).

There will be no charge for these events but we hope you will give a donation towards the cost of the Village Day.

Tea Towels – The Community Association have produced Tea Towels for the Millennium in Oakington, they will be available at the Village Talks and Village day at only £2.75 each.

Please note – The Millennium Mugs are available to ALL CHILDREN IN THE VILLAGE UNDER 16 – that is YEAR ELEVEN. (Children attending Oakington Primary School do not need to fill in form). The mugs can be collected on **Thursday 13 April** at Oakington School until **5pm**. Please complete the slip below and return ASAP.

COMMUNITY ASSOCIATION - The next meeting of the Association will be on **Tuesday 21 March** at **7.45pm** at the School. Will all village organisations please send a representative.

OAKINGTON BABY AND TODDLER GROUP are holding a Messy Play session on **Saturday 8 April** from **10 until 11 am** in the Playgroup Hut - all under fives welcome. The theme will be Easter and will include Easter biscuit decorating. Another date for your diaries is the Easter Party on **Tuesday 11 April from 2 – 3.30pm**. We will be having an Easter Egg hunt and Easter Hat competition. Please sign the list in the Playgroup Hut to give us an idea of numbers, or please phone Claire Edwards on **233682**.

ST ANDREWS CHURCH. On Mothering Sunday **2 April** at **10.15am** there will be a service in the Village Church to celebrate family life and receive God's blessing on it. Do come ! The service lasts just under the hour and is an informal service for children and families.

Easter celebrations at St Andrews:
❖ **Good Friday, 21 April – 10.00am.** Meditations on the Cross.
❖ **Easter Day, 23 April**
  10.15am. Praise for the Resurrection and receiving of New Life.
  6.30pm – Festival Evensong.

PLEASE COMPLETE FORM FOR ALL CHILDREN UNDER 16 NOT AT OAKINGTON PRIMARY SCHOOL

NAME:.. **AGE:**.................... **SCHOOL YEAR:**..........................
ADDRESS:.. **TEL No:**....................................
I can/cannot collect my Millennium mug on Thursday 13 April.   Please return form to 14 Orchard Way or Oakington School.

Association

This is the type of society where people have only a superficial relationship other people, seeing them only at work for instance, but never outside (having a single-role relationship). There is little sense of belonging to any community, and people are prepared to move away with little regret.

Tonnies' community and association

	Community	Association
Relationships	People are very close, and know each other	People know few others and their relationships are generally impersonal
Values	People share the same basic values and this usually promotes harmony	There are a number of competing values held by different groups – this can lead to conflict
Actions and behaviour	People act in traditional ways and take into account the good of the community	People look after their own interests and are more likely to accept new ideas
Most important institutions and organisations	The family and the local village or area is the focal point of a person's sense of belonging	The workplace provides a basis for casual friendships
The basis of people's status	People are seen in terms of their family background (what sociologists call 'ascribed status')	People are seen in terms of what they earn or own (what sociologists call 'achieved status')
The basis of social control	People behave because they are concerned about other people's views of their behaviour	People behave because of fear of the police and the law
People's feeling about the locality	The place they live is important to them and they feel they belong	The place they live is just that, a place to stay in and they have no particular loyalty to it

Question

According to Tonnies, rural areas have community while urban areas are characterised by association. Do you think this is true?

Community in the city

According to Tonnies, rural areas have community while urban areas are characterised by association. But many sociologists have criticised this simple division arguing instead that most people who live in large urban areas have a sense of their own 'neighbourhood' and this fills the role of community for them. Furthermore, groups of people join together into clubs based on leisure interests and sport. All this pulls people together.

The changing community and urban life

This extract examines the view that there was once a thriving working-class community in the cities which has been destroyed.

The common view is that urbanisation has broken up traditional social bonds, replacng them with *anomie* (a breakdown in law and order) and *alienation* (people feel they do not belong); the past represents human warmth and close relationships, the present coldness and isolation. But a recent study challenges this view. Most people do still have social relationships with people who live nearby. A sizeable minority have relatives living close at hand, have friends within ten minutes' walk and the overwhelming majority have friendly dealings with their neighbours.

It is therefore wrong to suggest that urban communities no longer exist. But there are pressures on it. The growth in mobility is one. More people own and move house, thus dispersing family and friends. One clear finding from research to date is that the sense of community is not more common in small towns than in cities. The size of a place or the numbers of people living there has nothing to do with it. What does count is people's length of residence. The longer they live in a place, the stronger and more extensive their links.

So newer places are likely to have weaker social networks. But physical layout is important too. Redevelopment of the inner cities has broken up ... traditional working class communities and has often replaced them with types of housing developments which weaken community. ... people in high rise flats, for instance, are more likely to say there is 'no community' in their area. ...

The upshot is that whereas in the past community attachment was particularly strong amongst the working class residents, it may now be stronger amongst the middle class. The traditional community, a densely-woven world of kin, neighbours and friends, is being replaced by the new neighbourhoodism in which people set out to join local organisations and make new friends. Middle class people are more enthusiastic joiners, everything from the local tennis club to the 'Stop the Bypass' campaign. In this sense they are more involved and active in the community than the working class.

Source: Adapted from J. Lawrence, 'The unknown neighbourhood', *New Society*, 6 June 1986

1 What is the traditional view of city life?

2 Does recent research bear this out?

3 Name three factors which influence the creation of a sense of community.

4 In the past, it has been the working class who have had the stronger community life. What is happening now, according to the extract?

5 Do you feel a sense of 'belonging' to where you live? Ask your family/neighbours if they feel there is a 'sense of community' in your area. Do they know the names of most of the people in the street? Is there a focus for the local community? Does it fit the evidence in the extract above? Ask them where the boundaries of their local community are

Community life in rural communities

The author of this extract examines the changes which have taken place in rural communities.

In the countryside … Most commonly the conflict is over housing, particularly where a village is within commuting range of a large city. Local people working in a low-wage economy cannot afford to buy houses once more affluent incomers bid prices up. The younger generation is forced either to take substandard living conditions (sharing, caravans, 'seasonal lets') or move out. In areas of natural beauty, retired people move in and affluent city people buy holiday homes which then remain empty most of the year. The age-profile of the settlement becomes distorted, the local school gets closed, the shop cannot pay its way, services and collective activities decline.

Even in less extreme situations there is tension, because incomers are different. Typically they are wealthier, more educated, and not in agriculture. They take over the running of clubs and local councils. Their way of life is distinctive, usually embracing an image of the village as a community that should not change. They want peace and quiet in preference to new jobs in rural development industries or even smelly farming.

Source: Adapted from G. Payne, 'Community and community studies', *Sociology Review*, September 1994

The extract describes village life.

1 What is the most common reason for conflict?

2 What are the effects of affluent newcomers arriving, and why is the change in age-profile so important?

3 Do newcomers fit easily into village life? Explain your answer.

Activity

List the advantages and disadvantages for the rural community of people moving into villages from towns. (The extract above is rather biased and only gives part of the story. Think what would happen without affluent outsiders coming with money to spend, and also find out if agriculture as a provider of employment is expanding or declining.)

Main points ▸ Urban means town and city life; urbanisation means the growth of towns and cities; de-urbanisation means the movement of people out of towns; suburban means the outer areas of towns and cities; rural means country and village life.

▸ From the eighteenth to mid-twentieth centuries, towns and cities grew in size as the job opportunities were there. Agriculture declined and industry grew.

▸ Since 1951, there has been a movement away from cities and a move towards smaller towns and the country.

▸ When talking about urban areas, we must be careful to remember that there are very different areas with them, including:
  – poor inner-city zones and social housing estates
  – affluent areas such as the richer suburbs and the redeveloped, expensive inner-city zones inhabited by the very rich.

▸ Both urban areas and rural areas have social problems, though these are different. The towns have crime, pollution, noise and poverty. The countryside has conflict between newcomers and the local population, poverty and a decline in services.

▶ Sociologists have suggested that there are different bases on which groups of people interact with one another. The two best known are community and association.

▶ Community refers to a group of people living in a neighbourhood who share a sense of belonging.

▶ Association refers to a group of people living in a neighbourhood who have no sense of belonging, but need each other for services and jobs.

▶ Some sociologists argue that rural life is characterised by community and urban life by association. However, others criticise this and say that you can find neighbourhoods in urban areas which are based upon community.

9 CHAPTER SUMMARY

1   Demography is the study of the composition of the population.

2   The information is important for the government for planning a range of services (including health, social services, housing and transport) for society.

3   The population size of a country is determined by the numbers of births, the numbers of deaths and the numbers of people entering or leaving the country.

4   Births: Overall, in the twentieth century, and at the beginning of the twenty-first century, the numbers of births has declined. This is caused mainly by changing attitudes of women who wish to work and to have a higher standard of living for themselves and their children.

5   Deaths: Everyone dies, so the numbers of deaths cannot decrease, but the number of people dying before retirement age has declined. People live longer. The reasons are higher standards of living and better health.

6   In the last 30 years more people have come to live in Britain than have left to live in other countries.

7   There is a continuing shift of the British population from the north to the south-east. This is resulting in problems of declining towns and cities in the north, and pressure on housing in the south-east.

8   There has been a movement away from living in large towns and cities to smaller towns and villages.

9   Both urban and rural areas suffer from social problems, though these are different sorts of problems.

10 There is great debate amongst sociologists over whether the basis of social life in cities is based on community or association.

Test Your Knowledge

1   What determines the size of the population at any one time?

2   Explain why the study of demography is important for a government.

3   Why has the birth rate fallen?

4   In your own words, explain why some groups are more likely to have better health and live longer than other groups.

5   Explain what is meant by the term 'burden of dependency'.

6   What problems are there in urban areas? Do all neighbourhoods in the urban areas have these problems to the same extent?

7   Explain the terms 'community' and 'association'. Is it true that community is the basis of social life in rural areas and association is the basis in the urban areas?

Chapter 10

EDUCATION

Chapter contents

- **An outline of the British education system**

  The chapter begins with a clear outline of how the British education system is organised and how it has changed over time. This is important because it shows us how changes in education both reflect changes in the wider society and also may help bring about change too. Two debates are examined in depth – first, whether comprehensive schools have 'worked' and, secondly, whether people should have the right to pay for their children to attend private schools.

- **What is education for?**

  We see that 'simple' societies do not have a formal education system, and so we find out what education provides for society. This turns out to be largely: teaching skills and values, then grading children by ability. There is little argument that this is what schools do, but there is considerable debate over whether it is a good thing or not.

- **Educational inequality**

  We note the extent of differences between social classes, ethnic groups and sexes. The key point is that educational success does not seem to reflect intelligence alone.

- **Social class and educational success**

  Taking the theme that educational success is only partly related to intelligence, we then go out and explore the bewildering variety of explanations on offer for the relative lack of success of children from poorer backgrounds. To make the explanations clearer, we put them into two categories – home background and the school. So, influences such as poverty and parents' attitudes are linked to the home background, while the attitudes of teachers, as well as the significance of 'streaming', are looked at under the heading of the school.

- **Ethnicity and educational success**

  Most, if not all, the influences on education which we discussed in the previous section are equally important when it comes to exploring ethnicity and achievement. But there are issues which are quite specific to ethnicity and so we examine them separately. These focus on racism in schools and cultural issues in the home.

- **Gender and educational success**

  Twenty years ago textbooks concentrated on why girls under-achieved compared to boys. How things have changed! Today, overall, female school students are more successful in education than boys. So this section is not about explaining under-achievement but what has happened to make girls so successful. The answer seems to lie in the changing role of women in society and the increase in confidence felt by them, as well as earlier maturity and a more positive approach to study.

  When it comes to exploring the educational success of boys, the story is very different. Boys are seriously under-achieving. The most important reason seems to be the values associated with 'masculinity', which includes the idea that studying is 'soft' and unimportant. We also examine how the changes in society which have benefited girls have done little for the self-regard of males.

- **Why males and females choose different subjects**

  Much of the discussion in the previous section is relevant for the interesting fact that male school students and female school students choose different subjects at school. We explore this and relate it to our previous discussions. Essentially, it seems that school subjects reflect the future career choices.

- **Truancy and exclusion**

  These are topics rarely discussed in textbooks, yet they are extremely high on the government's list of concerns over education. We look at the extent of truancy and exclusion, who is likely to be excluded and explore the reasons suggested by sociologists. What is particularly interesting is that the concerns over school failure and the differences between the ethnic groups, social classes and the sexes, all emerge here too in a very similar way.

An outline of the British education system

Getting through the British education system is a bit like climbing a mountain. As you work up through it, there are a number of choices. So although most climbers do succeed in climbing a good way up the mountain, it is still a minority who make it all the way to the top. This is partially because some people are better climbers than others, but also because people start at different points on the educational mountain and some have easier routes to the top than others.

The chapter will explore all the different routes and the different heights that people achieve on the educational mountain. It will come as little surprise to learn that there are clear differences in attainment depending upon differences in social class, gender and ethnicity.

The first stage in our discussion, however, needs to be an exploration of the nature of the British educational system.

The education system (our rockface) has the following clear stages:

- primary education
- secondary education
- further education
- higher education.

State education

Most of the schools, colleges and universities in Britain are provided by the government and paid for though taxation, although at universities, better-off students must pay a fee.

Primary education

This consists of infant and junior schools. Usually these schools take any child from a particular area and are co-educational, that is they take both sexes.

Secondary education

This consists of all schools taking pupils between the ages of 11 and 16 (the minimum school-leaving age), plus sixth-formers up to the age of 18.

Comprehensive schools

Ninety per cent of all secondary pupils attend comprehensive schools, which are supposed to take the entire range of academic ability. Attendance at a particular school is through a mixture of parental choice and geographical closeness.

Comprehensive schools can be very different in character, however, and usually the mix of students in the schools reflects the social profile of the area from which they draw their intake. Middle-class areas will have predominantly middle-class students, for example.

Since 1988 there has been a gradual move to introduce selection of students by a minority of schools which have been given greater freedom of action by the government.

City technology colleges

These were set up in 1993 to specialise in science and technology.

Specialist comprehensives

These comprehensive schools gain additional funding to specialise in a specific area of study, for example modern languages.

State grammar schools

A few education authorities (Essex, Kent and Gloucestershire, for example) have retained grammar schools, where the children who score highest in examinations at age 11 are sent.

Further education

Education beyond the compulsory age of 16 takes a variety of forms. From 16 to 18, students can attend sixth forms of schools, sixth form colleges or attend further education colleges.

Higher education

Higher education consists of universities. From the age of 18 onwards, people with appropriate qualifications can enter a university. About 40 per cent of 18-year-old school leavers now go on to study at university.

Private education

Definitions

Private schools – all schools which charge fees

Public schools – those higher status private schools which belong to an organisation called 'The Headmasters' Conference'

Primary education

Fee-paying pupils generally attend 'prep' schools which 'prepare' them for **private schools** or **public schools**.

Secondary education

The private or 'independent' sector includes schools, colleges and one university (see below). They receive no funding from the government, though they receive tax relief as they are registered as charities.

About 7 per cent of school children attend private or public schools.

Opponents of private education claim that these schools allow the children of the rich to receive a separate and special education, as the shared experiences of attending the most exclusive schools creates a sense of superiority and comradeship among the children of the rich. This sense of 'being special' is maintained throughout life, and as adults the ex-public school boys tend to help each other into positions of power, thus 'reproducing' another generation of rich and powerful people. Naturally they send their children to public schools and so the cycle is repeated. When they leave school, they are more likely than students from state schools to go to Oxford and Cambridge and from there into the top positions of our society, where they wield great power.

Defenders of private and public schools argue that people should have the right to spend their money in any way they want. If parents wish to economise in other areas in order to send their children to schools which charge fees, then in a free society they should be able to do so.

I think people should have the right to send their children anywhere they want. After all, if parents want to spend their money on their children's education, why shouldn't they? Other people spend it on holidays and smart cars, so what is the difference?

Besides, there is no choice in the state education system. Children have to attend their local comprehensive, good or bad. When they are there, they get taught the same subjects because of the National Curriculum. And, finally, parents don't seem to have any power in a state school. Who cares if they complain? After all the school gets the money.

Well, I think it is wrong that people should be able to pay to have their children educated privately. After all, most people simply cannot afford the fees, even if they do make sacrifices. And frankly, I think the majority of those who send their children to private schools don't have to make sacrifices anyway – they are well off. Private education is a way for the rich to ensure that their children have an educational advantage over most other children and gives them a head start in getting the top jobs. And it isn't just ability – ever heard of the saying 'the old school tie'? Connections, that is what gets the top jobs.

Who is right?

Higher education

There is one private university which is totally funded from fees and donations – the University of Buckingham.

Main points

▶ The education system in Britain is divided into four stages – primary, secondary, further and higher education.

▶ Educational establishments are either paid for by the government (state education) or by people paying fees (the private or independent sector).

▶ There is disagreement between people about the existence of private education. Some say it gives an unfair advantage to the children of the better-off, others that it is the right of people to spend money the way they want.

The development of education in Britain

Historical background

Before 1870

There was no organised education system. Children could possibly attend charity schools run by the various churches. The rich paid for private tutors or sent their sons to private schools.

The Forster Education Act 1870

This Act introduced a basic network of state-supported primary schools. Attendance was voluntary. It was introduced because Britain was falling behind its competitors (principally Germany) in industrial development. One problem was a lack of educated workers needed for the new technology of the time. This is similar to the situation today regarding IT skills and Britain's need to compete with other technologically advanced countries.

A summary of the situation before 1944

The education system was clearly based on class divisions. Children received a basic elementary education up to 14, but education beyond that age was restricted to the middle and upper classes. Middle-class children went to fee-charging grammar schools, with a few scholarships available to working-class boys. The upper class sent their children to expensive public schools.

1944–65

Definition

Meritocracy – a society where a person's social and financial position depends mostly upon their ability

In 1944, a new Act was passed, which became known as the Butler Act. It reflected the new values of **meritocracy**, where each child was to receive an education based upon his or her ability rather than his or her parents' ability to pay, as had occurred up to 1944.

Three types of school were introduced: grammar, secondary technical and secondary modern. Children were to be sent to the type of school most appropriate to their educational needs, based upon assessment in an examination at 11 (the '11+'). Because there were three types of school, the system was known as the 'tripartite system', though in practice only grammar and secondary modern schools were built in the main. The minimum school-leaving age was raised to 15.

The Act, introduced in the last year of the Second World War, was partly a response to the obvious unfairness of the pre-war period to which people were not prepared to return. Educational reform was part of a wider package of reforms including the National Health Service and the social security system. A second reason was that industry needed an increasingly high standard of education amongst the workforce, and there was far too great a waste of talent amongst clever children from poorer families.

In practice, the tripartite system became a means by which the middle class passed the 11+ and went to grammar schools, while the majority of the working class failed and went to secondary modern schools. The upper class continued to attend public schools. The 11+ examination was not a reliable or accurate test of a child's ability. Many bright children who failed the 11+ were sent to secondary modern schools where they were not *expected* to achieve much.

1965 onward

Comprehensive schools

In 1965, against considerable opposition, comprehensive schools were introduced. Three advantages were claimed:

- *economic* – one large school, it was argued, would be cheaper than a number of smaller ones and better facilities, such as swimming pools or craft workshops, could be provided
- *social* – there would be a breakdown of the class divisions in society by mixing the social classes in one school
- *educational* – children would no longer be sent to different types of school at

11, which many believed had resulted in children at secondary moderns failing to achieve their full potential, regarding themselves as less intelligent than grammar-school pupils.

Were comprehensive schools successful?

An educational sociologist criticised comprehensives after only a few years of their existence.

> There is, in short, no evidence that comprehensive education contributes to the breakdown of the barriers of social class which still divide adults and children alike. ... For schools reflect the structure and culture of the society as a whole. As long as we live in a class society then the influence of social class will be felt in the schools, determining the kinds of education children receive and the results they obtain from them.

Source: J. Ford, *Social Class and the Comprehensive School* (Routledge, 1969)

1 According to the writer, did comprehensive schools break down social class differences?

2 What reason did the writer give?

3 What is your opinion? Do you think that schools can change society?

4 So, what would you do?

Have comprehensive schools been successful?

Studies of comprehensive schools have not fully borne out the early hopes of the system. As we shall see later, there are noticeable differences educational attainment between groups in society. For, although the vast majority of children attend comprehensive schools, the schools vary greatly in the sorts of students they contain. So, comprehensives based in pleasant middle-class suburbs very often have a completely different atmosphere and examination success rate, compared to those in poorer neigbourhoods.

The contemporary system: league tables and the National Curriculum

Major changes in the education system in England and Wales were introduced with the 1988 Education Act. Changes included:

- the introduction of the **National Curriculum**
- the introduction of league tables
- changes in the funding and control of schools.

The National Curriculum

The introduction of the National Curriculum meant that for the first time in Britain, all school students were to study the same subjects and were to be tested against targets set by the Department for Education and Employment (DfEE). These tests are known as standardised attainment tests (SATs). Many argue that the National Curriculum has narrowed the range and variety of learning in schools, so that now schools are less about exploring and discovery and much more about training for skills and exams.

League tables

League tables of SATs results began to be published and, on the basis of these, schools were labelled as good performers or under-performers. Critics point out

---

Definition

National Curriculum – the subjects which the government says must be studied in all state schools

that these tables do not take into account the variations in student backgrounds we mentioned earlier, and encourage schools to compete with each other to obtain high places in the league tables. Increasingly schools are reluctant to take difficult or less able students who may lower their league table position.

League tables
The extract from the league table below shows the position of some schools in Cambridgeshire.

Performance tables 1999: GCSE results

	Pupils aged 15		GCSE Results			
	Total	with SEN	5+A*–C	5+A*–G	No passes	Average point score
LEA average			52.7%	89.4%	5.8%	40.3
England average			47.9%	88.5%	6.0%	38.1
Bassingbourn Village College	76	4	70%	95%	3%	48.4
Bellerbys College Cambridge	7		0%	0%	71%	2.1
Bottisham Village College	180		59%	91%	6%	42.1
Cambridge Arts and Sciences	6		33%	100%	0%	27.7

Source: DfEE website (1999)

1 Do you think that examination results tell you how good or bad a school is? Explain your answer.

2 What are the results for your school/college?

3 How does your experience compare with the position in the league tables?

Funding and control

Schools have gained more power over how to spend the money they receive from the government. Schools are encouraged to compete for students on the understanding that the more students they take, the more money they receive. This means that they are very keen to have high rankings in the league tables.

Change in higher education

The 1980s saw a massive demand for higher education, which the universities were unable or unwilling to meet. The government responded in the early 1990s by creating a huge swathe of new universities, so that most larger towns and cities in Britain have at least one university (sometimes two). This allows everyone who has appropriate qualifications and who wants to attend university to do so. Critics have pointed out that the new universities have poorer facilities than the older ones and that a two-tier system has developed with younger students with higher qualifications going to the old universities and more mature students and those with lower qualifications attending the new universities.

Main points ▸ The education system has gradually developed since about 1870. People have not always had the right to education.

▸ In 1944, the education system was changed to reflect the new belief in meritocracy.

▸ By 1965, people realised that the system was wasting the talents of too many children and the comprehensive school system was introduced.

▸ Many people believe the comprehensives have the great drawback that they reflect the neighbourhoods in which they are based, and so those based in middle-class areas are likely to be (or appear to be) more successful.

▸ The current educational system encourages competition between schools with the publication of league tables, based on SATs.

▸ There is much greater control over what is taught in schools with the introduction of the National Curriculum.

▸ There has been a huge expansion in further and higher education.

What is education for?

Skills and knowledge in 'simple societies'

In traditional societies, there were no schools or even 'education'. Knowledge, beliefs and skills were passed on from one generation to the next in the normal rhythm of everyday life. Children helped their parents undertake tasks and through practice learned how to do them. Values were learned by copying the behaviour of the adults and through stories told by parents which contained key beliefs.

Education in a tribal society 50 years ago

Children learn the tasks required of adults simply by doing them. General behaviour, attitudes, and values are not taught by any formal training. These are inextricably bound up with life in the society and become unconsciously adopted by anyone fully partaking in social life. ...

One night, while sitting in a hut, we watched a girl of seven learning to cook. Fermented porridge was needed for the baby and this the girl set out to make in a small pot in the presence of her mother and several other girls somewhat older than herself who happened to be there. When the water boiled, she put in some grain, twirling the porridge twirler between the palms as she had seen her mother do. She took the comments and criticisms of the company with good grace, even when they smiled at her awkwardness. Meanwhile, her mother mentioned to us how useful it would be to have someone who could cook the evening meal on days when she came home late or tired from fetching wood.

Source: J. and J.D. Krige, *The Realm of the Rain Queen* (Oxford University Press, 1943)

1 How do children learn to perform the economically necessary tasks?

2 Is it the same in our society? What do you think accounts for the differences?

3 Is the child an essential part of the economy? At what age does this happen in our society?

4 Who are the teachers in this tribal society? Is it the same today in our society?

Sociologists have suggested that there are three key elements to education in contemporary society:

- learning skills and knowledge,
- grading individuals by their abilities
- teaching values.

Skills and knowledge

The type of 'natural' education system found in simple societies cannot work in modern, industrial societies. We have a wide variety of employment skills, a vast and complex pool of knowledge and a diversity of values and beliefs. Above all else, these are rapidly changing. The knowledge and skills which are useful now might be outdated within ten years. For example, the astonishing developments in computers and information technology are revolutionising all aspects of social and economic life. It would be impossible for parents to teach their children relevant skills – indeed it is often the other way around when it comes to technology.

Schools and other educational establishments therefore developed in order to provide the high levels of skills and knowledge which was demanded.

But critics argue that different types of school teach different forms of knowledge. The National Curriculum requires all state schools to teach certain skills and topics – those the government think will be most useful to British society in the future. However, private and public schools do not have to teach the National Curriculum – they can teach what they think is most appropriate. Some critics argue that they are taught different skills and knowledge which will mark them out from state-educated students and give them an advantage in obtaining the top jobs.

Despite lack of funding, newly developing countries realise that they must have an education system if they are ever to have a chance to compete with the more advanced industrialised countries.

Grading by ability

Not all young people are of equal ability and it is important for society to get the most able people into the higher status jobs. We will all benefit from this. Schools and colleges act as 'sieves' to grade students by ability, with the more able progressing to university and then on to take the more skilful and demanding jobs.

Definitions

Streaming – grouping of students by their measured ability into classes, typically of about 30 school students

Setting (banding) – classes are formed from a wider range of ability

Mixed ability – students of all ability arc taught together

Examinations and **streaming** or **setting** are intended to achieve this, by allowing students to work at their own pace and by providing each ability group with the appropriate level of knowledge and skills for employment.

But critics argue that this description of the schools' grading activities is wrong. Although schools may have been created to give children the maximum learning opportunities, it is doubtful in practice that they actually do so. Setting, streaming and examination success do seem to be heavily influenced by such things as social class background, gender and race. We will examine the evidence for this claim later, but the evidence does seem to support the critics. So it is not just ability which determines your grading, but other social influences as well.

The relationship between school and work: a critical view

Two US sociologists, Bowles and Gintis, argue that that the education system does not grade children according to ability but reproduces the inequalities of society from one generation to the next.

How is this done? Children of the better-off attend public schools, where they are taught to believe they are superior, to think independently and to strive for the highest positions in society.

Bowles and Gintis compare this with comprehensive schools which teach conformity and obedience both in the official and hidden curriculum. The pupils learn to arrive on time, to cope with boring lessons and, most important of all, to accept society as it is, rather than criticise it. As a result of this, working-class people come to accept boring low paid employment without too much complaint.

1 What does the passage mean when it states that education helps to 'reproduce' the class system?

2 Which sort of schools do the children of the better-off attend?

3 What do they learn that helps them to be successful?

4 According to Bowles and Gintis, how do comprehensive schools prepare pupils for their future employment?

Transmitting values

Definition

Socialisation – the process by which people are taught to accept the values of society and to conform

For society to continue, there must be a common, cultural background – a common language, common beliefs, common expectations. As we saw earlier, traditional societies passed on their beliefs, values and knowledge from one generation to another through their social activities, but this became difficult as societies became complex and the pace of social change increased. In modern societies it is schools which play a key role in passing on what is seen as the key values and beliefs.

The school system knits children together from a wide range of different ethnic and cultural backgrounds into one flexible whole. Children learn not only a common culture, but just as importantly they learn the rules of society. Schools therefore reinforce **socialisation**.

But critics argue that all modern societies have a range of different values and beliefs, and critics agree that the values taught in school do bring people together and do ensure that most people behave in a 'correct' way. But the problem according to these more critical sociologists is that the role of the school is to pass on just *one* set of values and beliefs and these actually benefit a small proportion of society. They are taught not to question the way things are at the present and that the inequalities or power and wealth are 'natural'. The result is a *compliant* population, i.e. one that accepts the rules and values without question.

Schools therefore reinforce socialisation and impose a form of social control (see page 323) upon students. This prepares them for adulthood.

Boredom at school teaches you how to cope with boredom at work

Paul Willis in his book *Learning to Labour* explored the way that school students (particularly those who are not doing well at school) teach themselves various 'techniques' to get through the boredom of much of the school day and which are, in turn, extremely useful in coping with boring jobs later on.

Suggest any techniques which you notice. How do you think they might be useful in boring jobs?

Schools' values and the hidden curriculum

Definition

Hidden curriculum – a set of beliefs and values about the world and a person's place in it, which is taught by the school, although it is not part of the official learning

We have just seen that schools pass on values to their students and depending on your viewpoint these can be good or harmful (or, of course, a mixture of both!).

But whatever the sociologists' viewpoint on the types of values, they all agree that that underneath the formal values which teachers tell their students are important, there are also a wider range of hidden values (referred to as the **hidden curriculum**) which are passed on to students in the daily life and the routine expectations of the school. These values may well be more important in deciding the future lifestyles of the students than the formal rules and values of the school.

These values 'teach' the young people views on a wide range of issues from gender to ethnicity and even some claim that extremes of wealth and poverty are normal and should simply be accepted.

The content of the hidden curriculum

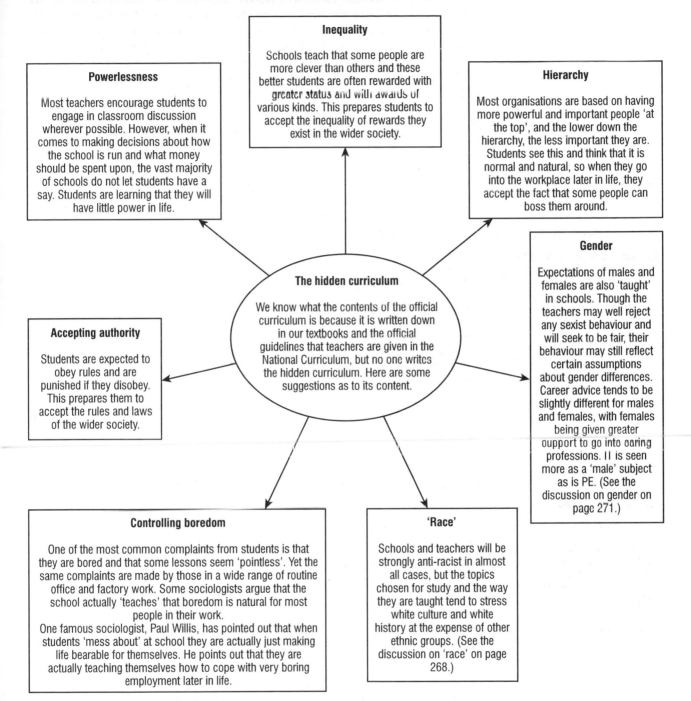

Inequality

Schools teach that some people are more clever than others and these better students are often rewarded with greater status and with awards of various kinds. This prepares students to accept the inequality of rewards they exist in the wider society.

Powerlessness

Most teachers encourage students to engage in classroom discussion wherever possible. However, when it comes to making decisions about how the school is run and what money should be spent upon, the vast majority of schools do not let students have a say. Students are learning that they will have little power in life.

Hierarchy

Most organisations are based on having more powerful and important people 'at the top', and the lower down the hierarchy, the less important they are. Students see this and think that it is normal and natural, so when they go into the workplace later in life, they accept the fact that some people can boss them around.

The hidden curriculum

We know what the contents of the official curriculum is because it is written down in our textbooks and the official guidelines that teachers are given in the National Curriculum, but no one writes the hidden curriculum. Here are some suggestions as to its content.

Gender

Expectations of males and females are also 'taught' in schools. Though the teachers may well reject any sexist behaviour and will seek to be fair, their behaviour may still reflect certain assumptions about gender differences. Career advice tends to be slightly different for males and females, with females being given greater support to go into caring professions. It is seen more as a 'male' subject as is PE. (See the discussion on gender on page 271.)

Accepting authority

Students are expected to obey rules and are punished if they disobey. This prepares them to accept the rules and laws of the wider society.

Controlling boredom

One of the most common complaints from students is that they are bored and that some lessons seem 'pointless'. Yet the same complaints are made by those in a wide range of routine office and factory work. Some sociologists argue that the school actually 'teaches' that boredom is natural for most people in their work.
One famous sociologist, Paul Willis, has pointed out that when students 'mess about' at school they are actually just making life bearable for themselves. He points out that they are actually teaching themselves how to cope with very boring employment later in life.

'Race'

Schools and teachers will be strongly anti-racist in almost all cases, but the topics chosen for study and the way they are taught tend to stress white culture and white history at the expense of other ethnic groups. (See the discussion on 'race' on page 268.)

Vocational education

Since the late 1970s, the education system in Britain has changed considerably regarding what it is considered important to learn. The government believed that the system was failing to deliver an adequate *vocational* education to the majority of British school pupils, as there was not enough training of young people with the technical skills needed for an advanced economy. The education system appeared to value academic, abstract teaching and to give relevant work-oriented training and education a low priority.

As a result, the government began to introduce a range of changes to education. The first of these was the National Curriculum mentioned earlier. Secondly, there has been a growth in alternative qualifications to A-levels, towards more vocational courses with an emphasis on work-oriented skills, which provide qualifications known as GNVQs (General National Vocational Qualifications) or NVQs. To ensure that the skill training is concentrated on those people most needing it, the government insists that those leaving school with no qualifications and no employment at the age of 16 must undertake recognised training programmes in vocational skills and work experience. If a young person refuses to take up the offer, then he or she cannot claim state benefits.

Supporters argue that as Britain has fallen behind other nations because of an unskilled workforce, the new courses will help remedy this problem. Critics point out that unemployment in Britain is not caused by lack of skills at all, and that increasingly it is skilled workers who are becoming unemployed. They see the new vocationalism as more of a way of creating cheap labour for employers and of keeping young people off the unemployment statistics.

Conclusions: What is education for?

Education then consists of three key elements:
- knowledge about the world
- skills for employment
- a set of values and attitudes which people take into their adult lives.

Whether the knowledge, attitudes and skills are to benefit the individuals themselves or the interests of the more powerful in society is a matter of considerable debate within sociology and you must decide for yourselves!

Main points ▶ Education in simple societies was learned during everyday life.

▶ In contemporary societies, life is too complex for education to be so informal.

▶ There are three elements to education in contemporary society – learning skills and knowledge, grading individuals, teaching values.

▶ Whether these are good or bad things is a matter of debate.

▶ What students learn at school is a divided into:
  - the formal curriculum which is what the school says it teaches (the National Curriculum)
  - the informal or hidden curriculum, which consists of values and ideas which are integral to education.

▶ The hidden curriculum contains such things as ideas about gender, ethnicity and inequality for example.

▶ In recent years there has been a move towards vocational education

Educational inequality

Most people assume that the educational success that a person obtains is a result of her or his individual intelligence and, apart from some people who are unfortunate, the majority of the population pretty much get what they deserve. In other words, Britain is a meritocracy.

However, this does not seem to the case. If we look at success it does seem to be associated with membership of different social groups. So, for example, more affluent people are successful than poorer people; more girls are successful than boys; more white and Indian students are successful than Bangladeshi or African-Caribbean students. Sociologists argue that this is not because the people who belong to the more academically successful groups are more intelligent, it is just that there are more barriers in the way of the less successful. Sociologists have seen it as their job to identify these barriers – and that is what we shall be doing in this section.

Students in further and higher education

Students in full-time further and higher education, United Kingdom

Thousands

	Males				Females			
	1970/71	1980/81	1990/91	1997/98	1970/71	1980/81	1990/91	1997/98
Further education (FE)	116	154	219	416	95	196	261	448
Higher education (HE)	241	277	345	498	173	196	319	554

Source: Adapted from *Social Trends 30* (The Stationery Office, 2000)

1 What is the difference between FE and HE?

2 Look at the students attending FE and HE. What change has taken place between 1970/71 and 1997/98?

3 Which sex has increased its numbers more rapidly in FE and HE?

Who goes to university?

Percentage of 18-year-olds from each social class attending university, Great Britain

Percentages

	1991/92	1992/93	1993/94	1994/95	1995/96	1996/97	1997/98	1998/99
Professional	55	71	73	78	79	82	79	72
Intermediate	36	39	42	45	45	47	48	45
Skilled non-manual	22	27	29	31	31	32	31	29
Skilled manual	11	15	17	18	18	18	19	18
Partly skilled	12	14	16	17	17	17	18	17
Unskilled	6	9	11	11	12	13	14	13
All social classes	23	28	30	32	32	33	33	31

Source: Adapted from *Social Trends 30* (The Stationery Office, 2000)

1 What percentage of young people from 'professional' backgrounds attended higher education in 1992/93 and 1998/99?

2 What percentage of young people from a skilled non-manual backgrounds attended higher education in 1992/93 and 1998/99?

3 Overall, what has happened to the proportion of young people attending higher education from backgrounds other than 'professional'?

4 What pattern still remained in 1999 which reflects the differences in social class in Britain?

Exam achievement

In all ethnic groups, girls do as well as, or outperform, boys at GCSE level. In England and Wales, the greatest difference in performance between boys and girls in 1998 was for pupils from the Black group. Twenty-four per cent of Black boys achieved one to four GCSE grades A* to C compared with 42 per cent of Black girls, while 23 per cent of Black boys achieved five or more GCSE grades A* to C compared with 35 per cent of Black girls. A greater proportion of Indian boys and girls achieved five or more GCSE grades A* to C than those in any other group. The performance of Indian pupils also outstripped that of other pupils at A-level. In 1998, 36 per cent of Indian pupils achieved two or more A-levels compared with 29 per cent of White pupils.

Examination achievements of pupils[1] in schools: by gender and ethnic origin, 1998, England and Wales

Percentages

	5 or more GCSEs grades A* to C	1–4 GCSEs grades A* to C	No graded GCSEs
Males			
White	43	25	7
Black	23	24	7
Indian	52	23	2
Pakistani/Bangladeshi	29	29	6
All males	42	25	7
Females			
White	51	25	6
Black	35	42	7
Indian	55	28	3
Pakistani/Bangladeshi	32	45	6
All females	51	26	6

[1] Pupils aged 16.

Source: Adapted from *Social Trends 30* (The Stationery Office, 2000)

1 Which ethnic group is most successful in obtaining 5+ GCSEs?

2 Which group is least successful in obtaining 5+ GCSEs?

3 Make two columns, heading one male and the other female. Rank the ethnic groups by success in obtaining 5+ GCSEs. Do the ethnic groups remain in the same order?

4 According to the text, which ethnic group performs best at A-level?

Achievement at GCE A level or equivalent[1]: by gender, United Kingdom

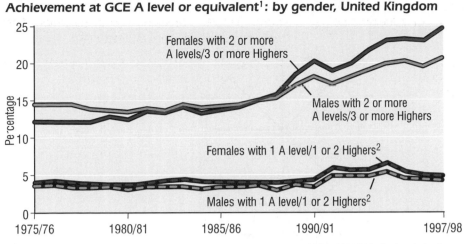

Females with 2 or more A levels/3 or more Highers

Males with 2 or more A levels/3 or more Highers

Females with 1 A level/1 or 2 Highers[2]

Males with 1 A level/1 or 2 Highers[2]

1 Based on population aged 17 at the start of the academic year. Data to 1990/91 (1991/92 in Northern Ireland) relate to school leavers. From 1991/92 data relate to pupils of any age for Great Britain while school performance data are used for Northern Ireland from 1992/93. Figures exclude sixth form colleges in England and Wales which were reclassified as FE colleges from 1 April 1993.
Excludes GNVQ Advanced Qualifications throughout.

2 From 1996/97, figures only include two SCE Highers.

Source: Department for Education and Employment; National Assembly for Wales; Scottish Executive; Department of Education (Northern Ireland)

Source: *Social Trends 30* (The Stationery Office, 2000)

1 Who gets more A-levels (or Highers), males or females?

2 Has the percentage of people getting A-levels increased or decreased between 1975 and 1997/98? By how many?

3 These 'facts' are well-known by teachers. In your opinion, do you think that this influences them in any way, in their teaching? Give examples.

Does intelligence determine educational success?

Of course, success depends upon intelligence. Look at me, with an IQ of 160, I was always one of the better students at my school, and at home I was always reading the books my mother bought for me. I could even beat my father at chess by the age of 17. I worked hard at school and did everything my teachers told me to. I was chosen to represent the school in a national competition once. Since going into my business I have risen to the very top.

Surely, educational success is only partially caused by our intelligence. What about other things like the home background and the quality of the school and teaching. There are some concerns too about the claim of some people that IQ scores can measure intelligence. Some would argue that IQ scores just say that the person is good at quizzes.

1 According to the university lecturer (on the right), what things other than 'intelligence' can affect educational success?

2 Is there anything that the businesswoman said that might actually support his comments?

Try some IQ
questions
yourself

30 Insert the missing letters.

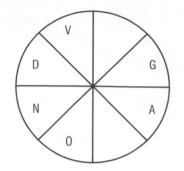

31 Insert the word that means the same as the word outside the brackets.

ARMOUR (. . . .) POST

32 Insert the missing number.

82   97   114   133   ?

33 Insert the missing word.

DRUM (LUMP) GULP

SLIP (. . .) GODS

34 Find the odd man out.

PEPLA

AANNAB

GENINE

PERRAGITUF

35 Insert the missing number and letter.

2	E	8	?
B	5	H	?

Source: H.J. Eysenck, *Check Your Own IQ* (Penguin, 1966)

The answers are on page 281.

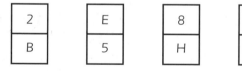

Social class and educational success

The statistics are quite brutal and quite clear – the better-off your parents are, the greater your chance of being successful in the education system. Those from poorer homes are much less likely to do well in SATs, to obtain GCSEs, A and AS-levels and higher grades in GNVQs, and finally to attend university, when compared to students from middle-class backgrounds.

The explanations for these differences stress:

- the home and community
- the school.

Sociologists agree that both of these are important, but one group argues that the effects of the home and the neighbourhood are more influential than the effects of the what happens in school, whilst others stress the school as being more important. Reading this for the first time, you might think that it is a bit ridiculous squabbling over which is more important, if both groups agree that the school and home are influential. The *implications* of the debate are very important however, for if it is the home background that is more important then the government needs to put effort in *combating deprivation*. If, on the other hand, it is the school which impacts more on the student's success, then more ought to be done to improve the *quality of schools*.

The home and community

Poverty

The lack of amenities at home can make it difficult for a child to study or even attend school. Lack of money can mean a cold and damp house, inadequate levels of nutrition, overcrowding and general deprivation. These can lead to poor school attendance through illness and inability to study at home. When they are at school the poor nutrition can affect a child's ability to concentrate. The parents may not be able to provide the learning opportunities which can come from buying books, computers and CD-ROMs. They may not go on holidays or have new positive experiences which broaden their horizons and give them something to aspire to.

Poverty and its effect on education

Children from disadvantaged backgrounds are much less likely to succeed in education ... On 'difficult to let estates' one in four children gain no GCSEs and rates of truancy are four times the average. ...

Abbeydale Grange draws its children from a wedge of deprivation ... 30% of children come from families on income support, 12% of the adults are diagnosed as suffering from depression and 25% of the children live in homes officially deemed to be overcrowded.

The poverty invades the school like water flooding a ship, reaching into every weak point. Poverty often means parents who gained nothing from school and expect nothing more from it for their children.

Poverty steers children off course long before they reach secondary school. Of the 115 11-year-olds in last term's Year 7 at Abbeydale Grange, 25 of them arrived at school with a reading age of less than eight. ... The effect on the rest of their schooling is catastrophic.

Poverty does its worst damage with the emotions of those who live with it: parents who are too tired or depressed, too stretched trying to juggle too many young children, too damaged to cope.

Source: *The Guardian*, 14 September 1999, Internet edition

Poverty is an issue too. Children can't study if they're cold or hungry, and they may not be very motivated if they don't feel they're going to get a job at the end of it.

Source: *The Telegraph*, Internet edition, no date given

1 What do the extracts tell us about the chances of educational success and coming from a deprived background?

2 What is the impact of poverty on the parents of the children who attend Abbeydale Grange?

3 List all the factors mentioned which affect the motivation of the poorer children attending the school?

Parents' attitudes

But children from poor backgrounds are not automatically guaranteed to fail. The degree of interest and encouragement parents show in their children's education can be a very important in affecting educational success. Indeed, according to some sociological studies, it can overcome poverty and deprivation. Often too, these parents have not been successful at school themselves and do not value education.

But poverty itself has an important effect on the parents, often 'grinding them down' with the constant problems they face, so that there is little time to support their own children.

The importance of parents and community

A lot of learning goes on in the home, but if parents haven't got the skills – if they're not comfortable with books for example – they won't be able to help no matter how supportive they are.

Source: *The Telegraph*, Internet edition, no date given

The view of education in the poorer communities is often not neutral, but hostile.

Source: *Times Educational Supplement*, 5 October 1999

According to these extracts, is it just poverty which hinders a child's education?

Cultural capital and cultural deprivation

It has been suggested that children from particularly poor backgrounds and deprived communities may suffer at school because they are not introduced to a range of cultural and learning activities which middle-class families might regard as being normal. This does note allow them to 'pick up the cultural cues' which teachers are referring to (such as comments about famous authors, artists or buildings) and which mark children out as being more 'educated'. This is known as *cultural deprivation*.

On the other hand, those middle-class students who have a background which is immersed in the appreciation of the arts and possibly the sciences have a huge advantage.

The sociologist, Bourdieu calls this possession of a knowledge of culture *cultural capital*, like financial capital which allows those who possess it a better start in life.

The headteacher recalled the children who had failed to turn up for school during the world cup matches ... [when she contacted the parents to find out why] ... Some of the parents had insisted that the children were right to stay at home. "They thought football was more important than school." The trouble is that education is a middle-class value which we are trying to operate in a working-class culture.

Source: *The Guardian*, 14 September 1999, Internet edition

Another aspect of culture is the ability to express oneself clearly in speaking and writing, which is a crucial component of success in our education system. Those parents who explain their actions and discuss them with their children help to develop language skills and reasoning ability which gives them success later at school. Sociologists believe that this situation is more likely to occur in middle-class homes.

The school

Teaching quality

The government is convinced that the quality of teaching in British schools is not as good as it should be and that by increasing the control over what happens in the classroom, those from poorer backgrounds can be helped to improve. The Department for Education and Employment has used this as the reason for many initiatives including the National Curriculum, standardised testing and very strict inspections of schools by **OfSTED**.

> ### Definition
>
> **OfSTED** – Office for Standards in Education – an official government body which monitors schools' performance and carries out inspections

The influence of the school

Teachers who blame everyone but themselves for the poor performance of pupils are holding up the drive to raise standards, Chris Woodhead, the [now ex-]Chief Inspector of Schools, told MPs last week.

The "culture of excuses" in education allowed teachers and local education authorities to blame everyone else for the continuing failure of some schools.

Mr Woodhead said: "We are talking about a minority of schools still where there continues to be a culture of excuses, a culture of low expectations. They blame the Government for a lack of resources, they blame parents for not producing intelligent enough pupils."

... He echoed the Prime Minister's warning last month against using poverty as an excuse. He said. "The notion that a child from a council estate needs a council estate curriculum I find obnoxious. All children need the same structure, the same rigour, teachers with high expectations of their pupils, consistency of approach and visible leadership.

Source: *The Daily Telegraph*, November 1999

1 What was meant by 'the culture of excuse'?

2 Who is the Chief Inspector of Schools blaming for poor attainment?

3 Does he agree that the home is the main cause for school failure? What does he think is the solution?

4 Carry out a small survey of the teaching staff as to the three most important factors they think account for school failure. Where do the teachers lay the blame?

The relationships between teachers and students

Students spend between 11 and 14 years of their lives in school, and consequently it is an extremely important part of their development. Their attitudes towards themselves and their abilities are heavily influenced by the attitudes of teachers towards them.

> They know you are going to argue. Teachers shouldn't shout, it makes you feel stupid ... They would embarrass me and shout at me at school, say I was stupid. I had to rebel, otherwise I'd feel stupid.
>
> *Janine (Camberwell)*

Source: T. Bentley and K. Oakley, *The Real Deal* (Demos, 1999)

Young people defined by teachers as troublemakers or as lazy are affected by these definitions and some sociologists have argued that they may well come to believe in this 'label' which is applied to them.

This *labelling* process follows a pattern. Children who are neat and tidy, conscientious and polite are much more likely to be labelled by teachers as 'clever', whether they are or are not. Awkward, untidy and less polite ones are far less likely to gain the teachers' approval. But there is one more level to this. Those awkward students are more likely to come from poorer backgrounds. The result is that students from poorer homes are less likely to be encouraged by the teachers.

This results in what sociologists call a *self-fulfilling prophecy* in which teachers are convinced that certain children are less able, put less effort into helping them, and find that they were right all along because the children do not do as well in tests.

Labelling and the self-fulfilling prophecy

Stephen Ball (in *Beachside Comprehensive* [Cambridge University Press, 1981]) studied a comprehensive school in Sussex in which school students were placed into three 'bands'. Ball found that the bands largely reflected the social class backgrounds of the students. Over time the attitudes of the students polarised between the bands, with the top becoming more eager and able, the bottom band students becoming more troublesome and disinterested in their studies, whilst the middle band students were very variable in their attitudes. Ball noticed that the teachers perceived the students in the different bands very differently and described the top band to him in terms like 'academic potential', 'bright and alert' and 'keen to get on'. They described the lower band as 'not interested' and 'troublesome'.

The students in the two bands also were aware of differences between them. Top band students were described in terms like arrogant and unfriendly by the lower band, while the top band described the other bands as 'thick'.

But, when the band system was abolished and mixed ability teaching took place, the labelling by teachers continued within mixed ability groups.

1 What did the bands reflect?

2 How did the teachers view the different bands?

3 What happened over time:

    a) between students?

    b) between students and staff?

4 Why do you think this was?

5 Did this stop when mixed ability teaching was introduced?

Streaming and setting

This process is formalised in the practice of streaming or setting students, where students are very publicly labelled by the school as to how able they are in particular subjects.

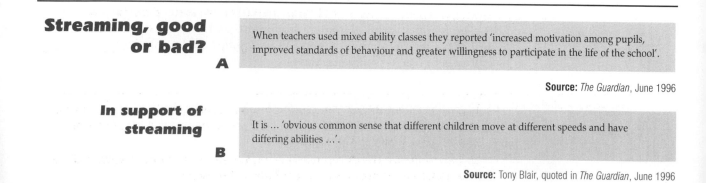

Streaming, good or bad?

A When teachers used mixed ability classes they reported 'increased motivation among pupils, improved standards of behaviour and greater willingness to participate in the life of the school'.

Source: *The Guardian*, June 1996

In support of streaming

B It is ... 'obvious common sense that different children move at different speeds and have differing abilities ...'.

Source: Tony Blair, quoted in *The Guardian*, June 1996

Grouping by ability

C

Percentage of classes in which children are grouped by ability

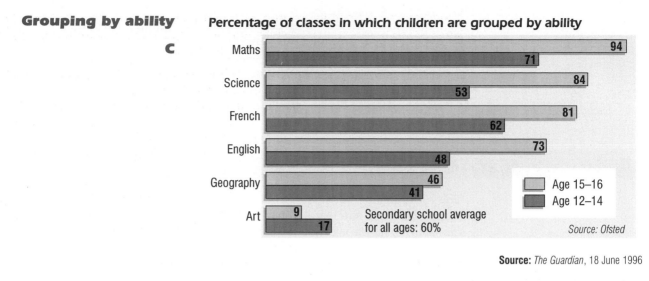

	Age 15–16	Age 12–14
Maths	94	71
Science	84	53
French	81	62
English	73	48
Geography	46	41
Art	9	17

Secondary school average for all ages: 60%

Source: Ofsted

Source: *The Guardian*, 18 June 1996

D

Children ... "kept in the wrong stream ... take on the characteristics of [the] stream ... academic performance deteriorated if [he/she] were in too low a stream and improved in too high a stream."

Source: National Foundation for Educational Research, 1991

1 Explain what is meant by the term 'grouping by ability'. Give two different examples of this form of dividing students.

2 What is meant by 'mixed ability'?

3 Look at C. At what age are school students more likely to be streamed? Which two subjects are they more likely to be streamed in? Why do you think this might be?

4 What do you think – should school students be streamed for all subjects? For some subjects? If so, which ones? Why?

5 Explain the meaning of D. Does this provide support for streaming or against it (or possibly neither)?

Arguments for teaching by ability groups and mixed-ability teaching

Teaching by ability groups	Mixed-ability teaching
School students can be taught at the correct academic **level**.	Students in lower streams feel humiliated.
They can be taught at the appropriate **pace**.	Teaching in mixed ability groups takes away the 'labels' which school students have according to their stream.
They can be taught the **appropriate subject matter**.	
Those who want to learn won't be **distracted** by those who do not want to learn.	Students learn to co-operate and to help each other.
Teachers will be able to **adapt their teaching** to the needs of the particular stream.	No problem with unmotivated lower stream school students, instead there is a sense of community and belonging.

Main points ▶ There are noticeable differences in the educational attainment, measured by exam success, between the social classes, between and within ethnic groups, and between the sexes.

▶ Explanations for the differences are extremely complex but basically divide into home-based reasons and school-based reasons.

▶ Home-based reasons stress poverty, parental attitudes, language deprivation and cultural differences.

▶ School-based explanations for differences in educational attainment include: teaching quality, labelling by teachers, streaming and setting.

▶ There are differences between educationalists over the advantages and disadvantages of mixed ability and streamed teaching.

Ethnicity and educational success

The relationship between ethnic background and educational success is complex. As we saw earlier, it is not true to say that those from the ethnic minorities perform worse than the majority, white population. Rather *different ethnic groups* have different performance levels, and *within ethnic groups* there are further variations by social class and gender.

For example, students from Pakistani and Bangladeshi backgrounds are less successful in the education system, with the females from those backgrounds performing worse than the males. On the other hand, females from Indian backgrounds are amongst the most successful in the state education system. Males from African-Caribbean backgrounds are less successful than average and have particularly high levels of school exclusion (see page 280). Finally, children from Chinese backgrounds are also particularly successful.

Explanations for differences in educational attainment by ethnic group

Explanations for the differences in educational attainment between different ethnic groups include:

- deprivation
- the impact of teachers' labelling of students
- institutional racism
- home backgrounds
- cultural differences.

Deprivation

When trying to explain why particular ethnic groups do particularly well or badly in the education system, people may mistakenly focus on ethnicity, because this is the most obvious difference between people. But what we should also remember is that ethnic groups differ greatly in income, housing standards and level of jobs. Many sociologists argue that these inequalities are the real cause of the differences in education and there is some evidence for this argument in that those ethnic groups which do particularly badly are also those which have the highest levels of deprivation.

Labelling by teachers

The attitudes of teachers to school students is often crucial in motivating them and giving them a sense of their true abilities. A number of studies have concluded that white teachers tend to have lower expectations of certain groups, and in particular of African-Caribbean students. Although most sociologists reject the view that this is the result of direct racism on the part of teachers, some suggest that white teachers have 'hidden prejudices' which mean that they treat black children differently.

Which is the really important influence: deprivation or ethnicity?

A

A study [published in 1999] by the National Foundation for Educational Research of 5,000 pupils in London primary schools concluded that "black pupils are just as likely to underachieve because of their social class or gender as for reasons of race." For example, "White girls from advantaged backgrounds were the single highest achieving group but many working-class white girls performed lower than many ethnic groups."

Source: *Times Educational Supplement*, 19 March 1999

Gillborn and Gipps in a study for the government's Office for Standards in Education (OfSTED) in 1996 argued that:

B

teachers often view Asian pupils as better behaved, more highly motivated and more able than black children. By contrast, there was often conflict between black pupils and white teachers.

Teachers may, the report says, play an active "though unintended" part in creating conflict with African-Caribbean origin pupils, "thereby reducing black young people's opportunity to achieve."

Source: Gillborn and Gipps, *Recent Research on the Achievement of Ethnic Minority Pupils* (OfSTED, 1996)

1 What explanation for educational attainment by junior school pupils does extract A support?

2 What stereotyping of pupils by ethnic group takes place according to the research described in B?

3 According to this argument what effect do white teachers have on 'black young people'?

4 Did teachers intend to have this effect?

5 How might this relate to the terms 'self-fulfilling prophecy' and 'labelling'?

Institutional racism

Definition

Institutional racism – where an organisation (such as a college or company) has procedures and regulations which, by their very nature, discriminate against certain groups in the population

The Commission for Racial Equality and OfSTED inspectors have suggested that there is **institutional racism** in British schools, in the sense that the behaviour expected of students are based on white, European ideas and that more boisterous boys from African-Caribbean backgrounds are more likely to be looked upon as troublemakers. Also subjects like history and English literature are likely to focus on the success of white British people.

Applicants to study medicine at university

In 1998:
3,874 white students were accepted out of 6,680 (57 per cent success rate)
1,275 Asian students were accepted out of 3,215 (39 per cent success rate)
73 black students were accepted out of 402 (18 per cent success rate).

Dr S. Everington vice-president of the Medical Practitioners Union said he believed the NHS as a whole was institutionally racist and that simply having an Indian surname made a candidate for a junior doctor post only half as likely to be offered an interview.

Source: Based on information in *The Daily Mail*, 9 June 1999

1 In what different ways could you interpret the statistics?

2 How might the quote support one of those interpretations?

3 Can you think of any examples of institutional racism which might affect the training of medical staff from ethnic minorities?

Home backgrounds

Jones found that the educational success of the child, of whatever ethnic group, was closely related to the educational standards of the parents.

African-Caribbean parents taking control

The emphasis on parental encouragement and the resulting success of many Indian school students has led some to argue that there is inadequate interest by African-Caribbean parents. But ...

Four out of 10 black parents support the idea of racially separate schools, according to government funded research today. The study, based on the views of African-Caribbean families in Leicestershire, found that 39.3% of parents thought that separate schooling was the only means by which their children could receive a decent standard of education. The majority of parents identified education as their greatest concern, far ahead of other issues such as health, housing or equal opportunities.

The study ... said that parents found it 'increasingly hard to accept such low standards of attainment and were losing confidence in ordinary schools'.

A volunteer-run Saturday school for black children was proving increasingly popular. Some parents said their children were treated unfairly at school, and maintained that teachers did not understand black pupils' 'cultural needs'.

Source: *The Daily Telegraph*, 16 August 1996

1 What does the extract tell us about the views of African-Caribbean parents regarding education?

2 Who or what do they blame for their children's lack of success?

3 What do you think the parents are referring to when they talk about 'cultural needs'?

Cultural differences

The majority of ethnic minority school pupils attending British schools were born in Britain, but many may well have parents who are not fluent in written or even spoken English and may not have the shared cultural values and backgrounds which help their children to succeed.

Activity

The following are headlines taken from the newspapers. Using information in the text, write the beginning of a story to fit each one.

a) West Indians fail because teachers expect them to...

Source: *The Daily Telegraph*, 6 December 1996

b) Race chairman attacks 'white bias' in lessons

Source: *The Daily Telegraph*, 6 January 1998

c) Schools accused of institutional racism

Source: *The Daily Telegraph*, 11 March 1999

Conclusions: ethnicity and education

The debate is a minefield of passions and misunderstanding. The statistics which have been collected seem to point to significant inequalities in education success which largely reflect material inequalities and differences in 'cultural capital'.

A forgotten ethnic minority

... Gypsy Traveller children formed 18% of the school roll, but represented 50% of the statemented [having particular educational problems requiring attention] pupils in the school – over half of the Gypsy Traveller pupils were on the SEN [special educational needs] register. In the second school, 74% of the Gypsy Travellers pupils were on the SEN register.

In half the schools [in the survey] no Gypsy Traveller child has yet sat for GCSE.

Of the four groups in the survey (Bangladeshi, Pakistani, Black Caribbean), Gypsy Traveller children are the most at risk in the education system.

Source: OfSTED, *Raising the Attainment of Minority Ethnic Pupils* (1999)

Your local district or county council will have a Traveller Liaison Officer. Contact her/him to find out the particular problems faced by gypsy traveller children. Use the explanations we have explored here to ask questions.

Main points ▸ There are quite complex differences between members of different ethnic groups and educational success in Britain.

▸ A number of explanations have been suggested for this. They include:
  – differences in deprivation and affluence between people from different backgrounds
  – the way teachers hold stereotypes about children from certain ethnic backgrounds – this labelling can impact on their behaviour and attainment.
  – the claim that British schools are institutionally racist in the way they operate and what they teach
    the home backgrounds of children from different ethnic groups vary considerably in terms of support and encouragement
  – cultural differences may still exist amongst certain families and ethnic groups which might hinder the success of children in the education system.

Gender and educational success

- Females perform better at school than boys in all subjects apart from physics.
- Almost 50 per cent of females get five or more GCSEs (grades A–C), compared to approximately 40 per cent for males.
- Just under 25 per cent of females obtained three or more A-levels, compared to just over 20 per cent of males.

Explanations for the success of females in education

Explanations which have been suggested for the change in the success of females in education include:
- changing perceptions of the woman's role
- equal opportunity in school
- growth in female employment opportunities
- increased motivation
- earlier maturity of behaviour and outlook.

Exam success by gender

Examination achievements of pupils in schools: by region and gender, 1997/98

Percentages

	2 or more GCE A levels		5 or more GCSEs grades A*–C		No graded GCSEs	
	Males	**Females**	**Males**	**Females**	**Males**	**Females**
England	27	33	41	52	8	5
Wales	23	30	40	51	11	8
Scotland	25	33	50	61	5	4

Source: Adapted from *Social Trends 30* (The Stationery Office, 2000)

Which is the only category in which the males outnumber the females in the statistics above?

Changing perceptions of women's role

Traditionally, women had expected to be housewives and mothers, possibly with a part-time job. Their horizons were limited and there was a general acceptance of the more important role played by males. The feminist movement challenged these notions and gave women self-belief, raising their expectations and allowing them to reject the limited horizons of mother and housewife. This self-belief has filtered down to education where girls are more confident in their ability.

Equal opportunity in school

At the same time, the women's movement pressured governments to change the way schools discriminated against girls in the way they operated:

- Traditionally girls were encouraged to study such things as office skills and domestic science, rather than other more 'academic' subjects. Now both sexes have identical opportunities
- Traditionally girls were portrayed doing caring and household tasks in books, whilst boys were more likely to be seen in dominant roles. This is no longer the case.
- It is no longer acceptable for teachers to stereotype school students by gender.

Female employment opportunities

The passage of laws on equal opportunities and equal pay have gradually had some effect (even though women still earn less than men on average, see page 300). Today, there are many more opportunities for women in the employment market compared to 20 years ago. This provides female school students with a realistic ambitions to achieve high level positions. These aspirations are closely linked to the increasing self-confidence of females in school.

Changing aspirations

Sue Sharpe studied changes in girls attitudes and aspirations in the 1970s and 1990s. She found many changes.

In my early research, girls from four Ealing schools described job expectations ... most of which fell into the general realm of 'women's work' ... forty per cent of these were in some sort of office work. The next most popular jobs were teacher, nurse, shop assistant or bank clerk: these accounted for a quarter of their choices. When receptionist, telephonist, air hostess, hairdresser and children's nurse or nanny were added to

these, this range of jobs accounted for three quarters of their job expectations.

Almost twenty years later, girls from the same Ealing schools similarly cited about thirty jobs they expected to go into, and like the generation before them, these were predominantly in 'women's work'. Increased awareness of gender issues and rights, and equality of opportunities, did not seem to be reflected in expanding

job expectations. There were, however, some significant differences. For example, the expectation or desire to do office work had shrunk to a fraction of its previous size. Hardly anyone specified wanting to be a secretary or to work in an office, and jobs like receptionist and telephonist were also missing. Many young girls declare their intention of avoiding 'a boring office job'.

... growth was more apparent in girls' personal horizons. They placed a great stress on equality with men, and on their own needs. I constantly detected an increased expression of assertiveness and confidence, and an emphasis on women's ability to stand on their own feet. They almost all agreed with the importance of having a job or career, and not having to depend on men.

Source: S. Sharpe, *Just like a Girl* (Penguin, 1994)

1 In her earlier research, what sort of jobs did the school students want to do?

2 What (a) had changed in girls' aspirations and (b) what had not changed?

3 What explanations could you suggest?

4 What factors can you pick out from Sharpe's

research which could have explained the increasing success of females in the education system?

5 How could you find out if Sharpe's description of the way young women think is true? Once you have decided, conduct a small piece of research to check the validity (truth or accuracy) of her research.

Motivation and behaviour

Girls are simply different from boys in their attitude to education. All the evidence shows that females are more motivated at school and are more likely to do their homework, to have better attendance, to be better organised and to work harder in class. These qualities lead to higher success rates. They may be more likely to have these skills because of the fact that females are still expected to help in the home more than boys; and are more closely controlled by parents, being made to stay at home, where they are more likely to do school work.

But they are also more mature in their outlook, and better behaved in class, so that teachers are less likely to have to spend time controlling , or attempting to gain their attention.

Main points

▶ Overall, females are more successful than males in the British educational system.

▶ Explanations for this include:

– women's perceptions of their role have changed – they want to have decent jobs and successful careers. Education is therefore important to them

– schools now provide equal opportunities for males and females, whereas traditionally girls were discriminated against

– there are far more employment opportunities available for females and this has provided them with role models and the possibility of successful careers
– girls appear to have greater motivation than males
– girls are mature earlier than boys and apply themselves to their studies.

Why males are less likely to be successful in the education system

It is important to remember that government statistics indicate that both males and females of all ethnic groups are improving their levels of examination success as measured by SATs and public examinations such as GCSEs. However, *relatively* females are becoming increasingly more successful than males. The following reasons have been suggested for the relative decline in the success of males:

- masculinity
- change in male role in society
- changing employment patterns
- teacher expectations.

Masculinity

Masculinity is a set of values which is associated with being a male. These include such values as 'being tough'; being good at (or at least interested in) sport; demonstrating their lack of interest in education; and 'having a good time'. Boys who do not demonstrate these values have low prestige in the eyes of the other boys and are looked down upon. Therefore the pressure on all the boys is to exhibit these 'masculine' values. Being interested in class and working hard for exams is definitely not part of masculinity.

Why are young men more likely to fight than any other group in society? Can this help us to understand 'masculinity'?

What boys think about themselves

In 1999, a study was published of what 11–14-year-old boys at school thought about themselves and their education. These are some of the conclusions.

The key finding was a concern with the idea of 'hardness'. Although only a small proportion of boys saw themselves as being 'hard', they believed that this was the image they ought to have.

The expectation to be 'hard' meant that it was not 'done' to be seen to work too eagerly at school. "If they worked in the library at break time they said they would have the 'mick' taken out of them. There was a strong emphasis on playing and knowing of football. Boys used it as a key way of differentiating themselves from girls."

The majority of those interviewed thought that race was not an important thing in their lives, but according to the author "African-Caribbean boys were almost described as supermen by white boys. They were seen as being particularly good at sports and envied for wearing designer clothes and being sussed and streetwise. White boys felt anxious that they were not like that and so admired and feared them."

Source: Adapted from R. Pattman, *Emergent Masculinities* (1999)

1 What image are boys keen to demonstrate?

2 Why do you think this is?

3 How does this affect educational success?

4 Where there any 'race' differences? Could this have any significance, do you think, for African-Caribbean boys. (You might want to look back to the section on labelling on page 268.)

Change in the male role in society

We saw earlier the new-found confidence of girls and women as a result of the women's movement. But, for males, this changing role of women has challenged traditional ideas of what men are and what their role in society is.

Young men have responded in different ways. First was the idea of the 'new man' who helped around the home and was 'caring'. However, during the 1990s a much more attractive role model for young men emerged that of *laddishness*, which emphasised having fun and taking risks. Laddishness does not support education and study as attractive role models, rather bars and football. Clearly it is closely linked to the idea of masculinity.

Changing employment patterns

Traditional 'male' manual jobs have been in rapid decline in the last 20 years and have been replaced by office and service work (such as selling) – traditionally the work of women. This has led some sociologists to argue that the traditional **patterns of transition** for males have broken down.

By patterns of transition we mean the traditional way in which many communities have provided a clear route from childhood to employment, so son follows father into similar employment, and he bases his childhood and adolescence on his future identity of miner, steel worker or builder for example. This continuity and identity has been smashed by the pace of technological change which has destroyed the certainty of future employment in particular industries.

Definition

Patterns of transition – the traditional ways in which many communities have provided a clear route from childhood to employment for young people

Labelling and teacher expectations

Within the classroom, it has become normal amongst teachers to expect boys to be more disruptive than girls, and teachers have a choice whether to *confront* the boys or whether to *accept* this behaviour. Confrontation means that the teacher loses learning time so very often the teachers just ignore the boys' poor behaviour. The boys, of course, then lose out.

Teachers also have lower expectations of boys, so that they are less likely to push them to achieve .

Main points ▶ Overall, males are less successful in the education system than females.

▶ Explanations which have been suggested include:
- the concept of 'masculinity' which includes values that see studying as being less important than being sporty and 'hard'
- there has been a change in the role of men in society. Some people argue this has left young males less confident and clear about what they want to achieve
- jobs which have traditionally been seen as 'men's work' have declined and the expectation by men that they should gain promotion over women is no longer true. This may have contributed to the lack of confidence, it is claimed, shown by young males
- teachers expect less from male students at school, and it may be that this helps bring about the relative failure of boys.

Why males and females choose different subjects

We have seen that there are differences in attainment at school by gender. However, the actual subjects studied, and attainment levels in these subjects, are related to gender as well, despite the fact that the National Curriculum ensures that all students must follow a core of compulsory subjects.

Females are more likely to study arts and social sciences such as English Literature, history and sociology. Males are more likely to take scientific or technology courses. The further on in the education system the students move, the greater the difference in choice becomes.

Why do the male and female school students choose different subjects?

The answer to why they choose different subjects takes us back to the discussions earlier about the roles of males and females in society and self-image. We can pick out three themes which are of particular importance:
- gender socialisation
- gender stereotyping
- masculinity.

Gender socialisation

Despite the huge changes in the attitudes towards females in society, the process of socialisation of children is still influenced by their gender. We know that girls are more closely controlled by parents and expected to help more in the house, for instance. Both sexes can also see the way their parents divide household tasks and all research indicates that it is the woman who still takes the primary role in doing and organising housework.

These influence attitudes to life in general and to study in particular. It seems that this is partially responsible for certain technical subjects being seen as male and caring (or social science) subjects being seen as female.

Gender stereotyping

The division is strengthened by expectations of careers. Girls may have higher aspirations, but they are more likely to be in a narrow variety of jobs which link to the caring role. Female employment rates are very high in teaching, nursing, social work, the media and charitable organisations, for example. Teachers and careers advisers may well strengthen this in their advice as to appropriate subjects to study if they want to work in these areas.

Masculinity

We saw earlier that many young men subscribe to a set of values which have been put together under the term 'maculinity', and this continues to influence both their choice of subjects and their idea of future careers. Scientific and technological subjects tend to be chosen because they are seen as being more 'manly' than discussion subjects such as English Literature or a GNVQ in Health and Social Care.

Main points

▶ Males and females choose different subjects to study.

▶ Girls are more likely to study languages and social sciences, whilst boys are more likely to choose sciences and maths.

▶ Reasons for this include:

   – differences in gender socialisation which direct boys and girls into different areas of interest (and later employment)

   – students choose subjects to enable them to follow a career of their choice. Employment patterns of males and females are still quite distinct from each other

   – masculinity – this seems to encourage males into studying subjects regarded as more 'appropriate' for males, such as technical subjects.

The influence of the home

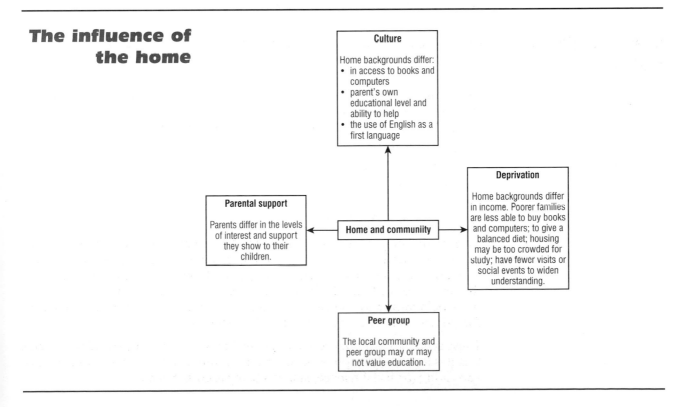

Culture

Home backgrounds differ:
- in access to books and computers
- parent's own educational level and ability to help
- the use of English as a first language

Deprivation

Home backgrounds differ in income. Poorer families are less able to buy books and computers; to give a balanced diet; housing may be too crowded for study; have fewer visits or social events to widen understanding.

Parental support

Parents differ in the levels of interest and support they show to their children.

Home and community

Peer group

The local community and peer group may or may not value education.

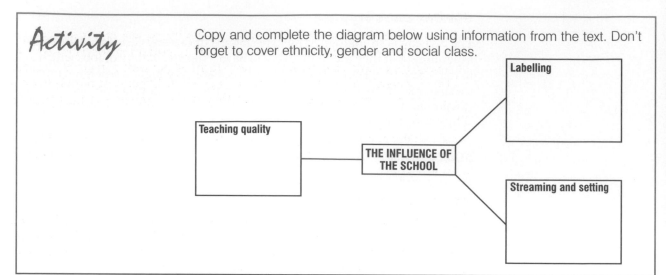

Activity Copy and complete the diagram below using information from the text. Don't forget to cover ethnicity, gender and social class.

Truancy and exclusion

On any one day, 400,000 pupils who should be in school are absent – that is 5 per cent of the school population, or 50,000 pupils. Every year, over one million students truant.

Why does truancy matter?

The children lose out because they stop learning ... Both truancy and exclusion are associated with a significantly higher likelihood of becoming a teenage parent, being unemployed or homeless late in life, or ending up in prison.

... the wider community suffers because of the crime into which many truants and excluded pupils get drawn ... For example, in London it has been estimated that 5% of all offences are committed by children during school hours. 40% of robberies, 25% of burglaries, 20% of thefts and 20% of criminal damage ... were committed by 10–16 year olds.

Source: *Report on Truancy and Social Exclusion* (Social Exclusion Unit, 1998)

Truancy

Who truants?

According to government's Social Exclusion Unit, the following students are more likely to truant:

- older school students – the further along the period of compulsory education, the higher the truancy rates
- students from poorer home backgrounds – those from low skilled, low income families living on local authority housing estates have particularly high levels of truancy
- certain minority groups – most notably traveller children, one third of whom have attendance levels of less than 50 per cent, and an unknown number not even registered for schools.

Reasons for truancy

There are three overlapping causes:

- the home
- friendship networks
- school.

The home

When we examined reasons for educational success, we saw that parents' interest in their children's education was a very important factor. This seems to be important in truanting as well. In one study, 44 per cent of truants believed that their parents knew they were truanting, while 48 per cent of non-truants were held back from truanting because they were frightened of their parents finding out.

Reasons why parents may support truanting include using their older children to look after the younger ones and expecting their children to stay at home to do housework.

Friendship networks

Government research has shown that there is a very close relationship between truancy and having friends or siblings (brothers and sisters) in trouble with the police. This suggests that friends and younger family members may have an influence on school children encouraging them to truant.

The school

The single most common reason given by truants for missing school is bullying, with one third of girls and one quarter of boys stating that they are afraid to go to school at some time for fear of being bullied.

There also appears to be a relationship between poor school performance and truanting. This links with a further reason for not attending which is that those who truant are more likely to say that they find school boring and irrelevant to their lives.

School exclusion

There are two types of exclusion:

- fixed term, which last for between 5–15 days
- permanent, when the school student is not allowed to return to the school.

The number of school exclusions

At any one time, 100,000 students are temporarily excluded from school and 13,000 are excluded permanently.

Percentage of students excluded from school, England, 1998

White	0.17
Black Caribbean	0.76
Black African	0.29
Black Other	0.57
Indian	0.06
Pakistani	0.13
Bangladeshi	0.09
Chinese	0.05
All	0.18

Source: *Social Trends 30* (The Stationery Office, 2000)

1 Which group is most likely to be excluded from school?

2 Which are the two groups least likely to be excluded?

3 Using the main text, what explanations are there for the different levels of exclusion amongst ethnic groups?

Who is excluded?

In terms of numbers, most excluded students are white, male youths in the later years of compulsory education. However, there are some specific groups which can be identified.

- Those with special needs are six times more likely to be excluded than average.
- African-Caribbean school students are almost seven times more likely to be excluded than average.
- Young people in care are ten times more likely than the average to be excluded.
- Males are far more likely than females to be excluded, comprising 85 per cent of those excluded.
- Older school students are more likely to be excluded with half of all those excluded aged 14 and 15. However, junior school exclusions have been increasing at a rate of about 18 per cent each year.
- Schools in areas of high deprivation are more likely to have high rates of exclusion.

Ethnic minority students and exclusion

Sixteen per cent of permanently excluded children are of ethnic minority origin and half of all these are African-Caribbean, yet African-Caribbean students make up only 1 per cent of the school population.

An OfSTED report suggested that these African-Caribbean young people who were excluded were more likely to have a lone parent, but also were of higher or average ability though the school was more likely to classify them as 'underachieving'.

The report also pointed out that there was much less evidence of disruptive behaviour by the excluded students when they were younger.

The review suggested that in secondary schools there appeared to be a 'high level of tension, even conflict' between white teachers and African-Caribbean students. The report gives examples of negative stereotyping, when teachers complained about 'troublesome' African-Caribbean students, and that there was a self-fulfilling prophecy at work when the school students were identified by teachers as being of low ability and disruptive.

The reasons given for exclusion

Summary of reasons offered by schools for exclusion (per cent)

Bullying, fighting and assaults on peers	30.1
Disruption, misconduct and unacceptable behaviour	17.0
Verbal abuse to peers	14.9
Verbal abuse to staff	12.0
Miscellaneous	8.1
Theft	5.5
Defiance and disobedience	5.0
Drugs (smoking, alcohol, cannabis)	4.0
Vandalism and arson	2.4
Physical abuse and assault on staff	1.2

Look at the reasons for exclusion – and read the main text. What links are there between the idea of 'negative stereotyping' and exclusion?

Source: *Report on Truancy* (Social Exclusion Unit website)

Main points ▸ Truancy is a growing problem in schools.

▸ The main influences on truanting are home background, the peer group and problems in the school.

▸ School exclusions are not evenly spread across young people, but appear to be more likely amongst some groups than others.

▸ There is some possibility that exclusions of certain ethnic groups are linked with negative stereotyping by teachers.

Answers to the IQ questions, page 262

30 A and B – to read the word 'vagabond' in a clockwise direction
31 Mail
32 154 – add the numbers 15, 17, 19, 21 respectively
33 DIPS – the first letter of the word in brackets is the third letter of the second word, the second is the third letter of the first word, the third is the fourth letter of the first word, the fourth is the fourth letter of the second word.
34 Engine – apple, banana and grapefruits are fruits
35 $\frac{K}{11}$ – the letters and numbers go up by three places and alternate in being above or below line.

10 CHAPTER SUMMARY

1 The British education system is divided into four stages – primary, secondary, further and higher.

2 Over 90 per cent of school children attend state schools, which are free. The rest attend private schools.

3 The education system has gradually developed since about 1870. One of the main reasons for the changes was the need to use all the talents of the population.

4 The system changed to its present one of comprehensive schools after 1965.

5 Many people believe the comprehensives have the great drawback that they reflect the neighbourhoods in which they are based, and so ones based in middle-class areas are likely to be (or appear to be) more successful.

6 Since the 1990s there have been changes to schools to encourage competition between them, to give them greater control over their own spending and to make them teach the same subjects (the National Curriculum).

7 Education in simple societies was learned during everyday life, but in contemporary societies life is too complex for education to be so informal.

8 There are three elements to education in contemporary society – learning skills and knowledge, grading individuals, teaching values.

9 But there is great debate over whether these three elements actually benefit the students attending school, or whether they are just being prepared for jobs and to do what they are told.

10 There are noticeable differences in the educational attainment, measured by exam success, between the social classes, between and within ethnic groups, and between the sexes.

11 Explanations for the differences are extremely complex but basically divide into:
  – home-based reasons which stress poverty, parental attitudes, language deprivation and cultural differences
  – school-based explanations for differences in educational attainment which include teaching quality, labelling by teachers, streaming and setting.

12 An additional factor affecting the success of females appears to be the changing role of women in society, which seems to have given females greater confidence.

13 Girls are more likely to study languages and social sciences, whilst boys are more likely to choose sciences and maths.

14 Reasons for this include differences in gender socialisation and future career choices which direct boys and girls into different areas of interest and employment.

15 Truancy is a growing problem in schools and is linked to the home background, the peer group and problems faced by children in school.

16 School exclusions are not evenly spread across young people, but appear to be more likely amongst some groups than others.

17 There is some possibility that exclusions of certain ethnic groups are linked with negative stereotyping by teachers.

Test Your Knowledge

1 What are the arguments for and against private education?

2 Why have comprehensive schools been less successful in giving all children equal opportunities, than originally expected?

3 What are schools for in modern societies?

4 What do we mean by vocational education, and how have schools changed to become more vocational?

5 Give three reasons why schools can have a great impact on a child's education.

6 Give three reasons why the home background can have a great impact on a child's education.

7 Why do males and females choose different subjects to study at school?

8 What reasons have been suggested for children truanting from school?

WORK, UNEMPLOYMENT AND LEISURE

Chapter contents

- **The influence of work on our lives**

  When students first find out that they are expected to study 'work' for their sociology course, they are often quite surprised – after all that is the subject matter of business studies or economics. But work is centrally important to our lives as individuals, and to the community we live in. Work is not just an economic activity, it is a social one too.

- **Work, employment and economies**

  We look at the way in which work is organised in our society. The first point to emerge is that there are lots of different forms of work, which can include legal and illegal, part-time and full-time, paid and unpaid work. The aim of this section is simply to open our eyes to the complex nature of work in Britain today.

- **The changing occupational structure**

  Given that there are many types of work, we explore what typical occupations people are engaged in and what implications this has for society.

- **The impact of changing technology**

  Britain was the first country in the world to industrialise. The effect of the changing technology on the nature of society and social relationships was immense. Industrialisation helped create a whole new world of politics, education, family life, leisure patterns and levels of income. Over the last two hundred years, there have been many changes in technology bringing about social changes. This section of the chapter provides a framework for understanding all these changes and introduces terms such as post-Fordism and globalisation, and even McDonaldisation! These terms are all ways of capturing the social and technological changes which are still happening as a result of automation and information technology.

- **The experience of work**

  How people experience work is a major element of most people's lives. What sociologists have found is that whereas some people work just for the money, others do so for a variety of social reasons – they might enjoy the job, or they may want to escape from a boring home life. Those who enjoy the job are generally those with skills or who are professionals, but for all those others, time at work can pass slowly and so employees develop strategies to help them cope with the work. It is this social aspect of work we will concentrate on.

- **Gender inequalities at work**

  As in most aspects of social life, women and men are treated differently and have different experiences of work. We explore some of these differences, which are also discussed in Chapter 4. The key point to emerge is that women are discriminated against at work in terms of access to top jobs and equal pay.

- **Industrial relations**

  Capitalism is an economic system which, by its very nature, pits employees against employers. Good employers might try to pay their employees well and provide decent working conditions, but other employers squeeze as much as they can from their workers. Our discussion on industrial relations explores how employees can express their views through a variety of means other than strikes and how the membership of unions, traditional defenders of the rights of workers, have changed over time.

- **Unemployment**

  No discussion of employment would be complete without a complementary discussion of unemployment. If having a job is more than having an income, losing a job can cast a person out of mainstream society. We examine this, and look at how different groups are more or less likely to become unemployed and what their responses are to unemployment.

- **Leisure**

  It is often claimed that Britain is becoming a 'leisure society', where leisure and consumption are replacing work as a 'central life interest'. We need therefore to explore leisure and its place in modern society. We begin by defining leisure and untangling it from work – no easy task. We then move on to look at the patterns of leisure and at the influence which a variety of factors such as age, occupation and income have on our free time. Finally, we wrap the chapter up with a discussion on the future of leisure.

**Work,
consumption
and leisure**

The following is a part of a newspaper report into working conditions in the factories of the companies supplying T-shirts and other goods for the Disney Corporation.

Disney staff in China work 112 hours a week
The researchers discovered that in some factories workers spent up to 16 hours a day at their posts, seven days a week. In four factories investigated, employees could be fined for lateness or taking time off, and they had to pay a deposit when they took the job.

Source: *The Guardian*, 23 February 1999

The influence of work on our lives

As individuals

The impact of work on our lives does not end at the office or factory door; it spills over into many aspects of our lives. In very broad ways, our occupation determines our social status and our income and, often, our identity. Differences in income cause different standards of living, and differences in social status influence the way people treat us. In narrower ways, too, our occupation influences our daily lives. The number of hours we work determines how much time we spend with our family or in leisure. The demands of our job influence our personality and leisure activities. The income and social status associated with our jobs also give us a sense of who we are, for example, a successful businesswoman or a retired teacher.

Communities

Occupations do not only influence us as individuals, but whole communities too can be affected. A good example is the way in which traditional mining communities were pulled together by the close bonds of the miners' working relationship, and how those communities collapsed when the mines were closed.

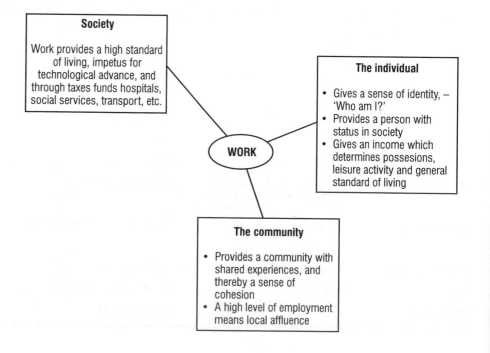

Work, employment and economies

The first thought to pop into anyone's mind at the mention that someone is 'working' is of a 'job' (usually employed by somebody), that there is a wage and that it is full-time. This is true – millions of people work in just this way. But also millions of people are working in very different ways in part-time work, in work which is not paid, in self-employment and in illegal work.

To understand this we need to look at 'economies' and occupational structures.

Economies

There are two sorts of economy in Britain:

- the **formal economy**
- the **informal economy**.

The formal economy

This consists of people who are employed, part-time or full-time, or who work for themselves. They are officially considered to be employed, and pay insurance contributions and tax, and are covered by laws governing health and safety.

The informal economy

This consists of activities by people who do not receive a wage, though they may get money for what they do, and who are not covered by employment laws, rarely pay tax and receive no official recognition for what they do. These people usually work in one of two types of informal economy:

- *the hidden (or underground) economy* – the huge number of money-earning activities which people get up to outside the taxable and often legal framework. It can vary from builders doing jobs 'for cash' to drug dealing
- *the household/communal economy* – characterised by people performing unpaid tasks which could include 'housework', caring for a relative or volunteering to work in a charity shop.

Characteristics of formal and informal economies

Work characteristics	Formal economy	Hidden economy	Household/communal economy
Place	Usually in office or factory	Anywhere, but usually informal place, e.g. home, street, pub	Usually in the home or community setting
Time	Office/factory hours	Anytime, but often outside 'normal' working hours	Anytime
Remuneration	Wages	Cash in hand	Love/duty or a 'favour owed'
Age	Usually 18–65 range	Any age	Any age
Legal framework	Legal framework – hours of work, safety and conditions subject to the law of the land	No legal framework	Often no clear legal framework
State benefits	Eligible for all state benefits	Eligible for some state benefits	Eligible for some, but usually different state benefits (e.g. carer allowances)
Official statistics	Appear in official statistics	Do not appear	Usually do not appear
Tax	Pays tax	Usually does not pay tax	Usually does not pay tax
Legal status	Legal	Legal and illegal	Legal

The changing occupational structure

Definition

Occupational structure – the sorts of jobs which people do within the formal economy

There are approximately 26 million people employed in Britain today, and (at the time of writing) approximately 2.5 million people who are not employed, but would like to be.

There are three types of industry in which people are employed:

- primary (or extractive) industries, which exploit our natural resources, including agriculture and fishing
- secondary (or manufacturing) industries, which involve making objects for our use, such as cars or electrical items
- tertiary (or service) industries, which provide services for us, such as banking, Internet companies, shops or restaurants.

Where the jobs are

Workforce: by selected industry, Great Britain

1 There was no Census in 1941
Source: Census, Office of National Statistics

Source: *Social Trends 30* (The Stationery Office, 2000)

1 Which two 'industries' have undergone the fastest decline during the twentieth century?

2 Which one 'industry' has increased? When did the increase occur?

3 Search the main text – what term is used to describe a shift from manufacturing to service industries?

Since the early part of the twentieth century, there has been a gradual shift from primary and manufacturing industries to service industries. Fifty-five years ago, shortly after the end of the Second World War, 70 per cent of the workforce had jobs in the manufacturing and construction industries, and the single largest type of employment was **manual work**.

Today, by contrast, over 70 cent of the workforce is in service industries, with about 20 per cent in manufacturing. The agricultural sector is now so small that it only employs about 1 per cent of the workforce. In the last 20 years, Britain has undergone period of rapid **de-industrialisation**, which is reflected in the changing patterns of employment.

Definitions

Manual work – work which mainly uses physical force, with varying degrees of skill

Industrialisation – the growth of factories and large-scale manufacturing which took place in the nineteenth and early part of the twentieth centuries

De-industrialisation – the decline in manufacturing and the growth of offices and commerce, which began taking place from the 1970s onward

Automation and increasing competition from more recently industrialised countries, such as China and South Korea, mean that fewer workers are needed for industry. There has also been a growth in the industries such as insurance and banking which employ white-collar workers.

The effects on society

The result of these changes has been the decline of manual workers and of the traditional working-class communities based on heavy industry such as steel, coal and the docks, with their emphasis on the extended family and trade union solidarity. As an increasing proportion of the workforce moves into white-collar jobs, they are less likely to view themselves as working-class, even if their wages are no higher than those of the remaining manual workers.

Increasingly, the new jobs in the service industries are being filled by women, for although women have only a quarter of jobs in manufacturing, they have two-thirds of service industry jobs – usually the lowest paid, it should be added. Nevertheless, it does mean more women are working than ever before. This will affect family relationships as increasingly women become the breadwinners.

People most likely to become unemployed are those who can be replaced by automated machinery and those in the declining manufacturing and primary industries. They are most likely to be young people, who find it difficult to get work in the first place, and the older unemployed, who are regarded by employers as not worth retraining.

Main points ▶

▶ Work influences our lives in many ways. It also influences the community and society in which we live.

▶ Work is difficult to define, as it has many elements to it, for example it can be full or part-time, take place in a factory, office or the home, be paid or not paid.

▶ There are two very different economies which exist – the formal and the informal.

▶ The formal economy includes all the employment which is legal and taxed.

▶ The informal economy has two elements – a hidden economy which is non-taxed work and a household/communal economy where work is done for love or duty, but is generally not paid.

▶ The occupational structure refers to the types of jobs undertaken in society.

▶ It is divided into three sectors – primary (agriculture and mining), secondary (manufacturing) and tertiary (service industries).

▶ The twentieth century saw a shift away from primary and secondary sectors to the tertiary sector. This has a considerable number of social effects.

The impact of changing technology

Britain was the first country in the world to industrialise. During the eighteenth and nineteenth centuries, it was transformed from an agricultural society, with the majority of the population living in the countryside and farming for their living, to an industrial society where almost all the people work in offices, shops and factories, while living in towns and cities.

But the shift from agriculture to industry was not simply an economic change, it was a profound social change too. The growth of cities as we know them now, of newspapers and later electronic media, the ability of the 'ordinary' person to read and write, the development of compulsory education, social class differences and the widespread ownership of consumer goods, even democracy as it is now, were caused, or at least influenced, by the process of industrialisation.

Factories needed a large workforce near at hand which led to the growth of towns. In turn, these attracted traders and so the towns grew into cities, and eventually into **conurbations**.

In order to work the machines and perform the clerical tasks, workers needed to be able to read and write, just as now we need to know how to use computers. Consumer goods were invented and produced at a price that eventually was within the reach of most of the employed.

The overwhelming power of the employers led to the counterforce of the trade unions. Finally, the fact that huge numbers of workers were pushed together in factories and cities in a common condition of employment helped to form social classes.

Not only has industrialisation produced major changes in society, but so too have changes in the technology of production. These changes include the move from craft production to mechanisation on to automation.

> **Definition**
>
> **Conurbations** – when cities expand and 'swallow up' neighbouring towns

The impact of industrialisation on work

> **Definitions**
>
> **Craft production** – manufacture of articles by hand
>
> **Mechanisation** – manufacture or articles by machine

Industrialisation replaced agricultural work and **craft production** (the manufacture of articles by hand) with **mechanisation**. Production by machines meant that large numbers of items could be made at a low price, and so gradually people were able to afford to buy them and achieve a higher standard of living.

The assembly line

Robert Linhart worked for a year on the Citröen production line. This is his description of assembly line work.

Each man has a well defined area for the operations he has to make … as soon as a car enters a man's territory, he gets to work. A few knocks, a few sparks, then the welding's done and the car's already on its way out of the three or four yards of his position. And the next car's already coming into the work area. And the worker starts again. Sometimes, if he has been working fast, he has a few seconds' rest before a new car arrives: or he intensifies his effort and 'goes up the line' so that he can gain a little time. And after an hour or two he's amassed the incredible amount of two or three minutes in hand, that he'll use to smoke a cigarette, looking on like some comfortable man-of-means as his car moves past already welded. If, on the other hand, the worker is too slow, he 'slips back', carried progressively beyond his position, going on with his work when the next labourer has already began his. The first car followed too far and the next one already appearing at the usual starting point of the work area, coming forward with its mindless regularity. It's already halfway along before you're able to touch it, you're going to start on it when its nearly passed through and reached the next station: all this loss of time mounts up. It's what they call 'slipping' and sometimes it's as ghastly as drowning.

Source: Adapted from R. Linhart (translated by M. Crossland), *The Assembly Line* (John Calder, 1981)

However, there were tremendous social costs involved for those who worked with machines or on assembly lines. Probably the worst of these, which remain today for factory workers, is the fact that workers constantly repeat the same task, which leads to dreadful boredom and lack of work satisfaction. Not only this, but the worker loses any control over the pace at which he works, as this is set by the management. Furthermore, as the machine produces an identical product each time, regardless of the interest or ability of the worker, then all sense of pride and craftmanship is lost. The resulting boredom and frustration has often created the conditions for industrial action, such as strikes, as the workers try to obtain higher wages in order to compensate for the boredom of their work.

Globalisation

Definition

Globalisation – the opening up of the world in terms of economic production and consumption. So that trade takes place right across the world

The organisation of the workforce into trade unions, and the needs of democratically elected governments, amongst other reasons, led to rising wages and working conditions in Europe and the USA. In the search for cheaper ways of producing articles, companies began to turn to poorer developing countries where costs were much lower. They were able to do so because of developments in communication technology and by the faster, newer means of transport which allowed executives to fly around the world and products to be delivered in large, fast ships.

Globalisation has had a major impact upon the societies of the world's poorer nations and has led to changes, in much the same way that British society was altered by the original industrialisation process.

Globalisation: a summary

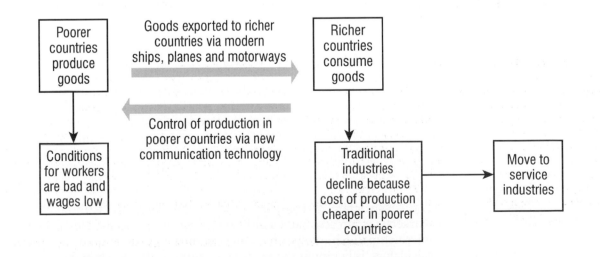

The globalisation of trade and employment

The globalisation of trade and employment is now a reality. Multi-national organisations have switched production of many articles from Europe and the USA to poorer countries in Asia and Central America because of extremely low wages, weak trade unions and lack of health and safety regulations there. Many of your favourite clothes (which are often very expensive) are produced by people who work long hours for low pay in conditions which would be unacceptable in Europe. Have a look at the labels on your clothes for example.

The diagram below shows where the money goes from the price of a pair of trainers made in a developing country.

Trainer labour: who gets what from the sale of a £50 pair of trainers

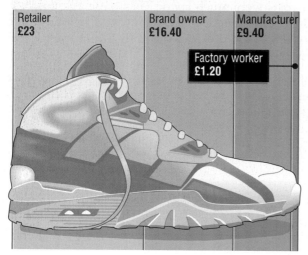

Source: *The Guardian*, 28 September 1996

1 What are working conditions like?

2 What is a 'brand owner'. Give four examples.

3 Construct a pie chart to show how much each the retailer, the brand owner, the manufacturer and the worker receive.

4 How is globalisation made possible by newer forms of communication and technology?

5 What might be the impact of globalisation on British and European employment?

Automation and information technology

Automation is the process where machines produce items with only a minimum of supervision by workers. Generally the machines have been programmed to repeat the same task to a high standard of accuracy, and can even reject items which are not of the required standard. An example of automation is the simple welding machine which is used in car production to perform a number of welds in set spots to car bodies as they pass along the production line.

The construction of complete products by machines without the need for workers has already had a considerable effect on society. However, the use of micro-chip technology, the tiny 'brains' inside home computers and calculators, is beginning to cause even more profound changes.

Technologically, the micro-chip allows machines to be controlled by computer to undertake highly skilled, as well as routine, tasks and to reach a standard of output of high quality. It is possible to manufacture virtually the whole of a car with automated machinery which needs only a few workers.

Cars being constructed in an automated plant

The use of micro-chip technology extends far beyond manufacturing though, for it allows many services to be performed by machine. Examples of this are the cash dispensers found outside banks and building societies, in effect replacing bank counter staff. In offices, too, a wide range of tasks have been replaced or improved by computers. Furthermore, the use of the new technology in communication equipment has meant that tasks can increasingly be performed anywhere in the world.

It is not an exaggeration to call this micro-chip-controlled automation the 'second industrial revolution'.

The social effects of automation and IT

In themselves, automated production and the use of computers are neither good nor bad, it just depends on how they are used. We know that they could be used to eliminate boring and dangerous tasks, and to cut down the numbers of employees in offices and factories. This could be excellent for society, if workers are moved to more interesting work, or if they are given greater

Definition

Deskilling – the skills needed for a job are lost when the computer-controlled machine takes them over

leisure, with the income to enjoy it. Or it could be bad, if the workers are simply made redundant or their skills taken away by computers.

It can be seen ,therefore, that automation and IT is a two-edged sword, which could free workers from the drudgery of boring work and produce a wide range of high quality articles at low prices, as well as offering new services such as armchair shopping. But it could also lead to unemployment, **deskilling**, and lower wages.

Activity

Social Consequences of New Technology

POSITIVE
- ✓ Dull, repetitive work eliminated.
- ✓ New interesting jobs created.
- ✓ More opportunities for women.
- ✓ Better quality and more varied products produced – at lower prices.
- ✓ Quality of life is improved through better communication and leisure equipment.
- ✓ Increase in leisure as workers are able to produce same amount in less time.

NEGATIVE
- ✓ Loss of skills as computers undertake skilled work
- ✓ Higher unemployment as automated machinery takes over jobs
- ✓ Fewer opportunities for male workers
- ✓ Increase in poverty as employees are divided into high-skilled, in-demand workers and low-skilled marginal workers.
- ✓ Political tensions caused by widening gap.
- ✓ Crime levels rise as a result of widening gap.

1 Add any other advantages and disadvantages you can think of.
2 In your opinion, what do you think the evidence points to – a better or worse society?

Post-Fordism and de-industrialisation

Employment patterns in Britain have been changing very rapidly over the last 20 years. The most obvious change has been the decline in the number of people working in industry and the growth in those working in offices which provide us with services.

Alongside this shift from industry to office work is another change – the way we organise how people work.

When industrialisation came, the 'social organisation of work' took the form of large factories where people went to work. They were all graded, from managers down to production line workers, and there was a clear distinction made between office workers and factory workers. This reached its peak with the 'efficient' methods used by the Ford factories for car production. The term **Fordism** was used to describe this form of work.

However, new technology has allowed a much more flexible method of production, which has been copied from Far Eastern economies. This new flexible production approach meant that workers (like the raw materials) were not needed at the factory, office or supermarket all the time – only at certain busy periods. After all, why pay workers if they are not working flat-out? Instead, workers are brought in or sent home when they are needed. So, a new attitude to work and workers has therefore developed amongst employers. They want relatively few permanent, full-time workers and much greater numbers of part-time, temporary or 'contract' workers.

Many new jobs in Britain are now of this type. Instead of employment being seen as a job for life, it is now a series of short-term and part-time jobs, with the likelihood of unemployment or under-employment. Increasingly it is women who are employed in these new, flexible jobs. This new approach to work has been called **post-Fordism**.

The social implications of the changes in employment as a result of post-Fordism are quite noticeable. The Welfare State will become more important as a means of supporting people through the periods of under-employment and unemployment. The class structure is fragmenting as traditional industries decline. Families and households need to adapt to the fact that women increasingly need to go out to work to take part-time employment.

Definitions

Fordism – a method of producing identical products cheaply using production lines on which people did one small task

Under-employment – not having as many hours' work as you would like

Post-Fordism – a new form of work pattern where workers are expected to be flexible and to be employed only when there is work for them. There is no expectation of employment for life

McDonaldisation

Definition

McDonaldisation – in service industries where the product and the style of service are identical

As industry has altered and become more flexible; service industries appear to have changed and become less flexible. The term **McDonaldisation** has been used to describe this. Just as the McDonalds fast-food outlets are identical and the service you receive is identical, so the people who work there have to learn to do tasks exactly the same way and in exactly the same 'pleasant' manner. This standardisation of work and the customer-pleasing attitude has now been adopted across all service industries.

The social consequences of technological change

Mass consumption
Factories and machinery led to the production of cheap articles on a large scale. Eventually this caused a decline in prices and, by the 1950s, the growth of mass consumption. The majority of the population could own articles previously thought of as luxuries.

Education
Workers needed to read and write as industrial processes were complicated. This led to the introduction of compulsory schooling in 1870s.

Leisure
Initially, the long hours of work in factories prevented leisure. Eventually the workers obtained shorter working hours, which led to the development of modern leisure activities.

Colonies
There was exploitation of the colonies for cheap raw materials for the factories in Britain. This led to the poverty of the Third World. It created a sense of racial superiority and eventually in the 1950s, influenced the patterns of immigration to Britain.

INDUSTRIALISATION

Urbanisation
The growth of cities, with their slums ad social problems of poverty and crime, and later the need to improve conditions, led to redevelopment and New Towns. Decline in the inner cities later linked to riots of the 1980s.

Production
This moved from agriculture to factories and machines. Working conditions were appalling – long hours for little pay. The relationship of employer and employee was one of conflict.

Politics
Large numbers of workers drawn together, in factories and towns in poor conditions, led to growth of political activity, notably the development of the Labour Party. The factory owners replaced landowners and the leaders of the Conservative Party.

Health
The growth of the cities with large numbers of people living close together forced improvements in public hygiene – sewers, water supplies, etc. Advances in medicine occurred. These, plus the rise in the standard of living, improved health standards and lowered death-rates. People lived longer.

Transport
Modern, fast means of transport, first the railways and much later cars, led to travel, holidays, suburbs, commuting and eventually the development of factories away from the towns.

Women working
De-industrialisation has increased the numbers of women working and the percentage of the workforce composed by women.

Offices
The main place of work in industrial societies is the factory. This is replaced in de-industrialised factories by the office.

DE-INDUSTRIALISATION

Automation

Globalisation

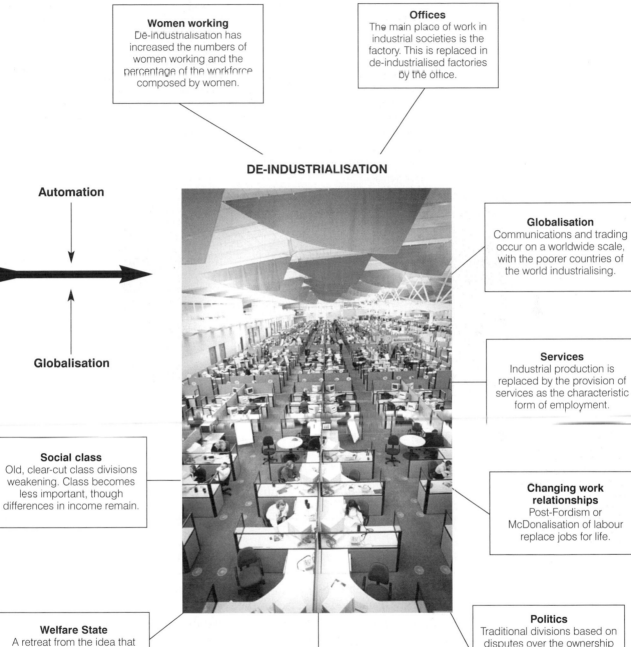

Globalisation
Communications and trading occur on a worldwide scale, with the poorer countries of the world industrialising.

Services
Industrial production is replaced by the provision of services as the characteristic form of employment.

Social class
Old, clear-cut class divisions weakening. Class becomes less important, though differences in income remain.

Changing work relationships
Post-Fordism or McDonalisation of labour replace jobs for life.

Welfare State
A retreat from the idea that welfare should be from 'cradle to grave', so people are strongly encouraged to look after themselves.

Consumption
Leisure time grows and the buying of goods and services becomes an ever important component of life and identity.

Politics
Traditional divisions based on disputes over the ownership and control of industry disappear. Parties now focus on the individual characteristics of the party leaders. A growth of a 'new social movements' which are concerned more about lifestyle choices.

The future of work

Low-paid jobs

It is clear that the information age will not eradicate poverty. All predictions of the future suggest that there will be a continuing growth in low paid jobs.

The jobs created (in the service economy) are poorly paid and often offered on a short-term and part-time basis. That is why there is a growing demand for women workers.

Other occupations are emerging as we move into those which are as arduous as any found in traditional manufacturing....The most obvious of these are the jobs provided by fast-food outlets. In these, work tasks are as mechanised, routinised and subject to forms of strict supervisory controls as any of those likely to be found in factories.

The Rise of Call centres:

Call centres have emerged directly as a result of developments in information technology. Essentially they provide services over the telephone, which can range from booking airline tickets to the provision of financial services.

In call centres, work is organised according to very strict routines; staff handle customer enquiries by reference to a computer driven format. The work is done on shifts and performance is measured by reference to tightly imposed quantity and quality standards. Wages are low and the workers are fully aware that their jobs are continually at risk in what is an international labour market.

Source: Adapted from R. Scase, 'The future of work', *Sociology Review*, November 1998

Call centres as sweat shops

The health and safety executive said yesterday that it intended to investigate working practices at telephone call centres after unions claimed they were sweat shops. Workers had complained of intolerable stress due to 'unachievable targets' and constant monitoring by superiors. ... Some union officials have described the centres as 'wired workhouses' because of workers being monitored via electronic surveillance.

Source: *The Guardian*, 30 November 1999

1 Why are women workers used for service sector jobs?

2 What is McDonaldisation (see main text) and how is it relevant here?

3 What is a call centre?

4 What advances have made call centres possible?

5 What are the conditions of work like?

6 About 500,000 people now work in call centres in Britain and the figure is growing. What image of the future of work do the extracts give?

Main points ▶

▶ Changing technology has a very great impact on the social way in which work is organised and also on the wider society.

▶ Industrialisation fundamentally altered the nature of British society by creating large factories in which people (though mainly men) worked, brought about educational change, helped create large cities and even strongly influenced the nature of family and communities. It also brought into being the two major political parties.

▶ The method of production associated with industrialism was known as Fordism and described a situation of production line manufacture.

▶ The latter part of the twentieth century saw major changes in work as a result of automation and IT. In factories, automated manufacture took over many of the jobs of unskilled and semi-skilled workers.

▶ In offices, IT helped the development of completely new ways of dealing with office work.

▶ Some sociologists have argued that new types of work relationships exist now. In factories they describe the working conditions as post-Fordist, and in shops and offices they suggest that the term McDonaldisation is appropriate.

▶ Another major change in world trading has been globalisation, which means that new means of communication allows goods to be made cheaply in poorer countries by companies based in richer countries, who sell the cheaply produced goods in the richer countries.

▶ Globalisation has been a major reason for the decline in manufacturing industry in Britain.

The experience of work

Definitions

Intrinsic satisfaction – employees gain pleasure from their jobs

Extrinsic satisfaction – employees find little satisfaction in their work and have to seek their pleasure outside their jobs

For millions of people, the majority of their waking time is spent in work, or work-related activities (such as commuting), so the experience of work is fundamental to a person's enjoyment of life. Sociologists have, therefore, studied workers' attitudes to, and enjoyment of, their jobs. The results of the studies show that attitudes to work fall broadly into two broad categories:

- intrinsic satisfaction
- extrinsic satisfaction.

Intrinsic satisfaction

This is usually found in skilled or intellectually demanding jobs, ranging from craftsmen to professional people, such as doctors. Their jobs are fulfilling and creative, with a great deal of variety. Satisfaction is therefore found inside their employment.

Extrinsic satisfaction

This is usually found in boring, repetitive jobs, such as assembly lines in factories, or routine clerical work in large offices. Jobs fail to stimulate or interest employees, stunting rather than stimulating their personalities. Employees therefore turn to the wage packet for their satisfaction. They try to earn as much as possible and gain their pleasure through spending their earnings on leisure pursuits and shopping. Satisfaction is therefore found outside their employment.

Why people work

Alienation

Karl Marx, the nineteenth-century writer, suggested the term *alienation* to describe the situation where workers experience work as something to be hated. Marx argued that, in an ideal world, our work ought really to be an extension of our personality, yet for the majority of the population this is simply not true. As two sociologists writing about work once commented that '87 per cent of workers...expend more mental effort and resourcefulness in getting to work than in doing their jobs'.

The alienated workers

Alienation at work affects a person's life outside work.

Meaninglessness
Regards work as pointless and boring: 'Why am I doing this? The only thing I get out of work is the wage. I might as well be in prison eight hours a day.'

Self-estrangement
Feels that his/her true potential is not being fulfilled: 'Anyone could do this work. I'm just like a machine.'

Isolation
Worker feels cut off from his/her companions, both physically and socially: 'It's so noisy in here. I can't hear what anyone says. Anyway, the other workers are so unfriendly, I can't be bothered being sociable.'

Powerlessness
Feels lack of control over working conditions: 'The bosses just push us around. They never listen to what we have to say. The only way of getting back at them is through the union or by "accidentally" breaking the assembly line.'

Do you think it is possible to apply the idea of alienation to:

a) studying at school or college?

b) family life?

c) a part time job (if you have one)?

Make comments under the four headings of meaning-lessness, self-estrangement, isolation, powerlessness.

Making work more fulfilling

Employers recognise that bored workers are often bad at their jobs and so they have tried to overcome this by introducing a range of initiatives.

However, employees too have strategies which they use to make life bearable. These are summarised in the diagram below.

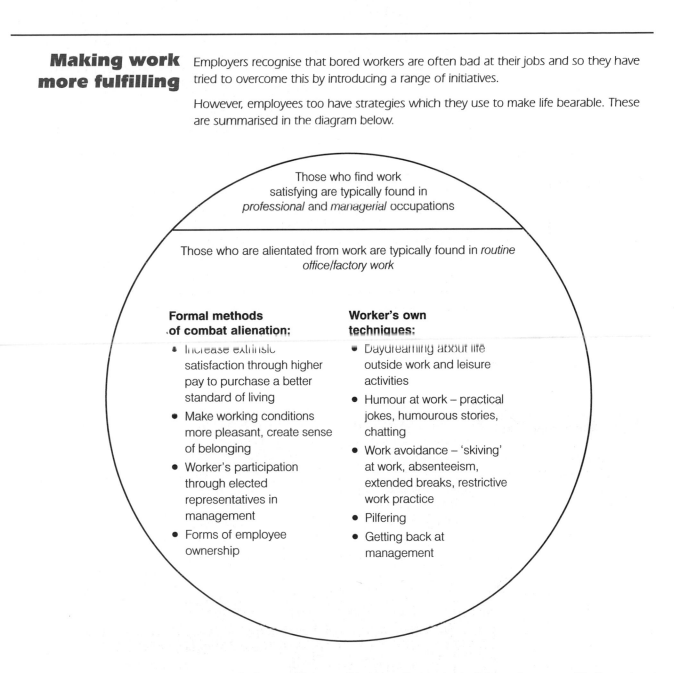

Those who find work satisfying are typically found in *professional* and *managerial* occupations

Those who are alientated from work are typically found in *routine office/factory work*

Formal methods of combat alienation:

- Increase extrinsic satisfaction through higher pay to purchase a better standard of living
- Make working conditions more pleasant, create sense of belonging
- Worker's participation through elected representatives in management
- Forms of employee ownership

Worker's own techniques:

- Daydreaming about life outside work and leisure activities
- Humour at work – practical jokes, humourous stories, chatting
- Work avoidance – 'skiving' at work, absenteeism, extended breaks, restrictive work practice
- Pilfering
- Getting back at management

Schools and colleges, in some ways, are similar to offices and factories in that students need to be motivated to study and accept the discipline of the school.

1   How does the school/college formally motivate students?

2   How do students informally cope with the school day?

3   Use the ideas given in the text as a basis for your answers plus your own experience.

This is an extract from a study of women working in a tobacco factory. It describes how women workers in dead-end jobs deal with their boredom.

> Val: I goes to sleep. I daydream. But when we don't talk for two hours, I starts tormenting the others, pulling the rag about, muck about sort of thing. With the Irish, you know, I picks on them. About Ireland – take the soldiers back, the bombings, all that – only mucking about like, I don't mean it. But then we have a little row, but we don't mean what we says. But I get so bored, I got to do something, or I start going out the back and have a fag. (Music comes on.) It's the best part of the day when the records come on.

Source: A. Pollen, 'Girls, wives, factory lives', *New Society*, 22 October 1981

1 Identify the ways in which Val copes with her boredom.

2 Some sociologists have talked about the 'culture of the workplace'. Using the information given in the extract, explain what this term might mean

---

Main points ▶ People work for different reasons: some for money, some for interest, some for status.

▶ Sociologists divide these into extrinsic reasons (people work for reasons other than the financial reward) and intrinsic reasons (people have a real interest in their job which keeps them doing it).

▶ Alienation is a term first used by Karl Marx to describe a situation where a person's job is of no interest to them. He thought this was wrong and that all work should be of interest to the person doing it.

▶ In order to make work more interesting, people engage in a whole range of activities ranging from daydreaming to making fun of colleagues. These are informal methods of coping with boredom. Formal methods are those used by companies to encourage their workers. These could include incentive schemes and pleasant working conditions.

Gender inequalities at work

Women

Women suffer from four major disadvantages compared to men in their working lives:

- *They are paid less than men.* On average, women receive 80 per cent of the wages received by men. There are three reasons for this:
  - They are more likely to be in part-time work.
  - They are more likely to be employed in the sorts of jobs which are lower paid.
  - They are less likely to be promoted than men.

  Since 1975 it has been illegal to pay women less than men for doing the same level of job, as a result of the 1970 Equal Pay Act.

- *They are more likely to be in part-time employment.* Ninety per cent of part-time workers are women. Part-time working reflects the fact that women are still expected (and themselves expect) to care for children. Typically, women give up full-time employment when they have children, work part-time when the children are young and then may return to full-time employment when the children are at secondary school.

Women tend to have higher absenteeism than men because they need to stay away from work to care for any member of family who is ill. Many women face role conflict (see page 7) at work, having to balance their employment responsibilities with those of being a mother. The growth of lone-parent families headed by women has increased the pressure on women.

- *Women are concentrated in the sorts of job 'sectors' which are lower-paid.* Women are largely concentrated in caring professions or in routine office or service work, all of which are low paid sectors of the job market. This concentration of women in caring work illustrates the continuation of traditional views on the role of women as more capable of providing care than men .

Over half of all women are in routine office or service work which is usually low paid. When women do have professional jobs, it is usually in the lower-paid professions such as nursing (92 per cent of nurses are women) or primary school teaching.

- *Women are less likely to be promoted to senior positions.* Only about 15 per cent of women were in the higher professions or senior management. The fact that they are less likely to be promoted and to be stuck at a level of middle management is referred to as the **glass ceiling**.

> **Definition**
>
> **Glass ceiling** – women cannot get promoted beyond a certain point in organisations

Gender inequalities in the workplace

Employment[1]: by gender and occupation, 1999, United Kingdom

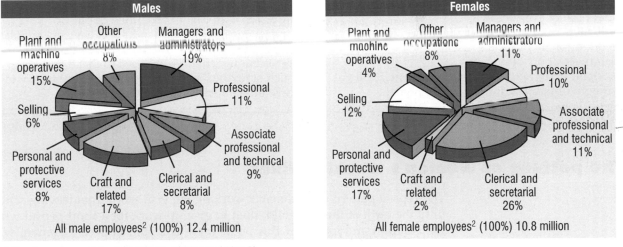

1 At spring each year. Males aged 16 to 64, females aged 16 to 59
2 Includes a few people who did not state their occupation. Percentages are based on totals which exclude this group.
Source: Labour Force Survey, Office of National Statistics

Source: *Social Trends 30* (The Stationery Office, 2000)

1 What percentage of male employees were engaged in management and administration?

2 What percentage of women employees were in management and administration?

3 Which area of work were women most likely to be concentrated?

4 Which area of work were women least likely to be employed in?

5 What differences can you see overall in male and female employment patterns?

The employment expert who is always busy

A day in the life of Kate Brearly, 42, a partner at the law firm Stephenson Harwood, where she specialises in employment law

5.30am: Get up. If I am writing a book, I will probably work for an hour and a half.

7.00 to 8.00am: This is my time with the children. I will get them dressed, have breakfast with them and catch up with their news.

8.00am: I will either go straight into office or work from my home office. If I have to go to a school play or event in the morning, I will work from home so that I can fit everything in.

9.30am to 6.30pm: I am usually in the office and will work through lunchtime, usually having a salad or sandwich at my desk.

6.30pm: If I have to attend a client event, I will go straight from work. If not I will go home.

7.30pm: The children are already in bed, so I cook dinner for my husband and myself. I might eat it while I am on the telephone with a client and my husband might take his upstairs to eat while he is working.

8.30pm to11.30pm: I will work. Sometimes, if I need to, I will work into the night. There have been occasions when I have had to work through the night, got the children ready and then turned round and gone back into work without going to bed.

Weekends: I may work early in the morning while the children are still in bed. If we go out to somewhere such as Legoland, I will have my mobile phone with me and may have to take calls from clients but my children are used to that. I don't see much of my husband during the week but we try to make time for each other at the weekend.

Source: *The Times*, 25 August 1999

The pattern of women's working lives

The typical pattern of a woman's working life is to work from leaving school until the birth of the first child, then to give up work for a short period while the children are young. At this point there is a split between women, with better-paid women in the professions and management returning to full-time employment in order to pursue a career, while other women in less interesting or well-paid jobs will be more likely to work part-time.

Despite the fact that it is illegal, their interrupted pattern of work means that many employers are less likely to promote women or train them for a career. Many employers still believe that women are less likely to remain with the company than a male worker.

Domestic labour

Earlier we discussed different economies and we saw that apart from employment, there was also the community/household economy. **Domestic labour** is work which most women do on top of their employment, and the

Definition

Domestic labour – housework and childcare

amount of work they do after they come home from their job varies, but certainly equals the number of hours in full-time employment. When women do domestic labour as their only or main work, and have no paid employment, the research shows that the majority of women regard it as often boring and seemingly never-ending. It can also be exhausting and, as they are often 'trapped' in the home with young children, they can feel isolated.

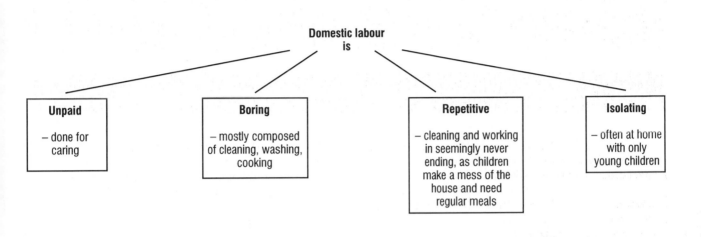

Domestic labour
is

Unpaid

– done for caring

Boring

– mostly composed of cleaning, washing, cooking

Repetitive

– cleaning and working in seemingly never ending, as children make a mess of the house and need regular meals

Isolating

– often at home with only young children

Part time work

Full and part-time employment: by gender, United Kingdom

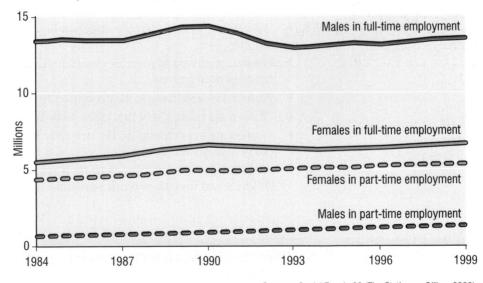

Source: *Social Trends 30* (The Stationery Office, 2000)

How many of the following were there in 1999:

a) women part-time employees?

b) male part-time employees?

c) male full-time employees?

d) female full-time employees?

Part-time work, post-Fordism and paternalism

This is part of a letter written to **The Guardian**.

1. Virtually all the part-time jobs created in the past 5–10 years have been the low-wage service sector. The growth of these jobs primarily reflects the flexible exploitation of employees by enterprises faced with fluctuating markets. Because demand for luxury goods and personal services is fickle, workers in high-street retail, fast-food chains, hotels and catering are increasingly employed only for the specific hours, days or months that they are most needed, and they must often be available at short notice. In this context 'flexibility' actually means insecurity.

2. 80–90 per cent of part-time workers are women. ... the majority of these women belong to households in which there is already a wage earner. This means that a considerable proportion of female part-timers can "afford" to work part-time.

3. Meeting women's preference for part-time jobs and a favourable balance between work and home may obscure a more fundamental imbalance. Many women do not look for full-time work because their exclusive responsibility for housework and childcare prevents it. ... This strengthens the male monopoly on secure, permanent, full-time work.

What we should be doing is demanding a reduction of working hours across the whole of society.

Source: Adapted from *The Guardian*, 25 January 1994

1 What does the term 'service sector' mean? Who is more likely to be employed in the service sector – men or women?

2 Explain in your own words the meaning of 'flexible exploitation of employees by enterprises faced with fluctuating markets'. What implications does this have for job security?

3 How does any of this relate to the concept of post-Fordism we looked at earlier?

4 What percentage of women work part-time? What explanations could you suggest from the main text and from the extract?

5 How can lowering the number of working hours for full-time employees be of help to women?

Main points ▸ Women suffer considerable disadvantages compared to men in their working lives.

▸ Women are likely to earn less than men and be concentrated in a narrow range of occupations.

▸ Women are less likely to be promoted to senior positions than men.

▸ Women are more likely than men to be in part-time employment.

▸ Women are expected to do the majority housework whether they are in paid employment or not.

▸ Women tend to have a break in their employment when they have children and may then work part-time. This disrupts careers.

Industrial relations

Definition

Capitalism – companies are owned by individuals or groups of people (shareholders), who try to make profit out of their companies

British society is based on the economic system of **capitalism**. This means that industry and commerce are owned by groups of individuals.

Employers and employees have some common interests, as both want the company to continue to exist and to make profit. But they also have different interests. The owners wish to make as much profit as reasonably possible and therefore wish to keep their costs, which include wages, as low as they can.

Employees, on the other hand, wish to obtain the highest possible wage for themselves and to work in the best conditions possible. The resulting conflict between the two groups as a result of their different wishes is known as *industrial conflict*.

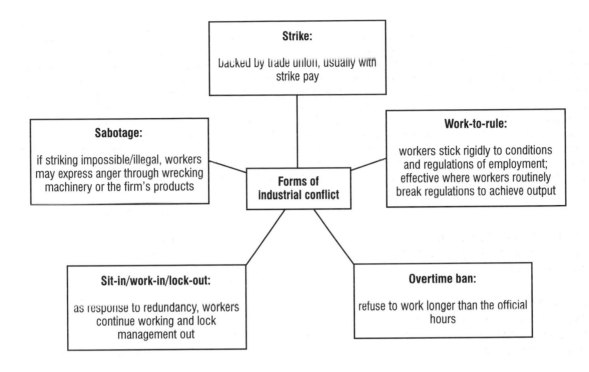

Two views on industrial relations

A Ford official publication

Industry is organised to make profit. Most people accept this as fact and recognise that the more profit their company makes the better chance it has of providing a good standard of living and security for its employees and their families. This is not only because everybody's future earnings depend on the Company continuing to make a profit, but because a good profit encourages more investment – a good safeguard for the future.

A shop steward

'It's just the situation they (management) are in. They've got to make a profit or they're finished. It's as easy as that. They've got to screw the blokes or they get screwed. That's the way it is ... '

Source: H. Benyon, *Working for Ford* (Pelican, 1984)

The extracts illustrate that employers and employees have things and in common and also competing interests. How do they show this?

The decline in strike action

Since the early 1980s the numbers of strikes in Britain has declined. The explanations are both negative and positive.

- *Negative reasons* are that strict laws now control employees' ability to strike. Secondly, the growth in flexible or insecure employment and in globalisation have meant that people are frightened of losing their jobs if they strike. Companies can simply move to another country with lower wages.
- *Positive reasons* include the fact that employers have attempted to improve the quality of the working environment to make work more meaningful and pleasant and, for the last 20 years, those in secure employment have seen wages rising.

Strike action   Labour disputes: working days lost, United Kingdom

Source: Office of National Statistics

Source: *Social Trends 30* (The Stationery Office, 2000)

1 In which year was the highest level of strikes? How many strikes were there?

2 Since 1950, which period saw the highest number of strikes?

3 What happened to the level of strikes in the 1990s?

4 In your own words, explain the positive and negative reasons for these changes.

Trade unions

Trade unions represent the workforce, negotiating working conditions and wage levels with the management.

Since the 1950s considerable changes have taken place in the trade unions. The number of trade unions has declined. There are now fewer, but bigger, unions and the total membership of the trade unions has fallen. The traditional view of trade unionists as male manual workers is now out of date. The growth area in trade union membership is in female, white-collar workers, reflecting the change in the whole employment structure with the move from industrial work to office and service employment, and the related growth in the numbers of women working.

The declining unions

The membership and power of the unions were concentrated in those industries, such as shipbuilding, steel, mining, and engineering, that suffered most from the industrial crisis of the 1970s, or in occupations, such as printing and dockwork, transformed by technical change.

When employment started to rise again, it did so in occupations concerned with consumption and services rather than production, in areas such as distribution, marketing and finance, which are much harder for the unions to organise. Furthermore, these occupations tended to recruit

part-time workers, women, the young, groups that are less likely to join unions than the full-time, adult, male workers typical of the traditional industries. There has also been a dispersal of employment to small units, and to small towns and rural areas, which has reversed the process of

concentration [in factories] that had earlier facilitated union organisation. Finding it difficult to recruit new members to replace those they have lost, the unions have resorted to mergers instead [so there are fewer unions with few members in total].

Source: J. Fulcher, 'A new stage in the development of capitalist society', *Sociology Review*, November 1991

Make a list of the changes in employment which have brought about a decline in union membership.

The professions

The professions are organisations that represent the interests of the jobs which are traditionally considered as the most skilful and which carry the highest status, such as medicine and the law.

There are two views concerning professions.

- One group of sociologists argues that the professions are organisations which are just middle-class trade unions, protecting the interests of their members by restricting the number of new entrants. As there are few professionals about, they can demand high fees.

- A second group of sociologists take a slightly kinder view of the professions and argue that they exist to protect the public by placing very high standards on behaviour in these jobs.

Main points ▶ British society is based upon capitalism which implies that owners of companies and their employees have some things in common, but also a number of conflicting interests.

▶ There are a number of different forms of industrial conflict, as well as strikes, including work to rule and sabotage of equipment.

▶ Strike action has declined very considerably over the last 20 years.

▶ The decline in strike action is partly as a result of better industrial relationships between workers and management, and partly because the service industries in which people are employed control their employees very strictly.

▶ Trades unions have a declining membership because the traditional industries in which they were very strong have closed.

▶ The professions have grown in size.

▶ There are two views on the nature of professions.

  – One group of writers see them as existing to protect the public by maintaining high standards.

  – The other approach sees them as simply middle-class trades unions, looking after their members' interests.

Unemployment

Unemployment is much more significant to most people than simply not having a job. It also has a range of social consequences too. These social consequences are linked to:

- income
- status
- self-respect.

Income

Unemployment means relying upon a very limited income provided by the government. Without money, it is difficult to buy all the consumer goods, or enjoy the leisure activities which are regarded as being part of a normal lifestyle.

Status

One of the first things people ask adults is what they do – meaning what job they have. Partly based on this, people tend to look up or look down upon people. So our social status is often linked with our job. Another element of social status are the clothes we wear and lifestyle we lead. As we saw before, those without money cannot make a claim for very high social status.

Self-respect

Status and income are important components of our identity – that is, how we see ourselves and the self-respect we hold for ourselves. A 'good job' and a successful career makes a person feel important and successful. Of course, employment is not the only thing which makes up our identity. Other things, such as family, leisure, success in sport or any other area, are all important too.

We can see then that having a job or being unemployed is extremely important to how we see ourselves and how others see us.

Measuring unemployment

Measuring the extent of unemployment is not as easy as it looks. The official statistics record only those who are registered as looking for work. But some people who work part-time would like to work full-time – including many women with young children. Secondly, people on the various government training schemes are not included. People who are disabled or long-term sick may also want to work, but are excluded from the statistics, as are people over 60.

The 'true' unemployment statistics are therefore probably higher than the official ones.

The causes of unemployment

Globalisation means that there has been a great decline in manufacturing industry and so those people, usually men, who worked in the traditional British industries have been made redundant and their skills are no longer needed. This is because the new jobs which are being created are in service industries and in technologically advanced companies, neither of which demand the skills these men have.

To make matters worse, where there are new industries, these tend to be highly automated and require far fewer workers.

Regional unemployment

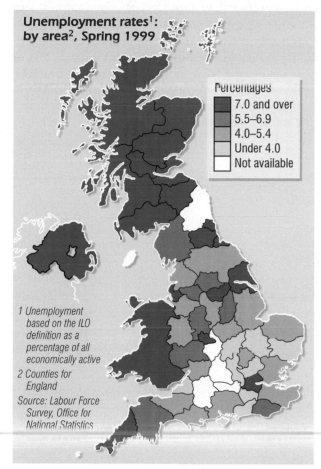

Unemployment rates[1]: by area[2], Spring 1999

Percentages

- 7.0 and over
- 5.5–6.9
- 4.0–5.4
- Under 4.0
- Not available

1 Unemployment based on the ILO definition as a percentage of all economically active

2 Counties for England

Source: Labour Force Survey, Office for National Statistics

Source: *Social Trends 30* (The Stationery Office, 2000)

The map shows there are differences in the unemployment rate in different parts of the country. Unemployment is not spread equally over the country – areas with the highest rates tend to be areas in which employment was provided by traditional industries, such as steel, mining and heavy engineering. As a result of globalisation these have now declined.

Look to see where you live. What is the level of unemployment?

1 Which areas have the lowest rates of unemployment?

2 What level of unemployment does London have?

The unemployed

Unemployment hits people at each end of the labour market: the young and the old.

There is disagreement over the extent to which women are affected by unemployment. As they are generally employed in the lower-paid jobs and are more often likely to have part-time work, it seems that they are more likely to work than men, and indeed outnumber men in the workforce. But many lone-parent women who would like to work are unable to do so because of child-minding costs and the fact that they will earn very little more in employment than they would staying on benefits.

Also, as we saw before, the official statistics do not include any married women who would like to work but are not eligible for benefits, so they seriously under-estimate the extent of female unemployment.

One major change that has taken place has been the growth of underemployment, by which we mean that people who work part-time (90 per cent of whom are women) may, in fact, really want full-time work, but are unable to do it.

The different experiences of unemployment

The experience of unemployment will not be the same for each social group. For a man of 50, for example, who has worked since leaving school, unemployment can be devastating. We know that men in particular take much of their identity from their job. Lack of work can lead to crisis of identity. For women workers who see their primary identity as a wife and mother, loss of employment need not be so devastating a blow to identity, although it will be just as harmful financially! However, for those women who see employment as an escape from the home, their return to domestic labour may make them feel a loss of identity in exactly the same way as men.

Experiences of unemployment

A

A man, in his fifties, reflecting on his experience of unemployment after having been made redundant, said:

'It affected me a lot when I was unemployed. ... It was very degrading. I have worked all my life and got angry. People who have never been unemployed don't know what it is like; they have never experienced it ... When you are unemployed you are bored, frustrated, and worried, worried sick: at least I was ... '
(Sinfield, 1981, p. 41)

Source: N. Abercrombie and A. Warde, *British Society* (Polity Press, 1994), quoting A. Sinfield, *What Unemployment Means* (Oxford University Press, 1981)

B

... the conversation between Stephen Woods, who was unemployed, and his 19 year old girlfriend, the mother of his child. He was anxious for them to set up home together. But not too anxious to work!

Girlfriend: 'I says to him, "Why should I work?" when he should work. He should support wer, not me support him and the bairn, then meself. Like if he got a job, I would like get a part-time job when she's one or two.'

Stephen: 'But you've got a better chance of getting a proper job 'cos you're the lass. Lasses can be on supermarket tills and what have you. You could get a start tomorrow, but they wouldn't start me there with us having a criminal record and that.'

Source: N. Abercrombie and A. Warde, *British Society* (Polity Press, 1994), quoting from *Youth Unemployment and The Family: Voices of Disordered Times* (Routledge, 1992)

1 What emotions did the unemployed man in extract A have?

2 Why do you think that is?

3 What were the views of the two younger people?

4 Why do you think they were different? (You may need to look in the main text for help.)

Young people without a lifetime of work behind them may well find the result of unemployment very different from the middle-aged. It could be argued that living on state benefits, freed from the drudgery of work could be, for a short time at least, a pleasant life. However, all this is marred by a number of hidden problems that develop individually and socially the longer unemployment lasts. The first problem facing many young people is that they need to remain at home, continuing to receive financial support and are, therefore, subject to attempts at control by their parents. Friction soon develops and the traditional way out, finding a flat or getting married, is no longer available. Paul Willis in a study of youth unemployment in the Midlands has found that some girls deliberately get pregnant in order to escape from their family, relying upon the state for support.

Young people, who have wholeheartedly embraced the ethics of the consumer society, increasingly expect to have consumer goods, fashionable clothes and enjoyable leisure. Unemployment robs youth of the legitimate ways of obtaining these goods, and may tempt some into crime.

'Consumerism' and unemployment have combined to create another feature of our current high streets, the groups of youth who are just hanging around. They have nothing to do and little money to spend. So they gather in the place where they can see and be seen by others of their age. In doing so they present a 'threat' to the middle-aged and 'respectable' shoppers. The police are called in to move the youth out and so develop the origins of resentment against the police.

The effect of unemployment on society

Unemployment

Individual

- Loss of self-worth
- Poverty
- Lack of respect from others
- Poverty linked to ill-health

The family

- Poverty – impacts upon the children particularly
- Stress and possible violence

The community

- High unemployment leads to a decline in sense of community, and to decay of buildings and local services
- Higher levels of crime and anti-social behaviour

Society

- High unemployment means lower tax revenues for government and therefore less to spend on NHS, social services, police, etc.
- Increase in social problems, e.g. drugs, racism, political unrest

Main points ▶ Unemployment is not simply about losing a job, but has three consequences for the person involved. They lose their income, their identity and their social status.

▶ The official statistics of unemployment may not give the true picture and many people argue that the statistics are higher than the official ones.

▶ Unemployment is caused by the decline in manufacturing industries, as a result of globalisation, and by automation.

▶ Those who remain unemployed tend to be the younger and the older workers – both without the skills needed.

▶ Unemployment is experienced differently by different groups of people.

Leisure

In modern industrial societies there is a strict division between what we consider to be 'work', that is paid employment, and what we consider to be 'leisure'. People work for a set number of hours each day and then at 5 p.m. they finish, and their leisure begins. This has not always been so. In most societies, throughout history, there was no clear distinction between work time and leisure time. To survive, people had to work in the fields or hunt. They performed these tasks until they had obtained enough food to eat, and adequate clothes and shelter. This work was not planned to happen at special times. As far as we know, there has never been a tribal society in which all the members started to hunt at 9 in the morning, stopped for an hour for lunch and then continued until 5 p.m!

Leisure, as we understand it, is related to the development of industry. Employers wanted a workforce that arrived at a particular time, so that the work of the machinery and employees could be co-ordinated. Work was so brutal and unpleasant that the few hours each day when people were not in the factories and offices was spent in trying to recuperate. Work then became separated from ordinary life; it became a fixed period of unpleasant labour each day. Work was time regarded as 'lost' from people's lives.

Gradually, the trade unions won shorter working days for their members and so the hours of non-work, or leisure, increased. However, the distinction in our lives between work, which is not expected to be enjoyable (for a large portion of the workforce), and leisure, which is expected to provide us with our fulfilment, has come to be seen as normal and natural.

Defining leisure

Although it may seem a very easy idea to define, leisure is a very slippery concept to grasp. It is not just time spent out of work, because we often have things to do which are forms of work in this time (for example, I wrote this book in my 'leisure' time). It is certainly not just activities, for one person's leisure is another's job. For example, some people dance for fun, others do it for a living. In the end, we have to say that there are certain characteristics more often found in leisure than in work, though these characteristics overlap.

There is, however, a fairly simple distinction between unemployment and leisure. Leisure means free time you have chosen to spend doing something you want, and having the finances to do it. Unemployment means free time not of your own choosing and with little money to spend. So here the difference lies in choice and finance.

The characteristics of work and leisure

Characteristics	Leisure	Work
Paid	No	Yes
Freedom	Yes	No
Choice	Wide	Limited
Self-imposed	Yes	No
Relationships with others based on power	No	Yes
Pleasurable	Yes	Only for those in skilled work

- Looking after children can be work or leisure.
- Cooking can be work or pleasure.
- Sexual activity can be work or leisure.
- Dancing can be work or leisure.

1 How can these statements be true?

2 Identify three other activities which could be work or leisure.

3 What does it tell us about ideas of work in society?

The influences on leisure patterns

Leisure activities are clearly the result of individual interests and choices, but these individual choices are themselves strongly influenced by other social factors. The most important are:

- social class and income
- occupation
- age
- gender.

Social class and income

Question

For people in advanced capitalist economies (such as Britain) work not just to survive, but to live in particular ways and to display the evidence of their success and status.

Source: A. Tomlinson. 'Buying time: consumption and leisure', *Social Studies Review*, January 1991

What does this quote tell us about the importance of leisure in Britain?

Historically, the different social classes have differences in their incomes and standards of education and probably some difference in cultural standards. This meant that traditionally they tended to have different leisure pursuits. However, as society has changed in the last 30 years, and class boundaries have become fluid, the differences are increasingly difficult to identify. Nevertheless, social differences in income and interests still exist, and these have important influences on leisure choices.

Changes in leisure over time

In Victorian England leisure habits were sharply class-divided. Professional men and their families took no part in the street culture of working-class areas. There are still some socially exclusive pastimes. Hopeful show-jumpers need rich fathers. But the most popular leisure activities, such as watching television and taking holidays away from home, are now classless.

Paid vacations were still a middle-class perk in many firms throughout the inter-war years. Since then middle-class holiday entitlement has grown slowly, if at all, while manual workers have almost closed the gap. (On average today senior managers and the self-employed work longer than men on the shop-floor.) There is no longer any sense in which our economic and political elites can be labelled a 'leisure class'.

This trend towards a leisure democracy has been strengthened as class differences in leisure tastes and habits have grown smaller. The middle classes still do more, but usually more of the same things that occupy working-class leisure. Class divisions in styles of holiday-making have collapsed. The main divisions now follow age, rather than class divisions. Discos cut across class barriers and it is the public in general, rather than high society, that dictates trends in fashion.

Source: Adapted from K. Roberts, *Youth and Leisure* (Allen & Unwin, 1983)

1 Why do you think that leisure patterns were so sharply divided along class lines in Victorian England?

2 What do you think the author means when he talks about the 'leisure class'?

3 Is leisure now divided along class lines?

4 What divisions are now stronger than class? Do you agree?

Occupation

If social class and income differences create broad divisions in our choices of leisure pursuits, occupation influences us in more specific ways.

It has been suggested that there are three sorts of relationships between work and leisure:

- extension
- neutrality
- oppositional.

Extension

This is when the job a person does is interesting and fulfilling. The person will allow work to intrude on leisure, and vice versa. This relationship is typical of people in professional occupations, such as social workers who may help doing voluntary work in their spare time or teachers who have a particular interest in their subject.

Neutrality

This is when the job a person does is basically uninteresting and is seen as just a way of getting money to pay for an adequate style of life. In leisure, the person may emphasise the family and social enjoyment. Typical occupations are clerical workers and semi-skilled workers.

Oppositional

This is when the job a person does is exhausting and involves periods of intense physical effort. In leisure, the person looks for the complete opposite of work in order to refresh themselves. Typical occupations are manual workers and building site labourers.

The relationship between work and leisure

Why is it that [deep sea] fishermen drink so much? In many cases it is not even true to say that they do drink more than the average man, they are merely concentrating their drinking [while ashore]. ... Is it that they are trying to forget the cold, black void of the Arctic which awaits them once again? Fishermen say: 'Of course fishermen get drunk. Anybody who does what we do has to drink to stay sane.'

Source: J. Tunstall, *The Fishermen* (McGibbon & Kee, 1962)

Parker has suggested three relationships between work and leisure – oppositional, extension and neutrality. Which one of these relationships is illustrated in the extract?

Age group

As we pass through certain ages of life, our tastes, income and abilities alter:

- Childhood is usually spent in play, but with very limited income.
- In youth, people have a considerable amount of uncommitted money (no household bills to pay), which can be spent on the pursuit of style and excitement.
- Young couples use money to purchase/renovate houses and to spend on young children. Leisure is family-based.
- In middle age children leave home and both partners often work, so this is the most affluent period of life. Luxury items and holidays are purchased.
- Over 65, income and physical abilities decline. Home-based activities, such as reading, watching television and going for walks, are favoured.

Consuming leisure

Eighty per cent of all leisure time is spent in or near the home, and a survey on the nature of home-based leisure ... reported that 86% of all 'leisure events' took place in the home. As Sue Glyptis put it, 'The home dominated the lifestyles of all social groups, and especially women, single parents, people of retirement and pre-retirement age, the professional class and the unemployed.'

Young people and employed working-class adult males are revealingly absent from this list, no doubt still seeking traditional forms of excitement and escape in the public spaces of the youth market and long-established male preserves such as the pub, the club and the sports field.

Source: A. Tomlinson. 'Buying time: consumption and leisure', *Social Studies Review*, January 1991

1 Where does most leisure take place for older people?

2 Where do younger people engage in leisure?

3 Why do you think this is?

4 In your household, keep a log for one week of household leisure activities for members of the family. What are your results?

Gender

As the culture of our society stresses different expectations of males and females, this influences their choices of leisure. Males are far more active than females in virtually every area, particularly sport, which is regarded as more appropriate to males. Females are more likely to go dancing, engage in keep-fit and yoga. Most importantly, women have less leisure time than men as they are expected to the bulk of the housework, even if they have a full-time job.

Women's leisure

... in general men in this country have more leisure time available to them than women. The least leisure time available is found amongst employed women, followed by employed men. Unemployed and retired women have less leisure time than their male counterparts. ... It is not just leisure time and quality which is differentiated by gender but also patterns of leisure. Whilst men's leisure is often out of the home and may revolve around sport (more often spectating rather than playing) and informal group activities like going for a drink, women tend to spend more leisure time at home. Women's at-home leisure often consists of things which are inexpensive, can be done in short, often unpredicted and interrupted time-spells or are easily combined with household work

Source: R. Deem, 'Women and leisure: all work and no play?', *Social Studies Review*, March 1990

1 Who has most leisure time?

2 What sorts of leisure do men engage in?

3 What sorts of leisure do women engage in?

4 Can you suggest reasons for these differences in time and activity?

Consumption and leisure

The percentage of household income spent on leisure

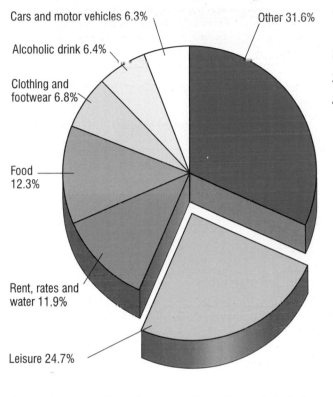

Cars and motor vehicles 6.3%

Alcoholic drink 6.4%

Clothing and footwear 6.8%

Food 12.3%

Rent, rates and water 11.9%

Leisure 24.7%

Other 31.6%

1 What is the single largest element of spending which is specifically named?

2 Does the answer surprise you? Explain why.

3 Do you think the pie chart as any weaknesses?

4 Work out what proportion of (a) your own and (b) your family's budget (if different) goes on leisure. (How you define leisure may be an interesting exercise in itself.)

Source: A. Tomlinson, 'Buying time: consumption and leisure', *Social Studies Review*, January 1991 and *Leisure Management*, Vol. 9, No. 5, 1989

Leisure: the future

In the future, the numbers of workers and the hours they will be required to work will decrease, as increased automation occurs. Sociologists have realised that this will make a significant impact on the role of leisure in society.

The optimists see the increase in leisure as giving us a chance to become more fulfilled. Increased time can be spent on the arts and on educating ourselves. The social class divisions caused by occupational and income differences will disappear as fewer and fewer people work.

The pessimists disagree. Where, they ask, will all the money come from for these leisure pursuits? In our society, people either receive a salary with which they can purchase leisure, or they live on state benefits which are not enough to purchase leisure. Leisure is usually provided by large profit-making companies. Unemployment will lead to boredom for the majority.

The growth of freedom

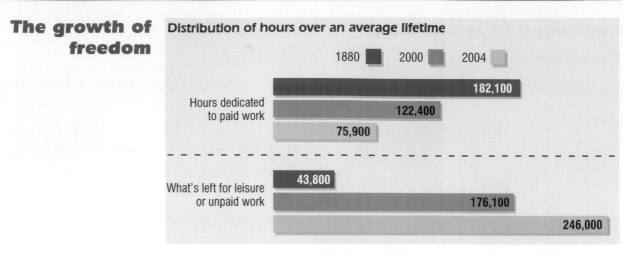

Distribution of hours over an average lifetime

1880 ■   2000 ■   2004 ■

Hours dedicated to paid work
- 182,100
- 122,400
- 75,900

What's left for leisure or unpaid work
- 43,800
- 176,100
- 246,000

Source: *The Guardian*

1 What has happened since 1880 to the number of hours dedicated to paid work?

2 How many hours left for leisure (or unpaid work) are there in 2004, and were there in 2000?

3 What implications do you think this might have?

Retirement

In the last 20 years a very quiet revolution has been taking place – the growth in early retirement. Roughly the same number of men over the age of 55 are now retired as are working, for example. As people can expect to live longer, the trend to early retirement and later death means that a significant part of people's lives are now happening after work.

Sociologists have identified this trend as having both positive and negative consequences.

Advantages	Disadvantages
The chance to enjoy new interests and renew relationships	It can be a time of poverty with low pensions and having to rely upon state benefits
The opportunity to learn new life skills, to travel	
The chance to move away to more pleasant areas of the country away from offices and factories	The person may not be well enough, after a lifetime of work, to enjoy increased leisure
The opportunity to undertake charity and voluntary work	The person may not have an adequate income to move house
More time to look after grandchildren	No family may live nearby to offer help to
	Loss of friends at work can mean social isolation

Main points ▶ Unemployment is not simply about losing a job, but has three consequences for the person involved. They lose their income, their identity and their social status.

▶ The official statistics of unemployment may not give the true picture and many people argue that the statistics are higher than the official ones.

▶ Unemployment is caused by the decline in manufacturing industries, as a result of globalisation and by automation.

▶ Those who remain unemployed tend to be the younger and the older workers, both without the skills needed, but they experience unemployment in a very different ways

▶ Leisure is a modern idea which developed with the growth of industry and with fixed hours of work.

▶ It is difficult to define leisure as it overlaps with work.

▶ Leisure patterns are influenced by four key elements: social class and income, occupations, age, gender.

▶ Income allows people to buy different sorts of leisure activities.

▶ People often respond to their occupation by either seeking leisure which is linked to work or by leisure that allows them to escape completely from it.

▶ Age is particularly important as leisure patterns alter over a person's lifetime.

▶ Males and females undertake different leisure patterns.

▶ There is a dispute over the future of leisure, with some seeing it as becoming the central life interest of people, while others see it as dividing people according to income.

▶ Retirement is a period which can open up new opportunities or be a time of poverty and isolation.

11 CHAPTER SUMMARY

1 Work influences our lives in many ways. It also influences the community and society in which we live.

2 Work is difficult to define, as it has many elements to it, for example it can be full or part-time, take place in a factory, office or the home, be paid or not paid.

3 There are two very different economies which exist:
   - The formal economy includes all the employment which is legal and taxed.
   - The informal economy has two elements – a hidden economy which is non-taxed work and a household/communal economy in which work is done for love or duty, but is generally not paid.

4 The occupational structure refers to the types of jobs undertaken in society. And is divided into three sectors – primary (agriculture and mining), secondary (manufacturing) and tertiary (service industries).

5 The twentieth century saw a shift away from primary and secondary sectors to the tertiary. This has a considerable number of social effects.

6 Industrialisation fundamentally altered the nature of British society socially, economically and politically

7   The later part of the twentieth century saw major changes in work as a result of automation and IT. In factories, automated manufacture took over many of the jobs of unskilled and semi-skilled workers.

8   Some sociologists have argued that new types of work relationships exist now. In factories they describe the working conditions as post-Fordist, and in shops and offices they suggest that the term McDonaldisation is appropriate.

9   Another major change in world trading has been globalisation.

10 People work for extrinsic reasons (people work for reasons other than the financial reward) or intrinsic reasons (people have a real interest in their job which keeps them doing it).

11 Alienation is a term first used by Karl Marx to describe a situation where a person's job is of no interest to them.

12 Employees and employers both find ways to make work more interesting.

13 Women suffer considerable disadvantages compared to men in their working lives. They are likely to earn less than men; to be concentrated in a narrow range of occupations; are less likely to get the top jobs and are more likely to be in part-time employment.

14 Women tend to have a break in their employment when they have children and may then work part-time. This disrupts careers.

15 British society is based upon capitalism which implies that owners of companies and their employees have some things in common, but also a number of conflicting interests. This can lead to industrial conflict

16 There are a number of different forms of industrial conflict. As well as strikes, these can include such things as work-to-rule and sabotage of equipment.

17 Strike action has declined very considerably over the last 20 years, partly as a result of better industrial relationships between workers and management, and partly because the service industries in which people are employed control their employees very strictly.

18 Trade unions have a declining membership because the traditional industries in which they were very strong have closed down, while professions have grown in size.

19 There are two views on the nature of professions. One group of writers see them as existing to protect the public by maintaining high standards. The other approach sees them as simply middle-class trade unions, looking after their members' interests.

20 Unemployment is not simply about losing a job, but has three consequences for the person involved. They lose their income, their identity and their social status.

21 The official statistics of unemployment may not give the true picture and many people argue that the statistics are higher than the official ones.

22 Unemployment is caused by the decline in manufacturing industries, as a result of globalisation and by automation.

23 Those who remain unemployed tend to be the younger and the older workers, both without the skills needed, but they experience unemployment in a very different ways.

24   It is difficult to define leisure as it overlaps with work.

25   Leisure patterns are influenced by four key elements: social class and income, occupations, age, gender.

26   There is a dispute over the future of leisure, with some seeing it as becoming the central life interest of people, while others see it as dividing people according to income.

27   Retirement is a period which can open up new opportunities or be a time of poverty and isolation.

Test Your Knowledge

1   Identify and explain the importance of (a) work and (b) unemployment in people's lives.

2   Explain three consequences of industrialisation on society and three consequences of de-industrialisation.

3   What do we mean by globalisation?

4   Explain the meaning of the term 'alienation'. What are its key elements?

5   Women suffer from four major disadvantages compared to men in their working lives. What are they?

6   What is domestic labour? What characteristics does it have?

7   Name four types of industrial action.

8   Why is it difficult to define leisure?

9   What relationships exist between a person's occupation and leisure?

Chapter 12

SOCIAL CONTROL, DEVIANCE AND CRIME

Chapter contents

● Social control

We explain the nature of social control and how it operates to ensure that society controls any forms of deviance which emerge. Social control is a continuation of the socialisation process, ensuring that not only do we know what to do, but that we really do it!

● Deviance

Society can only run smoothly if people conform fairly closely to common forms of co-operative behaviour. Deviant acts, that is acts which are unusual or culturally odd, challenge this smooth running. Yet, people constantly seek new challenges and different ways of behaving. Often, over time, what is deviant becomes normal and conversely what was once normal comes to be seen as bizarre. The chapter explores this 'relative' view of deviance and suggests some of the reasons why views on deviance change over time.

However, not all things which are deviant come to be seen as normal, some become criminal. So, we also need to explore just why some deviant acts are acceptable, if 'odd' and some deviant acts are simply not acceptable to society, such that laws are drawn up to forbid them, and punish anyone who acts in a deviant manner. This discussion will take us deep into sociological territory and we will examine such things as 'labelling' and 'moral crusades'.

There is always someone who decides what is deviant and what is not. And what that means is that there are differences in power between groups when making decisions over illegal and deviant actions.

● Explanations for crime and anti-social behaviour

We look at some of the key explanations as to why some people commit deviant acts and others do not. We focus our discussions on four key areas of interest: age, gender, social class and place. This is because most crime is committed by young males from less well-off backgrounds who come from large, deprived housing areas. This is not a rule that all young males from these areas are criminal or anti-social, merely that official statistics point to a higher chance of these young men engaging in deviant acts. Having identified this, we go onto explain what factors may be involved in causing this association between age, deprivation and criminality.

● White-collar and corporate crime

Blaming young males for crime is hardly surprising, but this part of the chapter suggests that there is as much deviance and criminality amongst the middle class – it just takes a different form. We explore two related issues. First, how ordinary middle-class people engage in theft, but somehow it is not regarded as a major threat to society. Secondly, we examine how companies engage in dishonest and sometimes 'borderline' behaviour in their search for profits.

● Criminal statistics

Much of the discussion so far, and certainly that about young males engaging in anti-social behaviour, relies upon official statistics of crime. We look rather more carefully at how crime statistics are constructed. The result is a rather cynical view of the figures. Finally, we just note how sociologists go about trying to find out the 'true' crime rate.

● Victims of crime

Most people think that being the victim of crime is just bad luck, but this is not so. There are very clear patterns. Basically, young, poorer people in socially deprived areas are more likely to be victims. Being a victim is a reflection of the power differences in society. The poorer and less powerful a person, the greater their chance of being a victim.

Social control

Definition

Social control – people learn the expectations and values of society (culture) through socialisation and if they do not follow the guidelines of society, then they are punished in some way (social control)

When we speak and write in English, we are aware that it has a grammar (a set of rules), even if we are not sure how to explain it. We work within these rules, maybe using different words in different combinations, but always working within a framework of grammar that we have learned since childhood. We make mistakes, and we have different dialects in different parts of the country and amongst different social classes. In the end, however, we know that there is a clear distinction between English and French or Italian, and you do not need to be an academic to know it.

Society too has its own 'grammar', or culture, which guides us in our actions, even though we may not be aware of it. No one disputes that, in language, grammar is a good thing, but the situation is different when it comes to social rules. Sociologists are divided in their opinions of who exactly benefits from the rules and values of society. Some sociologists argue that we all benefit from having a common set of values, as life is predictable. Others disagree, claiming that the rules guiding our behaviour are to the benefit of those who are more powerful and wealthy, because they persuade us to act in the ways they want us to. **Social control** is the process through which people are encouraged to conform to the common expectations of society.

Types of social control

There are two types of social control:

- informal social control
- formal social control.

Definition

Peer group – a group of a person's own age who are important to them; the group exerts influence over individual members; most often used when referring to young people

Informal social control

This form of control is based on the approval or disapproval of those around us whose view of us we regard as important, for instance family, friends and **peer group**. If they disapprove of our behaviour we usually alter it to conform to their expectations.

How is informal social control enforced?

People around us may tell us they do not like our behaviour, they may ridicule us, they may argue with us, they may play practical jokes on us, or they may even 'send us to Coventry'.

Informal social control is part of the socialisation process by which we become a truly 'human' being, by learning the expected patterns of behaviour in society.

Formal social control

Whenever we are given rules to follow, as in school or the laws which are the legal system of society, then this is an example of formal control. One difference between formal and informal rules is that formal rules are almost always written down.

How is formal social control enforced?

Usually, formal control is enforced through official sanctions, such as a fine for speeding, or being sacked for coming to work late too often.

Social control – every society needs ways of gently persuading people to obey rules.

Social control in action

We have seen that social control operates in two ways, formally and informally. In society, there are a number of institutions, or agencies, which impose social control upon us.

The most important are:
- the family
- the school
- the peer group
- the mass media
- the workplace
- the legal system
- to a much lesser extent, religion.

The family

> ### Definition
>
> **Socialisation** – the process by which people are taught to accept the values of society and to conform

The basic **socialisation** takes place in the family and it is here, through parents and relatives, that we learn the accepted morality of society, to distinguish between right and wrong. Not only do we learn what is right and wrong in general, we also learn the expected behaviour for males and females (gender roles). Delinquency has been linked to the failure of parents to socialise their children correctly.

The school

The process of socialisation continues – formally in the content of the lessons we are taught and informally in the expectations of us by the teachers and fellow pupils. Pupils are divided into successes and failures, and they develop appropriate attitudes to cope with these situations.

The peer group

People of our own age to whom we look for approval are crucial in forming our attitudes to society. Peer groups develop in school and studies have shown how pupils divide themselves into those who accept the school rules and those who do not. The groups appear to develop from the different streams as a result of teachers' differing attitudes and expectations of high- and low-stream pupils.

The mass media

The term 'mass media' includes such things as newspapers, radio and television, cinema and the Internet. These influence us by providing models of behaviour which we copy, and by condemning other deviant forms of behaviour. Although they do not affect us directly, in the sense that seeing something on television does not immediately make us want to copy it, they do create a certain climate of opinion regarding acceptable behaviour.

The workplace

At work, conformity is ensured by the fact that if we are troublemakers, or 'weird', then we may not be promoted, or in some certain circumstances even sacked. Amongst our work colleagues, if we fail to conform to their values, they may well use such things as practical jokes at our expense to show us we ought to change our behaviour.

The legal system

The most powerful institution dealing with social control is the legal system, by which we mean the police and the courts. People breaking the law are arrested and judged. Usually the law is reserved for what many people regard as the more serious breaches of our values. It has a whole range of punishments including fines and imprisonment.

Religion

Historically, the Church was one of the major forms of social control. Each week, people used to attend church and through the sermon were advised on the way to behave. In contemporary society, the influence of Christian religion has waned for the majority of the British population, although for other religious groups, such as Muslims, religious teachings have retained their importance.

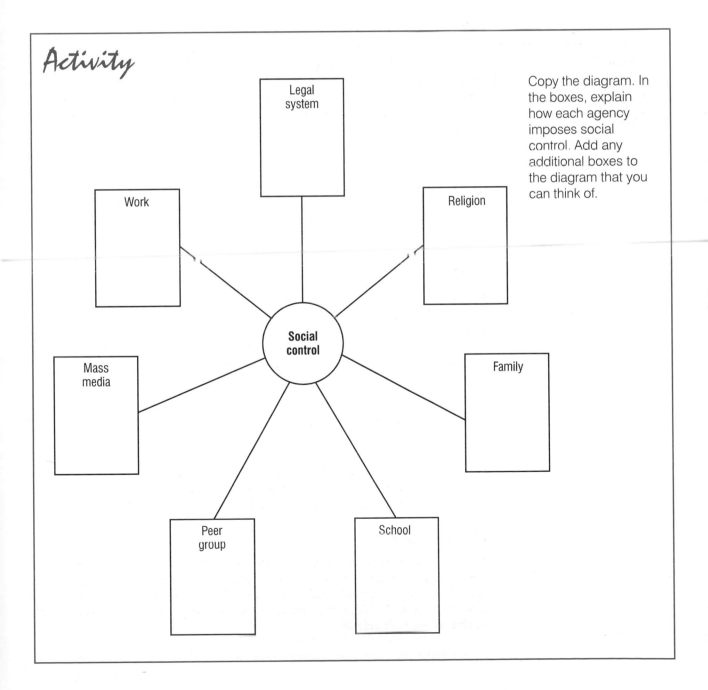

Activity

Legal system

Religion

Work

Social control

Mass media

Family

Peer group

School

Copy the diagram. In the boxes, explain how each agency imposes social control. Add any additional boxes to the diagram that you can think of.

Socialisation and social control

The process of social control cannot be separated from the process of sociali-sation (see pages 8–10). As children grow up, they are constantly learning the correct and most appropriate way to behave – from family, school, media, religion and peer group, and this is known as socialisation. Social control is the 'iron fist within the velvet glove' of socialisation – it exists to make sure that rules are followed even if socialisation has not been completely effective. Whereas socialisation teaches, social control guides behaviour more firmly and ensures that, at the extreme, people who deviate will be punished.

socialisation = learning to conform
social control = maintaining conformity

Power and social control

What we have seen is that society exists because there are rules and regulations which ensure order, and help prevent chaos But who benefits most from the order imposed by the social rules? Some sociologists argue that we all benefit from having social rules, and a common set of values because they make life predictable and so help society to work smoothly.

Others disagree, claiming that the rules guiding our behaviour are to the benefit of those who are more powerful and wealthy, because they persuade us to act in the ways that they want.

In most societies, some have more power to control than others.

Main points ▶ Social control is the process by which people are made to conform to social rules.

▶ There are two types of social control – formal and informal.

▶ Informal control takes place in most situations, but there are no written rules. Enforcement is by such things as making rude comments or by ignoring someone who breaks the 'unwritten rules'.

▶ Formal control is usually written rules and is enforced by official sanctions. The most important example of formal social control is criminal justice system.

▶ Social control is enforced by the family, the school, the peer group, the mass media, the workplace, the legal system and religion.

▶ Socialisation and social control are closely related. Socialisation is learning and social control is enforcing.

▶ Some people have more power to enforce social control than others.

Deviance

Social control exists to prevent deviance, that is behaviour which is considered to be threatening or disruptive to the order in society. **Deviant behaviour** includes an enormous range of actions which appear to have little in common. It can include, for example, crime, mental illness, unusual sexual activities, strange religious rites, and bizarre ways of dressing. Although all very different, what they share is the fact that they challenge normal behaviour in one way or another.

Deviance: in the eyes of the beholder

Most behaviour is not deviant in itself, it is how people define and respond to the behaviour which makes it deviant. It is rather like beauty, in that it exists in the eye of the beholder! What is considered deviant in one situation is not in another. Take, for example, a man with a large amount of make-up on, who is dressed in strange clothes, and keeps pretending to throw water over people who look at him. Strange behaviour perhaps in the streets, but quite amusing in a circus tent!

Sociologists have spent a great deal of time trying to explain the circumstances in which certain acts are tolerated and others regarded as deviant, or even criminal. The following factors have been suggested as important.

Place

Where an action takes place is important. Lovemaking, for instance, is regarded as deviant if it takes place public, but 'normal' in private. Even arguments are seen as private things which ought to take place indoors.

Society or culture

Views on what is appropriate behaviour varies across different societies. For example, in Italy, it is considered very bad manners not to shake hands on meeting friends, even if you have seen them only a couple of days before. In Britain, shaking hands is usually reserved for the first meeting, or on meeting someone after a long time. In Italy, it would be quite normal and acceptable for (male or female) friends to kiss.

Period of time

What is considered appropriate behaviour alters over time, It was only recently that being gay or lesbian has been regarded as acceptable and it is still not considered 'normal' by some. In the last 20 years attitudes towards the use of drugs have changed, so that today, although illegal, cannabis use is widespread amongst younger people. It is possible that in another 20 years it will be regarded as so normal that laws may even be changed.

Who commits the act

An act is considered deviant or not depending upon who is doing it, For example, it is considered normal in our culture for an adult to drink alcohol, yet wrong and even criminal to give alcohol to children.

Power

The more powerful a group is in society, the less likely it is that their activities will be seen as deviant. Gangs of working-class youths chasing stray cats or dogs across towns in order to beat them to death would cause a public outcry. Yet fox-hunting is defended as a British tradition by many people, when carried out by affluent people in the countryside. Only recently has it come to be seen by the majority as being cruel.

Accepted values

The further away from accepted values an act is, the greater the chance of it being labelled as deviant, even if it does no harm. For example, travellers are often persecuted in Britain because people regard them as dishonest. Much of this prejudice may come from the fact that they have a different lifestyle from the majority of the population.

Deviance varies

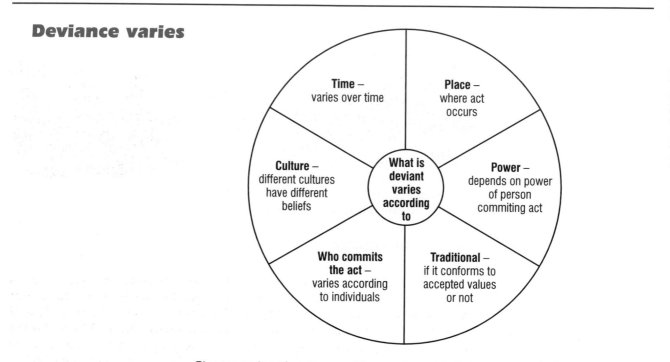

Give examples of your own of how acts vary in being seen as deviant, according to each of the 'segments' above.

The relationship between crime and deviance

Most forms of deviant behaviour are merely disapproved of and dealt with by informal means of social control. However, in certain circumstances deviant behaviour can become illegal.

The following seem to be very important in tipping an act into the category of criminal, rather than just being disapproved of.

Clash of values

The most obvious example of this is where an action is so strongly disapproved of by the majority of the population, that it is made illegal. Therefore murder and rape are against the law, and attract long prison sentences.

In this sense, the labellists are saying the cause of deviancy is often not the action itself, but the reaction of others to it. It is possible, they say, that social control, far from preventing crime, can help cause it.

But critics argue that it fails to explain people's actions before they are labelled. After all, why do some commit crime in the first place and others not? It is not just labelling which determines a person's life.

A tragic story of crime, labelling and ... cleaning

The story of Student Anne

Steals lots of textbooks and takes loads of drugs   Has lots of fun   Gets good results   And is now a famous lecturer in Sociology – lucky Lecturer Anne

The story of Student Brenda

Had just one puff, stole just one book   Sent to prison   Never got a degree, and no one wants to give an untrustworthy drug-taking thief a job   Now cleans Lecturer Anne's house – unlucky Cleaner Brenda

What does the cartoon tell us about the difference between reality and labelling?

Main points ▶ Deviance is when people do not conform to what society expects. Social control exists to limit deviance.

▶ Deviance is not a fixed thing, but varies across a number of dimensions including place, culture, time, who commits the act, power and how far from accepted values an act is.

▶ Not all deviant acts are criminal. The relationship between something going from being deviant to criminal is quite complicated.

▶ The key factors in making something deviant become criminal are a clash of values with accepted values of society, moral crusades and power.

▶ Moral crusades are when groups of people campaign for something to be made illegal.

▶ Labelling is when a group of people are marked out as bad or deviant and then punished.

▶ Labelling can lead to people being unable to re-enter society and so it can cause even greater deviance.

Crime patterns

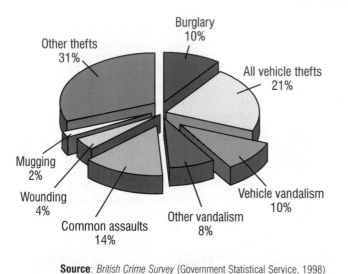

1 What is the most common form of crime?

2 What percentage of crime does burglary form?

3 What percentage of crimes appear to be violent?

Source: *British Crime Survey* (Government Statistical Service, 1998)

Explanations for crime and anti-social behaviour

Four key elements emerge from looking at the official statistics on crime. These are that criminality and delinquency are related to:

- age
- gender
- class
- place.

Age

The Henley Centre for Forecasting estimates that the cost to households and businesses of burglaries, car thefts and arson committed by 18–21-year-olds is over £3.8 billion.

The period in a person's life when they are most likely to commit a criminal offence is 14–20. Youth is a period when there is a great stress on excitement and 'having a laugh'. This search for a 'good time' can often lead to clashes with the law. It is also true to say that youth is a period when social control is weak. It has been suggested that the weakness of social control, coupled with the search for excitement, can lead to a drift into delinquency.

Age, gender and frequency of offending

Offenders[1] as a percentage of the population: by gender and age, 1997–8, England and Wales

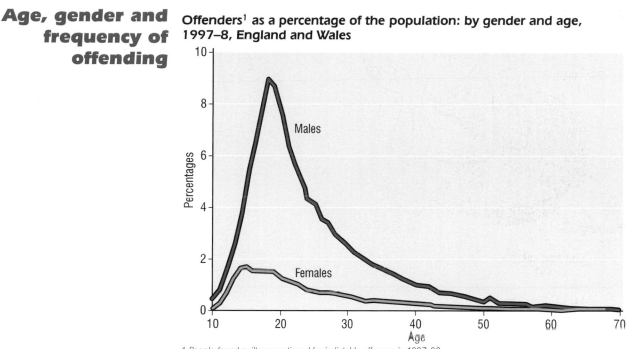

1 People found guilty or cautioned for indictable offences in 1997-98

Source: Social Trends 30 (The Stationery Office, 2000)

1 Who commits more crime, males or females?

2 Between what ages are (a) males and (b) females more likely to commit crimes?

People move away from delinquency as they get older because of the stability provided by marriage, family and employment. (Of course, this suggests that if rates of unemployment stay high for young people, then they may not move out of crime.)

Gender

There is a marked difference between the crime rates of males and females, with the male rate being about five times higher than the female rate.

The different expectations we have of boys and girls leave their mark on us as we grow up. Typically, masculine values, such as toughness, can lead directly to fighting, for instance. On the other hand, feminine values stress conformity, and success in relationships and, often, education. These are not values which lead directly to anti-social behaviour.

Gender and crime

In *Women and Crime*, Frances Heidensohn argues that much of the explanation for the conformity of women is that they are far more constrained than men, particularly by the roles they are expected to play in society:

'It's hard to bring off a burglary if you're pushing a twin baby-buggy and its contents; caring for a demented elderly relative hardly gives a woman time to plan a bank robbery. In fact women are burdened with duties which act as a constraint. ... In public, appropriate behaviour for females is different than it is for men. For example males virtually have a monopoly over the use of force and violence in society. ... It is unacceptable for women to be violent, yet relatively normal for men to be so.'

There is evidence to suggest that police treat female criminals differently. They tend to think that females are 'naturally' more law abiding than males and therefore have been 'led astray' into crime. Police too are sometimes more lenient on females than males. For example, two girls fighting is less likely to result in arrest than two males fighting, as it is not regarded as so serious. Once again this is related to police officers' views on male and females as different.

1 Explain how the social role of women is supposed to explain the low proportion of crimes committed by women.

2 Given the importance of gender roles, what sort of crimes do you think women are most likely to commit?

3 Why do police treat female offenders differently?

4 Have you ever seen the police dealing differently with males and females? Explain what happened.

Gender and convictions

Gender and convictions, England and Wales, 1998

	All aged 10 and over (thousands)
Males	
Theft and handling stolen goods	152.6
Drug offences	96.0
Violence against the person	51.7
Burglary	37.2
Criminal damage	12.4
Robbery	5.6
Sexual offences	5.5
Other indictable offences	74.3
All indictable offences	435.9
Females	
Theft and handling stolen goods	56.8
Drug offences	11.5
Violence against the person	8.9
Burglary	2.0
Criminal damage	1.3
Robbery	0.6
Sexual offences	0.1
Other indictable offences	15.0
All indictable offences	96.1

Source: *Social Trends 30* (The Stationery Office, 2000)

1 What is the total number of 'indictable' (more serious) offences that (a) females commit and (b) males commit?

2 As a proportion of their crimes, is there any differences in the types of crimes which women and men are likely to commit?

Class

Most delinquents and criminals arrested by the police are drawn from the less affluent groups in society. Crime and delinquency are directly related to social class, with working-class youth, for instance, having a crime rate eight times higher than upper middle-class youth.

The following explanations have been suggested:

- subculture
- poor socialisation
- anomie
- status frustration.

Subculture

Some sociologists have argued that a small proportion of young people develop strong anti-social attitudes which are different from the mainstream values of society and which can lead them into crime.

Poor socialisation

The majority crimes are committed by a very small proportion of the population. Some sociologists have suggested that these are people who have been poorly socialised into the values of society.

Anomie

Modern societies are based on the belief that if a person works hard, he or she will have a good chance of being successful in life. However, for many people in inner cities or large housing estates where there is little opportunity of decent employment, people can feel bitter and frustrated Some may possibly turn to crime. This happens particularly in periods of high unemployment. The term 'anomie' refers to a situation where large numbers of people fail to follow generally accepted values, instead adopting various deviant forms of behaviour, such as theft or drug-taking.

Status frustration

Working-class youths are more likely to fail at school and be in lower streams. They feel that everybody looks down upon them and so they express their frustration in delinquent behaviour, which helps them to 'get their own back' on society.

Criticism

One law for the rich and one for the poor: Marxist writers suggest the explanations given so far miss out the obvious and centrally important point that the wealthy and powerful pass the laws which benefit themselves at the expense of others, so it is bound to be the working class who commit most crime. For instance, the theft of money from a bank is quickly pursued by the police, but stock exchange swindles and tax avoidance are rarely punished or even investigated.

Chapeltown: an example of place and subculture

The lure of the frontline is made more attractive by the sight of older drug dealers pulling up in the Hayfield car park in their BMWs, decked out in gold bracelets and chains and with state-of-the-art mobile phones in their back pockets.

"There's no jobs around in Leeds and if you're from Chapeltown nobody will even give you a chance. They just think, 'Oh, the place is lull of black muggers and drug dealers'. What other options have we got?" asks Luke.

"The police can't really explain the high crime, a sociologist would probably be able to give a better answer. There's unemployment, lack of benefits, lack of opportunity."

... "I can't blame the guys on the frontline, because there are very few options available if you come from Chapeltown. There's a lot of talented people out there but they are not getting the chances. ...

The former affluence of the area can be seen in the handsome Victorian buildings, but the more affluent people moved out during the 1950s, abandoning Chapeltown once Yorkshire's mills and factories began closing down … deprivation set in and Chapeltown became just another blighted inner-city area left to rot.

"Hash, you want good hash? Want some weed?" visitors are asked by the groups of young men huddled around their cars or lurking in the Hayfield's elegant doorways. Others plant themselves on the wall, mobile phones in hand, busy arranging another deal or waiting for the drive-bys, people pulling up in cars and looking to score and cruise out of the area as quickly as possible.

By late afternoon Luke, aged 15, and a dozen friends have gathered, chatting in huddled groups, smoking joints and planning the evening's work. The bookmakers and post office provide fruitful pickings for the mob – one of several that patrol the frontline looking for fresh victims or re-acquainting themselves with old ones.

Like most of his friends Luke has not attended school for 18 months. He admits that favourite victims are elderly Asian women or white men in suits. Dressed in expensive Nike trainers, hooded top, baggy jeans and with intricate patterns carved on his cropped head, Luke says he works the frontline because "it's better than school and you get more money than working."

He shows me the tools of his trade – a chair leg or lump of wood, which can easily be ditched on to the street or in a garden if the police approach, and can be explained away as everyday inner-city rubbish.

… Luke will not say if he was part of the pack I saw on Saturday evening lurking by a bus stop on Chapeltown Road, kicking their heels and surveying passers-by that followed an elderly man who got off the bus carrying three bags of shopping, saw the hungry mob and instinctively started running. He didn't get far, soon he fell under a hail of punches and kicks, his shopping scattered, his jacket ripped, wallet and watch snatched from him: another sad chapter in Chapeltown's recent troubled history.

Source: Adapted from *The Guardian*, 1 November 1994

1 The description of a subculture 'in action' gives a vivid account of life on the streets and how this may eventually lead to permanent criminal lifestyle. From the extract, find as many points as you can to illustrate the diagram on page 339.

2 Do you have any sympathy for Luke?

3 If you were asked to propose a solution for the problems described here, what would you suggest?

Place

Crime rates are significantly higher in inner cities and in large, deprived housing developments than in the suburbs or the country areas.

Where crime takes place

**Proportion of households which were victims of crime:[1]
by type of crime and type of area,[2] England and Wales, 1997**

Percentages

	Inner city	Urban	Rural
Vehicle crime (owners)			
All thefts	23.7	16.2	12.0
Vandalism	9.2	7.2	4.9
Bicycle thefts (owners)	8.9	5.2	2.4
Burglary	8.5	5.9	3.4
Home vandalism	4.3	3.7	2.6
Other household	8.4	6.8	5.4
Any household offence	32.2	28.6	22.8

[1] Percentage victimised once or more.
[2] Area type classification based on CACI ACORN does, copyright CACI Ltd 1994.

Source: *Social Trends 30* (The Stationery Office, 2000)

1 What percentage of households in inner cities were the victims of thefts from cars?

2 What percentage of urban households experienced a burglary?

3 Where are people most likely to be the victims of crime?

4 Where are they least likely to be the victims?

5 Why do you think this is?

Crime rates are higher in inner-city areas and some 'problem' housing estates, because the people concentrated in these areas are often poorer and have more social problems than the bulk of the population. Consequently, the explanations which we have just looked at regarding the working class are especially true here.

An alternative explanation put forward by many sociologists is that policing in inner city areas and on large housing estates may be much tougher, and young people there may face higher chances of arrest.

Explaining crime and delinquency

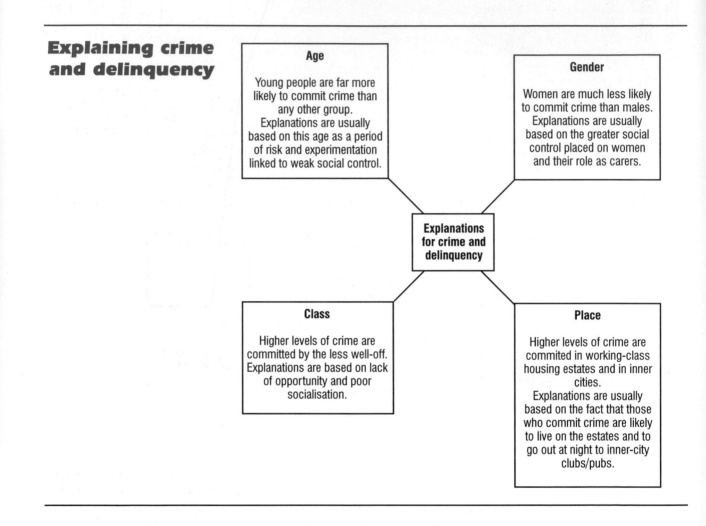

Age

Young people are far more likely to commit crime than any other group. Explanations are usually based on this age as a period of risk and experimentation linked to weak social control.

Gender

Women are much less likely to commit crime than males. Explanations are usually based on the greater social control placed on women and their role as carers.

Explanations for crime and delinquency

Class

Higher levels of crime are committed by the less well-off. Explanations are based on lack of opportunity and poor socialisation.

Place

Higher levels of crime are commited in working-class housing estates and in inner cities. Explanations are usually based on the fact that those who commit crime are likely to live on the estates and to go out at night to inner-city clubs/pubs.

From street crime to serious crime: crime as a process

All these explanations can be very confusing and can they all be right? One sociologist, David Farrington, has suggested that it is better to see crime as a 'process'. He means by this that young people may start criminal or anti-social activity for one reason, for example poor socialisation by the family, and may then continue (or drop out) for different reasons, for example the subculture they belong to. Finally, he points out that most young men stop committing crime in their early twentiess when they are working and in a settled relationship. Those few who remain may become serious, career criminals. So, we can have a number of different explanations for crime, which will be important at different stages in a person's life.

From street crime to serious crime

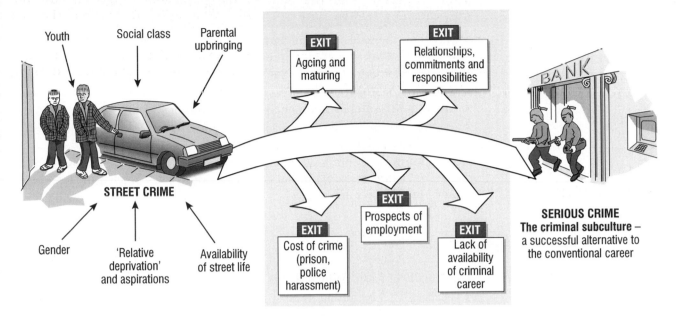

Taking each of the factors mentioned above, copy and complete the diagram below, explaining everything in your own words.

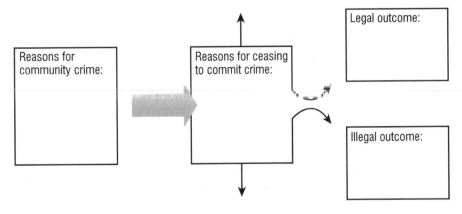

***

Main points ▶ The majority of crimes committed are property crimes. Serious crimes of violence and sexual attacks are relatively rare.

▶ Four key elements help us to understand crime and anti-social behaviour:
  – age – it is young people who commit most crime
  – gender – it is males who commit most crime
  – social class – less well-off young males are the most likely to commit crime, possibly because they feel that they have little chance of having the socially expected standard of living by legal means
  – place – large working-class housing estates and inner cities have higher rates of crime.

▶ A number of specific explanations have been put forward for crime. These include subculture, anomie, poor socialisation, status frustration.

▶ Crime can be viewed as a sort of career or process, with young people starting with minor criminal acts and then progressing onward either stepping out of crime or heading for a regular life of crime.

White-collar and corporate crime

When we talk about crime, most people think of things such as burglary or car theft. However, there are other types of more subtle crime which cost more to society than the value of all the burglaries and bank robberies put together. This hidden crime consists of three types of overlapping offences:

- white-collar crime, where the employee uses his or her position in a company to steal
- fraud, where money is obtained by deception of some kind
- corporate crime – the routine abuse of the law by companies in order to make greater profits.

No one knows for sure how much money is obtained through these sorts of crimes, but estimates suggest that it might amount to as much as *three thousand million pounds each year!*

White-collar crime

This usually consists of such things as:

- *Fiddling* This is routine in most organisations, and usually consists of such things as claiming false expenses, or claiming things are broken or lost when they have been sold privately
- *Pilfering or small-scale theft* Again this is most common. For most shopping chains, more is actually stolen by staff than by shoplifters. This is known as 'shrinkage' and can add up to 10 per cent to the cost of articles to the shopper. Studies on bakeries, shops and restaurants have all shown that employees routinely pilfer articles for themselves.

Fraud

This includes:

- *Computer crime* This is increasing as more financial transactions are conducted via computers, giving those controlling the computers the opportunity to alter codes and steal. More common than this, however, is the use of stolen or false credit cards.
- *Tax fraud* This consists of giving false information on earnings to the Inland Revenue for income tax or to the Customs and Excise for VAT. It is relatively common amongst self-employed people.

Corporate crime

Businesses may commit crime as well as individuals. Often they are not caught, but if they are, they are more likely to be described as 'infringing regulations'.

It is easiest to look at the different types of corporate crime by breaking it down according to the victims.

The customer is the victim

This may consist of very direct crime, for example, where costs are saved by not following safety laws in providing public transport, or ignoring food and hygiene regulations in the production or sale of food.

The employee is the victim

The employee may be harmed when a company tries to save money by not paying full wages, for example, by avoiding the minimum wage or by flouting health and safety regulations. Each year in Britain, over 500 people die from work-related accidents and it is estimated by the government that two-thirds of these are the result of failing to comply with the health and safety regulations.

Society as a whole as the victim

Here all of us suffer either directly or indirectly because of the actions of companies. The clearest example is the polluting of the environment by chemical companies.

Main points

▶ White-collar crime is often not viewed as such a great a problem as that posed by burglary and street crime, even though huge amounts of money are lost to the public because of it.

▶ White-collar crime is best thought of in three categories: white-collar crime, fraud and corporate crime.

▶ White-collar crime consists of pilfering and fiddling.

▶ Fraud consists of obtaining money by deception.

▶ Corporate crime is where companies cheat people, either taking their money or by placing them at risk.

Criminal statistics

Definition

The dark figure – the difference between the real number of crimes committed and the figure in official statistics

All the discussion on crime and delinquency so far has made the assumption that the official statistics of crime accurately reflect the amount and type of crime committed and the people responsible. This may not be true. Sociologists studying the accuracy of official crime statistics have come to a surprising conclusion – only a small proportion of crimes are reported to the police. For example, less than a quarter of acts of vandalism are reported. The difference between official statistics of crime and what actually occurs is known as **the dark figure**.

The social construction of official statistics

There are three stages in compiling official statistics:

- *the reporting of crime* – for the police to know a crime has been committed somebody has to tell them and not all crimes are reported
- *the recording of crime* – even if the police have been informed that a crime has been committed by a member of the public, they may decide not to record it
- *the activities of the police* – apart from the public making complaints, the only other way that crimes are reported or recorded is by the police force itself.

Reality and recording

The chart below shows the difference between police records of crimes and the actual number of crimes.

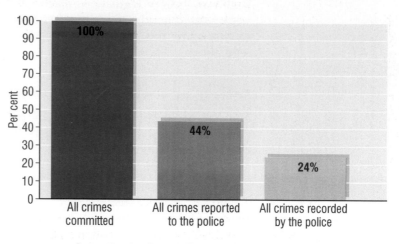

Source: Based on figures in *The British Crime Survey* (Government Statistical Service, 1998)

1 What percentage of all crimes were reported to the police?

2 What percentage of crimes were recorded by the police in their official statistics?

3 What percentage of all crimes never get to be recorded by the police?

4 After you have read the explanations in the main text, explain in your own words why you think that:

  a) 97 per cent of vehicle theft is reported to the police

  b) 45 per cent of wounding is reported to the policed

  c) 35 per cent of theft from the person is reported to the police.

5 After you have read the explanations in the main text, explain in your own words why you think that:

  a) 29 per cent of theft from the person which is reported to the police is actually recorded by them

  b) 63 per cent of wounding which is reported to the police is actually recorded by them.

6 How might a 'moral panic' influence the crime statistics?

Reporting of crime to the police

People often fail to report crimes because:
- they regard them as too trivial (a scratch along the side of a car)
- they do not believe the police can do anything (a wallet stolen in a busy market place)
- they regard it as a private matter (theft by a member of the family from another family member)
- they feel humiliated (rape).

But people do report crime when it is insured (car theft) and there is some evidence to suggest people make false claims in cases of burglary in order to claim larger amounts on the insurance.

Recording a crime

Police use their discretion in deciding whether an act is worth defining and recording as criminal. Sometimes they feel that they do not want to be involved, for instance, in a dispute between husband and wife. On other occasions, they regard the offence as too trivial, meriting only a warning to the person involved (riding a bicycle on the pavement).

As laws or society's attitudes change, so the police may change their approach too. This may mean that an increase or decrease in offences can in reality be a reflection of enforcement.

For example from the early 1990s onward many, if not most, police forces in Britain began ignoring the possession of cannabis in small amounts. The police had accepted that use was so widespread amongst young people that arresting them for possession was pointless and would not prevent continuing use of the drug.

Finally, when a person comes to a police station to complain that an offence has been committed, it is up to the police to decide which category the offence should be put into. For example, if a house is broken into and little of value was taken, the police may categorise it as 'breaking and entering' (less serious) or 'burglary' (more serious).

Fiddling the crime figures

Crime experts say at least 220,000 crimes including burglary, assault, theft and car crime vanished from official statistics last year as a result of police manipulation of the figures. ...

• Victims of violent attacks, previously classed as actual bodily harm, are having the crimes described by police as common assault, a civil offence which does not feature in official crime statistics.

• Attempted burglaries are logged as criminal damage to windows and doors and not put down as crimes.

• Thieves caught breaking into cars are being charged with tampering – which is not a recordable offence – rather than theft.

• A whole category of offences such as malicious telephone calls, assaults, deception and minor criminal damage are not classified as crimes because police say they are too trivial to record.

Home Office figures reveal that only 57% of the nearly 10 million reported crimes in England and Wales were recorded in official statistics. A spokesman said the government could not explain why the proportion of recorded crime was falling. Police chiefs and experts, however, said the practice is the inevitable result of recent Whitehall [government] pressure on police to improve crime statistics.

Source: *The Times*, 16 October 1994

1 What percentage of 'reported' crime is not being recorded by the police?

2 How many other 'crimes' are claimed to have 'vanished' from official statistics?

3 According to the article who does this?

4 Give three examples of how the official statistics are manipulated.

5 Why do you think this occurs?

6 What warning can we draw from this article about relying upon official statistics of crime?

Activities of the police

More police are used to patrol inner-city districts. This leads some to argue that they therefore discover more crime, simply by being there! Police officers work with certain assumptions about 'criminal types'. This leads them more often to stop working-class youths, for instance, and so this might account for the high proportion of these youths in the official statistics. Similarly, racist attitudes on the part of some police have led them to pick on black youths.

A further point is that the police are often influenced by the media and may become 'sensitised' to certain types of crime (or suspect). This leads to a blitz, or moral panic on these crimes or those suspected of committing them, and so the figures for this form of offence grow alarmingly.

The method of policing is important too. In recent years the police have engaged in 'pro-active' policing. This means that they choose one particular form of crime, for instance burglary, and then spend a period, perhaps as long as a year, gathering information on suspects. They then make mass arrests on one chosen day. The result is a sudden upsurge in people arrested for burglary.

How sociologists find out the real crime rate

The diagrams we looked at earlier, and the discussion we have just had on the reporting and recording of crime, all demonstrate that the real crime rate is much higher than the official statistics. So sociologists need ways to uncover the true extent of crime. Two main techniques have been used:

- **self-report tests**
- **victim surveys**.

Self-report tests

These are lists of criminal or deviant acts which are given to people and they are asked to tick off the activities which they have committed. It is always given anonymously so that people can feel free to admit to crimes. It is very helpful in that it avoids the embarrassment of an interview, so that people are more likely to admit to crimes, and it also allows researchers to measure the proportion of crimes committed by people who have never been arrested or charged by the police.

Victim surveys

These are usually large-scale surveys of the population in which people are interviewed and asked what crimes had been committed against them in the previous year. These are likely to be accurate for most crimes, because this form of survey cuts out the problems associated with official statistics, such as the failure of people to report crime to the police and the failure of the police to record crime.

Although victim surveys are generally very accurate, it is often claimed that they under-estimate certain categories of crimes where the victim is embarrassed to tell the interviewer, such as sexual offences, or where the victim is not interviewed, such as in cases of child abuse.

The most well-known example of a victim survey is the **British Crime Survey**, a national survey undertaken every five years. The diagram on page 342 is taken from the British Crime Survey.

How criminal are you?

This is an example of the sorts of questions asked in a self-report test.

- I have driven a car or motor bike/scooter under 16.
- I have been with a group who go round together making a row and sometimes getting into fights and causing disturbance.
- I have played truant from school.
- I have travelled on a train or bus without a ticket or deliberately paid the wrong fare.
- I have taken money from home without returning it.
- I have taken someone else's car or motor bike for a joy ride.
- I have broken or smashed things in public places like on the streets, cinemas, clubs, trains or buses.
- I have insulted people on the street or got them angry and fought with them.

- I have broken into a big store or garage or warehouse.
- I have broken into a little shop even though I may not have taken anything.
- I have taken something out of a car.
- I have taken a weapon (like a knife) out with me in case I needed it in a fight.
- I have started a fight with someone in a public place like in the street, or club.
- I have broken the window of an empty house.
- I have used a weapon in a fight (like a knife or a razor or a broken bottle).
- I have drunk alcoholic drinks in a pub under 16.
- I have taken things from big stores or supermarkets when

the shop was open.
- I have taken things from little shops when the shop was open.
- I have dropped things in the street like litter or bottles.
- I have bought something cheap or accepted as a present something I knew was stolen.
- I have got into a house and taken things (even though I didn't plan it in advance).
- I have taken a bicycle belonging to someone else and kept it.
- I have stolen school property worth more than about £5
- I have stolen goods from someone I worked for worth more than about £5.
- I have trespassed somewhere I was not supposed to go, like empty houses, railway lines or private gardens.

- I have had sex with someone for money.
- I have taken money from slot machines or telephones.
- I have taken money from someone's clothes hanging up somewhere.
- I have got money from someone by pretending to be someone else or lying about why I needed it.
- I have taken someone's clothes hanging up somewhere.
- I have smoked cannabis or ecstasy.
- I have used a heroin or cocaine
- I have got money/drink/ cigarettes by saying I would have sex with someone even though I didn't.

Main points

▶ There is considerable debate about how accurate the official statistics of crime are.

▶ A majority of crimes committed are not recorded by the police.

▶ There are three factors which affect the accuracy of the statistics:
  – reporting of crimes by the public – people may decide not to report a crime
  – recording by the police – even if people report what they consider to be a crime, the police may not take it seriously
  – the activities of the police – the way the police operate can strongly influence the crime rates.

▶ Sociologists attempt to find the true rate of crime by using either self-report tests or victim surveys.

Victims of crime

Most of us have been victims of crime at one time or another. We think that we were unlucky or perhaps plain stupid to put ourselves in a position to become a victim, but generally we believe that victims are chosen at random. This is not true, however. Some people are far more likely to be victims than others.

Who is more likely to be a victim?

Proportion of households victims of burglary, by household characteristics, 1997

	% victims once or more		% victims once or more
Age of head of household		**Tenure**	
16–24	15.2	Owner occupiers	4.2
25–44	6.5	Social renters	8.0
45–64	4.8	Private renters	9.7
65–74	3.5		
75+	4.1	**Accommodation type**	
		Detached house	4.1
Head of household under 60		Semi-detached house	5.0
Single adult & child(ren)	11.2	Mid terrace	6.5
Adults & child(ren)	5.3	End terrace	7.1
No children	6.4	Flats/maisonettes	7.2
Head of household over 60	4.0		
		Hours home unoccupied average weekday	
Head of household employment status		Never	5.2
In employment	5.4	Less than 3 hours	4.8
Unemployed	10.0	3 but less than 5 hours	5.9
Economically inactive	8.8	5 or more hours	6.2
Household income			
<£5k	8.3		
£5k to <£10k	5.8		
£10k to <£20k	5.3		
£20k to <£30k	4.6		
£30k +	5.0	**All households**	**5.6**

Source: Adapted from *British Crime Survey* (Government Statistical Service, 1998)

Using the information from the statistics provided above, copy and complete the table opposite, stating the characteristics of victims and adding any comments you might wish to make.

Victim characteristic	Information from statistics on page 346
Age	
Household type	
Employment	
Income	
Tenure	
Accommodation	
Hours unoccupied	

Taking all the information into account, what do you think it tells us about a person's social status and chance of being a crime victim?

People more likely to be victims of *property theft* are:

- the less well off
- those living in large local authority housing estates (and near to them)
- those in inner cities
- the young.

According to sociologists, the reasons are that these groups are the ones without the income to 'defend' their property with such things as burglar alarms and decent locks. Furthermore, they are more likely to be living near those who commit crimes, and we know that criminals are more likely to break into properties in areas which are more familiar to them.

Those more likely to be victims of *violence in the streets* are young men. The reason for this is that young men are more likely to be out at night and are perceived as 'fair' victims by the aggressors – who happen to be other young men!

Finally, there are two other groups of victims who are likely to be attacked in their own homes:

- women
- children.

Most violence against women and children is by other, male family members – usually the male partner/father.

Domestic violence

Incidence of domestic assault:[1] **by gender, England and Wales**

Percentages

	Males	Females	All
In lifetime			
No domestic assault	85	77	81
Chronic levels of assault	5	12	9
Intermittent levels of assault	10	11	10
All	100	100	100

[1]The survey was carried out in 1996. Respondents were aged 16 to 59.

Source: Adapted from *Social Trends 30* (The Stationery Office, 2000)

1 What percentage of females are subjected to 'chronic' (extreme and often) assault?

2 Is this higher or lower than for males?

3 Approximately, percentage of partners intermittently use violence in their relationship? Does this surprise you?

Main points ▶ Crime victims are not distributed randomly across the country. Certain groups of people are more likely to be victims than others.

▶ In terms of property crime, victims are likely to be younger, poorer people, living in privately rented properties on large estates or in the inner cities.

▶ In terms of violent crime, victims are likely to be young men, in inner cities at night.

▶ However, women and children are more likely to be victims in their homes as the result of domestic violence.

12 CHAPTER SUMMARY

1 Social control is the process by which people are made to conform to social rules

2 There are two types of social control – formal and informal.

3 Informal control takes place in most situations, but there are no written rules. Enforcement is by such things as making rude comments or by ignoring someone who breaks the 'unwritten rules'.

4 Formal control is usually written rules and is enforced by official sanctions. The most important example of formal social control is the criminal justice system.

5 Socialisation and social control are closely related. Socialisation is learning and social control is enforcing.

6 Some people have more power to enforce social control than others.

7 Deviance is when people do not conform to what society expects. Deviance is not a fixed thing, but varies across a number of dimensions.

8   Not all deviant acts are criminal. The key factors in making something deviant become criminal are a clash of values with accepted values of society, moral crusades and power.

9   Labelling is when a group of people are marked out as bad or deviant and then punished.

10 The majority of crimes committed are property crimes. Serious crimes of violence and sexual attacks are relatively rare.

11 Less well-off young males are the most likely to commit crime, possibly because they feel that they have little chance of having the socially expected standard of living by legal means.

12 A number of specific explanations have been put forward for crime. These include subculture, anomie, poor socialisation, status frustration.

13 White-collar crime is often not viewed as such a great problem as that posed by burglary and street crime, even though huge amounts of money are lost to the public because of it.

14 There is considerable debate about how accurate the official statistics of crime are, as the majority of crimes committed are not recorded by the police.

15 There are three factors which affect the accuracy of the statistics: reporting of crimes by the public, recording by the police, the activities of the police.

16 Sociologists attempt to find the true rate of crime by using either self-report tests or victim surveys.

17 Crime victims are not distributed randomly across the country. Certain groups of people are more likely to be victims than others.

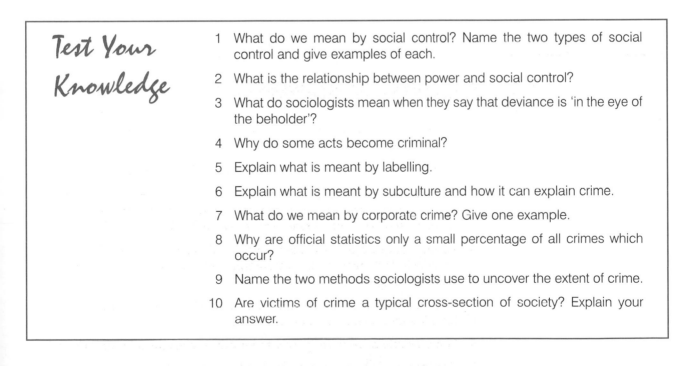

Test Your Knowledge

1   What do we mean by social control? Name the two types of social control and give examples of each.

2   What is the relationship between power and social control?

3   What do sociologists mean when they say that deviance is 'in the eye of the beholder'?

4   Why do some acts become criminal?

5   Explain what is meant by labelling.

6   Explain what is meant by subculture and how it can explain crime.

7   What do we mean by corporate crime? Give one example.

8   Why are official statistics only a small percentage of all crimes which occur?

9   Name the two methods sociologists use to uncover the extent of crime.

10 Are victims of crime a typical cross-section of society? Explain your answer.

Chapter

13

POLITICS AND POWER

Chapter contents
● Politics and power

Whenever I tell students that we are going to study politics, a groan goes up. The usual comment is that it is 'boring' and that 'I'm not interested in politics'. Politics affects your life in every way imaginable – you are seriously ill and the hospital says that you will have to wait for 18 months because there are no doctors available; you lose your job because of 'competition from abroad' and then you are told that you will have to live off your savings because there are no state benefits; or you are told that there is no money for teachers/computers/new school buildings. These are all the direct result of politics! Governments make choices how to spend money and how much to raise in taxes, and this affects how good the education system, the social security system and the education system is ... and every other aspect of your life. But politics is only one aspect of power, which is the general term we use when people have different wishes and one person's view wins out. This happens daily in a person's life, disputes with parents and children, between colleagues at work and students in class. In this first section we undertake a clear discussion of what power and politics are.

● Power and authority

Sociologists have suggested that power can be divided into two types. The first, coercion, is just getting your way in whatever way you can. The second, authority, is when you can persuade people that you have right to have your way. We look at how people can be persuaded to let others boss them around, and we see that people can gain authority over others in a number of ways.

● Political systems

Politics affects almost every aspect of people's lives, so most people want to have a say in political decisions. In Britain, we have a democracy which allows us to influence politicians' decisions. However, many other societies in the world have dictatorships or monarchies, where the views of the people are not taken into account. These are known as totalitarian societies. We look at some of the characteristics of both democracies and totalitarian societies.

● Political parties and ideologies

This brief section provides an overview of the different political beliefs known as 'ideologies', and their relationship to the main political parties in Britain.

● The British political system

Although most of the chapter is concerned with understanding the theories and concepts of politics, it is difficult to apply any of these without understanding the way that the British political system is organised and operates. This section works through the British democratic system to provide a clear and accurate overview.

● How democratic is British society?

Some critics argue that actually Britain has a ruling class that hides behind the image of a democracy. Governments may come and go, but the powerful group, usually those who went to the top public schools, continue to occupy the most important positions in the courts, the civil service, in politics, army and the financial institutions. So, is Britain really a democracy?

● Political socialisation

Political socialisation is how we learn our views on politics and politicians and come to accept the political system which exists. In British society, political socialisation occurs in exactly the same way as our general socialisation, and so our views develop through the family, the media and the school. In other societies, particularly totalitarian ones, people are taught that the state is more important than their family or friends and they are often indoctrinated in specific organisations to ensure that they do what they are told (which brings us back to authority, which we discussed earlier).

● Voting

One of the key elements of a democracy is the ability to vote. Surprisingly, between a third and a half of the electorate don't bother to vote in elections. We start off by finding out the reasons for this. We then move on to look at the different types of voters (those who change their mind and those who always stay loyal for example), and having classified them, we then explore the influences on their voting choices. The reasons people vote for a particular party seems to be a complicated mixture of self-interest, social class/ethnic background and an image of the political party and its leader. Interestingly, specific policies do not seem to be too important.

● Democracy in action: pressure groups and social movements

Politicians are elected more or less every five years, and they are elected on very general policies. But although voters may agree that the general approach of a particular party is one which seems good, they may disagree on many specific policies. Pressure or interest groups develop to fill this gap. They are organisations which are concerned with one very specific issue and they try to pressure whichever government is in power to adopt their viewpoint on this issue. We look at how the pressure groups go about their business and suggest that the answer to whether or not Britain is a democracy lies very much in the effectiveness of pressure groups to reflect a wide variety of interests. In recent years, many people have become rather disillusioned with the rather limited choice of political parties and have wished to alter a broad set of values or attitudes which are common to both major parties, for example the fact that discrimination was accepted against women and gays/lesbians. Broad coalitions of people joined together to demand a different sort of lifestyle and these are known as social movements. They have been particularly effective in the area of gay rights, women's rights and ecology.

● How political parties stay in touch with the views of the electorate

This final section explores the methods political parties use in order to find out what the majority of the population think about them. There are two main approaches used by all political parties – focus groups and opinion polls. We explore how these techniques work and how they influence both policy-making and how people vote.

Politics and power

When we think about power, we generally think of party politics. But the two things, although related, are quite different. Party politics concerns 'groups of people' (or parties) seeking election in a democracy where people vote one of the parties into government.

However, power is much broader than this and is something that is used and experienced every day by all of us. If we obey someone else, we do so because they have power over us. So parents, teachers, police officers, bullies at school and referees in hockey games all make us obey them, although why we do so is very different in each case.

Sociologists are interested in power in all its senses, not just as something related to politics and government.

The whole idea of social relationships involves the notion of power. Whenever two or more people are engaged in some activity, potential conflicts will arise and will have to be resolved.

Questions of obedience and disobedience arise in families, in the classroom, between couples and at work, as well as in dealings with the law.

Source: Adapted from 'Power and authority', *New Society*, 21 February 1985

Power and authority

At the beginning of the twentieth century, Max Weber suggested that to understand how some people get others to obey we ought to distinguish different types of power, because the reason why people obey others varies. Weber suggested that, first of all, it is important to distinguish between **coercion** and **authority**.

- Coercion is when we obey people because they can threaten us (with punishment or penalities of some kind) if we ignore their wishes, for example: the power of prison officers over the inmates (from the prisoners viewpoint, that is), and the power of kidnappers over their victims.
- Authority is when we willingly obey people because we believe it is right for them to boss us around, for example the authority of parents over their children, and the authority of managers over their employees.

Types of authority

Weber distinguished between three types of authority, arguing that we willingly obey someone for one of three reasons:

- *Charismatic authority* This is when a person is so impressive and forceful that they can make people act in certain ways, almost by force of personality. Examples of this sort of leadership include Adolf Hitler and Ghandi.
- *Traditional authority* A second explanation as to why people obey others is when the person or group giving orders has always been obeyed. In traditional societies, this would be the king, or tribal chief or perhaps the priestly caste of the Brahmins in India.
- *Legal-rational authority* This is the type of authority which modern day people recognise. Here the person is being obeyed because the position they hold in society or in a company/organisation is the position which we agree should be obeyed. However, the leader is not obeyed for any personal qualities but simply because they are the holder of the 'office'. There are also strict limits as to the power of the leader – they can only demand obedience to tasks which are accepted as in the power of that office. If this sounds difficult, it is much easier to give an example. Most students accept the right of the teacher in the classroom to tell them what to do regarding behaviour in class and how to study. But that is the limit to the authority of the teacher. Beyond the school, the teacher has no authority. So most people in most jobs have their authority based on this legal-rational idea.

Look at each person in the photos above. In your opinion, what form of authority does each have – charismatic, traditional or legal-rational? Explain the reasons for your answer.

The nature of power

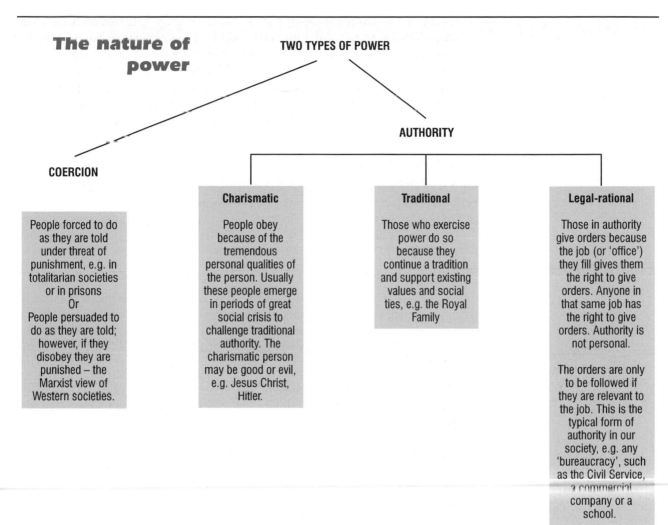

TWO TYPES OF POWER

COERCION

People forced to do as they are told under threat of punishment, e.g. in totalitarian societies or in prisons
Or
People persuaded to do as they are told; however, if they disobey they are punished – the Marxist view of Western societies.

AUTHORITY

Charismatic

People obey because of the tremendous personal qualities of the person. Usually these people emerge in periods of great social crisis to challenge traditional authority. The charismatic person may be good or evil, e.g. Jesus Christ, Hitler.

Traditional

Those who exercise power do so because they continue a tradition and support existing values and social ties, e.g. the Royal Family

Legal-rational

Those in authority give orders because the job (or 'office') they fill gives them the right to give orders. Anyone in that same job has the right to give orders. Authority is not personal.

The orders are only to be followed if they are relevant to the job. This is the typical form of authority in our society, e.g. any 'bureaucracy', such as the Civil Service, a commercial company or a school.

1 Give two examples of power in everyday life.

2 What does coercion mean?

3 Give an example of country/area where coercive power is used

4 What is the major difference between coercion and authority?

5 What are the three types of authority?

6 What is the difference between the reason for obeying a figure like Hitler and obeying your college tutor?

7 Why do people listen to what Prince Philip or Prince Charles have to say?

8 Why do Marxists disagree with the argument that the form of power in democracies is 'authority'?

Main points ▶ Power is a much wider concept than politics and refers to how people get their way in a wide variety of social and personal situations.

▶ In this widest sense, power can be divided into two types: coercion and authority.

▶ Coercion refers to a situation where the people who are told what to do only obey because they are forced to do so.

▶ Authority refers to all situations where the person who is told what to do believes that the person giving orders has a right to do so.

▶ There are three different types of authority – charismatic, traditional and legal-rational.

Political systems

Definitions

Democracy – where the ordinary people elect their leaders and have the right to express their views without fear

Totalitarian society – where the political leadership does not allow elections or free speech

Societies vary in the amount of power ordinary people have to influence the decisions of the government. In some societies the people have very little say indeed and these are generally described as **totalitarian**. On the other hand, societies which try to give ordinary people a strong influence in what decisions are made are known as **democracies**.

The nature of the power in totalitarian societies is usually coercion, as people have not freely chosen the government. In democracies the nature of power is generally accepted to be based upon authority.

Totalitarian societies

Totalitarian societies are those controlled by a very few people who usually arrange the society for their benefit. The rulers refuse to allow the population any say in the important decisions that affect them and they may well ensure their view holds by controlling the police, courts and the mass media. Criticism is forbidden.

Types of totalitarian society include:

- *monarchy*, where a king or queen has absolute power, as in Britain in the Middle Ages
- *dictatorship*, where one person (the dictator) holds absolute power, for example in Germany in the 1930s and early 1940s under Hitler
- *oligarchy*, where a few people rule, as in the case of the People's Republic of China.

A dictatorship

Burkina Faso, Africa

... In 1992 Compaoré stood unopposed as President; in 1997 he had his rubber-stamp national assembly change the constitution (which allowed a president only two terms) so he could be elected 'President-for-life'.

'What will the President do to impose himself on intellectuals who are wise to the extent of his dictatorship and its tragic implications for our people? ... There is only one thing he can do: put them in prison, kill them, make them disappear.' So wrote Norbert Zongo, editor of the newspaper *L'Indépendant*, who fearlessly exposed corruption in the Government and nepotism in Compaoré's family. A month after the 1998 elections Zongo was himself murdered ...

Freedom
Key opposition figures have died or disappeared and the judiciary is compromised. Amnesty International has criticized the climate of impunity.

Politics: NI ASSESSMENT
Blaise Compaoré has dominated the political landscape for more than a decade. After the revolutionary interlude of the 1980s he has ensured the return of politics and business as usual and has enriched his family and coterie. The movement for democracy has become stronger over the last year; everyone, not least the poor, badly needs this to gather even greater momentum.

Source: *New Internationalist*, May 2000

What elements of a totalitarian society can you find in this extract?

Democratic societies

A true democracy would be a society in which every decision made by the government was voted on by the members of society, but this is not practical as it would be too complicated. Instead, most democratic societies have a system called 'representative democracy', in which certain people (MPs in Britain) are elected to represent the interests of communities (known as 'constituencies' in Britain). This is the model used in Britain, the USA and in Europe, for example. We elect Members of Parliament to represent constituencies of about 60,000 people.

But a democracy is more than just voting once every five years for an MP. It also involves freedom to express opinions critical of the government, to have an uncensored media, free from government control, and an independent legal system. If all these things exist, it is likely that the laws passed by the government and the decisions made by it will reflect the will of the people.

A checklist of the elements of a democracy

	Yes	No
Is there more than one political party competing to gain power?		
Are there regular elections?		
Do the majority of people have the right to vote?		
Is it possible to express criticism of the government openly?		
Is there a range of opinions expressed in the newspapers, on radio and television?		
Are the mass media free of government control?		
Is there any way in which ordinary people can communicate with the decision-makers (such as MPs) between elections?		
Are the police and the courts free of direct government control?		

For a society to qualify as democratic all the answers ought to be 'Yes'.

1 According to the checklist above, is Britain a democracy?

2 Give two other examples of democracies.

3 Find two nations where the majority of the answers to the checklist are 'No'. (The **New Internationalist** magazine has a useful section on political rights. Your school/college library should have copies.)

Political parties and ideologies

Political parties are organised groups who share a common **ideology**, or set of views about how to solve societies' problems. Political parties try to win political power, usually aiming to form the government of a country.

The main political ideologies are communism, socialism, conservatism, social democracy and fascism.

Definition

Political ideology – an explanation of how society works and a plan of action for solving any problems based upon this explanation

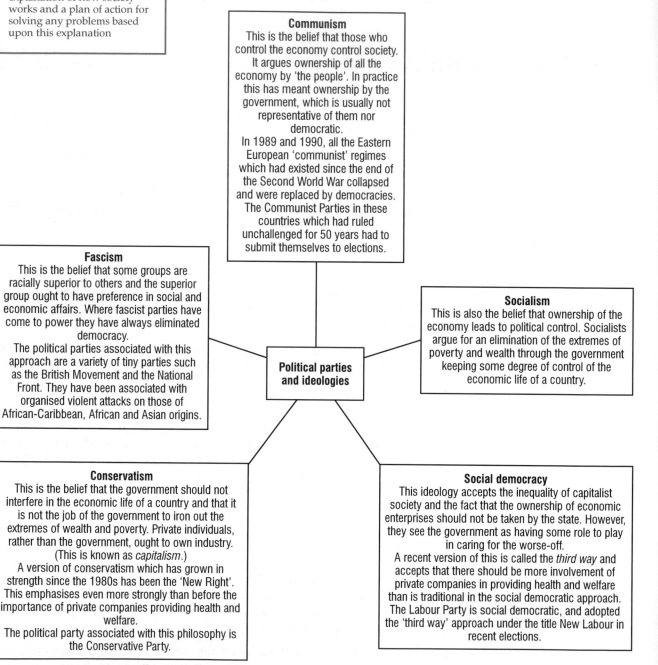

Communism
This is the belief that those who control the economy control society. It argues ownership of all the economy by 'the people'. In practice this has meant ownership by the government, which is usually not representative of them nor democratic.
In 1989 and 1990, all the Eastern European 'communist' regimes which had existed since the end of the Second World War collapsed and were replaced by democracies. The Communist Parties in these countries which had ruled unchallenged for 50 years had to submit themselves to elections.

Fascism
This is the belief that some groups are racially superior to others and the superior group ought to have preference in social and economic affairs. Where fascist parties have come to power they have always eliminated democracy.
The political parties associated with this approach are a variety of tiny parties such as the British Movement and the National Front. They have been associated with organised violent attacks on those of African-Caribbean, African and Asian origins.

Political parties and ideologies

Socialism
This is also the belief that ownership of the economy leads to political control. Socialists argue for an elimination of the extremes of poverty and wealth through the government keeping some degree of control of the economic life of a country.

Conservatism
This is the belief that the government should not interfere in the economic life of a country and that it is not the job of the government to iron out the extremes of wealth and poverty. Private individuals, rather than the government, ought to own industry. (This is known as *capitalism*.)
A version of conservatism which has grown in strength since the 1980s has been the 'New Right'. This emphasises even more strongly than before the importance of private companies providing health and welfare.
The political party associated with this philosophy is the Conservative Party.

Social democracy
This ideology accepts the inequality of capitalist society and the fact that the ownership of economic enterprises should not be taken by the state. However, they see the government as having some role to play in caring for the worse-off.
A recent version of this is called the *third way* and accepts that there should be more involvement of private companies in providing health and welfare than is traditional in the social democratic approach. The Labour Party is social democratic, and adopted the 'third way' approach under the title New Labour in recent elections.

Main points ▶ There are two main types of political system – democracies and totalitarian societies.

▶ Totalitarian societies are those where only a few people rule and they forbid elections and do not allow people to express their opinions.

▶ Democratic societies are those where the people choose who rules and can express their views about politics without fear of being arrested.

▶ There are a number of political ideologies which exist. These include communism, socialism, social democracy, conservatism and fascism.

The British political system

The British political system is a democratic monarchy, which means that there are elected parliaments in London and Edinburgh with an unelected Queen as Head of State. There are also elected assemblies in Wales and Northern Ireland.

There are three key components of the British version of democracy:
- the decision-making bodies or parliaments
- a bureaucracy that carries out the decisions – the civil service
- an organisation that enforces the law – the police and judiciary (the courts).

Parliament

The House of Commons is the more powerful parliament as it has representatives from the whole of the UK. These Members of Parliament (MPs) are divided along party lines. Normally the party that has the most MPs elected at a general election forms the government.

Scotland also has a parliament with Scottish Members (SMPs). This has power over most things except for defence and foreign affairs. Northern Ireland and Wales also have assemblies which have a range of powers.

There is also the House of Lords which is not elected.

Many critics have pointed out the unrepresentative nature of MPs. They are still mainly male, white and middle class, with very few members from ethnic minority groups. These critics argue that this makes it makes it more difficult for them truly to reflect the will of the people.

The civil service

The civil service is the bureaucracy that runs the state on behalf of the government In total there are over 600,000 civil servants. The civil service is expected to be non-political and entirely neutral in how it approaches its job. When a government changes and new policies are introduced, the civil service is expected to implement the changed policy, even though many civil servants may privately disagree with these policies.

Some sociologists have commented on the power of senior civil servants over ministers. They have argued that ministers, who are the politicians appointed by the Prime Minister to run civil service departments, are themselves controlled by the civil servants.

Whereas ministers rarely stay in one ministry (government department) for more than two years, civil servants spend their whole careers there. They are, therefore, able to manipulate the ministers into taking the decisions that they want them to. The result is that the country is run more by the civil service than by elected politicians. These top civil servants are even less representative of the population as a whole than the politicians, with about one third of all top civil servants coming from public school backgrounds – usually a sign of an upper or upper middle-class family.

The judiciary

The judiciary, composed of judges and magistrates (who judge lesser offences), have the role of interpreting and fairly applying the law passed by parliament. They are completely independent of the government and can criticise it or judge that it is acting illegally if that is their opinion. Judges too are drawn from a very restricted social class background, just like senior civil servants, and have generally attended public schools. Some critics argue that although they may not be deliberately biased, they do share a particular set of values and backgrounds which make them conservative.

The British political system: a summary

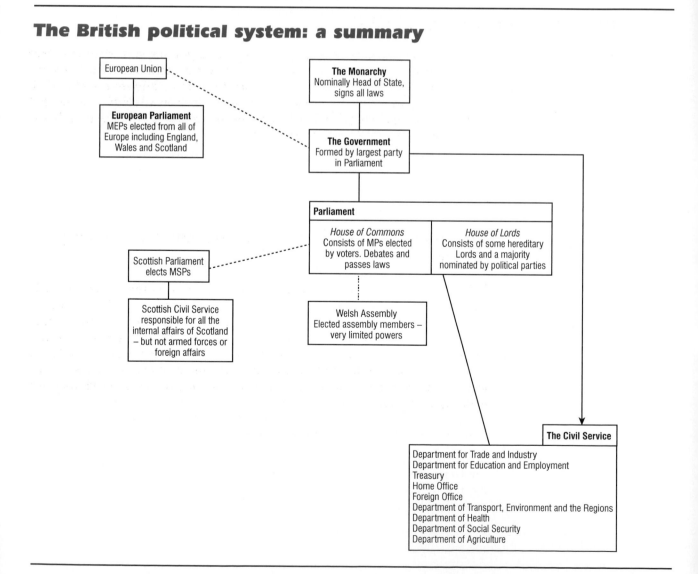

How democratic is British society?

We have seen that Britain is a democratic society and that governments are voted in by the people approximately every five years. But is it right to say that by voting every five years the population actually have much control over the government?

Sociologists agree that voting every five years is not that effective in ensuring the wishes of the people are met. But although they agree on this, they go on to disagree.

- One group of sociologists go on to argue that Britain still is a democracy because there are other ways in which people influence the government. This approach is known as **pluralism**.

- Another group say that power is maintained in the hands of a relatively small number of people – a **ruling class** or **elite**, who actually control our society.

Pluralism: Britain is democratic

This approach suggests that power is spread right across society and that everybody, in some way, is able to influence government decisions. They can join a political party or pressure group, vote in elections and see their local MP if they have any views or problems. The term 'pluralism' simply means that there is more than one (plural) centre of power. According to this approach, the government reflects the will of the people.

The ruling class approach: Britain is controlled by a relatively small number of people

This approach argues that power lies in the hands of very few people, the rich, and that the vast majority of the population really have no effective way of influencing the decisions of the government. Supporters of this view point to the great differences in resources and contacts between the pressure groups representing the interests of industry and those representing the ordinary person. They also point out how control of the media by very few people can lead to their views (generally in support of the rich) being imposed upon the majority of people.

MPs' backgrounds

The new parliamentary Labour Party, by occupation and education, 1997

Occupation

This new intake, more than any before, seals Labour's decisive shift from a blue-collar to a white-collar party

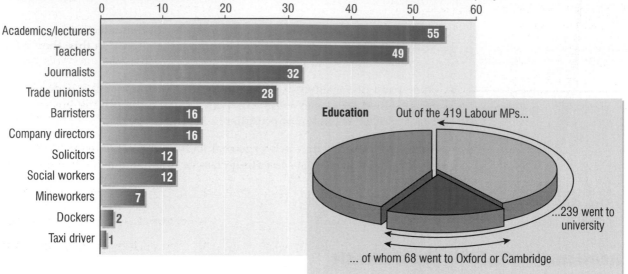

Occupation	Value
Academics/lecturers	55
Teachers	49
Journalists	32
Trade unionists	28
Barristers	16
Company directors	16
Solicitors	12
Social workers	12
Mineworkers	7
Dockers	2
Taxi driver	1

Education Out of the 419 Labour MPs...
...239 went to university
... of whom 68 went to Oxford or Cambridge

Source: J. Williams, 'Research roundup', *Sociology Review*, Vol. 7, No. 1, September 1997, originally from *The Observer*, 4 May 1997

The Labour Party has traditionally represented the working class, but Labour MPs are rarely from the working class.

1 How many MPs came from working-class backgrounds?

2 How many went to Oxford or Cambridge universities?

3 How many went to university?

4 What was the most common profession of Labour MPs?

Women MPs

After the 1997 General Election, there were 651 MPs in Parliament. Of these, 18 per cent were women.

Women MPs, 1997

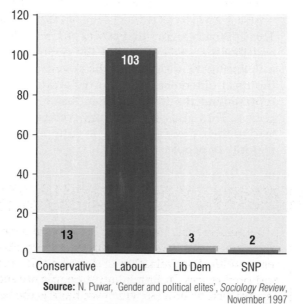

Party	Value
Conservative	13
Labour	103
Lib Dem	3
SNP	2

Source: N. Puwar, 'Gender and political elites', *Sociology Review*, November 1997

1 What was the total number of female MPs in 1997?

2 Approximately half the population of Britain is female. Are women therefore fairly represented?

3 In your opinion, does this matter?

4 If you feel it is unfair, how would you change the situation?

The distribution of power in society

The case for the ruling class view:

On the face of it, we are a grossly unequal society, with the top 10 per cent, for instance, owning 60 per cent of all personal wealth. ... Our top institutions are dominated by people from privileged social backgrounds, educated in the main at public schools and the universities of Oxford and Cambridge.

The mass media are controlled by fewer and fewer hands. One man, Murdoch, owns four Fleet Street newspapers, for instance.

In their studies of television news, the Glasgow University Media Group have argued that by careful selection it presents a pro-establishment point of view while appearing to be neutral and objective.

The case for the pluralists:
But pluralist writers are not convinced by these arguments. This evidence might prove the existence of a British establishment, but it fails they say to prove 'that it rules'.

A study by Christopher Hewitt of 24 major policy issues faced by

successive British governments over a 20-year period found that no one significant group managed to get its way on most issues. Indeed on only one issue did Parliament go against public opinion and that was when it stopped capital punishment for murder.

In a detailed study of the influence of the Confederation of British Industry, the organisation which speaks for most of the large British companies, Grant and Marsh, found that 'the CBI's ability to influence events is limited by the government's

need to retain the support of the electorate and by the activities of other pressure groups.'

The debate continues:
But the reply of many of those who believe in the idea of a ruling class has been to develop the idea of 'non decision making', which is the ability of the powerful to ignore or suppress all but the safest of issues, and to ensure that threats to their own most important interests (such as redistribution of private property) are never seriously debated in parliament.

Source: Adapted from *New Society*, 21 February 1985

1 What do sociologists mean by the term the 'ruling class' and what evidence is there to support its existence?

2 What evidence do pluralists put forward to refute this?

3 What does the non-decision-making approach argue?

Activities

1 Find out who the MPs for your area are. What party do they belong to? What is their majority of votes over their opponents? Check the local papers to see what their views are on major topical issues. Are there any clear influences of pressure groups on them?

2 Delegate a small group to arrange a visit with your local MP. Devise a questionnaire for him or her concerning such things as the rights of women, education, the public service, the power of the civil service, whether an establishment exists.

3 Is there a local issue of great importance currently being debated in your town? If so follow the history of it, find out which groups are influential and what the outcome of the issue is.

Political socialisation

Definition

Political socialisation – the process of learning political values and preferences

Just as individuals learn about the general beliefs and values of society and the correct forms of behaviour, they also learn about political values. We use the term **political socialisation** to describe this process of learning political values and preferences. In Britain, most people are socialised into an acceptance that the democratic process which we have is the best political system. Within this, however, they are socialised differently in their preferences for political parties.

In just the same way that they learn ordinary social values, people learn their political preferences through:

- the media
- the family
- the school
- the peer group/social class.

The media

Newspapers in Britain generally support conservative values. They are usually part of large companies, the sorts of institutions that would lose out under a radical socialist government, for example. They are also careful to reflect the views of the readership which they are trying to sell their newspapers to.

Radio and television stations, which are controlled by British law, are not allowed to support any particular political party. In general, they support the 'establishment' view of the world, which is basically to keep things as they are.

There is little evidence to show that people's voting choices are determined by the media. However, it is clear that general opinions about political events are influenced by the way in which they are portrayed by the media. Support of the British capitalist, democratic system is constantly expressed in the way world events are described. So people learn to interpret the world around them through the framework provided by the media.

The family

The most important agency of socialisation is the family. It is where we first learn the expectations society has of us and these lessons stay with us throughout our lives. Political views, if not taught openly, are often contained within the general socialising process that children are subjected to. Although there is a considerable change in voting attitudes between generations, a significant proportion of people vote the same way as their parents.

The school

At first it may seem surprising that school has any political influence on us. Yet here we learn a particular version of history, one in which Britain plays the part of the 'goodie', a belief in the value of British society as it is, the habit of obeying rules, the need to compete against each other, and the acceptance that the more successful ought to take higher rewards. These may not appear to be political at first sight, but they are all values on which our political system is based.

Some writers influenced by Marxists argue that western democracies are really based on coercion, but the ruling class have managed to trick the population into accepting that the political and economic system is really to the benefit of everybody. Consequently, they rarely have to resort to open threats and violence. The task of persuading people to believe in the system is usually dealt with by the education system and the media.

The peer group/social class

The people we mix with in our daily lives reinforce or weaken our own opinions. Usually the people with whom we mix (peer group) are drawn from the same social class and as the experiences of social classes are so different, people in each class develop very different views on political events.

Main points ▶ Britain is a democracy which is headed by a monarch.

▶ There are three elements to the British state – parliament, the civil service and the judiciary.

▶ There is a parliament elected for the UK as a whole and a separate one for Scotland. There are assemblies in Wales and Northern Ireland.

▶ The civil service exists to carry out the wishes of the elected members of parliament.

▶ The judiciary consists of the magistrates and judges and these are independent of parliament.

▶ Some critics argue that Britain is not as democratic as it seems. They argue that politicians, top civil servants and the judiciary are mainly drawn from the higher social classes in society and have generally been educated in public schools.

▶ This has led to a debate between:
  – those who argue that the best way to describe power is that it is dispersed across the society – the pluralist view
  – those who argue that there is a ruling class who control society.

▶ People are socialised into understanding politics and having views on the subject by a range of agencies including the media, the family, the school and their peer group/social class.

Voting

It's Neck and Neck

Polls open TODAY until 9.00PM
You DON'T need your Polling Card to vote
If YOU need a lift - ring 01954 780964

Liberal Democrats

1 elect **Derek Ford** **X**

Printed by Glisson Printers 4, Glisson Road, Cambridge and published by R Martlew Leylands, Caldecote, Cambridge

In a representative democracy, such as Britain, the government is chosen by the electorate and people vote for the party which they prefer.

In most of Britain, the first-past-the-post system of voting is used. Each voter is allowed to choose one person to represent them. The person who amasses the most votes is the winner. People can vote or not vote as they wish.

Non-voters

In recent years, the number of people choosing not to vote has increased very considerably. At general elections approximately 30 per cent of the electorate do not vote, and in local and European elections the figure rises as high as 60 per cent. Non-voting is highest in the most socially disadvantaged constituencies, and perhaps reflects a belief by the people who live there that politicians are simply not interested in doing anything for them.

Why don't people vote?

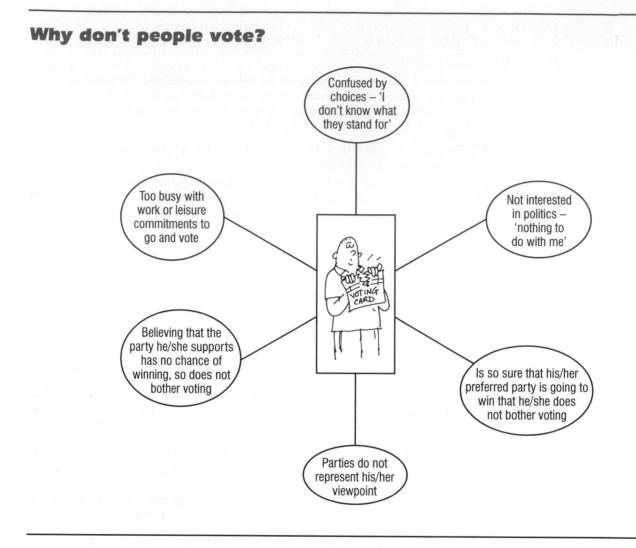

Confused by choices – 'I don't know what they stand for'

Too busy with work or leisure commitments to go and vote

Not interested in politics – 'nothing to do with me'

Believing that the party he/she supports has no chance of winning, so does not bother voting

Is so sure that his/her preferred party is going to win that he/she does not bother voting

Parties do not represent his/her viewpoint

Types of voters

Sociologists have suggested that there are four types of voter and each type is influenced by different things in deciding which way to vote.

- *Floating voters* change their vote in different elections.
- *Abstainers* do not vote.
- *Loyal voters* tend to vote for the same party at each election.
- *Tactical voters* are people who may support one party, but decide that as this party is unlikely to be successful in their particular constituency will vote for a third party in order to stop their most disliked party candidate from getting elected. For example, Voter X hates Labour, so she votes Liberal Democrat because she knows that the Conservative candidate will not be elected and she prefers the Liberal Democrats to the Labour Party! In the 1997 election about 25 to 35 seats were lost to the Conservatives by tactical voting.

Influences on voting

1997 vote (change on 1992 in brackets)

	Conservative		Labour		LibDem	
All Great Britain voters	31	(-12)	44	(+9)	17	(-1)
Men	31	(-8)	44	(+6)	17	(-1)
Women	32	(-11)	44	(+10)	17	(-1)
AB voters	42	(-11)	31	(+9)	21	(0)
C1	26	(-22)	47	(+19)	19	(-1)
C2	25	(-15)	54	(+15)	14	(-4)
DE	21	(-8)	61	(+9)	13	(0)
1st time voters	19	(-16)	57	(+17)	18	(-3)
All 18–29	22	(-18)	57	(+19)	17	(0)
30–44	26	(-11)	49	(+12)	17	(-3)
45–64	33	(-9)	43	(+9)	18	(-2)
65+	44	(-3)	34	(-2)	16	(+2)
Home owners	35	(-12)	41	(+11)	17	(-3)
Council tenants	13	(-6)	65	(+1)	15	(+5)
Trades union members	18	(-9)	57	(+7)	20	(+2)

Source: J. Williams, 'Research roundup', *Sociology Review*, Vol. 7, No. 1, September 1997

1 Was there any significant differences in the voting patterns of men and women?

2 Which social class of voters were more likely to vote (a) Labour and (b) Conservative?

3 Overall, is there a relationship between social class and voting?

4 What does class de-alignment mean? (Read the main text.) Is there any evidence for it here?

5 What voting preference do trades union members have? Why do you think this is?

6 Which age group is most likely to vote Conservative?

Voting behaviour

Voting and class loyalty

Until the 1970s, many working-class people voted for the Labour Party, while most middle- and upper-class people voted Conservative. Only the Liberal Democrat Party drew its limited support from across the main social classes. This reflected the clear-cut class structure which existed then.

Class de-alignment

From the mid-1970s, a great change took place in the voting patterns. What has happened since then is that the class loyalty broke down. From 1979 people began to switch across parties in their voting in greater numbers. Nevertheless, it is still true to say that the middle class are more likely to vote Conservative and the working class are more likely to vote Labour. Those who straddle the border between the two groups – the routine white-collar workers, seem most likely to shift allegiance.

> **Definition**
>
> **Class de-alignment** – the decline of social class as the main influence on voting behaviour

The term **class de-alignment** has been used to describe this situation where social class is only one influence on voting behaviour, rather than *the* influence. It seems that in the future voting will become less and less influenced by these traditional social class patterns as social class itself is fragmenting and the distinctions are increasingly blurred.

Partisan de-alignment

Partisan de-alignment is the term used by sociologists to explain the way that people are gradually shifting votes away from the two traditionally dominant political parties – Labour and Conservative. In the last 20 years, their share of the vote has declined and the votes of other parties such as the Scottish and Welsh Nationalists and the Liberal Democratic parties have increased.

Self-interest

A second explanation is that people vote for the party which they perceive as being better for them. Few people know what the policies of the political parties actually are, so what they have instead is a perception concerning what the political parties stand for. The voters then work out rationally which party they think will look after their interests.

Party image

Few people know what the policies of political parties are. Instead they have an 'image' of what a party stands for. If this matches their views they are likely to vote for it. It is therefore very important for political parties to ensure that the image they have is one which is attractive to voters. The Labour Party is generally regarded as being for supporting and improving welfare and education, whilst Conservatives are generally seen as 'tougher' on issues of law and order.

The media

But where do the images of the political parties come from? The answer is that people broadly speaking gain their impressions from a mixture of their own experiences and from the information provided by the media.

There is no evidence that the media has a direct and immediate impact on most voters during election campaigns, but there is considerable evidence that the public is influenced by the general tone of the media over a long period of time.

The political parties have become so aware of the importance of the media as the lens through which the population see the political parties, that they invested considerable effort in 'spinning' the news to their benefit and weaving images of themselves to appeal to the electorate.

The Labour Party during the late 1990s transformed itself into 'New Labour' in a successful bid to break away from its image of representing the image of the working class. The new image has made it far more classless in outlook, and resulted in electoral success.

Definition

Partisan de-alignment – the decline of support for just the two major parties and the readiness of electors to turn to other parties

Leader's image

As politics has changed from one based on the differences between social classes, so the rigid divisions between political parties have weakened. For voters, seeking a clear-cut difference between the parties which will give them a reason to choose one of the competing parties, this can lead to some degree of confusion. What seems to have happened, as in the United States, is that voters are influenced by the image of the leader of the particular party. If a leader is seen as trustworthy and sympathetic, then they are likely to attract votes.

Media bias

When dealing with media bias, it is essential to distinguish between print and electronic media. The electronic media are required to be balanced and impartial, while newspapers can be as partial and party political as they like. We will deal first with the easier case of the print media. There are four main reasons why British newspapers usually have a particular ideological leaning.

1. The press is mostly controlled by multimillionaires and multinational companies which often (but not always) have the same economic and political interests.

2. Generations of British press barons have pursued not money, but power. They have frequently controlled the editorial policy of their newspapers, even written the editorials themselves.

3. At the same time, newspapers and commercial TV rely heavily on advertising income, and are unwilling to bite the hand of the business interests that feed them.

4. Since the late 1950s, the British press has tried to carve out a media market which is distinct from television's. TV is required to be balanced and impartial, so the tabloid press has increased its party political bias, and the quality press has increasingly presented in-depth commentary and analysis of the news.

The result is that the British press as a whole is party political compared with that in most other Western countries. If there were strong party competition between papers this might not matter. But the press weighs heavily on the side of Conservative economic interests and Conservative politics.

Source: I. Budge, I. Crewe, D. McKay and K. Newton, *The New British Politics* (Addison Wesley Longman, 1998)

1 Describe in your own words the four reasons for the bias of the newspapers.

2 Which party are they more likely to sympathise with?

Geographical location

In England, people in the north are more likely to support Labour and in the south to support the Conservatives. In Scotland and Wales the most popular parties are Labour, Scottish and Welsh nationalists and Liberal Democrats.

Voting is also related to city, suburbs and countryside, with Labour being most popular in the cities and Conservatives most popular in the countryside.

It may well be that it is not so much where people live which influences them, but more that different areas vary in their social class composition. For example, the inner cities of the north are more likely to have less well-off, working-class voters living there.

Variations in voting across the country

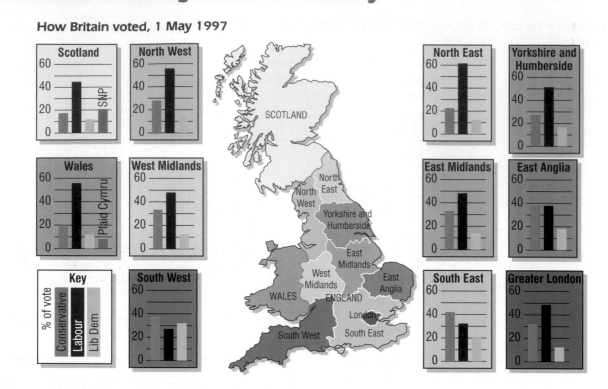

How Britain voted, 1 May 1997

Source: 'Focus', *Sociology Review*, Vol. 7, September 1997, originaly in *The Sunday Times*, 4 May 1997

1 In the 1997 election was there any area of Britain which voted Liberal Democrat?

2 Which part of Britain was most likely to vote Conservative?

3 Which part of Britain was most likely to vote Labour?

4 Can you suggest any reasons for this?

5 Which parts of the country had other parties apart from Conservative, Labour and Liberal Democrat, which received a substantial number of votes? What parties were they? How does this illustrate 'partisan de-alignment?

Ethnicity

There is a close link between membership of a minority ethnic group and Labour voting. This is because Labour is perceived as being more supportive of ethnic minorities than the Conservatives. Over 70 per cent of voters of Asian origin voted Labour and over 90 per cent of voters from African-Caribbean backgrounds.

Ethnicity and voting

Per cent intending to vote for given parties among Asians and Blacks who decided to vote, 1996–7

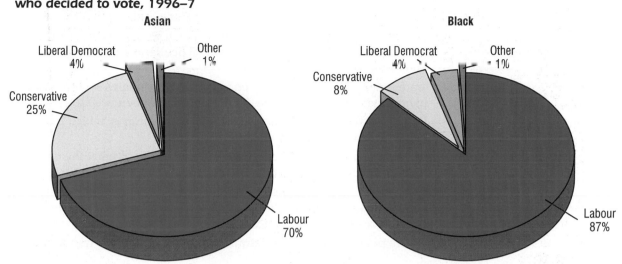

Asian

Liberal Democrat 4%

Other 1%

Conservative 25%

Labour 70%

Black

Liberal Democrat 4%

Other 1%

Conservative 8%

Labour 87%

Source: I. Budge, I. Crewe, D. McKay and K. Newton, *The New British Politics* (Addison Wesley Longman, 1998)

1 Which party received the highest percentage of support from ethnic minorities? What are the percentages

2 What proportion of Asians voted Conservative?

3 What proportion of 'Blacks' voted Conservative?

4 Suggest reasons why these voting preferences exist.

Influences on voting behaviour

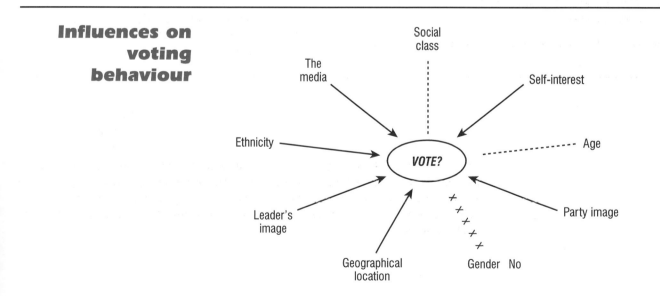

Social class

The media

Self-interest

Ethnicity

VOTE?

Age

Leader's image

Party image

Geographical location

Gender No

Write a sentence explaining each of the points in this diagram.

Main points ▶ A significant number of electors choose not to vote. This is influenced by a number of factors including lack of knowledge or interest in politics.

▶ There are four types of voters – floating voters, abstainers, loyal voters and tactical voters.

▶ There are many different influences on how people choose to vote.

▶ People are less loyal to the one political party, and more likely to choose different parties. This is especially true in Scotland and Wales. This is known as partisan de-alignment.

▶ Traditionally social class has been important. It remains so, but is declining in importance. The term class de-alignment has been used to describe this.

▶ People are strongly influenced by self-interest – that is, which party will benefit them and their family.

▶ Increasingly, people are influenced by their image of what the party stands for and the personal qualities of the leader.

▶ The media play a very important role in creating images of political parties and leaders. Traditionally, the majority of newspapers have been supportive of the Conservative Party.

▶ Where people live and their ethnic backgrounds are also important.

Democracy in action: pressure groups and social movements

As we saw earlier, democracy involves more than just the right to vote in elections every five years. Most important of all, it involves a constant flow of communication from the people to their representatives in Parliament. In many cases this simply involves MPs meeting their constituents (the people who elected them) and listening to their views.

Political action

The most authoritative study of the extent to which people undertake political action shows that, apart from voting (75–80 per cent in general elections, about 40 per cent in local elections), most action is stimulated by social groups. About 14 per cent of adults take part in informal group activity and 11 per cent in organised group activity to do with politics (like writing letters or distributing leaflets to express concerns). Twenty-one per cent had contacted a local councillor and almost 15 per cent had attended meetings to protest against some policy. Sixty-three per cent had signed a petition. Most people do not do these things very often: three or four of them are undertaken in a five-year period. When they do, however, it is generally at the prompting of some group which organises the action.

Source: I. Budge, I. Crewe, D. McKay and K. Newton, *The New British Politics* (Addison Wesley Longman, 1998); percentages are from G. Parry, G. Moser and N. Day, *Political Participation and Democracy in Action* (Cambridge University Press, 1992)

1 List the activities which people engage in.

2 What is the most popular activity?

3 What proportion of people engage in an organised group activity to do with politics?

4 What does the term 'organised group activity' mean? Give an example.

Pressure groups

However, far more important are the activities of organised groups who agitate in order to persuade Parliament to pass laws which benefit them or they believe would improve society. These groups are known as **interest groups** or **pressure groups**.

Types of pressure group

There are two types of pressure group:

* those which *defend their own interests*, such as trade unions or the Confederation of British Industry (the CBI, representing the owners of industry), these are known as *protective* or *defensive pressure groups*
* those which *promote new initiatives*, which they argue will benefit society, known as *promotional groups*. Examples include the Child Poverty Action Group, which campaigns for better benefits for low-income families, and Greenpeace which campaigns for less pollution and a better environment.

In reality, the division between the two types of group is not completely clear-cut. Some pressure groups might wish to promote change in order to benefit themselves. For instance, those groups which have campaigned for longer opening hours for pubs and bars have been financially supported by the alcohol industry. Although the campaigners believe that longer hours prevent drunkenness, the brewers still hope to sell more alcohol.

Pressure groups and political parties

There are two main differences between pressure groups and political parties. Firstly, pressure groups generally do not try to win electoral power; they just wish to influence MPs or those in authority. Secondly, they generally concentrate on one issue rather than the wide range of issues supported by political parties.

Using the Internet, look up press coverage of the fox-hunting debate. What are the main arguments for and against fox hunting? What organisations can you find who are for and against fox hunting?

Look up the Countryside Alliance – a pressure group who claim to look after the interests of country people. What can you find out about it?

How pressure groups influence decision-makers

Lobbying

This involves sending representatives to see MPs, or whoever is in authority. The representatives try to persuade those in authority of the sense of their campaign. This is usually supported by leaflets, letters and documents. In recent years, there has been the growth of professional lobbying firms, who will lobby for any pressure group if paid to do so.

Retaining the services of those in authority

A number of Labour MPs are 'sponsored' by trade unions to look after their interests, and MPs from all parties are often asked to represent a particular industry (rather than a company) or professional association. There is rarely corruption, but the groups ensure that their interests are looked after.

Publicity

For many groups who have contacts with those in authority, the best way of gaining attention is to attract publicity. Pressure groups may give stories to the press or engage in newsworthy exploits. Greenpeace, the environmental group, is particularly good at this. The aim is not just to attract attention, but also to win public sympathy.

Pressure groups and new social movements in action

Protest

Demonstrations and public meetings within the law, as well as direct action outside the law, may attract publicity and bring pressure to bear on the authorities to change their attitudes. Protest is usually the method of the weakest, as the powerful generally have direct access to the politicians and civil servants. One group which has moved towards illegality in recent years is the animal rights movement, which protests against the use of animals in experiments. Activists break into laboratories, free the animals and harass employees of research companies. There are also hunt saboteurs and opponents of larger road schemes.

Criticism: differences in resources

The idea that the activities of pressure groups guarantee democracy has been most strongly criticised for the fact that it overlooks the real differences in resources that various pressure groups have at their disposal. The Confederation of British Industry, which represents the owners of British industry, employs over 400 people and is very rich. Yet other groups such as Help the Aged, a pressure group to look after the needs of older people, has only a tiny staff and little money.

Social movements

Pressure groups are usually concerned with only one particular issue. Pressure groups form and then disband after a time. But from the 1980s it became clear that a new form of political 'organisation' was emerging. Groups of people began to develop alternative ways of thinking and acting, which included challenging the traditional political structures of parties and pressure groups. The 'organisations' consisted of like-minded people who began to think and act in alternative ways from normal. There was no formal membership, nor was there any particular central organisation. Generally people followed their own ideas, but there were enough of these people 'sharing their own ideas', that they found they were a political force in their own right. These new ways of thinking and acting have been described as 'movements', and more specifically *new social movements*. The best known examples of these are the feminist movement, the green movement and the lesbian and gay movements.

> **Definition**
>
> **Social movement** – a loosely organised coalition of different groups who come together to bring about social change on a fairly broad scale

The movements promote alternative lifestyles, as opposed to clear political programmes, and they do not set out to put together political parties, or to win seats in Parliament. Within movements, there are many different strands with individuals sharing some beliefs and not others.

One recent example of a new social movement has been the increasing opposition to cruelty to animals in any form, including hunting, animal experiments, the mistreatment of animals before slaughter, even opposition to killing animals for food.

New social movements: an example

In 1999 the World Trade Organisation (an international organisation which decides on trading agreements between all countries in the world) met in Seattle, USA. For many people, the WTO is one of the major reasons why African countries are trapped in debt and unable to provide decent living standards for the people who live there. Protesters from all over the world, who had communicated by the Internet, gathered outside the conference centre to disrupt proceedings and to protest. The result was that the African nations refused to continue co-operating and started to demand certain rights.

The words of the chant and the drums beat around the walls of the jail all afternoon. It was 2 December 1999 and the Seattle protests against the World Trade Organization (WTO) had been raging all week. After mass arrests the day before, thousands of people besieged King County Jail. A deal was offered by the jail authorities: if the crowd would leave, lawyers would be allowed in.

This meant a decision had to be made – and so, naturally, the protesters held a meeting. This was no mean feat: for a start, the crowd was so large that not everyone could hear what was said, so each comment had to be shouted out, line by line, by those closest to the speaker. In the end the decision was made to leave, allow the lawyers to enter, and return the next day.

For the Seattle protesters, consensus meant involving everyone in coming to a collective decision. It does not mean unanimity, or submitting to binding commitments, but empowering people to share in group decisions. To act effectively in the chaos of tear gas and rubber bullets that week required co-operation and trust, not conformity to a fixed plan.

Meanwhile, in the WTO summit down the road, trade representatives of 134 nations were meeting.

As Dr Devinder Sharma, an Indian WTO negotiator, explains, the aim 'was to push the political agenda of the US and the richest trading bloc down the throats of the Third World countries'. Southern countries' efforts to introduce a one-country, one-vote system have been strenuously resisted.

That Thursday evening, as the crowd was dispersing from the jail, time began to run out on the WTO. The chanting at the jail changed to 'Africa Don't Sign!' until around midnight when the news arrived that with consensus blocked the talks had collapsed. The crowd erupted in triumph.

Source: T. Lloyd, 'Consensus games', *New Internationalist*, 24 June 2000

1 What are the protesters angry about?

2 Is there any particular pressure group or organisation controlling the protests?

3 How did they make decisions about calling off the protest outside the jail? Is this typical of most organisations?

4 Were they successful?

5 Find two other examples of direct action by social movements.

How political parties stay in touch with the views of the electorate

Opinion polls

Opinion polls are generally used to find out people's opinions on topical subjects, or to carry out market research on consumers' preferences. They involve asking questions of a typical cross-section of the population, and the results are then claimed to be an accurate representation of the views of the population. Opinion polls are widely used by political parties and newspapers to find out voters' intentions at elections. However, they have been criticised for possibly having an effect on the outcome of elections, rather than just providing information. For it seems that voters use the information given in opinion polls to engage in tactical voting. Voters, who realise that the party of their first choice has absolutely no chance of winning according to the opinion polls, may decide to switch votes. Opinion polls are then actually influencing the outcome of the elections, not just informing people of the situation.

Clever use of opinion polls by political parties becomes an important weapon in the electoral battle. They may release selective information to encourage people to use tactical voting. The result is that people vote into power not the party of first choice, but the one least disliked – a rather different matter. Of course, this all assumes that the opinion polls have actually predicted correctly the voting intentions of the electorate.

Opinion polls: an unfair political weapon?

Opinion polls have become a political institution. They influence four aspects of the political process:
• party morale
• the election date
• election campaigns
• policy formation.

Party morale
The steady publication of opinion polls forms a permanent background to the party political stage. When they are favourable, the party leader is confident and the MPs and media are respectful. When they are unfavourable, opponents in the government who wish to get power for themselves, flex their muscles and the media criticise. This inevitably affects the morale of the party.

Election date
The Prime Minister decides the election date and always seek a time most favourable to his or her party. Opinion polls guide the choice of date, as they give an indication of how the electorate feel.

Election campaigns
The political parties pay for private polls which tell them how the campaign is going and what issues they should concentrate on. Parties tailor their propaganda according to the information and feedback they receive through the polls.

All parties now leak selected information to the media about how the various candidates are doing, in the hope of making electors switch their votes tactically. For example, if it seems likely that Labour will win an election because voters who normally vote Conservative are considering voting for the Liberal Democrats as a form of protest (not because they want the Liberal Democrats to actually win, but to give the Conservatives a 'scare'), they may be frightened back into voting Conservative, on seeing the results of an opinion poll showing that Labour may actually gain the seat as a result of the protest vote. The same applies to Labour, and for slightly different reasons to the Liberal Democrats.

Policy formation
Political parties are strongly influenced by what people indicate they want in opinion polls. Indeed, the parties go so far as to change their policies to fit in with what the public wants.

1 What are opinion polls?

2 Are they always accurate?

3 In what four ways do they influence politics?

4 It has been suggested that opinion polls should be banned during elections (as they are for a certain period in the French elections). Why have people said this?

Focus groups

As an alternative to opinion polls, political parties have increasingly been turning to focus groups. Focus groups are small groups of people chosen from a variety of backgrounds who are asked their views on particular issues. A discussion follows which is recorded and then the key points are pulled out by the researchers. This information is then fed back to the politicians who use it to adjust their policies to make sure they are in-tune with the electorate.

Focus groups have been criticised by some commentators who argue that it is the task of government to lead the people on certain issues, but by using focus groups, the politicians substitute pleasing the electorate (who may be badly informed) for decision-making based upon the best information available.

Main points

▶ Voting for political parties is only one of a number of ways to participate in a democracy.

▶ Many people join pressure groups which are organisations concerned with a particular issue.

▶ There are two types of pressure groups – promotional and defensive.

▶ Pressure groups are different from political parties in that they are not seeking power to govern – they just want one issue resolved.

▶ Pressure groups use a number of tactics to influence politicians. These include gaining publicity, lobbying, paying powerful people and direct protest.

▶ Pressure groups are very unequal in the amount of resources they have to influence politicians.

▶ In recent years, social movements have developed which are much broader in membership and scope of interest than pressure groups. They are concerned much more about a lifestyle rather than one issue. They have no organisation.

▶ Political parties stay in contact with the views of the electorate by using focus groups and opinion polls.

▶ Opinion polls have been criticised for influencing the way that people vote.

13 CHAPTER SUMMARY

1 Power is a much wider concept than politics and refers to how people get their way in a wide variety of social and personal situations.

2 Power can be divided into two types – coercion and authority.

3 There are three types of authority – charismatic, traditional and legal-rational. All of these divisions classify the reasons why people obey others

4 There are two main sorts of political systems – democracies and totalitarian societies.

5 Totalitarian societies are those where only a few people rule. They forbid elections and do not allow people to express their opinions.

6 Democratic societies are those where people choose who rules and can express their views about politics without fear of being arrested.

7 There are a number of political ideologies which exist. These include communism, socialism, social democracy, conservatism and fascism.

8 Britain is a democracy which is headed by a monarch.

9 There are three elements to the British state – the parliament, the civil service and the judiciary.

10 There are parliaments elected for Britain as a whole and a separate one for Scotland. There are assemblies in Wales and Northern Ireland.

11 Some critics argue that Britain is not as democratic as it seems. They argue that politicians, top civil servants and the judiciary are mainly drawn from the higher social classes in society and have generally been educated in public schools.

12 This has led to a debate between those who argue that the best way to describe power is that it is dispersed across the society
   – the pluralist view;
   – those who argue that there is a ruling class who control society.

13 People are socialised into understanding politics and having views on the subject by a range of agencies including the media, the family, the school and their peer group/social class.

14 A significant number of electors choose not to vote. This is influenced by a number of factors including lack of knowledge or interest in politics.

15 There are four types of voters – floating voters, abstainers, loyal voters and tactical voters.

16 There are many different influences on how people choose to vote. These include social class, self-interest, images of the political parties and their leaders, the views of the media, where people live and their ethnic backgrounds

17 Partisan-alignment is where people are less loyal to one political party.

18 Class de-alignment is where people are less likely to vote for the party traditionally associated with their social class.

19 Voting for political parties is only one of a number of ways to participate in a democracy and many people join pressure groups or social movments.

20 Pressure groups are different from political parties in that they are not seeking power to govern, they just want one issue resolved.

21 Pressure groups use a number of tactics to influence politicians. These include gaining publicity, lobbying, paying powerful people and direct protest.

22 Pressure groups are very unequal in the amount of resources they have to influence politicians.

23 In recent years, social movements have developed which are concerned much more about a lifestyle rather than one issue. They have no organisation.

24 Political parties stay in contact with the views of the electorate by using focus groups and opinion polls.

25 Opinion polls have been criticised for influencing the way that people vote.

Test Your Knowledge

1 Identify and explain, with examples, the three types of authority.

2 What differences are there between a totalitarian and a democratic society?

3 Explain the terms 'social democratic' and 'conservative'.

4 What do we mean by the term 'ruling class'?

5 Why do some people not vote in a democracy?

6 Explain the difference between class de-alignment and partisan de-alignment.

7 What is a pressure group and how do pressure groups influence decisions?

8 How might opinion polls influence voting patterns?

Chapter

14

POVERTY AND WELFARE

Chapter contents

- **Poverty and social exclusion**

  We discuss of the nature of social exclusion and how it relates to poverty. Most people have an image of poverty as not enough money, and then seem to stop their analysis there. But poverty has a very wide-ranging impact on people's lives. Just to make this point clear, sociologists have used the term 'social exclusion' to try to incorporate all the problems and difficulties the poor face.

- **Defining and measuring poverty**

  There are all sorts of claims bandied about regarding how much poverty there is in Britain. As usual, once we start to look underneath these claims, it become really complicated! We discover that there are very different, competing definitions of poverty, and that each one suggests different numbers of people living in poverty. At its simplest, you can see poverty as either being absolutely without the necessities of life – perhaps the term 'destitution' best sums this up – or you can see poverty as missing out on what most people consider to be a normal style of life. Take your choice.

- **The extent of poverty**

  We have already seen that definitions vary, but in this section, rather than being confusing, we opt for the simple definition used by the government and then simply note, without comment, just how many people can be said to be poor in Britain. I think you will be surprised.

- **Poverty and the life cycle**

  There is a belief that people live in poverty all their lives, and so we can distinguish between poor people and the rest of us. This is not true – poverty can best be seen as a stage which many people enter and leave at different points in their lives. For millions of people on low incomes, some periods of their lives can be quite acceptable, and other periods of their lives can see them deep in poverty. We explore just why this should be so.

- **Who are at risk of poverty?**

  Following on from our earlier sections on the extent of poverty and the links between the lifecycle and poverty, we go on to look at just which groups of people are more likely to fall into poverty, and why. Some groups are obvious – the low paid, the unemployed – but others may puzzle us somewhat. Why do women and children provide the bulk of the poor?

- **The causes of poverty**

  At the end of our discussions on who is in poverty and the extent of it, we come to the question which most people ask – just why are people in poverty? The answer is complex and hotly debated. Some claim that it is the fault of individuals who cannot be bothered to work hard; others that there is a cultural problem which blocks some people off from success; still others who point to the fact that the poor are usually less powerful and that they are simply victims of a complex economic system. The debate is important, because if we can find out the causes then we may be able to find out how to prevent it.

- **The Welfare State**

  The Welfare State has, for well over 50 years, been the way to combat poverty and social deprivation. It was the creature of the Second World War and the memories of the terrible pre-war social conditions. But is it relevant for the world today? In this section we gain an overview of what the Welfare State does and how it operates.

- **Debates about the Welfare State**

  The final section of the chapter takes just two of many debates about the efficiency of the Welfare State and looks at possible alternatives. For a number of years, those with politically 'right-wing' views have been arguing that there is no need for the Welfare State anymore and it is just a waste of tax payers' money. Defenders of the Welfare State point to what an excellent job it is doing. We do not take sides in this discussion, just put forward the arguments and leave the decision to you.

Poverty and social exclusion

Most people think that poverty means not having enough money and having
to struggle to pay the bills. This is true, but poverty involves much more than
that – it infiltrates every aspect of people's lives, causing a range of social
problems from poor health to school failure. It is also closely associated with
crime, suicide and drug abuse. Sociologists therefore often refer to poor people
as being **socially excluded** from society, as they are excluded from the normal
pastimes and pleasures that the majority of the population take for granted.

Poverty and social exclusion

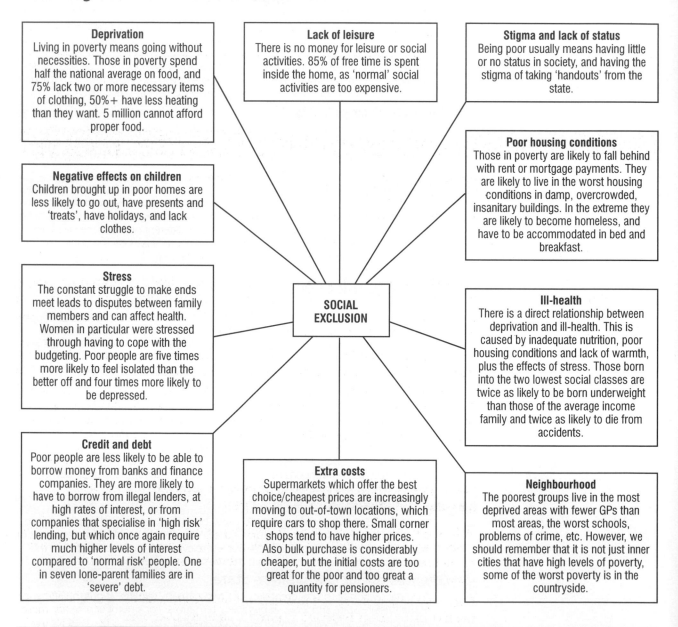

Deprivation
Living in poverty means going without
necessities. Those in poverty spend
half the national average on food, and
75% lack two or more necessary items
of clothing, 50%+ have less heating
than they want. 5 million cannot afford
proper food.

Lack of leisure
There is no money for leisure or social
activities. 85% of free time is spent
inside the home, as 'normal' social
activities are too expensive.

Stigma and lack of status
Being poor usually means having little
or no status in society, and having the
stigma of taking 'handouts' from the
state.

Negative effects on children
Children brought up in poor homes are
less likely to go out, have presents and
'treats', have holidays, and lack
clothes.

Poor housing conditions
Those in poverty are likely to fall behind
with rent or mortgage payments. They
are likely to live in the worst housing
conditions in damp, overcrowded,
insanitary buildings. In the extreme they
are likely to become homeless, and
have to be accommodated in bed and
breakfast.

Stress
The constant struggle to make ends
meet leads to disputes between family
members and can affect health.
Women in particular were stressed
through having to cope with the
budgeting. Poor people are five times
more likely to feel isolated than the
better off and four times more likely to
be depressed.

**SOCIAL
EXCLUSION**

Ill-health
There is a direct relationship between
deprivation and ill-health. This is
caused by inadequate nutrition, poor
housing conditions and lack of warmth,
plus the effects of stress. Those born
into the two lowest social classes are
twice as likely to be born underweight
than those of the average income
family and twice as likely to die from
accidents.

Credit and debt
Poor people are less likely to be able to
borrow money from banks and finance
companies. They are more likely to
have to borrow from illegal lenders, at
high rates of interest, or from
companies that specialise in 'high risk'
lending, but which once again require
much higher levels of interest
compared to 'normal risk' people. One
in seven lone-parent families are in
'severe' debt.

Extra costs
Supermarkets which offer the best
choice/cheapest prices are increasingly
moving to out-of-town locations, which
require cars to shop there. Small corner
shops tend to have higher prices.
Also bulk purchase is considerably
cheaper, but the initial costs are too
great for the poor and too great a
quantity for pensioners.

Neighbourhood
The poorest groups live in the most
deprived areas with fewer GPs than
most areas, the worst schools,
problems of crime, etc. However, we
should remember that it is not just inner
cities that have high levels of poverty,
some of the worst poverty is in the
countryside.

Living in poverty in Britain today: experiencing social exclusion

'I cannot go for a job interview even if I could get one, as after three years of unemployment my clothes are virtual rags, and I cannot buy any more, as it costs so much to keep my son decent – scruffy children have their lives made a misery at school and whatever else I do without, he will not have to go through that.

He wets the bed and has to wear nappies. His sheets and bedding must still be washed every day. When my washer broke, I asked if the DHSS [now DSS] could help and was told that the washer was not regarded as a necessity, and I should use the launderette.

He has not had either birthday or Christmas presents since he was two. He asks for Lego and cars from Santa, but Santa is dead in this house; how does one explain that to a child of five?

I have no chance of getting out to meet people; (I can't afford) ... a babysitter. I have no relatives to help out and since I can no longer entertain or go out, I have literally no friends. So I spend every day alone and every night.

I sat down and worked out roughly what you spend per week. And now you've got washing-up liquid, you got toilet paper, you got soap to wash with. Well, what is it, you go out and you think to yourself, now if I buy washing-up liquid I can't have a loaf of bread. Which do you do? Buy the loaf of bread or the washing-up liquid? You've got to keep yourself clean and you've got to eat. So which way do you sway?

Some days I just go into a corner and won't let anybody come near me. I just sit in a corner and bang my head against the wall. And say why me?'

Source: Adapted from J. Mack and S. Lansley, *Poor Britain* (Allen & Unwin, 1985)

Defining and measuring poverty

Sociologists have defined poverty in two different ways:

- **absolute poverty**
- **relative poverty**

Absolute poverty

Definition

Absolute poverty – not having the very basics to live

Towards the end of the nineteenth century, a number of concerned people began to argue that something ought to be done about the dreadful problem of poverty that existed. Most powerful people laughed at this, denying there was any serious problem (just as happens today).

To prove just how bad the situation was, Seebohm Rowntree conducted a survey to discover the extent of poverty in Britain. First, though, he had to provide a clear guide to the point at which people fell into poverty. He created a poverty line with which no reasonable person could disagree. He decided that the line was the income needed to ensure that a person was able to live healthily and work efficiently.

How is the poverty line calculated according to the absolute definition of poverty?

To find the amount of income to reach this point, Rowntree added together: the costs of a very basic diet; the costs of purchasing a minimum of clothes; the rent for housing. The poverty line was then drawn at the income needed to cover these three costs.

But critics have pointed out that this sort of definition fails to take into account the fact that what is regarded as poverty changes over time.

The advantages and disadvantages of absolute definitions of poverty

Advantages	Disadvantages
• It is absolutely clear and does not rely upon people's opinions about what is poverty. • It allows comparisons across societies, so that it enables sociologists to say just how many poor people there are in a poorer developing nation compared to richer developed nations.	• It fails to take into account the fact that what is regarded as poverty changes over time. What is a luxury today may be a necessity tomorrow. For example, a basic diet today is very different from a basic diet of 50 years ago. This also true for housing and clothes. • It is very hard to decide exactly what really are the minimum standard of clothes or the minimum acceptable diet.

Activity

a) Make a list of necessities for two adults and two children for one week. Find out the total sum of money they add up to. How much is needed each week, in your opinion?

b) Can you agree exactly what the 'necessities' are?

Relative poverty

Definition

Relative poverty – not being able to afford the standard of living considered acceptable by the majority of people

The criticism of Rowntree's definition led sociologists to create a different definition of poverty. This is based on the idea that poverty is really the situation in which some people are denied what most people normally expect to have. For instance, 40 years ago central heating in homes was a luxury for the better-off. Today it is regarded as a normal convenience for the majority of households. At that time televisions, telephones and cars were all luxuries. Are they today? And how long before anyone without a mobile phone will be poor? So, when Rowntree allowed a set of warm clothes, he did not take into account that they might need to be sufficiently fashionable. Today, however, fashion and the brand of the clothing are both very important.

The result of this was that sociologists began to search for a poverty line which reflected the fact that poverty is closely related to the general standards of living of the population.

How is the poverty line measured in relative definitions?

There are two ways of measuring poverty within the relative definition approach:

- **the relative income measure**
- **consensual definition measure**.

Definition

Relative income measurement of poverty – income less than 50 per cent of average income

The relative income measure

The most commonly used approach is to say that anyone (or any family) living in households which receive less than half the average British income is in poverty. This, of course, means that there is no way that poverty can ever be eliminated. This is how the British government currently measure poverty.

Half average household income:

for a family with three children = £260 a week
for a single person = £95 a week

Advantages and disadvantages of the relative measurement of poverty

Advantages	Disadvantages
• It relates the poverty to the expectations of society – reflecting the fact that people do measure themselves against the quality of life of other people in that society. • It gives a realistic picture of what is generally considered to be deprivation within any one society. • It broadens the idea of what poverty is, from lacking basic necessities to a range of other 'needs' that people expect to have in a society, and which makes life bearable.	• Taken to its extreme, this approach means that as long as there is inequality there is poverty. • It could be argued that just because a person does not have the 'extras' which most people have come to expect in contemporary Britain, they are poor. As long as they are fed, housed and clothed then they have all that is needed. • The relative approach is not really appropriate for the poorest countries in the world, for there it would seem to say that as long as person is not starving they are not because expectations are so much lower in these countries. This is clearly untrue. Most people in most of the poorest countries are poor, by any realistic standard. • If half average household income is used to measure poverty, then even if the whole society became very rich indeed, with extremely high standards of living, those below the average would be defined as poor.

Question   What other disadvantage apart from those listed above can you find from the text under the heading 'consensual measures of poverty'?

Absolute poverty definitions seem more useful when applied to the poorest countries in the world, whilst relative definitions are more useful for richer countries. Can you explain why?

Definition

Consensual measure of poverty – a measure based upon an estimate of the numbers who do not have a normally acceptable 'minimum' lifestyle

A consensual measure of poverty

Many people have concerns about saying that poverty is 50 per cent or below the average income. Why 50 per cent and not 60 per cent or 30 per cent, or any other figure? They say the percentage is arbitrary, that is, it has just been chosen 'out of the air'. They suggest instead asking people to rank in order of importance what they consider to be necessities. These are then put together, and as a result a list of necessities is produced which is agreed with by the large majority of people. Using these agreed (or 'consensual') necessities, they are then able to work out what most people regard as an unacceptable level of deprivation.

Mack and Lansley's list of necessities

In 1985 and 1991, Mack and Lansley asked over 1000 people what they thought 'necessities' were, and then from their replies made a list of the most commonly agreed necessities. Below is the list that Mack and Lansley produced from the first phase of their research, and which they then asked people to rank in order of importance.

New, not second-hand, clothes	Refrigerator	Celebrations on special occasions such as Christmas	Meat or fish every other day
Heating to warm living areas of the home if it's cold	Bath (not shared with another household)	Damp-free home	A dressing gown
Enough bedrooms for every child over 10 of different sex to have his/her own	A car	A warm water-proof coat	Children's friends round for tea/a snack once a fortnight
Leisure equipment for children, e.g. sports equipment or a bicycle	A holiday away from home for one week a year, not with relatives	Two hot meals a day (for adults)	Indoor toilet (not shared with another household)
Carpets in living rooms and bedrooms	Public transport for one's needs	A telephone	Friends/family round for a meal once a month
Presents for friends or family once a year	A garden	A packet of cigarettes every other day	Beds for everyone in the household
Three meals a day for children	A television	A roast meat joint or its equivalent once a week	Self-contained accommodation
Toys for children	A night out once a fortnight (adults)	A 'best outfit' for special occasions	A washing machine
	A hobby or leisure activity	An outing for children once a week	Two pairs of all-weather shoes

Source: J. Mack and S. Lansley, *Poor Britain* (Allen & Unwin, 1985)

1 As a group, try to come to agreement over what you collectively agree are the first five necessities.

2 Check your results against those of Mack and Lansley on page 405.

3 Do you agree with the order of 'necessities' according to Mack and Lansley?

Views on measuring poverty

A ... by almost every material measure it is possible to contrive: health, longevity, real income, ownership of consumer durables, number and length of holidays, money spent on entertainment, numbers in further education. ... not only are those with lower incomes not getting poorer, they are substantially better off than they have ever been before ...

B The picture which emerges is one of constant restriction in almost every aspect of people's activities. ... The lives of these families...are marked by the unrelieved struggle to manage, with dreary diets and drab clothing.
They also suffer from what amounts to cultural imprisonment in their home in our society in which getting out with money to spend on recreation and leisure is normal at every other income level.

[Poverty] is defined by reference to the actual needs of the poor and not by reference to the expenditure of those who are not poor. A family is poor if it cannot afford to eat. ... A person who enjoys a standard of living equal to that of a medieval baron cannot be described as poor for the sole reason that he has chanced to be born into a society where the great majority can live like medieval kings.

C

It is not just money that decides how people live — it is access to resources that makes the difference between drowning in poverty and managing just to keep your head above water. To measure poverty only by income is inaccurate — what facilities do people have and what social activities are they able to engage in, are the real indicators of poverty.

D

Source: R. Lister, *The Exclusive Society* (CPAG, 1990)

1 Copy and complete the table to identify the type of measure each quote is referring to.

Definition of poverty	Quote
Absolute definition	
Income measure	
Consensual measure	

2 Which of these do you feel is the most accurate? Why?

The importance of different definitions of poverty

Sociologists are concerned about defining poverty because the outcome of the work has very important results for poor people.

- If poverty is simply the level below which people cannot live and work efficiently, as Rowntree suggests, then very low levels of financial support are needed from the government, and the number of people considered to be in poverty is very low.

- On the other hand, if poverty is not having what is regarded as normal and desirable, as the relative poverty group argues, the level of financial support required from the government is much higher and the numbers of people defined as poor are very much higher too.

The government uses a measure called Households Below Average Income (HBAI), which is the relative income approach we discussed earlier.

Main points ▶ Being poor is one aspect of social exclusion, and the consequences of poverty include social and health problems as well as lack of money.

▶ Sociologists have two different definitions of poverty:

– Absolute poverty says that poverty is a lack of the necessities of life.

– Relative poverty says that poverty is lacking what most people regard as an adequate standard of living, and this changes over time.

> There are two different ways of measuring poverty within the relative definition approach:
> - The relative income measure says that poverty is having an income below half the average.
> - The consensual measure creates a list of normal expectations and says those who only have some on the list are poor.
> The debate over the different ways of measuring poverty is very important, as the government relies upon the figures to help determine its policies towards poverty.
> The government uses the relative income measure.

The extent of poverty

As we have seen, the numbers of people living in poverty will vary according to which definition and measure is used. But if we take the measure most commonly used by the government, that is the number of households with incomes below average income (HBAI), then *one quarter of the population, or 14 million people, are in poverty* (1999 figures).

The risk of poverty

A   The 'poverty line' in 1997/98 (April 1999 prices)

	1998 (excluding self-employed)
Single adult	£74
Couple with no children	£134
Couple with three children (aged 3, 8 and 11)	£224
All family types	£134

Look at A. The statistics are based upon 50 per cent of average income after housing costs.

1   In 1998, what was the income which formed the poverty line for a couple with three children?

2   What was the figure for a single adult? So, what would the average income be for a single adult, after housing costs?

B   Number of people in poverty in the UK

	Total population (million)	Number in poverty (million)	% of total population
1979	54.0	5.0	9%
1994/95	55.8	13.3	24%
1997/98	56.4	14.0	25%

Look at B.

3   How many people were in poverty in 1979?

4   What proportion of the population did this represent?

5   What had happened by 1997/98?

6   What does this tell you about the inequality of incomes in Britain over this period?

Source: Adapted from *Poverty: Journal of the Child Poverty Action Group*, Issue 106, Summer 2000

Poverty and the life cycle

When we talk about the poor, it gives the impression that there is a fixed body of people, separate from mainstream society, who live in poverty all their lives. This is true for some people, but the majority of the poor are people who live on the margins of poverty and who are more likely to be in poverty for certain periods of their lives, and to climb out of it during other periods.

For example, people with young, dependent children who have a low wage will probably be in great financial difficulties because of the financial burden of having children and they will, therefore, be likely to go into poverty – and of course their children will be poor too. Later as the children are able to do part-time work or later enter full-time employment, the parents may well move out of poverty (just!). However, as they grow old and their incomes decline again, and with little money saved, they may fall back into poverty.

Poverty and the life cycle

Who are at risk of poverty?

A **% of group in poverty, 1997–8**

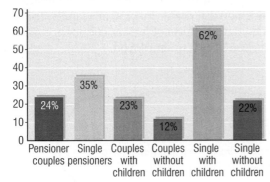

B **Number in poverty (% of total), 1997–8**

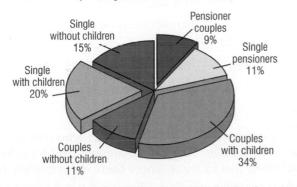

Look at A.

1 Which family type had the highest percentage of people in it in poverty? What percentage of that family type was in poverty?

2 Which group has the second highest proportion of its members in poverty? What percentage was it?

3 Which family type has the lowest percentage of its members in poverty? What is the percentage?

Look at B.

4 Which group formed the biggest percentage of people in poverty? What percentage is that? How many people is that?

5 Which group forms the second biggest percentage of people in poverty? What percentage is that? How many people does it comprise in total?

6 Which group provides the smallest percentage of the poor? What percentage is that? How many people does that comprise in total?

Source: Adapted from *Poverty: Journal of the Child Poverty Action Group*, Issue 106, Summer 2000

Lone-parent families

The number of lone parents has grown from just over a half a million at the beginning of the 1970s to about 1.7 million today. Over 60 per cent of all lone parents live in poverty in Britain. Almost all lone parents are women, who are caught in a trap of low wages or living on state benefits because they have to look after their child/children.

Lone-parent families are more likely to be poor for two overlapping reasons.

- Single women who come from poor socio-economic backgrounds, who live in social housing, or who live in areas of high local unemployment, are more likely to become lone mothers than others. So, they are already poor before they have children.

- Even if they are not poor before they have children, the problem of combining work with childcare means that lone mothers are likely to work part-time and claim additional state help, or not to work at all. In any case, the outcome is that they are likely to be in poverty.

The unemployed

About two-thirds of people with incomes below half the average are not working. Over two million children live in households where there is no one in employment.

The number of people who are out of work changes with the overall situation the economy. There are two types of unemployment:

- long-term unemployment
- short-term unemployment.

Those who are unemployed for a long time face much greater problems than those out of work for a short period. These problems include a lower level of income, the exhaustion of savings, and a gradual running down in the condition of clothing, furniture and general possessions. One study found that after three months of unemployment, the average disposable income of a family dropped by 59 per cent. Of course, the psychological effects of lack of confidence, stress and depression are more acute for the long-term unemployed.

You end up pulling your hair out because you can't ever get away for a night out like working people ... Tensions build when you get a bit of time on your own.

Source: C. Oppenheim, *Poverty: The Facts* (CPAG, 1993)

The low paid

In 1999, there were 2 million employees over the age of 25 who earned less than half the average male hourly wage. People who are low paid tend to be those with fewer skills and often live in areas where there are relatively few jobs, so that wages are kept low by competition. But an important element of low pay impacts particularly upon lone parents, and that is the growth of part-time employment, which is usually relatively low paid. Single mothers often have little choice but to take this work, as they have childcare responsibilities.

> I was earning roughly £35 to £40 a week. It was piece work, 13p per skirt — you had to sew hundreds to get to £35–£40 … I had to work sometimes until midnight, from nine in the morning just to pay rent, electricity and gas.
>
> *(Sevin, mother of three)*

Source: C. Oppenheim, *Poverty: The Facts* (CPAG, 1993)

The poverty trap

The poverty trap refers to the problem which many low income families receiving state benefits face when they get employment or receive higher wages, as state benefits cease when people reach certain levels of income. For many people, the loss of state benefits when their wages increased or when they find a job can mean that their actual real increase in income is extremely low. They might even, bizarrely enough, lose income when they get a higher wage. This situation has been termed the *poverty trap*. However, governments have made great efforts to 'taper' benefits so that now benefits decline much more slowly as income increases, reducing the problem of the poverty trap.

One of the biggest groups in this situation is that of lone mothers who need to pay for childcare and this may cost them more then they can earn.

Children

Forty per cent of children are 'born poor', that is born into low income families. In 1998 there were 4.4 million children living in poverty.

The majority of poor children come from households where there is no working parent. So, 10 per cent of all children of two-parent families had no parent in employment, and 58 per cent of children of lone parents had no working mother.

> The children are always asking for things — they say their friends have this and this … we have to say no, so the children get upset and we feel upset.

Source: C. Oppenheim, *Poverty: The Facts* (CPAG, 1993)

Children in poverty

Number of people in poverty in the UK (including self-employed)

	Total population (million)	Number in poverty (million)	% of total population
1979	13.8	1.5	10%
1994/95	12.7	4.0	31%
1997/98	12.9	4.4	34%

Source: Adapted from *Poverty: Journal of the Child Poverty Action Group*, Issue 106, Summer 2000

1 What percentage of children were in poverty in 1979? How many children was that?

2 What percentage of children were in poverty in 1998? How many children was that

3 Overall, is the situation improving or deteriorating?

In 1999, the Prime Minister pledged to eliminate child poverty by 2019.

Sick and disabled people

According to government statistics, there are 6.2 million adults (14 per cent of all adults) and 360,000 children (3 per cent of all children) who suffer from one or more disability. Of these people with disabilities, 34 per cent are living in poverty, and the average income for an adult, under pensionable age with a disability is 72 per cent of non-disabled people.

The reasons for the poverty of people with disabilities are:

- *limited work opportunities* – people with disabilities may be unable to work, or may be limited to particular kinds of low-paid employment
- *expenses* – a person with a disability has greater outgoings than a fully able person. He or she may need to have the heating on longer or may need a special diet, or special aids, for example.

Older people

About 18 per cent of the population (11 million people) are over retirement age. Women form over 65 per cent of older people. With the gradual raising of life expectancy, the number of older people in the population is likely to continue to increase until the end of the first decade of the twenty-first century.

Older people are often dependent upon pensions for their income. This means living in poverty for those 1.3 million who only receive the state pension, as this is so low. The state pension is, in fact, less than 20 per cent of the average male weekly earnings.

Poverty in old age is not something that happens to all pensioners. Rather the poverty reflects the divisions in employment, income and fringe benefits that exist throughout a person's employment. People who are poor in old age are most likely to be those who have earned least in their working lifetime. Therefore, the groups we looked at before – the low paid, the lone-parent families, disabled and unemployed people – are all poor in their old age.

People from ethnic minority groups

People of African-Caribbean and Asian origin have substantially higher rates of unemployment than the majority of the population. This holds true even if the black or Asian pensioner has the same educational qualifications as a white person.

People of African-Caribbean origin and a majority of those of Asian origin have a higher chance of earning lower wages than the majority population, and to work in the types of employment where wages are generally lower.

Women

The majority of the poor in Britain are women. In fact, in all the groups of poor people that we have looked at – the unemployed, the low paid, lone-parent families, the sick and disabled people, and older people – women form the majority of them.

Ninety-five per cent of lone parents on state benefits are women, and over three times as many women over pensionable age had to ask for additional state support compared to men. This is because they are less likely to have savings.

Main points ▶

▶ About one quarter of the population, or 14 million people, are in poverty.

▶ Most 'poor' people actually live on the margins of poverty and move in and out of poverty at different periods of their lives, depending upon the different responsibilities they have.

▶ Some groups are more at risk of being in poverty than others.

▶ In terms of family types, lone parents and households living on pensions are the poorest.

▶ In terms of employment, people who are unemployed or receive low pay are likely to be in poverty.

▶ In terms of individuals, children, women, sick and disabled, and members of ethnic minority groups have higher chances of being in poverty.

▶ The poverty trap occurs when people living on state benefits actually lose money, or earn little extra, when they enter employment. Although a significant problem in the past, it is gradually declining. One of the biggest groups in this situation is that of lone mothers who need to pay for childcare and this may cost them more then they can earn.

He wanted extra money off me which I couldn't give him, which led to rows and then in the end I were saying there were only the £5 electricity money left and he were taking it and spending it. And then on Monday when I cashed the family allowance, he wanted money out of that as well. So that didn't help.

(Carol, lone mother of three, expecting another)

He liked cars and drinking and there wasn't the money for it. Me and the kids used to go short on food and clothes because he spent the money.

(Vanessa, lone mother)

Source: C. Oppenheim, *Poverty: The Facts* (CPAG, 1993)

> ## *Question*
>
> How can a family be in poverty, even if the income is above the poverty line?

The causes of poverty

There are two explanations for the causes of poverty:

- The first stresses the process of dependency.
- The second stresses the process of exclusion.

Dependency

Explanations which centre around the concept of dependency often stress that people who are in poverty are there because of some failing in themselves or the particular social group to which they belong. Within this approach to explaining the causes of poverty, we can distinguish:

- blaming the individual
- the underclass
- the culture of poverty.

The individual

Quite simply poverty is a result of the failure of the individual to achieve success through his or her own efforts. People who are poor are lazy or incompetent, and should try harder.

The underclass

> #### Definition
>
> **Underclass** – a term used by right-wing commentators to refer to a group or 'class' of people who do not want to work, but prefer to live off state benefits

This is a rather more subtle development of the individual explanation, and suggests that a distinct '**underclass**' exists of people who are lazy and who make no effort to work or look after themselves. These people prefer to live off the state rather than having to work.

It is important to remember that the underclass refers only to those groups of poor people who make no effort to help themselves, and the people who put forward this explanation accept that there are poor people who are in this state through no 'fault' of their own. Nevertheless, the bulk of poverty is caused by those who do not make the effort to earn a living and/or squander what they do have.

The underclass

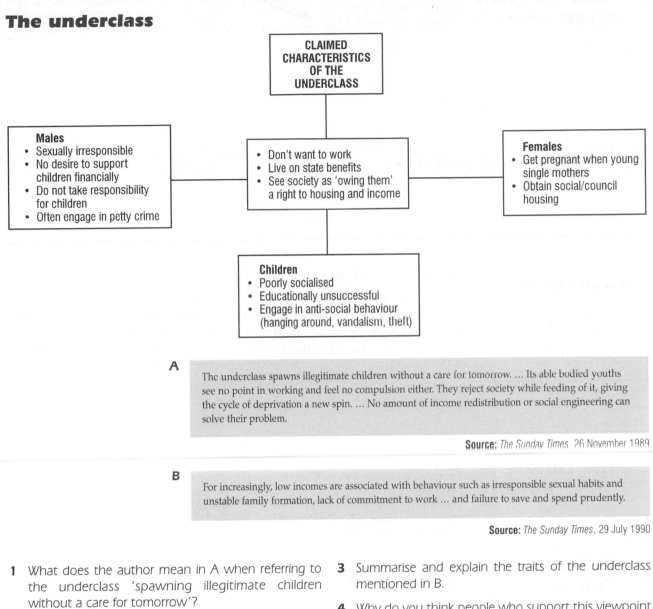

CLAIMED CHARACTERISTICS OF THE UNDERCLASS

- Don't want to work
- Live on state benefits
- See society as 'owing them' a right to housing and income

Males
- Sexually irresponsible
- No desire to support children financially
- Do not take responsibility for children
- Often engage in petty crime

Females
- Get pregnant when young single mothers
- Obtain social/council housing

Children
- Poorly socialised
- Educationally unsuccessful
- Engage in anti-social behaviour (hanging around, vandalism, theft)

A

The underclass spawns illegitimate children without a care for tomorrow. ... Its able bodied youths see no point in working and feel no compulsion either. They reject society while feeding off it, giving the cycle of deprivation a new spin. ... No amount of income redistribution or social engineering can solve their problem.

Source: *The Sunday Times*, 26 November 1989

B

For increasingly, low incomes are associated with behaviour such as irresponsible sexual habits and unstable family formation, lack of commitment to work ... and failure to save and spend prudently.

Source: *The Sunday Times*, 29 July 1990

1 What does the author mean in A when referring to the underclass 'spawning illegitimate children without a care for tomorrow'?

2 Explain also the reference to 'rejecting society while feeding off it'.

3 Summarise and explain the traits of the underclass mentioned in B.

4 Why do you think people who support this viewpoint claim that the Welfare State plays a large part in causing the growth of the underclass?

Criticism

The idea of the underclass has been strongly criticised as there is little or no evidence that there is an identifiable group of people with these distinctive values, who just want to sponge off the state. The majority of people want to work and support their family.

Not everyone agrees there is an underclass

What this research shows is not that poor people are alienated from society, have different values or behave differently, but rather their remarkable assimilation into the attitudes, values and aspirations of British society.

Source: A. Walker in C. Murray, 'The emerging British underclass', IEA *Choice in Welfare Series*, No. 2, 1990

According to the author of the extract, do poor people have different values and beliefs from the majority of the population?

Definition

Culture of poverty – refers to people who have a particular culture which prevents them being successful in society and so keeps them in poverty

The culture of poverty

This approach stresses that the way people act is the result of how they are brought up by their family. It differs from the underclass explanation because it does not see poverty as a fault of the person. It stresses that individuals are brought up in such a way that they never have a chance to escape the poverty of their parents.

The culture of poverty

'So I explained to her that the real problem was that she was suffering from the culture of poverty. She looked surprised and said that as far as she could tell she was suffering from lack of money.'

Usually a particular culture develops because it enables people to cope with their surroundings. Cultures are always changing, but the main outlines are passed on from one generation to another mainly by parents and those who influence people when they are young.

The culture of poverty represents an effort to cope with feelings of hopelessness and despair which develop from the realisation that there is no possibility of achieving a comfortable standard of living.

Once it comes into existence, it tends to perpetuate its effect on the children. By the time deprived children are aged 6 or 7 they have usually absorbed the basic values and attitudes of their subculture and are not psychologically geared to take full advantage of changing conditions or opportunities which may occur in their lifetimes.

According to the text, how does the culture of poverty argument differ from the underclass explanation for poverty?

The culture of poverty argument was first developed by Oscar Lewis when he studied very poor people in Central America. The values and behaviour (the culture) of these poor people was significantly different from the majority of the population. Lewis argued that this was because these particular values enabled the very poor to cope with circumstances which would otherwise lead to despair and hopelessness.

<table>
<tr><td>

Definition

Cycle of poverty – the way that certain groups of people 'pass on' poverty from one generation to another

</td><td>

The cycle of poverty

A development from the culture of poverty argument is the claim that a **cycle of poverty**, or a cycle of transmitted deprivation, exists. This explanation concentrated on the way in which some poor people failed to help and support their children, for example by not encouraging them to work hard at school. The result was school failure and another generation condemned to poverty.

</td></tr>
</table>

The cycle of deprivation, the culture of poverty and the underclass

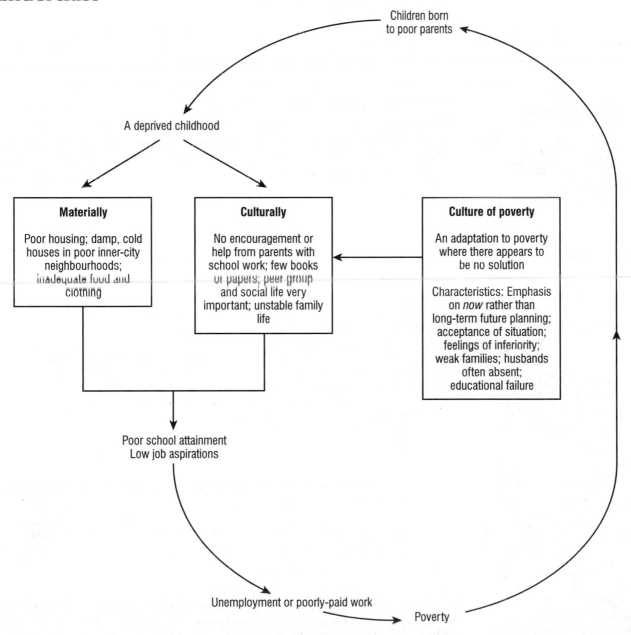

This explanation ignores the reason why some families start off poor.

Could it be that an unfair proportion of the wealth and resources of society are taken by the rich and powerful?

The Economic and Social Research Council commissioned a review of evidence about transmission of deprivation. The research by Rutter and Madge ... [concluded that] With respect to intelligence, educational achievement, occupational status, crime, psychiatric disorder and problem family status, there are moderate continuities over two generations ... yet ... Over half of all forms of disadvantage arise anew each generation. ... At least half of the children born into a disadvantaged home do not repeat the pattern of disadvantage in the next generation.

Source: Adapted from M. Banton, 'The culture of poverty', *Social Studies Review*, January 1990

What proportion of those from disadvantaged homes are themselves disadvantaged later in life?

Question   Do you think that poor people are unlucky, or it is their own 'fault? Give reasons for your view.

Exclusion

Definitions

Marginalisation – being forced to live on the edges of society and have your needs ignored

Dyswelfare – refers to the fact that some people lose out in society through no fault of their own

The second set of explanations for poverty are based on the idea of exclusion – meaning that the poor are in that situation because they are squeezed out of a decent standard of living by the actions of others. Another term for this process is **marginalisation**. This approach stresses differences in power between the various groups in society. Those who lose out – disabled people, older people, women, the ethnic minorities, and of course, children – have significantly higher chances of living in poverty.

Within this approach we can distinguish the:

- **dyswelfare** view
- economic system approach.

The dyswelfare view

Dyswelfare describes the process in which some people lose out in complex industrial societies, through no fault of their own. They are the casualties of industrial and social change. The 'victims' of dyswelfare include physically and mentally disabled people, single parents, etc. This approach emphasises that their poverty is blameless and is the result of the changes in the nature of society. For example, a physically disabled person may not be able to find an adequately paid job, despite trying.

However, this approach says that society does not deliberately discriminate against any group, but that it is inevitable that some people will lose out in any form of society, in which people compete for high income and a decent quality of life.

It is this explanation for poverty that largely underlies the foundation of the Welfare State, as it is the job of the Welfare State to look after these people.

The economic system approach

The final, and most radical, explanation for the continuation of poverty comes from those who argue that society is a competition between various groups. Some groups have considerably more power than others and are able to impose their will on the rest of society. Power and wealth generally go together, as do poverty and powerlessness. The groups in poverty are largely formed from the powerless, in particular women, children and the ethnic minorities. Low pay and poor state benefits are the result of the fact that to pay more would be harmful to the interests of those who are more affluent.

This approach contrasts with the dyswelfare explanation, because it says that the poverty is the result of the direct and intended outcome of modern western society.

Main points

▶ There are two groups of explanations for poverty.
  – Dependency explanations tend to stress that an individual is at fault and that they prefer to live off state benefits than work.
  – Exclusion explanations say that it is not a person's fault, but that things beyond their control have caused them to be in poverty.
▶ There are three explanations within the dependency approach. They are:
  – the individual explanation – it is a defect in the person
  – the underclass approach – that a new class of people exists who simply do not want to work
  – the culture of poverty approach – that some people have been born into a culture which prevents them being successful.
▶ The cycle of poverty refers to the situation when, for whatever reason, the poverty passes from one generation to the next.
▶ There are two explanations within the exclusion approach:
  – the dyswelfare explanation – people are poor because social change takes place around them over which they have no control (for example, unemployment caused by closing of the company), or because they have some form of disability
  – the economic system approach – people are poor because the rich ensure that they do not get a 'fair share' of the wealth.

The Welfare State

The Welfare State is a term used to describe the government departments and other organisations which are concerned with looking after the health and welfare of the population.

Origins of the Welfare State

The Welfare State as we know it can be traced back to the 1940s, when a government report (the Beveridge Report) said that the levels of poverty and ill health amongst the British population were so bad that the government must intervene and provide a range of services itself. Although there had been some limited provision of pensions and sickness benefits since 1908, people had not considered it to be a government's job to provide unemployed people with an income, or to build and run hospitals and pay doctors.

Beveridge said that there were five giant 'evils' which the government must combat with a Welfare State, which would provide help and support from 'the cradle to the grave

The tasks of the Welfare State, according to Beveridge

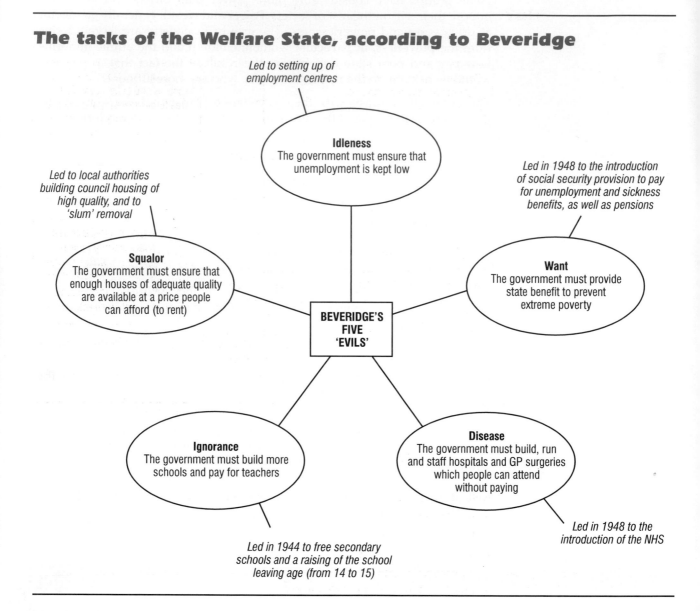

Led to setting up of employment centres

Idleness
The government must ensure that unemployment is kept low

Led to local authorities building council housing of high quality, and to 'slum' removal

Led in 1948 to the introduction of social security provision to pay for unemployment and sickness benefits, as well as pensions

Squalor
The government must ensure that enough houses of adequate quality are available at a price people can afford (to rent)

BEVERIDGE'S FIVE 'EVILS'

Want
The government must provide state benefit to prevent extreme poverty

Ignorance
The government must build more schools and pay for teachers

Disease
The government must build, run and staff hospitals and GP surgeries which people can attend without paying

Led in 1948 to the introduction of the NHS

Led in 1944 to free secondary schools and a raising of the school leaving age (from 14 to 15)

Social control and the Welfare State

Not everyone welcomed the Welfare State. Some have argued that it is a means by which the very rich can control the poor by giving them a small amount of help that is just enough to stop there being a revolution. So the Welfare State is really a means of social control.

> Throughout its [the Welfare State's] history, its primary role has been to uphold the operation of a capitalist labour market, with its social and sexual divisions of labour, and to control and contain the inequalities and poverty that result.

Source: Novak, 1988, quoted in M. Hill, *Social Security Policy in Britain* (E. Elgar Publishing, 1992)

What does the Welfare State do?

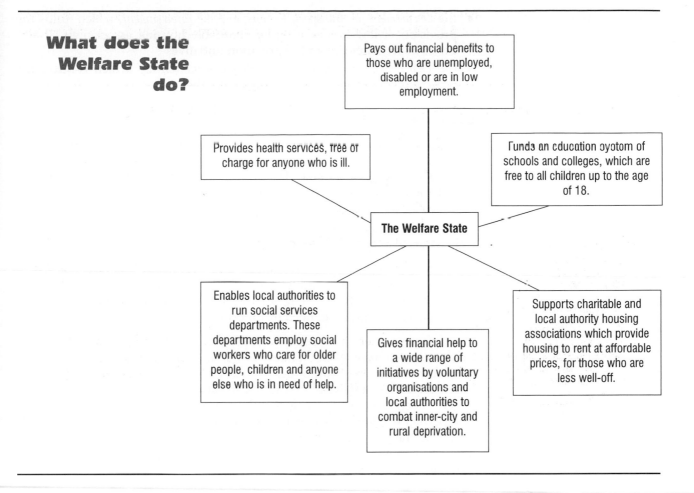

Pays out financial benefits to those who are unemployed, disabled or are in low employment.

Provides health services, free or charge for anyone who is ill.

Funds an education system of schools and colleges, which are free to all children up to the age of 18.

The Welfare State

Enables local authorities to run social services departments. These departments employ social workers who care for older people, children and anyone else who is in need of help.

Gives financial help to a wide range of initiatives by voluntary organisations and local authorities to combat inner-city and rural deprivation.

Supports charitable and local authority housing associations which provide housing to rent at affordable prices, for those who are less well-off.

Who provides the welfare?

Welfare is provided by:

- the government
- local authorities
- voluntary and charitable organisations
- commercial organisations
- family, friends and neighbours.

The government

The government departments most concerned with welfare provision are:

- the *Treasury*, which provides the funding for all the services from money obtained from taxation. It also gives the Working Family Tax Credits for lower earning households
- the *Department of Health*, which runs the National Health Service (NHS) and is ultimately responsible for the quality of the Social Work Departments of local authorities (local government) who employ social workers
- the *Department of Social Security* (DSS), which is responsible for paying out pensions and most state benefits which include:
  - Income Support for the unemployed
  - Family Credit for the low paid

- the *Department for Transport, Regions and the Environment*, which funds the provision of low-cost housing by charitable housing associations. It also funds many inner-city anti-deprivation initiatives
- the *Department for Education and Employment* (DfEE), which controls the provision of education and training across the country.

Local authorities

Local district and county councils are responsible for providing schools and for running social services departments which employ social workers. Local councils also run a wide range of other welfare services such as day centres for older people, as well as services for young people. Local councils also own and run housing developments for rent.

Voluntary organisations

There have always been tens of thousands of voluntary organisations where people give their time and effort for nothing, believing that they are contributing to society by doing so. Voluntary organisations provide help to every conceivable group in need of support.

> **Definition**
>
> **Mixed economy of welfare** – refers to the way that it is no longer the government which provides all welfare, but increasingly it does so in co-operation with voluntary organisations and with companies operating for profit

In recent years there has been a huge growth in voluntary organisations and charities which have taken on many of the tasks previously provided directly by government or local authorities. For example, housing for rent at affordable prices used to be built and run by local authorities, but this has now been largely taken over by housing associations which are charities and which receive their funding directly from the central government. This move towards providing help through voluntary organisations (and commercial organisations) as well as through the government is sometimes called the **mixed economy of welfare**.

 **Activity**

Either through the phone book or by visiting your local library, find out the names of three voluntary organisations and then contact them to find out what they do.

Commercial organisations

In recent years a number of companies which operate for profit have moved into the area of welfare. There have been private schools for a long time, but more recently there have been a growth in companies offering:

> **Definition**
>
> **Privatisation of welfare** – refers to the increasing amount of welfare being provided by companies for profit

- private pensions, which 'top-up' the state pension
- private health care provision
- care in nursing homes and old people's homes.

The growth of the private companies in providing welfare has been called the **privatisation of welfare**.

Question

Think of four examples of commercial companies providing health, welfare or financial support for people.

The National Council for One Parent Families is the leading charity working to promote the interests of Britain's 1.7 million one-parent families, helping lone parents to achieve their ambitions, and working to influence the policies that affect their lives.

POLICY AND RESEARCH OFFICER £26,000

Reporting to the Director of Policy, Research and Information and working as part of a small team, you will share responsibility for researching and analysing the position of lone parents, developing 'lone parent friendly' policies, and promoting them through campaigns, parliamentary work, and through working with other organisations.

Key tasks will include production of policy briefings and position statements, analysis of and responding to consultation documents from Government and others, commissioning and managing research projects and maintaining an up-to-date knowledge of research data. Ideally, you will already have specialist knowledge in one or more of: employment, housing, social security, family, education and childcare policy.

One Parent Families enjoys a strong reputation for policy and research work, and the organisation has a high profile in academic, government and media circles. If you are excited about joining a dynamic and ambitious charity with a strong social and political agenda, we would like to hear from you.

We offer a pleasant working environment, good leave arrangements and a contributory pension scheme. We strive to be an equal opportunities employer and operate a no-smoking policy. This post is available for jobshare.

For further information and an application form, contact National Council for One Parent Families, 255 Kentish Town Road, London NW5 2LX, email: orla@oneparentfamilies.org.uk, telephone 020 7428 5420, www.oneparentfamilies.org.uk.

Closing date for applications: 5pm Monday 18 December 2000

Interviews will be held on 11 January 2001

Tameside and Glossop
Community and Priority Services NHS Trust

Community Drug and Alcohol Team
Substance Misuse Worker

Primary Care and Intermediate Interventions

Salary will be on point between £21,350 and £24,620 p.a., based on 37.5 hours per week

Based in this busy and expanding multi-disciplinary service, you will be a qualified, experienced drug worker who will enhance the service to primary and secondary care sectors.

You will have a sound knowledge of substance misuse services particularly illicit substances, with well developed clinical, liaison and organisational skills. Full time RMN/RGN, DipSW or other professional clinically relevant qualification is required. Experience in planning and delivering training is advantageous, as this post is likely to involve delivering training to GPs and other primary care workers. You should have a basic competence with IT systems and be a car driver/owner.

For informal enquiries please contact Mary Hopper on 0161 339 4141.

For a job description and application form, please contact: The Personnel Department, Tameside & Glossop Community and Priority Services NHS Trust, Tameside General Hospital, Fountain Street, Ashton-under-Lyme, Lancs. OL5 9RW. Tel. 0161 331 5111 (24 hour answerphone), minicom 0161 831 5371, quoting reference number N447/ODP and stating where you first saw the advertisement.

Closing date: 15 December 2000

The Trust operates a no smoking policy in all its locations and is working towards creating a smoke free atmosphere.

The Trust is working towards being an equal opportunities employer.

Redbridge Council
for
Voluntary Service

Based in Ilford, in the London Borough of Redbridge, RCVS exists to support, promote and develop initiatives and activity within a strong, effective and independent voluntary sector, aimed at improving the quality of life for all in Redbridge.

CHIEF OFFICER
£28,140 – £30,198 (NJC PO4:41-44) + pension
35 hours per week

The Chief Officer faces the challenge of bringing RCVS Mission Statement and Strategic Aims into practice, while ensuring the effective day to day management, financial and general administration of RCVS.

Essential requirements include:
- 5 years experience of strategic and personnel management within the voluntary/statutory sector
- 3 years experience of managing an organisational budget in excess of 700,000 p.a.
- an awareness of the opportunities and difficulties facing the voluntary sector
- proven experience of policy development within voluntary organisations
- the ability to devise systems to monitor, evaluate and improve the quality and equality of RCVS' services
- good communication skills, public speaking and negotiation skills

RCVS is committed to equality of opportunity in employment and service delivery – the post holder will be required to adhere to this.

For an application pack please send an SAE (41p) to Recruitment, RCVS, First Floor, Broadway Chambers, 1 Cranbrook Rd, Ilford, Essex IG1 4DU. CVs will not be accepted.

Closing date: Wednesday 20 December 2000, 6pm

Interviews will be held during the week beginning 8 January 2001

Reg. Charity. No. 1005075

VOLUNTEERS NEEDED

Have you got a week to spare? *The Winged Fellowship Trust* is the UK's largest voluntary provider of respite care and quality holidays for people with physical disabilities. Volunteers are needed nearly all year round to help out at one of five purpose-built centres. As part of a team your role will involve accompanying guests on trips and outings, and generally helping to enhance the fun holiday atmosphere.

We welcome applicants of all ages over sixteen. No previous experience is required apart from a willingness to help out and full support and training is provided. Board, lodging and travel are paid for.

For further information please ring our Volunteer Department on either **0171 833 2594, 0115 981 3881 or 0181 343 2155.**

Alternatively write to; **the Winged Fellowship Trust, Angel House, 20–32 Pentonville Road, London N1 9XD.**

Reg Charity No. 295072

Look at each job advert. Which sort of organisation (private, voluntary, government , etc.) does each represent?

Families, friends and neighbours

A huge amount of welfare is provided informally by family members, by individual friends and by neighbours. The activities can vary from a neighbour keeping an eye on an infirm, older person to family members caring for a disabled relative, and even a friend lending some money to tide someone over. Sometimes this form of help is referred to as **informal welfare**.

Debates about the Welfare State

Make the Welfare State a safety-net?

A group of critics, known as the New Right, argue that the Welfare State is simply too expensive and big. The result is that it is too great a burden for the tax payer. They suggest that the answer is to privatise all or most of the agencies which provide welfare, which means that commercial, profit-making companies should compete to provide the services. The fees for their services would be paid by people who would have much lower tax bills as they were no longer paying taxes to support the Welfare State. The resulting system according to the critics would be efficient and would provide choice. Those who were very poor could fall back on a limited Welfare State which would act as a 'safety net'.

But supporters of the Welfare State argue that this would create a two-tier system of health and welfare. Those with money would have better, private health care and higher pensions. Those with low incomes would receive very poor quality care, provided by the state. This is morally wrong.

The cases for and against privatising the Welfare State

For privatisation	Against privatisation
• It is far too expensive.	• The Welfare State has been very successful in combating ill health and poverty.
• It costs the taxpayer too much precisely because it is expensive.	• It is actually cheap compared to commercial provision.
• It is not efficient – there are enormous waiting lists for hospitals for example,	• The family remains a very important informal provider of welfare and health care.
• It undermines the bonds which hold society together – because it is mutual help that cements the bonds of family and neighbourhood. If the government takes over all responsibility, people will not be interested helping each other.	• **The alternative to the Welfare State would be a two-tier system, in which the better-off would have good health and care while the poor would get little or nothing from a poor quality 'safety-net' system.**
• It takes away people's choice: people receiving welfare or health care have no choice over the services given to them.	
• **They propose instead that the Welfare State should simply be a 'safety net'.**	

An argument against the Welfare State

The Welfare State:

... has many harmful consequences. By multiplying public expenditure, it distracts finances from productive investment which would raise the general standard of living. By creating huge centralised bureaucracies, it weakens the vitality of the family, the local community and voluntary associations, which are the natural arenas of genuine mutual help. It fails to get help to those who most need it. The disadvantaged lose out to more sophisticated, better organised fellow citizens. It gradually reduces the capacity of the population for personal autonomy by schooling them to **welfare dependency**.

Source: Adapted from D. Marsland, 'Face to face', *Social Studies Review*, November 1989

> **Definition**
>
> **Welfare dependency** – when people prefer to rely upon the Welfare State rather than their own efforts

1 List the five arguments against the Welfare State. Explain them in your own words.

2 Do you agree with the writer?

Targeting versus universalism

A second debate, which is closely linked to the previous discussion about making the Welfare State a 'safety-net' system, is about just who ought to benefit from welfare. Those who support a safety-net version of welfare argue that only those who appear to be in real need should be helped (targeting), while those who support the current Welfare State system, argue that it is so difficult to find these, and so expensive to do so, that it is easier to give most people the benefits instead (universalism) – even though this might appear wasteful.

Targeting

What I say is - if a person can afford to smoke - well, they can't be poor!...

Targeting is the term used to describe a system of welfare provision that aims benefits at particular groups in the population – those who are identified as most in need. The very concept of 'most in need' usually has a moral element in it that says these people are the most deserving, as opposed to others who, if forced to, could escape from their poverty.

Targeting can be done by:

- *eligibility*, for example people receive disability benefits only when they can prove a certain level of disability
- *means-testing*, when a person must fall below a certain level of income to qualify for government help.

Universalism

The alternative to targeting through means-testing is to give benefits to everyone who falls into a particular category. Child Benefit, for example is not means-tested and everyone with a child under 18 receives it.

When everyone in a particular category receives benefits, then it is known as universalism. Those who argue for universalism claim they are defending the Welfare State, though very few benefits available since the Welfare State began are truly universal – the overwhelming majority of state benefits are targeted in some way.

The advantages and disadvantages of targeting and universalism

Targeting	Universalism
✔ It targets help to the most needy, and does not give money or services to the better off.	✔ It ensures that everyone who is in need obtains the benefits, and no one is omitted through their ignorance of benefits available or through fear of stigma.
✘ But means testing is complex and creates a large bureaucracy to administer it. Large bureaucracies cost a large amount of money.	✔ It is cheap to operate because there is no expensive bureaucracy working out entitlement through means testing.
✔ Providing help to targeted groups should cost less to the state, as fewer people should receive benefits.	✘ But the total cost is often higher because so many people receive benefits unnecessarily.
✔ The savings made could be spent on providing better services for the recipients, or it could be used by the government to lower taxes.	✘ The money spent should go to the most needy groups.
✘ But people often fail to take up the benefits because they feel embarrassed to ask (they feel 'stigmatised') or because they are ignorant of what they might claim.	✘ Giving people benefits which are not really needed encourages them to rely on the state rather than on their own resources.

Main points ▶ The Welfare State developed at the end of the Second World War in the 1940s.

▶ It was the result of the Beveridge Report, which said that the government would have to intervene to stop the five giant evils of want, squalor, idleness, disease and ignorance.

▶ The Welfare State refers to welfare provided by the government, or funded by the government.

▶ Today, welfare is provided by a range of people and organisations including the government, local authorities, voluntary and charitable organisations, family, friends and neighbours.

▶ The Welfare State has a number of critics, known as the New Right, who argue that the Welfare State is wasteful and ought to be replaced by commercial (for-profit) organisations and charities. The job of the Welfare State should be to help the very poorest who cannot afford to pay for their health or care services.

▶ Supporters of the Welfare State argue that it is very effective and without it the poorest would get very bad quality care.

▶ Critics of the Welfare State also argue that it is too wasteful in that it gives help to people who do not need it. They suggest that the Welfare State should target the very needy and help them only.

▶ Supporters of the Welfare State disagree and argue that targeting is expensive and makes people who receive benefits feel like they are receiving charity and they therefore feel stigmatised.

Results of Mack and Lansley's research (page 384)

Standard-of-living items in rank order	% classing items as necessity	Standard-of-living items in rank order	% classing items as necessity
1. Heating to warm living areas of the home if it's cold	97	18. New, not second-hand clothes	64
2. Indoor toilet (not shared with another household)	96	19. A hobby or leisure activity	64
3. Damp-free home	96	20. Two hot meals a day (for adults)	64
4. Bath (not shared with another household)	94	21. Meat or fish every other day	63
5. Beds for everyone in the household	94	22. Presents for friends or family once a year	63
6. Public transport for one's needs	88	23. A holiday away from home for one week a year, not with relatives	63
7. A warm water-proof coat	87	24. Leisure equipment for children e.g. sports equipment or a bicycle	57
8. Three meals a day for children[a]	82	25. A garden	55
9. Self-contained accommodation	79	26. A television	51
10. Two pairs of all-weather shoes	78	27. A 'best outfit' for special occasions	48
11. Enough bedrooms for every child over 10 of different sex to have his/her own[a]	77	28. A telephone	43
12. Refrigerator	77	29. An outing for children once a week[a]	40
13. Toys for children[a]	71	30. A dressing gown	38
14. Carpets in living rooms and bedrooms	70	31. Children's friends round for tea/a snack once a fortnight[a]	37
15. Celebrations on special occasions such as Christmas	69	32. A night out once a fortnight (adults)	36
16. A roast meat joint or its equivalent once a week	67	33. Friends/family round for a meal once a month	32
17. A washing-machine	67	34. A car	22
		35. A packet of cigarettes every other day	14

Average of all 35 items = 64.1
[a]For families with children only

14 CHAPTER SUMMARY

1 Being poor is one aspect of social exclusion, and the consequences of poverty include social and health problems as well as lack of money.

2 Sociologists have two different definitions of poverty – absolute and relative.

3 There are two different ways of measuring poverty within the relative definition approach – the relative income measure and the consensual measure.

4 The debate over the different ways of measuring poverty is very important, as the government relies upon the figures to help determine its policies towards poverty. The government uses the relative income measure.

5 About one quarter of the population, or 14 million people, are in poverty.

6 Most 'poor' people actually live on the margins of poverty and move in and out of poverty at different periods of their lives, depending upon the different responsibilities they have.

7 Some groups are more at risk of being in poverty than others.

8 The poverty trap occurs when people living on state benefits actually lose money, or earn little extra, when they enter employment.

9 There are two groups of explanations for poverty:

   – Dependency explanations include the individual, the underclass and the culture of poverty explanations.

   – Exclusion approaches include the dyswelfare and the economic system explanations.

10 The cycle of poverty is when poverty passes from one generation to the next.

11 The Welfare State developed at the end of the Second World War in the 1940s and refers to welfare provided by the government, or funded by the government.

12 It was the result of the Beveridge Report, which said that the government would have to intervene to stop the five giant evils of want, squalor, idleness, disease and ignorance.

13 Today, welfare is provided by a range of people and organisations including the government, local authorities, voluntary and charitable organisations, family, friends and neighbours.

14 The Welfare State has a number of critics, known as the New Right, who argue that the Welfare State is wasteful and ought to be replaced by commercial (for-profit) organisations and charities. They suggest that the Welfare State should target the very needy and help them only.

15 Supporters of the Welfare State argue that it is very effective and without it the poorest would get very bad quality care, targeting is expensive and makes people who receive benefits feel stigmatised.

Test Your Knowledge

1 What do we mean by the term 'social exclusion'?

2 Explain the two ways by which poverty is defined by sociologists.

3 Give any three criticisms of the relative income measurement of poverty.

4 What do we mean when we say that poverty is closely linked to the life cycle?

5 Why are lone parents more likely to be poor?

6 What is the underclass? Do all sociologists agree that it exists?

7 What do we mean by dyswelfare?

8 Give any four examples of what the Welfare State does.

9 What do the New Right argue should happen to the Welfare State?

Chapter 15

RELIGION

Chapter contents

• The relationship between religion and society

• Secularisation

• Religion, ethnicity and identity

• Sects, cults and new religious movements

The relationship between religion and society

In every society, throughout history and still today, people are frightened about the certainty of their deaths; they need some explanation for their brief stay here on earth. Surely it must all have some purpose? It is precisely this question that religion answers. Life does have meaning and there is a life after this one on earth. Not only this, but if people behave in the ways which the religion preaches, then there will be a reward for them after their death.

Although sociologists agree that religion does provide answers to questions about why we are here, what is the purpose of life and what happens after death, they also point out that religion does other things too, and we can summarise these into three views:

- that religion benefits society, by helping to draw people together, providing a moral framework for action, and creating a sense of community
- that religion can be used by powerful people to impose views to their benefit on the majority of people
- that, although religion often provides a sense of harmony, it can also bring about conflict and change in society.

Belief systems

> **Definition**
>
> **Belief system** – organised and coherent sets of values and beliefs which provide a framework for people to understand their place in the world and the meaning of life

But sociologists also point out that religion is not alone in doing these three things – so do other organised sets of beliefs, in particular political ideologies such as communism or the views of Nazis, or even perhaps modern-day environmentalists who see their job as saving the planet.

Sociologists suggest that religion is therefore just one type of **belief system**.

Sociologists are not concerned about the question of whether God exists or not – that is a question far beyond the powers of mere sociologists! They are only concerned with the role of religion in society.

Religion benefits society

This was the viewpoint of the nineteenth-century sociologist, Emile Durkheim. He pointed out that religion helps both society and individuals in different ways.

For society

Religion provides the moral backing to the rules and laws of society, placing them beyond question. The result is a generally accepted way of behaving, which pulls people together in a shared morality. Those who do not share these basic values are regarded as outsiders and deviants. The result is that religion plays a major part in keeping societies stable and preventing abrupt change.

For the individual

Religion can provide a sense of purpose and meaning in life. We are here because God put us here and after our death we will go on to an after-life. Secondly, it gives us emotional support in times of crisis. So, death is not such a tragic event if we know that the dead person has gone to Heaven. Thirdly, for many people the church provides them with a sense of community. They feel they belong to something that cares about them.

The benefits of religion and of belief systems

Religions and belief systems:
- provide a meaning for an individual's life
- provide a moral code
- explain why the world exists as it does
- provide a future goal for individuals and society
- provide emotional support in times of crisis
- explain how those who do not behave as the belief system wants are the cause of all unhappiness in the world
- provide a sense of belonging to a community.

1 What other benefits of a religion can you think of?

2 Give examples of how religions perform each of the benefits above.

Religion is a way of controlling people

This approach derives from the nineteenth-century sociologist, Karl Marx, who saw religion as a means by which people are tricked out of seeing the way they are being cheated and used by the rich and powerful. Although most people spend their lives working for the rich, they are comforted with the knowledge that if they cause no trouble and do their best to live a 'good' life (that is, to do what they are told), they will go to heaven after death. Religion then prevents them from ever questioning the way society is. For Marxists, religion acts as a form of **social control**.

Religion and social control

The Ragged Trousered Philanthropists, published in 1914, tells of the lives of a group of workers of that period. The author uses the book for some very bitter criticisms of British society. Amongst the objects of his attacks was religion.

'Then he goes to the workers and tells them that God meant them to work very hard and to give all the good things they make to those who do nothing, ... He also tells them that they mustn't grumble, or be discontented because they're poor in this world, but that they must wait till they're dead, and then God will reward them by letting them go to a place called heaven.'
  Frankie laughed, 'Do they believe it?'
  'Most of them do, because when they were little children like you, their mothers taught them to believe, without thinking, whatever the vicar said.'

Source: R. Tressall, *The Ragged Trousered Philanthropists* (Granada, 1965)

1 Which approach to religion is referred to here?

2 Why do you think that sociologists called religion 'an agency of social control'?

3 Today the influence of religion has declined. Are there any other agencies which have taken over the job of social control? If so, what are they?

Religion as a cause of social change

A criticism of both the above approaches is that religion can also lead to social change, as well as maintaining stability, and can be used as a focus by the poor and under-privileged to challenge their position in society. In Afghanistan in the late 1990s for example, the Taliban took over control of the country, founding a new government which is based on a strict interpretation of Islam.

Max Weber, writing at the beginning of the twentieth century, suggested that the idea that religion always plays a major role in maintaining social stability is not true. He argued that religious ideas are just as likely to bring about change as to prevent it.

Weber described how the ideas of a Protestant sect, the Calvinists, played a crucial part in bringing about industrialisation (production by machines in factories) in Britain more than 200 years ago. Calvinists believed that working hard and not spending money on enjoying oneself was the way to win God's approval. To be successful was taken as a sign of approval by God and an indication that one was likely to go to Heaven. The result of the Calvinists' hard work (and no play) was considerable savings, which they were able to invest in factories. People with other religions which stressed giving money away to the poor, for instance, which resulted in them having only small savings, would not have been able to finance the building of factories and machinery. So Weber concluded that the values of Calvinism led to savings which in turn led to industrialisation as we know it today.

It is important to remember that Weber was not saying that Marx and Durkheim were wrong, only that religion can bring about change as well as stability and that it is not always a way of manipulating people.

The relationship between religion and belief systems

As we have already seen, sociologists have pointed out that when we talk about religions they ought to be seen as just one example of belief systems, which set out to provide a guide on how best to live.

Throughout much of the twentieth century, for example, communism provided a total way of life for hundreds of millions of people. In many ways, communism was no different from a religion, as it answered all questions on the meaning of individuals' lives and providing a reason for the world as it is, and a clear moral framework on how to act. For many people, the collapse of communism in the 1980s and 1990s left them confused and they turned to religions for an alternative framework.

The need to believe

The following is a report on a television programme in Moscow about the religious conversion of a communist who had spied for Russia against Britain.

The British traitor, George Blake, who has lived in Moscow since his escape from Wormwood Scrubs Prison in 1966, appears in old age to have found the consolation of religion.

Blake, who was sentenced at the Old Bailey in 1961 to 42 years in prison for betraying Western secrets to the Soviet Union ... said that he had experienced a crisis when he lost the Christian faith of his youth. He had turned to communism, seeing in that ideology an attempt to build the Kingdom of Heaven on earth.

"Everything that happened to me was meant to happen," he said. "There were no other possibilities." Asked whether God or Marx had determined his fate, he said it was the "universal force", adding he would know that better when he died.

But the strong implication at the end of the programme was that, having been disappointed in Marxism, he had sought refuge again in God.

The programme ended with a shot of Blake, standing in clouds of incense, at the Orthodox Church in Kratova, outside Moscow.

Source: Adapted from *The Independent*, 12 July 2000

What impression does the interview with Blake give about his view of communism and religion?

Main points

▶ Religion is one example of a belief system.

▶ Belief systems, such as religion, provide a number of important benefits for society and for their members.

▶ All societies have some form of religion or belief system which helps to explain a person's place in the world and what the meaning of life is.

▶ Some critics argue that religion is way of controlling people so that they cannot see the truth about how they are exploited. Religion is a form of social control.

▶ Although religion can provide the conditions for harmony, it can also cause unrest and social change.

New Age movements

During the 1970s the opportunities for travel allowed thousands of young people to visit India and the Far East. At the same time, ethnic communities were establishing themselves and their own customs in Britain. The result of this was that British people became exposed to a whole range of 'new' (to Britain) medical, philosophical and religious ideas. These are now extremely common in society. Ideas brought in ranged from acupuncture to Feng Shui, and included yoga and meditation. This huge array of alternative lifestyles and philosophies are examples of New Age movements.

Activity

Look at the adverts in your local paper or visit a health food shop or alternative health centre. List as many as possible of these new activities and philosophies. If possible, arrange for a speaker to come in to talk to your class or group.

Secularisation

Definition

Secularisation – the decrease in importance of religion in people's lives

One hundred years ago, about 40 per cent of the population claimed to attend church each week. Today, the figure is a little over 10 per cent. The obvious conclusion drawn by some sociologists is that people are less religious today than in the past.

Furthermore, it is claimed by some that Christian religions have lost much of their influence in modern society. Fewer people believe in God and use religious values as their guidelines on how to behave. For example, 'traditional' teachings of the Christian churches on contraception, abortion, homosexuality and the marriage of Catholic priests, have all come under considerable strain over the last 20 years. Indeed, it seems that the reverse is true today and the churches follow the general change in attitudes. An example of this is the Church of England's acceptance of the right of people to divorce, and the ordination of women priests.

The political influence of the Church of England has declined too and is rarely listened to by those in power. The importance of religious teaching in schools has slowly eroded so that it no longer has an important place in most schools' teaching programmes, despite it being on the National Curriculum.

The functions of the churches have been lost to other agencies. Social workers, for example, paid by the state take the main responsibility for care of people with problems.

The status of the church has declined, particularly amongst young people. Church membership is seen by young people almost as an embarrassing thing to admit to. The rate of church attendance is far higher amongst older people than it is amongst the young.

All of this is summarised in the word **secularisation**.

Reasons for the secularisation of society

The reasons given for this decline are that people now explain the world in scientific terms. Rather than understanding such things as the creation of men and women in terms of Adam and Eve, people now understand it as a result of evolution.

In general, then people look for natural explanations for events rather than supernatural ones. This has also influenced the idea of sin and morality. For example, illness was once seen as punishment by God and having done something wrong. Today, we see illness simply as a physical thing, and so we go to the doctor. Of course, this has also weakened the importance of the clergy in the community.

> **Definition**
>
> **Modernism** – a way of describing a society based on rational and scientific thought

This is part of a general movement in societies towards what sociologists have called **modernism** – all of modern western societies' activities are now dominated by a way of thinking which is rational and logical. Scientific discoveries have created the belief that societies are based on the laws of nature not on the laws of God. In social affairs, too, the influence of the social sciences, political philosophies and economics have persuaded people that society can be controlled, and that it is not simply God-created and unchangeable in the way it is organised.

Along with the change in ways of explaining the world, there has also been a change in the values of society. Modern society stresses success as the ownership of as many things as possible. For example, a successful married couple is one with a large house, car and all the consumer goods that their family wants. The traditional values of stress on community and mutual help, strongly associated with the churches, have declined.

The continuing importance of Christian religions

It has been argued that the statistics, which so convincingly show a decline in religious belief, in reality only show a decline in attendance at church, which is a very different matter. After all, believing in God does not mean attending church.

If people are asked if they believe in God, over 62 per cent still reply that they do, and if asked which church they belong to, over 70 per cent of the British population claim membership of a church. This is despite the fact that only 23 per cent say that they have attended a religious ceremony in the last month.

> **Definition**
>
> **Rite of passage** – the ceremony that signifies leaving one stage of life and entering another

The majority of people still use churches for the major ceremonies and **rites of passage** of life and death – baptism, marriages and funerals are still religious ceremonies. For example, about two-thirds of first marriages take place in church.

Religion: still some life left?

Only 10 per cent of people say that they definitely do not believe in God, and a further 15 per cent are not sure.

Source: *Social Trends 30* (The Stationery Office, 2000)

The results of the survey [conducted by Opinion Research Business among a representative sample of 1,000 people] found that ... 62% of people believe in God, down from 76% in 1980, yet only 23% of people have attended a religious service in the past month – the same figure as a decade ago.

Most people retain their faith in family values and the institution of marriage, although there has been a move away from organised religion, with those regarding themselves as belonging to a particular religion falling from 58% in 1990 to 48% today, the Church of England suffering the biggest drop, from 40% in 1990 to 35%.

About 27% described themselves as "spiritual", rather than "religious", with 25% believing in reincarnation and 55% in fate. And despite the finding that 45% of Britons never attend church, 69% of the population believe they have a soul – up from 64% 10 years ago.

The survey also found that just over half the population believes in an afterlife, up from 44% a decade ago.

Although the belief in a personal god has consistently fallen over the past 40 years, from 41% in 1957 to 32% in 1990 and to 26% now, a larger proportion, 32%, still believe in the devil. While 52% profess to believe in heaven, only 28% are convinced that hell exists – figures that have changed little over the past 20 years.

A large number of people are in favour of church leaders speaking out on moral issues such as poverty (82%), racial discrimination (75%) and global inequality (70%).

A spokesman for the Archbishop of Canterbury said the survey results "seemed to go against the idea that religion is dead". He added: "Religion is far more important to people than a lot of commentators think."

Source: *The Guardian*, 29 May 2000

1 What does the extract mean when it says that people are more likely to view themselves as 'spiritual' rather than religious?

2 Does everybody who believes in God go to a religious service?

3 Which religion has had the greatest fall in membership?

4 What percentage of people definitely do not believe in God?

5 Do people still believe that religious leaders should speak out on moral issues?

6 Do you agree with the comment by the Archbishop of Canterbury?

7 Devise your own survey, constructing questions which will give you information to compare against the figures here.

In the past there was great social pressure on people to attend church each Sunday, because it was a sign of social respectability. People may have attended but not really believed in God. Today, not attending church is perfectly acceptable. Those who do attend, do so for the right reason – that they truly believe.

British society is still based largely upon Christian values, with almost 80 per cent of people questioned regarding seven or more of the Ten Commandments as applying to them in their own lives. The importance of religion in the lives of people is still very strong. This is shown by the way that the major rites of passage are still marked by religious ceremonies. Baptism, marriage and the funeral service are all important church rituals for most families.

Churches: the changing membership

Church membership, United Kingdom

Thousands

	1970	1980	1990
Trinitarian churches			
Roman Catholic	2,746	2,455	2,198
Anglican	2,987	2,180	1,728
Presbyterian	1,751	1,437	1,214
Other free churches	843	678	776
Methodist	673	540	478
Orthodox	191	203	266
Baptist	272	239	230
All Trinitarian churches	9,272	7,529	6,624
Non-Trinitarian churches			
Mormons	85	114	160
Jehovah's Witnesses	62	85	117
Other non-Trinitarian	138	154	182
All non-Trinitarian churches	285	353	459

Source: *Social Trends 30* (The Stationery Office, 2000)

1 Which church claimed the highest membership?

2 Which is declining fastest?

3 Are there any churches which are not declining?

Finally, and most importantly, the decline in church attendance usually refers to the more traditional churches, such as the Church of England or the Catholic Church. There has been a great growth in newer churches, such as the Mormons and Jehovah's Witnesses, as well as those which have a high attendance by people of African-Caribbean origin, for example, which have shown a growth in membership of more than 30 per cent since 1970.

Non-Christian religions are having an increasing impact upon British society, with a huge growth in the number of Muslims in Britain. There are also increasing numbers of Hindus and Sikhs.

The death of religion does seem to have been exaggerated. Clearly there has been an overall decline in the importance of Christian religion in British society, but to measure that solely in terms of church attendance is mistaken. However, much of the decline in attendance appears to be in the older-established churches, such as the Methodist, Church of England and Catholic churches. However, people still believe in God and still subscribe to values which are largely based on religious ideals.

Some of the more traditional ways of expressing religion are dying, but people are now more likely to explore alternative forms of spirituality.

Main points ▶ People used to attend church far more than they do nowadays.

▶ The influence of the church on how people act and on the government is declining.

▶ This decline in church attendance and influence is known as secularisation.

▶ Secularisation seems to be caused by the growth of rational thinking linked to the development of science.

▶ Societies based on scientific and rational thinking are known as modernist societies.

▶ However, religion still has great importance in people's lives. It is the more traditional Christian church which is in decline, not religion.

▶ The numbers believing in God and traditional values remain very high.

▶ There has been an enormous growth in non-Christian churches.

Religion, ethnicity and identity

Religion and the African-Caribbean experience

In the 1950s thousands of young people came to Britain from the West Indies and Guyana on the coast of South America to work. Most had been encouraged to come by employers who were desperate for hard-working employees. For many of the new arrivals, Britain was a not a welcoming place and they faced racial discrimination in employment and racism in ordinary life.

Pentecostalism

The young people who came to Britain from the West Indies were largely staunch Christians and they attended the Church of England. But the style of religious practice and the racism they encountered amongst many of the worshippers gradually persuaded them to set up their own churches. The new **Pentecostal** churches were lively places with fervent singing, powerful preaching and a dialogue between the preacher and the congregation, with the preacher calling out and the congregation answering back. Pentecostal churches are less concerned about rigid ideas about religion and more concerned with getting people to experience God 'within them'.

Rastafarianism

A different form of religion also developed, known as Rastafarianism. This originally developed in Jamaica in the 1920s and, drawing upon the Bible, it argued that the only way for black people to be saved from poverty and discrimination was for them to return to Africa where their troubles would be solved. Rastafarianism did not fully transplant to Britain and largely has become a much looser cultural movement. Rastafarians can be recognised by a particular style of dress and the wearing of (dread)locks.

> **Definition**
>
> **Pentecostal** – refers to Christian churches which stress experiencing God, rather than learning a lot of rules of faith

Ethnic minorities and non-Christian religions

As Britain has changed from a predominantly single culture to a multi-cultural society, reflecting the immigration of the 1950s and early 1960s, so there has been a large growth in non-Christian religions. The number of Muslims in Britain now totals around half a million, and there are a quarter of a million practising Sikhs and 140,000 Hindus, as well as the traditional British Jewish community which numbers about 100,000. While the number of actively religious Jews is declining, the growth of the other religions has been quite remarkable, with an threefold increase, for example, in the number of Muslims practising in Britain and a doubling of Sikh and Hindu numbers.

As these religions increase in numbers, the religious leaders are increasingly demanding that more account should be taken of their views and beliefs in the broader culture of Britain. They point to the fact that they have little political power, with only one Muslim MP and little influence on the content of the school curriculum.

Membership of non-Christian religions

Membership of Christian religions, United Kingdom

	1970	1980	1990
Muslim	130	306	495
Sikh	100	150	250
Hindu	80	120	140
Jewish	120	111	101
Others	21	53	87
All other religions	451	740	1,073

Source: *Social Trends 30* (The Stationery Office, 2000)

1 Which religion has increased at the fastest rate?

2 Which religion has declined?

Reasons for the growth in non-Christian religions

The main reason for the growth of the Islamic, Hindu and Sikh religions is that they all reflect the growth in size of the Asian communities in Britain. When Asian immigrants began coming to Britain in the 1950s, they brought with them their religions. The original numbers have been increased by the higher birth rate amongst some of the Asian community, particularly amongst Muslims, and by the continuing practice of arranged marriages, which bring brides or grooms over from the Indian sub-continent. So, growth in the Muslim, Hindu and Sikh religions do not reflect a substantial number of new converts from Christian or other religions, but an increase in the size of the Asian ethnic minority communities.

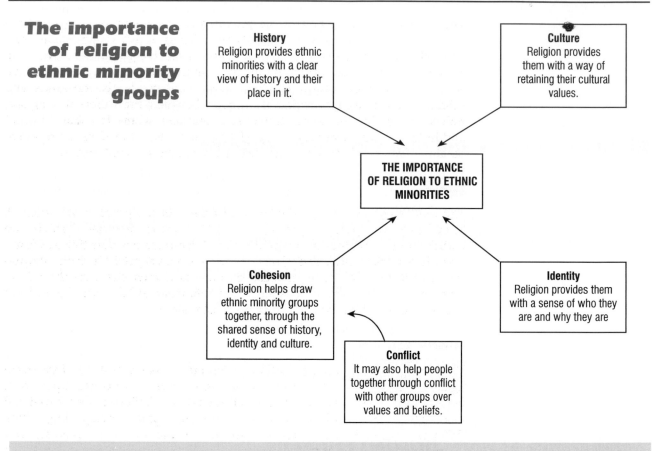

The importance of religion to ethnic minority groups

History
Religion provides ethnic minorities with a clear view of history and their place in it.

Culture
Religion provides them with a way of retaining their cultural values.

THE IMPORTANCE OF RELIGION TO ETHNIC MINORITIES

Cohesion
Religion helps draw ethnic minority groups together, through the shared sense of history, identity and culture.

Identity
Religion provides them with a sense of who they are and why they are

Conflict
It may also help people together through conflict with other groups over values and beliefs.

"Part of the British establishment hoodwinks itself into thinking this is a white, Anglo-Saxon, Christian country," says Moeen Yaseen, a spokesman for the Muslim Education Forum.

There are 250,000 Muslim school children in this country, the largest concentration of non-Anglican children after Roman Catholics. Most of them go to state schools. There are 28 private Muslim schools educating about 2,500 children. Most but not all of these want to join the state sector. About six of the schools for older children offer religious training for pupils preparing for a vocation. Two are schools for children of expatriate workers, well resourced and separate.

The Education Reform Act of 1988 says that RE syllabuses must "reflect the fact that the religious traditions in Great Britain are, in the main, Christian while taking account of the teaching and practices of other principal religions that are represented in Great Britain".

Dr Syed Pasha, secretary of the National Muslim Education Council of the UK, believes that stressing Christianity to Muslim children at best confuses and at worst undermines the spiritual teaching which the children receive at home, at the mosque and in the supplementary schools.

Like many other Muslims, he would like to see the emphasis on Christianity deleted from legislation. His organisation would like Islam taught to Muslim children in state schools by state-funded Muslim teachers.

"Our main idea is that RE should be done in such a way as to be acceptable to parents of all religious communities," he says. "At the moment it is tilted toward the Christian parents."

Source: *The Guardian* (Education section), 23 March 1993

1 How many Muslim school children are there in Britain, according to the extract?

2 In terms of religious faiths attending school, where does this place them, according to the extract?

3 Why is there a problem for them attending state schools?

4 What solution is suggested?

5 What is your view about teaching religion in school? How should it be done and which faiths should be taught?

The values of these religions have provided the Asians with a sense of their cultural identities. They unite the various Asian groups from particular areas and· help them to preserve their own values while living in Britain. The main religions are Islam, Hinduism and the Sikh religion. It is important to note that while each religion draws together those from similar backgrounds and origins, there is also considerable friction between the different religions, reflecting the divisions in the Indian sub-continent, where Pakistan (Muslim) and India (Hindu) have fairly poor relations and where the Sikhs are trying to obtain an independent state from India by sometimes violent means.

Islam

The followers of Islam are Muslims and believe in the prophet Mohammed. They believe that Jesus was not the son of God (whom they call Allah), but an earlier prophet and that the preachings of Mohammed overrule those of Jesus. Their holy book is the Koran (Qur'an) and they are very strict in their interpretation of it. One of the main social differences is their stress on the role of women, who are expected to be modest in behaviour and dress, and to defer to the authority of husbands or fathers in most matters.

Hinduism

The Hindus believe in reincarnation, which means that after death they return again on earth in another form. What you return as depends upon your behaviour in your previous lifetime. Hindus do not believe in one individual God (whom they call Brahman), but that God is part of everything, taking different forms. Socially, they too stress the importance of modesty and obedience in women. Traditionally, they believe in the caste system, in which people are graded according to their holiness and 'inferior' people must accept the superiority of others. These social rules appear to be breaking down in Britain.

Sikhs

The Sikhs come from Northern India and are instantly recognisable because of their turbans, long hair and beards. They gather for worship, which consists of readings from their holy book, the Granth, and then listen and sometimes discuss sermons based upon it. They believe in reincarnation, but not that people are punished or rewarded for their previous lives. They believe in one God and that all people are equal, in particular they believe in the equality of male and female. The religion frowns upon tobacco and alcohol.

Sikh holy men in New Delhi on their way to Punjab, where the founding of the Khalsa order of Sikhism is celebrated at Anandpur Sahib

Main points ▶ When people came from the West Indies to settle in Britain in the 1950s and 1960s, they faced considerable racism in society and the church.

▶ Part of their response to this situation was to form their own churches.

▶ Pentecostal churches are the more mainstream and involve more singing and involvement in the ceremony than in more traditional churches.

▶ Rastafarianism is a religion which originated in Jamaica and stresses the need for black people to find their own salvation through rediscovering their own roots and identity.

▶ The biggest growing religion is Islam. This was brought to Britain by Asian immigrants.

▶ The Hindu and Sikh religions were also brought to Britain by Asian immigrants in the 1960s.

▶ There are considerable differences between the various non-Christian religions.

Sects, cults and new religious movements

When discussing religion, people commonly talk about churches, meaning religious organisations that meet regularly to worship God. However, sociologists find this a little too vague and prefer to distinguish between different types of religious organisations: the church, the sect, the cult and the denomination. Sects which have grown in size, such as scientology, are increasingly being known as new religious movements.

Basically, the more formal, the larger, the more tolerant and the more conformist a religious organisation is, the more likely it is to be a church. It follows then that the smaller, the more radical and the stricter a religious organisation is, the more likely it is to be defined as a sect. In the middle lies the denomination.

Churches

A church is religious organisation with paid officials, usually fully integrated into the values of society. It has regular formal acts of worship in a special place put aside for that purpose. One of the major churches is generally linked to the state, and is known as the 'established church'; in England, this is the Church of England.

Sects

A sect is a religious organisation which is very strict in its beliefs and control of its membership. Usually they believe that only they have found the truth concerning God. There are rarely any paid officials. They are generally strongly opposed to the accepted values of society.

Examples of sects which have grown into new religious movements include Jehovah's Witnesses and Scientology. They have retained many of the sect features such as a degree of secrecy and strict discipline.

Denominations

A denomination is a religious organisation which is accepted by the wider society, although it has no connection with the state. It is smaller in size than a church and the running of it is far more in the hands of the congregation than in a church. Often denominations are sects that have grown in size and have become less critical of other religious groups. The Methodists are an example of a denomination.

Cults

A cult is an extreme version of a sect, but is much smaller and can actually exist within a wider church. It is usually based upon one charismatic leader.

Characteristics of cults: image or reality?

The following extract is from a news story about the alleged kidnapping of a 16-year-old boy by the Jesus Christians.

The Jesus Christians are an Australian-based cult. Their leader is David McKay who is thought to have been a member of the notorious Children of God sect before setting up the group.

The number of members in this country or worldwide is not known because members are secretive and reluctant to talk about their activities.

But one of its basic rules is that members have to break contact with their families and friends. They are also expected to hand over all their worldly goods.

In that they are similar to the Children of God, now called The Family. The late David Berg, an American who founded the Children of God in 1968, preached free sex to his followers. He also preached child abuse.

Graham Baldwin, who monitors the activities of cult groups, reckons there have been at least 1,000 set up in this country in the past 50 years.

Some are quite small with only a handful of followers. Others have members around the world.

One that has been known to leave some adherents with serious psychiatric problems is the Church of Christ.

It has branches around the country and its members believe they are the only true Christians. Every member has a discipler, another member who is consulted about every decision.

Mr Baldwin said: "The effect is that everyone is controlled by the cult and everyone is expected to hand over ten per cent of their income."

Source: Adapted from *The Daily Express*, 14 July 2000

Draw a diagram to illustrate the characteristics of the cult according to the extract.

The movement of sects to churches

Definition

Charismatic – describes a
person who has an extremely
unusual ability to dominate
people through force of
personality and persuade them to
do things which they would not
normally do

Over time the original founders of sects and new religions die, and as the dominance enjoyed by them over everybody else (known as 'charisma') in the sect declines, so rules of behaviour replace the orders of the founder. New recruits may not be as fervent as those of the first generation and gradually, as the sect grows in size, the radical ideas become watered down to attract yet more members. So, over a considerable period, the sect takes on the characteristics of a denomination. Methodism is an example of this. Christianity began as a small, radical sect in Palestine based upon the **charismatic** personality of Jesus Christ, and gradually over hundreds of years developed into the official religion of the Roman Empire.

The development of churches from cults

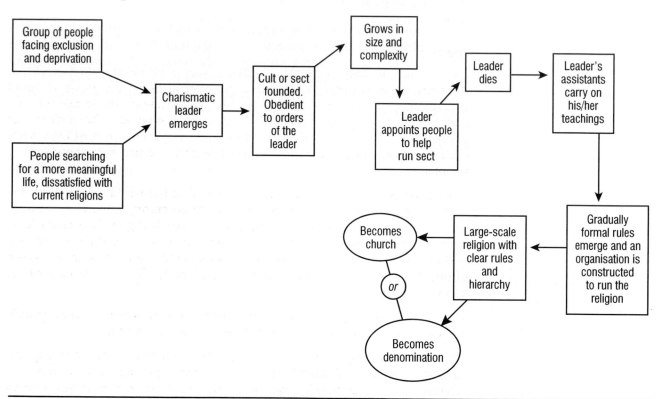

The changing face of religion

The most noticeable thing about the changing face of religion in Britain has been the decline of the older established churches, and the growth of sects and new religions. Sociologists have suggested the main reason for this is that sects are performing the functions that the older established churches are no longer providing. So the sects have taken their places. The small size of the sects, their discipline and stress on shared experience provides a home for those who are lonely, or searching for a creed full of certainty.

Conditions for the development of new cults

A new cult may develop where the following conditions exist.

- The beliefs and values of the main churches are too vague and unclear.
- The churches fail adequately to challenge the government and society on social issues.
- The churches are too impersonal and fail to make people feel they belong.
- Some people may feel that the churches are not welcoming, for example members of ethnic minorities.
- The churches ideas seem inappropriate and outdated for the problems of contemporary society.
- The traditional churches, their attitudes and services may seem dull and unattractive.

The membership of sects and new religions

Membership appears to be drawn from two very different groups:

- the rejecters
- the rejected.

The rejecters

The rejecters are those who feel that the values of society are wrong and that the modern stress upon ownership of possessions as the one gauge of value ignores the need for inner harmony and contentment. These rejecters are usually younger people from well-off homes who are themselves not financially deprived, but feel they need a sense of purpose in their lives. Sects such as the Moonies and Hare Krishna draw their recruits from these sorts of people.

One of the beliefs of these new religions is that as the world is so corrupt, the only way to achieve spiritual peace is by members cutting themselves off from society. Once new members join, they are expected to give their entire lives over to the religion, including working for it, handing over their possessions and possibly often living together. The leaders of the sects are seen as carriers of messages from God. Famous examples include the Rev. Sun Myung Moon and Guru Maharji.

The 'world-rejecting' religions recruit members from amongst those people who are unhappy with their lives and are seeking an escape.

The 'world-affirming' new religions do not contradict the values of society, but claim that personal fulfilment can only occur through religion. These religions typically do not demand full-time commitment or that members live in communal accommodation, but they do demand 'contributions' or fees from members. Often a form of meditation or 'exercises in human growth potential' are practised which aim to allow people to develop their potential to the full. The best known example of this type of world-affirming new religion is Scientology. Members often come from middle-class backgrounds and wish to find ways of achieving Western society's goals, of power, status or personal attractiveness.

The rejected

The rejected, on the other hand, are from the poorer, deprived groups in society who need comfort and explanation for their situation. In the United States, the Black Muslims started as a small sect and has now grown into a significant religion, as it provided an alternative and acceptable explanation for the poverty and social deprivation which the Black Americans living in the poor 'ghetto' areas of large American cities experience in their daily lives. The traditional, mainstream explanation for their poverty is that they are not interested in working hard and anyway are less able than the majority of Americans.

Sects and hope

In the USA, as in Britain, a considerable number of sects and new religions developed from the 1960s onward. One of these was the Black Muslims. Kaplan argues that the growth of this sect amongst poor Black-Americans was because:

It offers him a rebirth. He can shed his old despised identity. It offers him an emotional if not physical outlet for his hostility toward the white man. It offers him hope. Joining the highly moral and disciplined Black Muslims gives him the prospect of raising himself from his condition of poverty and frustration. It also provides him with the goal of building for a new glorious future in a united and powerful black society.

Source: Adapted from H.M. Kaplan, 'The Black Muslims and the Negro American's quest for communion', *British Journal of Sociology*, 20 June 1969

How I became a teenage cult member
I first met Hamid when I was at secondary school in Glasgow. I was 14 years old ... Like most young people, we were rebellious towards our parents and society. We were also vulnerable, impressionable and in search of identities.

When I met him, I was spinning in a world of teenage confusion. My best friend had cut off all communication with me six months previously after she had joined his group. I had been hurt and I was angry with him for taking her away, but I was also in awe of him.

I wanted my friend back. I felt like an outcast, rejected by my best friend and ostracised by members of his group. I was torn between my own family and my need for a "social" family, which he controlled. Hamid's ideas were spiritual and powerful and he seemed truly to believe in them – that was what made him so charismatic.

Source: Adapted from *The Independent*, 18 October 1994

Look at the first extract.

1   Why was it more likely that the membership of the Black Muslims should have been amongst the poor Black-Americans, than amongst the better-off Black-Americans in the USA?

2   According to the main text and to the extract, what categories of people are attracted to sects?

Look at the second text.

3   At what age did the writer become involved in the cult?

4   What does the term 'charismatic' mean?

5   In the main text we suggested that there are sects which attract rejecters and rejected. Do the extracts support this? How?

Main points

▶ There are a number of different types of religious organisations. These include churches, sects, cults and denominations.

▶ Over time, some sects or cults will grow in size and become churches or denominations. The Catholic Church is an example of this.

▶ Cults and sects tend to be far more radical than churches and denominations.

▶ People join sects and cults for a number of reasons, but often it is because traditional churches do not provide for the needs they have.

▶ Sects and cults can be divided into two kinds by the sort of people they recruit. Either they recruit people who feel rejected by society, or those who actively reject society.

15 CHAPTER SUMMARY

1   All societies have some form of religion or belief system which helps to explain a person's place in the world and what the meaning of life is.

2   Belief systems, such as religion, provide a number of important benefits for society and for their members.

3   Some critics argue that religion is way of controlling people so that they cannot see the truth about how they are exploited. Religion is a form of social control.

4   Although religion can provide the conditions for harmony, it can also cause unrest and social change.

5   People used to attend church far more than they do nowadays, and the churches had much greater influence than today

6   This decline in church attendance and influence is known as secularisation.

7   Secularisation seems to be caused by the growth of rational thinking linked to development of science.

8   However, religion still has great importance in people's lives. It is the more traditional Christian church which is in decline, not religion.

9   There has been an enormous growth in non-Christian churches.

10 People of African-Caribbean origin set up Pentecostal churches and continued with the Rastafarian religion, partly as a result of the racism they faced.

11 The biggest growing religion is Islam, which was brought to Britain by Asian immigrants.

12 The Hindu and Sikh religions were also brought to Britain by Asian immigrants in the 1960s.

13 There are a number of different types of religious organisation. These include churches, sects, cults and denominations. Cults and sects tend to be far more radical than churches and denominations.

14 Over time some sects or cults will grow in size and become churches or denominations. The Catholic Church is an example of this.

15 People join sects and cults for a number of reasons, but often it is because traditional churches do not provide for the needs they have.

16 Sects and cults can be divided into two kinds by the sort of people they recruit. Either they recruit people who feel rejected by society, or those who actively reject society.

Test Your Knowledge

1 What is a belief system? Give one example apart from religion.

2 Give four examples of how religion benefits society.

3 Explain the meaning of the term 'secularisation'.

4 What arguments have been put against the idea of that secularisation is occurring in Britain?

5 Who are most likely to attend Pentecostal churches? Why?

6 Which religions are growing in Britain today? Why?

7 Why do people join cults and sects?

8 Describe the process whereby sects might become churches or denominations. Give one example.

GLOSSARY

Absolute poverty	Not having the very basics to live
(People of) African-Caribbean/ Pakistani/Bangladeshi (origin)	Used when we wish to be more specific about the differences between groups. It also indicates that the people are most likely to be British born but of families who migrated here from those countries
Age status	The way that people receive different amounts of income and social prestige depending upon their age
Arranged marriage	Where the decision about whom to marry is made by the families, not only the individuals concerned
Ascription	Your place in society and how others act towards you is determined at birth and is based upon the social group your parents belong to, rather than any personal qualities you have, for example, members of the Royal Family in Britain
Assimiliation	When ethnic minority groups are absorbed into the majority culture, adopting mainstream values and behaviour
Asylum seeker	Someone who has 'well-founded' fear of being persecuted for reasons of race, religion, nationality or political views; *see also* **Refugee, Political asylum**
Authority	When we willingly obey people because we believe it is right for them to boss us around
Belief systems	Organised and coherent sets of values and beliefs which provide a framework for people to understand their place in the world and the meaning of life
Beliefs	Very general views on the nature of the world
Birth rate	The number of babies born in a year for every 1,000 people in the population. The higher the birth rate, the more babies are born
Bourgeoisie	The rich and powerful who own industry and commerce
British Crime Survey	A national, government survey which asks people which crimes have been committed against them
Burden of dependency	The costs of looking after older people
Capitalism	Companies are owned individuals or groups of people (shareholders), who try to make profit out of their companies
Case study	An intensive study of one particular group or situation
Casual employment	Insecure employment where the worker has no permanent job or job security
Charismatic	Describes a person who has an extremely unusual ability to dominate people through force of personality and persuade them to do things which they would not normally do
Class de-alignment	The decline of social class as the main influence on voting behaviour
Coalition	When different groups join together to look after their common interests
Coercion	When we obey people because they can threaten us if we ignore their wishes
Cohabitation	Partners with or without children, who are sharing a household but not married to each other
Community	A sense of belonging to a particular place and having something in common with other people who live there
Comparative study	Comparing two societies or groups of people to find out in what key ways they differ
Consensual measure of poverty	A measure based upon an estimate of the numbers who do not have a normally acceptable 'minimum' lifestyle
Content analysis	The detailed analysis of one or more of the media (such as newspapers, Internet sites or advertisements) in order to find how a particular group or event is being portrayed
Contraculture	A form of subculture which actively opposes the dominant culture of society; for example, terrorist groups; *see also,* **Subculture**
Conurbations	When cities expand and 'swallow up' neighbouring towns
Covert observation	Where the researcher does not tell the group members that he or she is a researcher; *see also* **Overt observation**
Craft production	Manufacture of articles by hand

Cross-cultural studies	Where sociologists gather information from different societies and compare them to see what similarities and differences there are in human behaviour
Cross-sectional survey	Covers the views of a group of people on a specific occasion
Cultural diversity	As society becomes more complex, there exists a wider range of values and beliefs about the correct way to behave
Culture	A whole way of life that guides our way of thinking and acting. People within a culture regard it as somehow natural; for example, the difference between British values and Italian values; *see also* **Subculture, Contraculture**
Culture of poverty	Refers to people who have a particular culture which prevents them being successful in society and so keeps them in poverty
Cycle of poverty	The way that certain groups of people 'pass on' poverty from one generation to another
De-industrialisation	The decline in manufacturing and the growth of offices and commerce, which began taking place from the 1970s onward; *see also* **Industrialisation**
De-urbanisation	The process of people moving out of larger towns and cities; *see also* **Urbanisation**
Death rate or mortality rate	The number of deaths each year for every 1,000 people in the population
Democracy	Where the ordinary people elect their leaders and have the right to express their views without fear
Demography	The study of the changes in the composition (size, age, distribution, sex balance) of the population
Deregulated labour market	Where workers have very few legal rights in their jobs to such things as paid holidays, good pensions, maximum working hours, etc.
Deskilling	The skills needed for a job are lost when the computer-controlled machine takes them over
Deviant behaviour	Actions which challenge conventional views on behaviour
Differentiation	The different ways people are treated according to the social group they are believed to belong to
Direct discrimination	When people are treated less favourably because of their 'race', gender or disability; *see also* **Indirect, Racial discrimination**
Disposable income	The money which someone has left to spend after the household bills and all other necessities have been paid for
Diversity	An acceptance of a range of different cultures which share some common features, but also value the differences
Domestic labour	Work which is done in the house and which is not paid
Domestic violence	The use of violence by one member of the household against another (or others). Usually it is men who use violence against their partners and/or children
Dyswelfare	Refers to the fact that some people lose out in society through no fault of their own
Emigration	The movement of people out of a country (or area); *see also* **Migration, Immigration**
Employment market	The opportunities and constraints which a particular group face in obtaining work
Ethnic minority groups, Blacks and/or Asians	Terms used where the writer wishes to compare the situation of all those members of these groups with the majority of British people
Ethnocentric	A way of looking at things from a particular cultural viewpoint and ignoring other possible ways of seeing the world. For example, seeing the history of the world only from a 'white' British viewpoint
Extended family	Three or more generations in close contact
Extrinsic satisfaction	Employees find little satisfaction in their work and have to seek their pleasure outside their jobs; *see also* **Intrinsic satisfaction**
Family life cycle	The changing relationships between the different generations of the family as they grow older
Feminist approach to sociology	A perspective which argues that much traditional sociology is the study of society from the man's point of view and by looking at it from a woman's viewpoint a whole range of findings of traditional sociology are brought into question, and a set of new questions also emerge
Fertility rate	The number of children born for every 1,000 women of child-bearing age (approximately 15–40 years of age)
Fordism	A method of producing identical products cheaply using production lines on which people did one small task; *see also* **Post-Fordism**

Formal economy	The activities of people who are in official employment and the companies which employ them; *see also* **Informal economy**
Formal welfare	When the help or care is provided by an organisation of some kind, usually the government
Fragmentation	Divisions within social classes
Gender	The way society expects people to behave on the basis of their physical difference; *see also* **Sex**
Glass ceiling	Women cannot get promoted beyond a certain point in organisations
Globalisation	The opening up of the world in terms of economic production and consumption. So that trade takes place right across the world
Hidden curriculum	The values which are taught to children in the school through the behaviour and expectations of teachers
Homogeneous	A single group with similar characteristics
Household	One or more people living in the same dwelling
Identity	A person's identity is composed of a mixture of personal experiences and wider images of the world and their place in it, provided by schools, the media and people who are important to the individual. It is usually linked to awareness of gender, race and social status, as well as an image of one's own body
Immigration	The movement of people into a country (or area); *see also* **Migration, Emigration**
Income	The money people live on which they obtain for their work, from state benefits or from their investments
Indirect discrimination	When a rule which appears to be equal for all actually discriminates against certain groups; *see also* **Direct discrimination, Racial discrimination**
Industrialisation	The process where a society becomes based upon factories and commerce, rather than on agriculture. In industrial societies, most people live in towns and cities and work in companies
Infant mortality rate	The number of children under one year of age dying for every 1,000 children born
Informal economy	The activities of people who are not officially employed; includes people working for cash and avoiding tax and also those 'working' in voluntary or caring tasks; *see also* **Formal economy**
Informal welfare	Help or care is provided by friends, neighbours or family
Instinct	Action which is 'genetically' programmed into our behaviour
Institutional racism	Where an organisation (such as a college or company) has procedures and regulations which, by their very nature, discriminate against certain groups in the population; *see also* **Racism**
Integration	When ethnic minority groups remain distinctive, but adapt and conform the majority values and behaviour
Interview	A series of questions or topics asked by a researcher directly to a person and the answers recorded by the researcher
Intrinsic satisfaction	Employees gain pleasure from their jobs; *see also* **Extrinsic satisfaction**
Joint conjugal role relationship	Where the partners share all household tasks and have leisure activities in common
Kin	The term used to describe all those family members related by blood or marriage or cohabitation. It is much wider than family
Learning	Behaviour acquired through socialisation and reinforced by social control
Life chances	The advantages or disadvantages people have which can affect them doing well or badly in society
Lone- or single-parent family	Only one parent living with the children. Ninety per cent of lone-parent families are headed by women
Long-range mobility	Movement up or down by two or more occupational groupings – the least common form of mobility; *see also* **Social mobility, Short-range mobility**
Longitudinal survey	Covers views over a considerable period of time, possibly years
Manual work	Work which mainly uses physical force, with varying degrees of skill
Marginalisation	Being forced to live on the edges of society and have your needs ignored
Marginalised	People who forced out of normal social life by poverty and unemployment
McDonaldisation	In service industries where the product and the style of service are identical

Mechanisation	Manufacture or articles by machine
Media (or the mass media)	All forms of written and transmitted communication to the public ('media' is the plural of 'medium' and so we say 'the media are …')
Meritocracy	A society where a person's social and financial position depends mostly upon their ability
Migration	The movement of people to live in a different place; *see also* **Emigration, Immigration**
Mixed ability	Students of all ability are taught together
Mixed economy of welfare	Refers to the way that it is no longer the government which provides all welfare, but increasingly it does so in co-operation with voluntary organisations and with companies operating for profit
Modernism	A way of describing a society based on rational and scientific thought
Moral crusades	When groups of people get together to change the law over a particular issue or, if there already is a law, to change the way it is enforced
Moral panic	When a social problem is hugely exaggerated by the media leading to a great public concern completely out of proportion to the real problem
Mortality rate	*see* **Death rate**
National Curriculum	The subjects which the government says must be studied in all state schools
New Right	A political and academic approach to understanding society which stresses that the government (which is paid for by hard-working tax payers) should not have to support people who have through their own decisions either chosen not to work or made themselves unemployable
Non-participant observation	Where the researcher follows and observes a group, but does not attempt to 'be one of them'; *see also* **Participant observation**
Norms	Socially approved ways of behaving
Nuclear family	Parent(s) and children only
Occupational structure	The sorts of jobs which people do within the formal economy
OfSTED	Office for Standards in Education – an official government body which monitors schools' performance and carries out inspections
Opinion polls	Surveys which are conducted by asking a small cross-section of the population for their opinion on a specific issue. 'Polling' was first devised in the USA
Overlap	Whereas once the divisions between the classes were clear, in terms of behaviour and income, today they are not and there is greater overlap at the edges of the classes
Overt observation	Where the researcher is completely open about the research; *see also* **Covert observation**
Panel survey	A more intensive form of longitudinal survey
Participant observation	Where the researcher joins the group and acts as one of them; *see also* **Non-participant observation**
Partisan de-alignment	The decline of support for just the two major parties and the readiness of electors to turn to other parties
Patriarchal family	A description of the family often used by feminist sociologists which suggests that the wishes of the husband/male partner are dominant and there is no sense of equality
Patriarchy	A society where the men hold more power than women
Patterns of transition	The traditional ways in which many communities have provided a clear route from childhood to employment for young people
Peer group	A group of a person's own age who are important to them; the group exerts influence over individual members; most often used when referring to young people
Pentecostal	Refers to Christian churches which stress experiencing God, rather than learning a lot of rules of faith
Pilot survey	A small-scale, dry-run for a larger survey
Pluralism	Power is diffused amongst many different people across society
Political asylum	When a person flees one country because they are being persecuted for their political views and asks to live in safety in another country; see also **Asylum seeker, Refugee**
Political ideology	An explanation of how society works and a plan of action for solving any problems based upon this explanation
Political socialisation	The process of learning political values and preferences
Positivism	Positivists believe that sociology should try to be a science and to use as many of the

	methods which the physical sciences use as is possible. They conduct surveys and gather statistics and, when possible, use experiments
Post-Fordism	A new form of work patterns where workers are expected to be flexible and to be employed only when there is work for them. There is no expectation of employment for life; *see also* **Fordism**
Power	When people can get others to do what they want (for whatever reason)
Pre-industrial or agricultural societies	Societies where the majority of people work in agriculture
Pressure (interest) groups	Organisations campaigning for a particular cause
Primary sources	All information that the sociologist has gathered him or herself; *see also* **Secondary sources**
Private schools	All schools which charge fees
Privatisation of welfare	Refers to the increasing amount of welfare being provided by companies for profit
Proletarianisation	The decline in working conditions, status and salary of the routine white-collar workers, to a level indistinguishable from the working class
Proletariat	All employees, no matter what grade, who work for the rich and powerful. A marxist term
Public schools	Those higher status private schools which belong to an organisation called 'The Headmasters' Conference'
Questionnaire	A series of written questions which people complete by themselves
Quota sampling	The cross-section is based on a statistical breakdown of the population, so that researchers are told to get a 'quota' of specific people to fill each statistical category
Race	A term which is rarely used in discussion but has its origins in the belief that there are biological distinctions between groups of people
Racial attacks	Use of violence against members of ethnic minorities motivated by racist beliefs
Racial discrimination	When people are treated unequally simply because they belong to a particular ethnic group; *see also* **Direct** and **Indirect discrimination**
Racial harassment	Actions and language which are intended to cause the victim, at the very least, to feel upset or uncomfortable in some way and, at worst, to lead to direct or indirect harm
Racial prejudice	When people are disliked simply because they belong to a particular ethnic group
Racism	The belief in the idea of the existence of distinctive 'races' and that some races are superior to others
Random sampling	The cross-section is found by randomly selecting people
Reconstituted family	A family which has at least one step-parent
Refugee	A person who has been accepted for asylum; *see also* **Asylum seeker, Political asylum**
Relative affluence	When people are quite well off compared to another group of people, even if they do not appear to have that much money themselves
Relative income measurement of poverty	Income less than 50 per cent of average income
Relative poverty	Not being able to afford the standard of living considered acceptable by the majority of people
Reliable	Each interview and questionnaire in a survey is carried out to a standard format, so that the researcher is sure that they are all the same
Rite of passage	The ceremony that signifies leaving one stage of life and entering another
Ruling class/elite	A relatively small network of powerful people who control society
Rural	Refers to the countryside; *see also* **Urban**
Sampling	A way of finding a small number of people who form a representative cross-section of the population in general
Sampling frame	The place, list or resource from which the sample is drawn
Scapegoating	Blaming certain groups of poorer or less powerful people for problems in society, instead of seeking out the real causes
Secondary sources	Information initially research by someone else and which the researcher uses; *see also* **Primary sources**
Secularisation	The decrease in importance of religion in people's lives
Segregated role relationship	Where the partners have separate tasks and leisure interests
Self-fulfilling prophecy	A belief (often incorrect) which leads a person to act in a way which makes the belief reality

Self-recruitment	Where the a person is in the same occupational group as their parents – this is very common, especially for the children who come from social class 1 backgrounds
Self-report test	A questionnaire which asks people what crimes they have committed
Self-segregation	When an ethnic minority group largely cuts itself off from the majority culture
Service 'class'	Professionals and managers
Service industries	Commerce which does not actually make anything, but instead provides some service, for example banking insurance, shops, leisure activities
Setting (banding)	Classes are formed from a wider range of ability
Sex	The physical characteristics based on genetic differences which distinguish males from females; *see also* **Gender**
Sexual bargaining	The negotiations which men and women make over 'how far' they should go sexually
Sexuality	Refers to our sexual behaviour and choice of partners
Short-range mobility	Movement up or down by only one occupational group – this is very common and it usually consists of people moving upward, as there has been a growth of middle-class jobs and a decline in working-class jobs; *see also* **Social mobility, Long-range mobility**
Social control	People learn the expectations and values of society (culture) through socialisation and if they do not follow the guidelines of society, then they are punished in some way (social control)
Social exclusion	Facing a wide range of physical, financial and social problems which make the quality of life very poor
Social mobility	The ability to move up or down the 'ladder' of social class; *see also* **Long-** and **Short-range mobility**
Social movement	A loosely organised coalition of different groups who come together to bring about social change on a fairly broad scale
Social role	A way of acting which is expected of a person in a particular position in society
Socialisation	The process by which people are taught to accept the values of society and to conform
Society	People acting in a particular set of predictable patterns (known as social roles) and who share a set of common ideas about the world (a culture)
Stereotype	To exaggerate differences between one group and another so that these differences are made to seem more important than the similarities. A problem with all research on social class and ethnicity
Stratification	The division of people into groups based upon how much wealth, social prestige and power they have
Streaming	Grouping of students by their measured ability into classes, typically of about 30 school students
Style	A term to summarise a way of dressing, appreciation of a certain type of music, use of particular speech expressions and a whole set of likes and dislikes which mark off a particular group as different
Subculture	Exists within a culture and is a distinctive set of values that marks off the members of the subculture from the rest of society; for example, youth (sub)culture; *see also* **Culture, Contraculture**
Subjectivists	Subjectivism is the approach in sociology which tries to get into the minds of groups of people by closely observing their behaviour and where possible joining in. It prefers this to using questionnaires and interviews
Symmetrical family	A family where the adults share household tasks, and see themselves as equals
The dark figure	The difference between the real number of crimes committed and the figure in official statistics
Totalitarian society	Where the political leadership does not allow elections or free speech
Transition	In sociology this means the period of change from being one age status to another; for example, the period of change from being a child to being a youth
Triangulation	Using a number of methods to carry out a research project
Unbiased	The personal views and biases of the researcher are kept out of the research
Under-employment	Not having as many hours' work as you would like
Underclass	A distinctive group or 'class' made up of men and women who have no interest in working, but prefer to live on state benefits and be housed by local authorities
Urban	Refers to towns and cities; *see also* **Rural**

Urbanisation	The process whereby the majority of the population gradually move from the countryside to live in towns and cities; *see also* **De-urbanisation**
Valid	The research measures what it is supposed to measure
Value diffusion	Similar attitudes and behaviour are common across social classes
Values	Ideas about the correct form of behaviour
Victim survey	Asks people what crimes have been committed against them
Wealth	The possession of things which, if sold, have great value. Wealth is often held in the form of stocks and shares, property and works of art
Welfare dependency	When people prefer to rely upon the Welfare State rather than their own efforts
White-collar work	Routine work in offices and shops which does not involve physical work (whether skilled or not)

INDEX